HISTORY OF NIGERIA

By Sir Alan Burns

HISTORY OF THE BRITISH WEST INDIES

COLONIAL CIVIL SERVANT

COLOUR PREJUDICE

IN DEFENCE OF COLONIES

HISTORY OF
NIGERIA

Sir Alan Burns

G.C.M.G.

George Allen and Unwin Ltd

RUSKIN HOUSE   MUSEUM STREET   LONDON

FIRST PUBLISHED IN 1929
SECOND EDITION 1936
THIRD EDITION 1942
FOURTH EDITION 1948
FIFTH IMPRESSION 1951
FIFTH EDITION (SIXTH IMPRESSION) 1955
SEVENTH IMPRESSION 1958
SIXTH EDITION (EIGHTH IMPRESSION) 1963

Sixth Edition © George Allen & Unwin Ltd, 1963

PRINTED IN GREAT BRITAIN
in 11-point Baskerville type
BY UNWIN BROTHERS LIMITED
WOKING AND LONDON

To Peter

PREFACE TO THE SIXTH EDITION

I went first to Southern Nigeria in 1912; thirty years later, in 1942, I acted as Governor of Nigeria.

I was present in the old Court House in Tinubu Square, Lagos, on January 1, 1914, when the amalgamation of Northern and Southern Nigeria was proclaimed. I was present also on October 1, 1960, at the Independence ceremony on Lagos Racecourse. There must be few, Africans or Europeans, who were present on both of these historic occasions.

I was for many years in the Nigerian Civil Service. When I served in other territories, and after my retirement, I continued to follow with interest the progress of Nigeria. It is a great satisfaction to me that I have been able to record in this revised edition the independence of Nigeria and to assert once again my confidence in the future of this great country.

I wish to record my gratitude to all those who have assisted me with information for the revision of this work, and I should like also to express my acknowledgement and thanks to those who have supplied me with portraits which are included in the book. His Excellency the Governor-General and the Prime Minister of Nigeria have kindly sent me their photographs. The portraits of Lord Lugard, Sir George Goldie and Richard Lander are from the National Portrait Gallery. The portraits of the Sultan of Sokoto and Chief Jaja were supplied by the editor of the *Nigeria Magazine*, that of Bishop Crowther by the Church Missionary Society, and that of Miss Mary Slessor by the Church of Scotland. For the portrait of Oba Akitoye I am indebted to the present Oba of Lagos.

The portrait of El Kanemi is reproduced from the frontispiece of Denham and Clapperton's *Narrative of Travels and Discoveries in Northern and Central Africa*, that of Sir John Glover from *Life of Sir John Hawley Glover* by Lady Glover, that of Mr Herbert Macaulay from a photograph supplied by the Olojo Photo Service of Lagos, and that of Sergeant-Major Belo Akure from *Nigeri a and the Great War*.

ALAN BURNS

London,
    September, 20. 1962

PREFACE TO THE FIRST EDITION

WHEN I first arrived in Nigeria, in 1912, Northern and Southern Nigeria were still separate administrations, with different traditions and distinct histories. Those Europeans who were interested in one Protectorate knew little of the other, and wasted no sympathy on their neighbours, while among the inhabitants of the country the lack of a uniform system of government had accentuated the already existing differences of race, religion and culture.

In no way was the difference between Northern and Southern Nigeria more marked than in the quality of their bibliographies. Several excellent books had been written on Northern Nigeria, and the history of the Protectorate was easily available to those who wished to study it. Of Southern Nigeria, on the other hand, there was not a single complete history, and information about the people of the country, and the early British administration on the Coast, was almost impossible to find.

Still more impossible was it to obtain, in a single volume, a history of Nigeria as a whole, and the amalgamation of January 1, 1914, made a book of this sort more than ever necessary.

Some years ago I began to collect the necessary materials for a history of Nigeria, but before this could be completed I was transferred to the Bahamas, where I languished for five years. During this period, for various reasons, work on the book made little progress, but it has at last been finished, and will, I hope, be published simultaneously with my return to Nigeria.

The book is designed to give to those who are interested in Nigeria, and particularly to such as are resident in the country, whether as missionaries, traders or officials, a short account of the history of its people and of their relations with the British Government.

It has been impossible to deal fully in a volume of this size with every incident, and those desirous of obtaining further details of any particular event are referred to the works mentioned in the notes. Those interested in ethnography should refer to the works of Mr P. A. Talbot and Mr C. K. Meek.

I have not attempted, in the spelling of Yoruba names, to follow the usual method of denoting the different sounds of the same letter. Thus Kosoko is printed without the usual dot beneath each 'o', which to the initiated would imply that the name is pronounced *Kawsawkaw*. Also where 's' (with a dot beneath it) is pronounced as 'sh' I have spelt the word as it is pronounced.

Lord Lugard had been good enough to undertake the writing of a Foreword to this book, which would have increased its interest enormously, but this was unfortunately impossible, as there was no time for him to read the proofs before it went to press. With characteristic kindness, however, and in spite of great private anxiety, he sent me a note of which I quote a few lines as further proof of his unfailing interest in Nigeria and his sympathy for all those who have tried to serve that country:

I regret that I should not have had an opportunity of reading the chapters which deal with events which I personally witnessed, but judging from these earlier chapters I confidently anticipate a volume which will serve as a textbook and authority on the history of Nigeria.

Owing to my departure for Nigeria it will not be possible for me to complete the revision of the proofs of the last few chapters of the book.

A. C. BURNS

St Leonards-on-Sea,
  January 25, 1929.

CONTENTS

MAPS

ILLUSTRATIONS

between pages 144–5

CHAPTER I

PHYSICAL FEATURES AND CLIMATE

Beware and take heed of the Bight of Benin,
Where few come out though many go in.

Old saying

The Federation of Nigeria consists of the three Regions of Northern, Western and Eastern Nigeria and the Federal Territory of Lagos.[1] Since October 1, 1960, the Federation has been an independent State, and is a member of the Commonwealth and of the United Nations.

The approximate area of Nigeria is 356,669 square miles, more than four times that of Great Britain. The total area is made up as follows:

	Square Miles
Northern Region[2]	281,782
Western Region	45,376
Eastern Region	29,484
Federal Territory of Lagos	27

The population was estimated in 1960 to be over 35 millions, greater than that of Australia, Canada and New Zealand combined, and much greater than that of any other State in Africa.[3]

The isolation for so many centuries of this rich and extensive country was due in the first place to the physical barriers set up by nature, a waterless desert to the north, and to the south a coast-line of seemingly impenetrable forest and swamp;

[1] Provision is made in the Constitution for increasing the number of Regions and for changing the existing boundaries between the Regions should this become advisable.

[2] This includes the area (about 17,500 square miles) of the northern part of the former Trust Territory of the Cameroons under United Kingdom administration, the population of which voted to join Nigeria as from June 1, 1961.

[3] The second most populous State in Africa is Egypt, with an estimated total of 26 million inhabitants.

in the second place to a hot and unhealthy climate unsuited
to European constitutions, and a number of insect-borne
diseases, the causes of which were not even guessed at sixty
years ago.[1]

Nigeria is situated on the west coast of Africa, on the shores
of the Gulf of Guinea. It lies between the parallels of 4° and
14° north, and is thus entirely within the tropics. It is bounded
on the south by the sea, on the west and north by the Republics
of Dahomey and Niger,[2] and on the east by the former German
colony of Kamerun, now the Republic of Cameroun.[3]

The greatest length of Nigeria, from east to west, is over
700 miles, and its greatest width, from north to south, over
650 miles; the coast-line is over 500 miles in length.

As is natural in a country of this size, the physical conditions
vary considerably. The volume of water poured into the Gulf
of Guinea by the River Niger has brought with it quantities of
sand, which in the course of ages has pushed the sea farther
and farther back, forming an immense delta. The sandbanks
are held together by the roots of the mangrove trees (*Rhizo-
phora racemosa*) which flourish in the shallow brackish water,
but the land is nowhere of any great elevation, and most of it
is mere swamp. Along the whole coast-line is a barrier of sand
upon which the Atlantic surf perpetually thunders. Where the
rivers cut through to find the sea this barrier takes the form of
a bar, which is an ever-present menace to shipping, but elsewhere it protects mangrove swamps or the tranquil waters of
shallow lagoons which in some cases are separated from the
turbulent ocean by only a few yards of white, glaring sand.
Where the mouth of a river breaks the white strip that marks

[1] Malaria was supposed to be caused by the bad air from the swamps,
hence its name, and the frequent reference in old books to the fatal 'miasma'.
The Sanitary Report on Lagos for the Year 1887 speaks of 'the possibility of the
admittance of the malarial poison to the human body by means of drinking-
water', and adds that 'the malarial poison is supposed, with reason, to be
developed in the soil' (C. 5249–17).

[2] Former French territories which became independent in 1960.

[3] This includes the former Trust Territory of the Cameroons under
French administration, which became independent in 1960, and the
southern part of the Trust Territory of the Cameroons under United
Kingdom administration, the population of which elected to join the
Republic as from October 1, 1961.

the coast-line the mangrove appears, from the offing, to be
growing in the sea, and a solid wall of green is all that is visible
to ships. Behind this wall, till the zone of tropical forest is
reached, there is scarcely anything but water and mud—and
more mangrove. Until the recent discovery of mineral oil there
was practically no production from this area, but it was always
important inasmuch as it gives access to the interior by an
unrivalled system of waterways and because the ports and
principal trade depots are there located. The branches of the
Niger delta, the estuaries of other rivers, and the lagoons
which lie between, are all connected one with another by
a multitude of creeks, the whole making a continuous navigable waterway from the western to the eastern borders of
Nigeria. In some of the creeks and the more sluggish of the
rivers the sudd (*Pistia stratiotes*) grows so thickly that the waterway is completely blocked, and even where it is not impenetrable launches are often brought to a standstill by the long
roots being wound around the propellers. In some places the
creeks are so full of sudd that no water is visible and a carpet
of green is stretched from bank to bank as far as the eye can
reach; over this carpet small birds and an occasional iguana run
lightly, while numbers of small frogs hop from leaf to leaf.

Farther inland is the zone of tropical forest, from 50 to 100
miles wide. Here are found evergreen trees of all descriptions,
mahoganies and other valuable furniture woods, and the principal asset of the country, the oil-palm (*Elaeis guineensis*).
Owing to the wasteful local system of farming and the extensive migrations of tribes in earlier times, the bulk of the vegeta-
tion consists of secondary growth, which has sprung up rapidly
in deserted clearings, and for this reason the number of different species growing together is very large. The undergrowth is
thick and in parts almost impenetrable, while ferns and mosses
flourish in the rich, damp ground, sheltered from the sun by
the dense foliage overhead. The ground is undulating and
there are a few hills; the country is intersected by rivers and
streams but, save where there is a village or farm, there are no
open spaces. A number of broad motor roads have been constructed by the Government, but some areas in this zone are
accessible only by narrow 'bush paths' along which a party
must proceed in single file. Although there is a considerable

amount of cultivation in the forest zone, very few farms are visible from the roads or paths, which are for the most part bordered by dense forest or undergrowth; the traveller can often hear the voices of the workers on the farms, screened from the road by the thick bush. In the forests there is an enormous variety of animal and bird life, and snakes are plentiful.[1]

North of a line drawn roughly through the towns of Abeokuta, Ondo, Onitsha and Afikpo, the forest begins to get thinner and the country gradually becomes more open and park-like, with little real forest save along the banks of the rivers. North of Ondo the country is hilly, and along the eastern border several ranges of hills occur of which the Oban hills are the most important. A line of hills to the east of the Niger forms the watershed between that river and the Cross river system. In this zone are found large expanses of open, undulating ground, covered with grass and studded with small clumps of trees, the general appearance being far different from what is popularly imagined as tropical country.

North of this zone is a great undulating plateau with occasional hills of granite and sandstone. The general elevation is about 2,000 feet, but to the south-west of Yola and in certain parts of the Bauchi plateau there are considerable heights, in some cases from 6,000 to 7,000 feet above sea-level. The southern portion of the plateau is clothed with thin forest, but the country becomes more and more open and sandy towards the north. Much of the country north of Zaria is covered with heavy loose sand and it is believed that the desert is gradually encroaching. On the east the plateau sinks to the plains of Bornu, which extend to Lake Chad.

The main physical feature of Nigeria is, of course, the great river from which it takes its name. The Niger[2] rises in the mountains to the north-east of Sierra Leone, about 150 miles from the sea, and flows in a north-easterly direction till it reaches Timbuktu. From this point it flows eastward for about 200 miles, and then flows in a south-easterly direction to Lokoja, about 340 miles from the sea. Here it receives the waters of

[1] The fauna of the country includes the elephant, the 'bush-cow' or dwarf buffalo, the hippopotamus, the rhinoceros, the giraffe, the lion, the leopard, the hyaena, and many forms of antelopes and gazelles.
[2] Known also as the Joliba, Kworra, Quorra, Kowara, or Fari'n Rua.

its principal tributary, the Benue,[1] on its left bank, and from here it flows due south to a point a few miles below Abo, where the delta commences. This delta extends along the coast for over 100 miles, and for about 140 miles inland; the river here forms an intricate network of channels, dividing and subdividing, and a multitude of creeks connect these branches of the Niger not only with one another but also with other rivers, so that it is difficult to say whether some of the streams are part of the delta or belong to some other river system. The length of the Niger is 2,600 miles, of which about two-thirds lie outside Nigeria, and the area of the river basin is estimated to exceed 500,000 square miles.

Both the Niger and the Benue are greatly affected by the rainfall, a difference of as much as 35 feet between high and low water being recorded. At high water the rivers form wide, navigable waterways, several miles in width from bank to bank, but in the dry season they shrink considerably, exposing large sandbanks which divide the shrunken rivers into several channels. Owing to the widely separated localities in which they rise the influence of the rainfall is felt at different times by the two rivers; the upper Niger rises in June, but below Timbuktu it reaches its maximum only in January, falling again in February and March and reaching its lowest point in April, with a slight temporary rise in August; the Benue is at its lowest in March and April, when it can be forded at several places, is at its highest in August and September and falls in October. Below the confluence the influence of both streams is felt; the lowest water is in April and May, in June there are great fluctuations, by the middle of August the water is rising rapidly, and the highest point is reached in September; the river begins to sink again in October and there is a slight temporary rise in January.

The other important tributaries of the Niger are the Sokoto river and the Kaduna, both of which join it above Lokoja, and the Anambara, which joins it at Onitsha; all of these are on the left bank. The Katsena and Gongola rivers are tributaries of the Benue, the former flowing from the south and the latter from the north.

[1] Known also as the Chadda, Tschadda, Shari, or Baki'n Rua. The Benue rises in the Republic of Cameroun.

The river valleys are all at a considerably lower elevation than the neighbouring plateau. The Benue at Yola, 800 miles from the sea, is no more than 600 feet above sea-level and at the junction with the Niger there is an elevation of only about 300 feet. The Kaduna Valley is about 500 feet above sea-level.

Apart from the Niger and its tributaries, the principal rivers are the Ogun, which flows into the lagoon behind Lagos island; the Benin,[1] which is formed by the junction of the Jamieson and Ethiope rivers at Sapele; the Escravos;[2] the Sombreiro; the New Calabar; the Bonny; the Antonio; the Opobo; the Kwa Ibo; and the Cross with its tributary, the Old Calabar river. The Cross river rises in the Republic of Cameroun, and at high-water forms a navigable waterway of nearly 200 miles. Between the Escravos and the Sombreiro are the numerous mouths of the Niger, which are known respectively, from west to east, as the rivers Forcados, Ramos, Dodo, Pennington, Middleton, Winstanley, Fishtown, Sengama, Nun, Brass,[3] St Nicholas, St Barbara, and St Bartholomew. Until recently the Forcados was the main channel, but in former years the Nun branch, on which the port of Akassa is situated, was the most important. Ocean steamers now enter the Niger by way of the Escravos river.

The chief watersheds of the country are formed by the Ondo hills, which separate the rivers flowing southwards into the Lagos lagoon from the Niger system, the hills which separate the Niger and Cross river systems, and the Bauchi plateau. From the last-named rivers run south-west, south-east and north-east; of these the most important are the Kaduna, flowing into the Niger, the Gongola, flowing to the Benue, and the parent streams of the Yobe, which flows into Lake Chad.

Lake Chad is on the north-east border of Nigeria and a portion of its area lies within the boundary; the lake receives the waters of the Yobe and of the Shari, which enters it from the east and, although there is no visible outlet the lake is obviously drying up, probably from evaporation. It is not unlikely that

[1] Also known as the Rio Formoso or Argon.
[2] = Slaves; often incorrectly spelt Escardos.
[3] So called from the importation by the people of that locality of European-made brass pans, known in the trade as 'neptunes', used for making palm oil and salt. *Memoirs of Captain Crow* (1830), p. 197.

Lake Chad was at one time connected with the Benue, and it was probably owing to a belief in this that the Benue was known for some while as the Chadda.

As might be expected, there is a very considerable difference in the climate between the dry, sandy country in the north of Nigeria and the low-lying, swampy coast. Both parts are hot, but while the heat of the north is dry, that of the south is damp and enervating. The seasons are, however, governed not by temperature but by rainfall, and there are only two seasons, which are, as a rule, well defined. The 'dry' season begins in the north in October and ends in April, while in the south it is of shorter duration and at Lagos generally lasts from November to March. It is characterized by the *Harmattan*, a dry, north-easterly wind, which brings along with it a thick haze[1] composed of minute particles of dust and shell from the Sahara. During the *Harmattan* the nights and early mornings are cold, but the days are very hot, and it is during this period that the maximum diurnal variations of temperature occur, a variation of as much as 50° being recorded within a few hours. It is in the north that the *Harmattan* is most severe, and it has been found that the difference in range between the maximum and minimum temperature is greater in proportion to the distance of a station from the coast. At the end of the 'dry season' numerous tornadoes herald the approach of the 'rainy season'. Before a tornado the air is oppressively close and heavy, but the tornado itself, which is generally scarcely more than a heavy squall, lasts but a short while, and is accompanied and followed by a thunderstorm and rain.

The rainy season lasts until October, with a slight break in August, and is followed by another short tornado season. In the south the prevailing wind during the rainy season is from the south-west, and with it comes the rain, which is remarkably heavy along the coast and decreases rapidly as it travels inland. At Akassa, Bonny, Forcados, and Brass the average annual rainfall exceeds 150 inches, at Calabar it is about 120 inches, and at Lagos over 70 inches; all of these towns are situated on the coast. At the inland towns of Ilorin, Lokoja, and Ibi the average rainfall is between 40 and 50 inches, while in the extreme north, at Sokoto and Maidugari, the average is under 28 inches.

[1] Known to the early navigators as the 'Smokes'.

That the distinction between the 'dry season' and the 'rainy season' is a very real one will be seen from the fact that at Maidugari not an inch of rain was recorded for the 37 years 1914–51 during the five months November to March; at Bonny, where the average rainfall is 172 inches, over 141 inches fall during the seven months May to November. June and July are generally the wettest months of the year.

The lowest mean temperature is recorded in July and August, and the lowest minimum temperature in December and January, during the prevalence of the *Harmattan*; the highest temperatures, both mean and maximum, are, as a rule, recorded in March and April. The temperature never rises as high on the coast as it does in the north of Nigeria, but the humidity of the air causes a damp and enervating heat which is more unpleasant than the greater but drier heat of the interior. The annual mean temperature in Lagos is approximately 80°, the absolute minimum about 60° and the absolute maximum 95°; at Maidugari the absolute minimum is about 43° and the absolute maximum 109°.

Frost is occasionally experienced in the neighbourhood of Lake Chad, and hailstorms have been recorded.[1]

That Nigeria is an unhealthy country cannot be denied, and the mortality among the Europeans who first visited the country justified the title of 'the white man's grave' which is shared with other parts of West Africa. Even among the natives of the country there is an excessive amount of disease and a high rate of mortality. The forests and swamps of the south are naturally more unhealthy than the open country of the north and, as will be seen in the next chapter, the stronger tribes have usurped the better lands and driven the weaker peoples down into the less healthy but less accessible forests.

[1] 'Friday, May 2nd, there was a hailstorm at 5 p.m.; the rare luxury of iced wine was partaken of.' English edition of *Iwe Irohin* of May 3, 1862. (This newspaper was published for some years at Abeokuta.) Sir Richard Burton, in a note to Night 764 of the *Arabian Nights* (1885), says: 'I have seen heavy hail in Africa, N. Lat. 4°, within sight of the Equator.'

CHAPTER II

POPULATION: (a) YORUBALAND

The African is not clay to be cast into Western moulds, but a living type which must develop in accordance with its own laws and express its own native genius.

J. H. OLDHAM: *Christianity and the Race Problem*, 4th ed., 1925.

The African population of Nigeria is divided into numerous tribal[1] and linguistic groups, great and small, speaking different languages, professing different religions, and differing one from another in manners and customs. Of the origin of these people little is known. Their ancestors have left them practically no written records or monuments, and their traditions, interwoven with myth and legend, are fragmentary and in many cases conflicting. Wave after wave of invasion appears to have swept over the country, and the weaker tribes have been driven back and scattered by successive conquerors. Although in the rugged fastnesses of the Bauchi plateau some of the aboriginal inhabitants have taken refuge and seen the wave of conquest surround and pass them by, for the most part the fugitives have been pressed southwards into the dense forests and swampy country along the coast, leaving to the stronger races the open and healthier plains of the north.

As we shall see, many of the people of Nigeria believe that their ancestors came from 'the East'—from Egypt or Arabia— and some almost certainly did. It is impossible to say who were the aboriginal inhabitants of the country and to what degree of culture they had attained, but there have been some important recent discoveries with some bearing on this problem. In 1931, at the village of Nok, south of Zaria, some pottery 'portrait' heads were found and similar discoveries have been made later in this area and on the plateau which lies north of the River Benue. Many of the figurines found are more than 2,000 years old and show an advanced technique. It has been suggested that 'Nok Society was a transitional culture between

---

[1] It is pointed out in the *Handbook of Commerce and Industry in Nigeria* (4th ed., 1960), that 'the term "tribe" is used in Nigeria not so much in its political or ethnic sense but as the distinguishing characteristic of language'.

stone and metals and reached its full development in the last two or three centuries B C', and that, in its later stages, Nok 'was the earliest iron-using culture in the region'. It is probable that the Nok people, responsible for these pottery heads and figures, 'were the direct ancestors of some of the peoples who live in central Nigeria today'.[1] It is probable that the art of Ife[2] and Benin[3] may have derived from the so-called 'Nok figurine cult'.

In the first half of the nineteenth century, when the interior of Nigeria first became known to Europeans, the open country had been for some time the home of Negroid and Berber peoples who had adopted the Muhammadan religion and formed powerful and comparatively civilized states. In the forest and mountain country, on the other hand, there dwelt a number of Negro tribes, addicted to cannibalism and human sacrifice, and with a few exceptions possessing no highly organized form of government. On the Bauchi plateau and in its immediate vicinity, within an area of less than 25,000 square miles, there were over 100 small tribes, and between the Benue and the sea there were nearly 100 more. The broken country afforded them a measure of protection from their stronger neighbours, but even in these wild regions 'where fragments of forgotten peoples dwelt' there was little security for life or property. Constant warfare raged, and thousands perished annually in slave raids, the captives being often utilized to provide the victims of a sacrifice or for a cannibal feast. In such circumstances it is little wonder that these people were unable to raise themselves from barbarism, and that the comparatively few years of ordered administration have not yet outweighed the centuries of chaos that preceded them.

Lord Lugard, writing in 1921, said that from the point of view of the administrator it was necessary to classify the people of tropical Africa into three groups, according to their social organization—viz. the primitive tribes, the advanced communities, and the Europeanized Africans. Such a division connotes a more real and profound difference than that of racial affinities, for intermarriage and concubinage with alien

[1] *Old Africa Rediscovered* (1959), by Basil Davidson, pp. 65–6.
[2] See page 36.   [3] See page 67.

captives and slaves have tended to obliterate tribal characteristics.[1] The Fulani, especially in the upper classes, afford a typical example of the effect of constant concubinage with

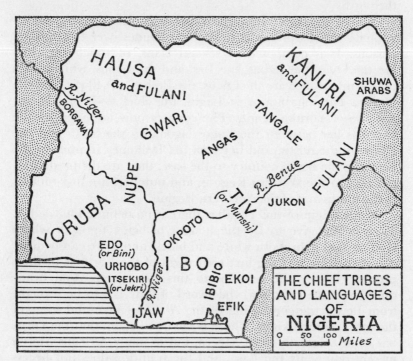

Negro slaves; they consider themselves[2] a white people, and those of the pastoral Fulani who have kept their blood pure possess a light bronze complexion and other physical characteristics of the Hamitic races, but the town Fulani are as dark as the pure Negro tribes, and to the superficial observer differ from them but slightly in other respects. It will be convenient

[1] *The Dual Mandate in British Tropical Africa* (2nd ed., 1923), by Sir F. D. (later Lord) Lugard, p. 72. Sir Frederick Lugard, as he then was, was High Commissioner of Northern Nigeria from 1900 to 1906 and Governor-General of Nigeria from 1914 to 1919.

[2] And are sometimes considered so by others. Sir Richard Burton, in *Wit and Wisdom from West Africa* (1865), p. 267, mentions the Yoruba ethnographical adage connecting the Fulani with Europeans: 'Eya oibo ni Fulani', which means, 'The Fulani are a tribe from over the sea', i.e. 'white men'.

to consider first the 'advanced communities', which are represented in Nigeria by the Yorubas and Binis (or Edo) in the
south, and the Hausa, Fulani, Kanuri, and Arab tribes in
the north.

One of the most important tribes is the Yoruba, which
with its various offshoots probably includes over five million
persons. It is composed of several clans, of which the chief
are the Oyos, the Egbas, the Ifes, and the Ijebus, while others
of less importance are the Owus, the Ijeshas, the Ekitis, and the
Ondos. The inhabitants of Lagos, the chief town of Nigeria,
are also of Yoruba origin. The country now occupied by the
Yorubas lies between the Lagos lagoon on the south and the
Niger on the north, and between the Dahomey frontier to the
west and the Benin country to the east; they are the predomin-
ant race in the Western Region, and numbers are to be found
in the south-west of the Northern Region.

Of the origin of the Yorubas there is no definite knowledge.
Their myths give to Ife the honour of being the spot where
God created man, both white and black, and there can be little
doubt that Ife was the first settlement of the Yorubas in their
present country. Ife remains to this day the spiritual headquarters of the race, and the sword of state has to be brought
from Ife for the coronation of the Alafin of Oyo and some of
the other Yoruba kings. There is the usual claim that the Yorubas came originally from Mecca, but to many Africans Mecca
merely represents the East, and the tradition does not neces-
sarily involve a suggestion that they sprang from the holy city
of Islam. A further tradition that they came from Upper Egypt
has better foundation; certain carved stones found at Ife, the
manner in which the dead are bound for burial, and the kind of
cloth used for this purpose, are supposed to indicate an Egyptian origin. Sultan Bello of Sokoto[1] states, in the work of which
Captain Clapperton obtained an extract, that the people of
Yoruba, 'it is supposed, originated from the remnants of the
children of Canaan, who were of the tribe of Nimrod. The
cause of their establishment in the west of Africa was, as it is
stated, in consequence of their being driven by Yaa-rooba, son
of Kahtan, out of Arabia to the western coast between Egypt
and Abyssinia. From that spot they advanced into the interior

[1] Died 1837. See below.

of Africa till they reached Yarba, where they fixed their residence. On their way they left, in every place they stopped at, a tribe of their own people. Thus it is supposed that all the tribes of Soodan, who inhabit the mountains, are originated from them, as also are the inhabitants of Ya-ory.'[1] Whatever

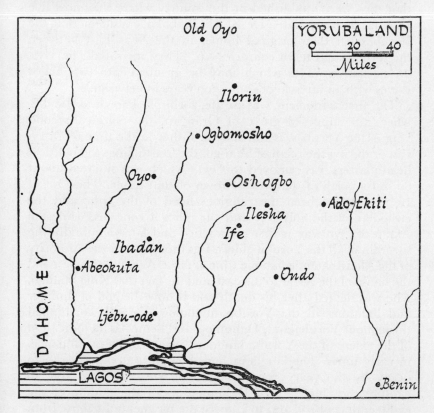

their origin, it is probable that the Yorubas were not originally of Negro blood, although, in the centuries during which they have occupied their present territories, they have so intermarried with Negro slaves as to have lost their early characteristics. Leo Frobenius, the leader of the German expedition which explored the antiquities of Yorubaland in 1910, thought

[1] See Appendix to *Narrative of Travels and Discoveries in Northern and Central Africa in the years 1822–4* (1828), by Major Denham and Captain Clapperton.

he detected a difference between the high-class Yorubas, 'men of finer stature, extraordinary slenderness and delicacy of limb, narrow heads, and fairer skins',[1] and those of the lower classes, who possess the usual Negro characteristics.

If the origin of the Yorubas is doubtful, it is at any rate clear that they were established in the country where they now live at a fairly early date. Dr S. O. Biobaku considers that the Yorubas left their original homes in the Near East between the seventh and tenth centuries AD. 'They migrated', he says, 'in successive waves which may be grouped into two major waves with an interval of about 300 years in between.'[2]

The first settlement was at Ife, formerly known as Ile Ife, where the supposed grave of Oranyan, the mythical second king of the Yorubas, is still shown. Either in the time of Oranyan or during the reign of Shango, the fourth king, the political headquarters was removed to Oyo,[3] which was situated about 80 miles north of the present town of that name. The Oni of Ife has always been the religious head of the tribe and the custodian of the holy city and the relics it contains, while the Alafin of Oyo was at first in practice and later nominally the suzerain of all the Yoruba chiefs. It is thought that the authority of the Alafin extended at one time as far as Accra to the west and the banks of the Niger to the east, and the fact that King Shango, who was deified after his death and is now the god of thunder and lightning in the Yoruba mythology, is still worshipped throughout Yorubaland, Dahomey, and Benin,[4] is an indication of the extent of the Yoruba kingdom, or at least of its influence, in early times. The kingdom had, however, already begun to decay by the year 1700, though the Yorubas were able to capture the chief city of Dahomey about the middle of the eighteenth century, and to enforce the payment of tribute from that country till about the year 1817.

Until this date the authority of the Alafin of Oyo had not

----

[1] *The Voice of Africa*, by Leo Frobenius (English translation, 1913), vol. i, p. 145.

[2] *The Origin of the Yoruba* (the first Lugard Lectures, 1955, broadcast in Nigeria).

[3] Also known as Eyeo and Katunga.

[4] *History of the Yorubas* (1921), by Rev. S. Johnson, p. 34. Mr Johnson was himself a Yoruba.

been seriously disputed by any of the Yoruba clans, although the allegiance of the provincial rulers was becoming more and more nominal. With the close of the long and peaceful reign of Abiodun, about the year 1810, the break-up of the kingdom began. Afonja, the governor of Ilorin, was an ambitious man, who desired to make himself independent of the Alafin, and in the reign of Abiodun's successor he made his bid for power. Besides being governor of Ilorin he held the highest military rank among the Yorubas, and the Alafin, who was well aware of his ambitions, and was moreover his personal enemy, set him the practically impossible task of capturing a hostile town which was believed to be impregnable. According to their military etiquette, a Yoruba general who did not succeed in his objective within a specified period was required to commit suicide, but Afonja was able to persuade his troops of the injustice of the Alafin's order, and the siege was raised. Led by Afonja, the army then marched on Oyo and after some negotiation the Alafin was invited to commit suicide, which he did after solemnly cursing his disloyal people. As soon as the Alafin was dead the soldiery sacked Oyo and then scattered to their homes, Afonja with his personal followers returning to Ilorin, where he established himself as an independent sovereign. To strengthen his position he invited a Fulani Muhammadan mallam, Alimi, to join him as his priest, and Alimi's Hausa slaves, with runaway Hausa slaves from neighbouring Yoruba towns, were formed into an army with which he succeeded in defeating a large Yoruba force sent against him. The excesses of his Hausa mercenaries, however, provoked much resentment among the Yoruba population, and Afonja at last determined to disband them, but this was by no means to their liking and they rose against him under the leadership of Alimi. Deserted by the other Yoruba chiefs, whom he had alienated, Afonja was defeated and killed, and Alimi became the ruler of Ilorin. To him flocked his Fulani and Hausa co-religionists, and Ilorin became an independent Fulani kingdom, the Emir yielding only a nominal allegiance to the Sultan of Sokoto.

It was on account of the mutual jealousy of the Yoruba chiefs, and the growing weakness of the central authority, that the Fulani were able to subdue a Yoruba population and set up a kingdom in one of the richest of the Yoruba provinces. Following the example of Afonja, the rulers of the various clans now asserted their independence and ceased to pay tribute to Oyo, leaving to the Alafin little but his capital. Even this he was not allowed to retain for very long. The Fulani from Ilorin made continual incursions into the Yoruba territories and finally captured and sacked Oyo. A little later the Emir summoned the Alafin to Ilorin and there compelled him to accept the doctrines of Islam, but this, and the indignities heaped upon him during his visit, stirred up the Yoruba people, who determined to avenge the insult to their titular head and to drive the Fulani from their country. A large army assembled, but divided counsels prevailed among the Yoruba leaders and the Fulani inflicted on them a crushing defeat, the Alafin being slain; Oyo was deserted and the people fled before the victorious Fulani who overran the country as far south as Abeokuta.

The disintegration of the kingdom was now complete. There was no central authority, and the increasing demand for slaves encouraged the various clans to fight one another and send their prisoners-of-war to the slave-markets of Lagos and Dahomey. Instead of uniting against their common enemies, the Yorubas sought to destroy one another. The Owus were attacked by the armies of the Ifes and Ijebus, assisted by some of the Oyo refugees, their towns were destroyed and they themselves almost annihilated.[1] A little later the allies attacked the Egbas, who were at that time established at Ibadan and in numerous other towns; the Egbas were outmatched and were compelled to retire in a south-westerly direction. They finally established themselves in their present town of Abeokuta about the year 1830, and were there joined by the remnant of the Owus. The abandoned town of Ibadan was occupied by the Oyo refugees, but a new Oyo was soon built by the Alafin Atiba, and Ibadan then became the military headquarters of the Yorubas, pledged to the defence of the country against the Fulani, and acknowledging the suzerainty of the Alafin. Ilorin

[1] Referring to this campaign in his *History of the Yorubas*, the Rev. S. Johnson says: 'The Ijebus were better armed . . . than any of the interior tribes, for, being nearest the coast, they had the advantage of obtaining guns and gunpowder from Europeans in exchange for slaves. . . . The older men . . . constituted the regular fighting column: being too old or too heavy to run away, they were obliged to be courageous.'

was in fact checked by the Ibadan forces in 1843, and for a moment it looked as though the ancient glories of Yoruba might be restored, but once again the demand for slaves started a fresh series of civil wars which nearly destroyed the people. Constant petty fights and unceasing slave-raiding became the order of things, and the harassed peasants had little time for agriculture or trade until the advent of British rule brought with it peace and prosperity.[1]

Though nominally subject to the Alafin of Oyo, each clan had been for some time past virtually independent, the government being in the hands of kings who, theoretically absolute, were in practice controlled by the council of elders which has always existed in every state, and is to this day possessed of considerable power. Although their choice is limited to members of the royal family, the council has the right of electing the king, and all matters of routine are dealt with by the king in consultation with the council; for matters of unusual importance a tribal meeting would be convoked. In the old days it was usual for the eldest son of the Alafin of Oyo to be more or less associated with his father in the government of the country, but in order to check a tendency to parricide it was a recognized law (until 1858) that the Aremo, as the eldest son was called, must commit suicide on the death of the Alafin. Among the Yorubas suicide was regarded as an honourable death, and those of whom convention required it seldom failed to take their own lives; should they hesitate their own relatives would kill them to avoid the disgrace to the family. Besides the Aremo, several of the king's household were required to end their lives by honourable suicide when he died: 'The custom is that each should go and die in his (or her) own home, and among his family . . . the house is full of visitors, mourners, and others . . . while the grave is digging, the coffin making, a parting feast is made for all the friends and acquaintances. . . . When everything is ready, the grave and the coffin approved of, they then take poison, and pass off quietly. But if it fails or is too slow to take effect, and the sun is about to set, the last office is performed by the nearest relatives (by strangling or otherwise), to save themselves and the memory of their kin from indelible

[1] The history of Yorubaland from 1843 is dealt with in Chapters X and XI.

B

disgrace.'[1] There were few of the kings themselves who did not end their own lives. Aole, the Alafin against whom the army rebelled in 1817, was sent an empty covered calabash,[2] which was intended for his head, and he took the hint and poisoned himself. Others received various symbolical messages to indicate that they were rejected by their people, and there is no recorded case of their failing to commit suicide.

Owing to the sanctity which was supposed to attach to the person of the king, it was impossible for any of his subjects to lay violent hands upon him, but no doubt a king refusing to commit suicide would have been dealt with in a suitable manner. To preserve respect for the monarchy and to avoid any chance of that familiarity which breeds contempt, the kings were not allowed to appear in public except on very special occasions, and some of the Yoruba chiefs wore bead veils to hide their faces from the vulgar eye. But there was another reason why the kings were not encouraged to appear in public; according to Yoruba etiquette, whenever a chief left his house he had to be followed by all his subordinates and, should a king go out, the normal life of his capital would be arrested as the whole population would be required to attend their sovereign.

In the old days the kings and members of the royal families shamelessly abused their positions and trampled on the liberties of the people, but in spite of this there were some who administered a crude form of justice which, peculiar as it may appear to modern eyes, apparently satisfied their subjects. Johnson refers to one of the Alafins, Adelu, who 'loved his people and would never allow any of the princes to distress the poor with impunity. An instance was given of a prince who fought with a commoner and cut off one of his fingers. This being reported to his father, he severely reprimanded the prince, and was determined to exact a full retaliation of the deed. But the constitution of the country forbade him to disfigure a prince, so he ordered someone to be brought from the family of his mother as substitute. A young virgin was met in the house beating corn, and she was summoned to the palace. The king ordered the executioner to lop off the same finger of the young

[1] Johnson, op. cit., p. 56.
[2] A gourd.

woman as that which the prince cut off from the man's hand. This was done instantly. Then said the king to her: "It is not my fault, it is your cousin who deprived you of your finger." This was his rude idea of justice. As that young woman and all the relations of the prince's mother enjoy great advantages under his auspices, so they should be ready to suffer for his crimes.'[1] We are not told what view the young virgin took of the matter.

The constitution of the Egbas is slightly different from that of the other Yoruba clans. Originally a small branch of the Oyo Yorubas, they were scattered in small hamlets under their own village head-men until the civil wars of the early nineteenth century compelled them to take refuge in a single town, the present Abeokuta, where the different quarters of the town still bear the names of the villages whence the first settlers came. The town now boasts four kings, three of them Egbas and the fourth the leader of the Owu people, who joined the Egbas at Abeokuta after their own towns had been destroyed. The Alake of Abeokuta, one of the kings, is recognized as *primus inter pares*.[2]

Although Muhammadanism and Christianity have been making progress in Yorubaland for a great many years, the people are still mainly pagan.[3] They believe in the existence of a Supreme Being, whom they term Olorun (the owner of the sky), but they consider Him too important and remote to be much concerned with the affairs of mankind; there are, however, a number of minor deities (Orishas) who are more directly interested in mundane matters, and frequent sacrifices are offered to these. They believe in a future state and also in the transmigration of souls, children frequently receiving the names of ancestors who are supposed to be reborn in them. The spirits of the departed are worshipped in different ways, chiefly through the medium of the priests and members of the Egugun or Adamuorisha societies, while the Oro, what-

[1] Johnson, *op. cit.*, p. 400.

[2] For the origin and early history of the Egbas, see *The Egba and their Neighbours, 1842–1872* (1957), by S. O. Biobaku.

[3] The word 'pagan' is loosely used in Nigeria (and in this book) to describe all who are neither Christian nor Muhammadan. The religion of most of the so-called pagan tribes is animistic.

ever its earlier significance, is now mainly a means of keeping
the female portion of the population in a state of proper sub-
servience to the stronger sex. A loud wailing noise, created by
a flat piece of stick carved in a peculiar way being whirled
round the head at the end of a piece of string[1] is the signal
that the Oro is abroad, and that all women must conceal themselves, on pain, in former years, of death, and nowadays of a
severe beating. Shango, one of the mythical Alafins of Oyo, is
worshipped as the god of thunder; the owner of any house
struck by lightning is required to pay heavy fees to avert the
wrath of Shango, which is considered to have been incurred by
the lies or perjury of the householder. It has been suggested
that many of the houses burnt during a thunderstorm are
destroyed by the agency of Shango's priests and not by lightning, and there is no doubt that the neoliths found by the
priests in the ground near the scene of the disaster are invariably
'planted' by them to give support to their claims. Sopona, the
god of smallpox, is one that needs much propitiation; the
priests of this cult bury the victims of the disease and claim
heavy fees from the relatives of the deceased, and it is believed
that on some occasions in the past they deliberately spread
the infection in order to increase the number of victims
and the amount of their fees. Johnson says that the number of
gods and goddesses recognized by the Yorubas is reckoned at
401, while 'sacrifices are also offered to whatever in nature is
awe-inspiring or magnificent, such as the ocean, huge rocks,
tall trees, and high mountains'.[2] Ifa is recognized as an
oracle.

The Ogboni is a religious council which is very largely concerned with political affairs, but as it is a secret society little
is known of its actual functions. Leo Frobenius, the German
ethnologist, claims to have been admitted as a member of the
Ogboni, and hints that ritual murder was practised by the
society.[3] That human sacrifice was a feature of the cult in
early years can scarcely be doubted.

The archaeological treasures of Ife are among the best
that have been found in Nigeria. They include well-carved

[1] Identical with the 'bull-roarer' of Australian aborigines.
[2] Johnson, *op. cit.*, p. 38.
[3] Frobenius, *op. cit*, vol. i, pp. 60–4.

monoliths, some of phallic significance,[1] one studded with metal nails, and others carved with characters of possible Phoenician origin; stone, terra-cotta, bronze heads and statues, and utensils of various kinds, are also to be seen.

[1] Traces of phallic worship are also found among other tribes, e.g. the Iyashi. See *Notes on the Tribes . . . of the Northern Provinces of Nigeria* (1919), by O. Temple, p. 161. Mr Talbot says that 'Phallic pillars of various sizes exist in great numbers, especially in the Cross River region'. See *The Peoples of Southern Nigeria* (1926), vol. ii, p. 22.

CHAPTER III

POPULATION: (b) LAGOS AND BENIN

... Power on silt,
Death in my hands, but Gold.
R. KIPLING : *A Song of the English*

No less than seven of the eight largest towns in Nigeria today are inhabited mainly by Yorubas.[1] The largest is Ibadan, with a population of over 600,000, and the next in size is Lagos, the population of which is about 364,000. Lagos is the capital and principal port of the country and, indeed, of West Africa. In the absence of any kind of written records we are entirely dependent on tradition for the early history of this place. If even tradition does not carry us back very far, it must be remembered that up to comparatively recent times Lagos was little more than a mudbank in the lagoon which now bears its name.[2]

The Lagos lagoon is a large shallow sheet of water formed by the River Ogun and a few smaller streams. The channel to the sea, about half a mile wide, is the only navigable opening in the coast-line between the rivers Volta[3] and Benin, and when the sea-borne trade of Nigeria began to become important it was inevitable that the value of Lagos as a port should be recognized. The island of Lagos and the smaller island of Iddo lie, moreover, immediately in front of the sea channel, and the current passing round these islands scours away the sand on the seaward side and ensures a deep-water anchorage. It was not, however, the value of Lagos as a port that attracted to it the first settlers. There was in those days no trade in that locality, and the island offered nothing save a refuge from enemies.

A band of Yorubas, led by a cadet of the royal family,

---

[1] Other than Ibadan and Lagos, the largest Yoruba towns are Ogbomosho (population, 140,000), Oshogbo (122,000), Ife (111,000), Iwo (100,000), Abeokuta (82,000), Ilesha (72,000), and Oyo (72,000). The Hausa town of Kano has a population of 130,000.

[2] Formerly known as the Ikorodu or Cradoo lagoon.

[3] In Ghana.

appears to have settled at Isheri, on the Ogun river, about 12 miles as the crow flies from the present town of Lagos; the settlers then spread southwards to Ebute Metta, on the mainland opposite Iddo island, where a town was built and farming was begun. Some time after this the outbreak of war among the Yorubas endangered the existence of the small community at Ebute Metta; the town was therefore abandoned and the inhabitants moved across to Iddo island, where they were more secure from attack. Iddo, however, was scarcely large enough to support the number of settlers, and as the farms on the mainland were considered too accessible to potential enemies, it was decided to begin cultivation on the neighbouring island of Lagos, which until then had been the resort only of fishermen. It was not very long after the move to Iddo that the first invasion from Benin took place: the inhabitants were fortunate that at this crisis their Olofin, or ruler, was a man of great courage and strong character, and under his leadership the King of Benin's soldiers were repulsed. Subsequent attacks met with no better success, and the Olofin gained in fame and influence. He is reputed to have had thirty-two sons, and 'one-half of these he made headmen, or petty chiefs; for they could not, if the one be excepted who succeeded his father, have deserved a higher title, considering how very circumscribed their territorial possessions were'.[1] Of the other sons, one succeeded his father as Oloto of Iddo, the title of Olofin falling into abeyance, 'probably because of the distinguished character of *the* Olofin, and the high regard entertained for him after his death';[2] four others were made chiefs of portions of the neighbouring mainland, and the island of Lagos was divided among the remaining ten. The custom of the Lagos chiefs to wear 'white caps' came originally from Iddo, and was introduced by the ten sons of the Olofin, whose successors still wear similar caps. In addition to the territorial chiefs who wore the 'white cap' in token of their position as landowners, there were certain court functionaries, appointed by the king, who also received permission to wear this distinguishing head-dress. The two classes of chiefs were, however, quite distinct.

Some little time after the Olofin's death there began the

[1] *Historical Notices of Lagos, West Africa* (1880), by Rev. J. B. Wood, p. 13.
[2] *Ibid.*

peaceful penetration into Lagos of settlers from Benin.¹ The
Binis probably realized that they would not be able to occupy
Lagos by force, as they had already been so decisively beaten
in their attacks on Iddo, and it is thought that they were also
prevented from further aggression by superstitious fear, the
dying wife of the Olofin having pronounced a terrible curse on
any further invaders from Benin. Whatever may have been the
reason, the immigrants from Benin arrived with no great show
of force, and permission was asked of the Lagos people for
them to land. This permission was granted, probably with no
very good grace, although at that time Lagos island was very
sparsely inhabited and there must have been room for many
more settlers. However, more and more people arrived from
Benin and, although the title of the original 'white cap'
chiefs to the land was never disputed, the Edos (or Binis)
gradually became the dominant faction in Lagos, and the
influence of Benin became more and more evident. It was
probably towards the end of the fifteenth century that the
Edos obtained the complete ascendancy and that Portuguese
vessels began to call regularly at Lagos. Some time after, the
Edos began to attack the people on the mainland, and the
leader of one of their marauding parties dying at Isheri, his
remains were conveyed to Benin by one of the Isheri chiefs
named Ashipa, who was anxious to secure the favour of the
powerful King of Benin. Ashipa was related to the ruling house
of Yoruba, and the King of Benin, desirous of consolidating his
hold on Lagos, appointed him king of that island. In his
appointment, for which there appears to have been no authority, the King of Benin showed great political acumen. The
appointment of a Yoruba of the blood royal to be their king
would not antagonize the original inhabitants of Lagos, while
the vassal monarch would be bound to his suzerain by ties of
gratitude. But to be on the safe side several 'advisers' accompanied Ashipa from Benin on his return, and these no doubt
saw that the interests of their country were not neglected.
Tribute continued to be paid to Benin for many years and it
was not till about 1830 that it was refused; by this time Lagos
was too strong to be attacked and the King of Benin had to be

¹ The people of Benin speak the Edo language and are called Edos. They
were formerly more often referred to as Binis.

content with occasional presents from the vassal state, which now was bound to Benin only by sentiment.[1]

With the appointment of Ashipa as King of Lagos the relative positions of Lagos and Iddo began to change. The Oloto of Iddo never acknowledged the suzerainty of Benin, and was inclined to look down on the ruler of Lagos as an upstart, but as the power and wealth of the latter increased, Iddo fell farther and farther into the background. It is not likely that the Oloto ever formally acknowledged himself as subject to the King of Lagos, but in practice that is what he became. Ashipa was succeeded by his son Ado, and he by his two sons, Gabaro and Akinshemoyin, successively. It was probably earlier than the reign of the last named that the Portuguese, who had neglected Lagos as their trade declined, again began to settle there, and it was they who gave it its present name.[2] Formerly it was known as Eko, which name it had received before any settlements were made on the island. The Portuguese were attracted to Lagos by its suitability as a slave-depot; creeks connected it on either side with Dahomey and Benin, while to the north lay the populous Yoruba country, where the disastrous civil wars were then commencing. These civil wars nearly destroyed the Yoruba nation, but they created the wealth of Lagos. From early in the nineteenth century to the date of the British occupation (1861) thousands of captives taken in these wars were brought to Lagos and sold in the slave-market, and large fortunes were accumulated by the Portuguese and Brazilian merchants who exported these unfortunate people. The kings took their share of the profits, and the town grew rapidly in wealth and importance.

Captain Adams, who visited Lagos in a slave-ship towards the end of the eighteenth century, tells us that

the horrid custom of impaling alive a young female, to propitiate the favour of the goddess presiding over the rainy season, that she may fill the horn of plenty, is practised here annually . . . one was impaled while I was at Lagos, but of course I did not witness the

[1] In 1851 the King of Lagos admitted to Consul Beecroft that he was a vassal of the King of Benin. See Chapter X.

[2] The Portuguese called it originally 'Lago de Curamo' (see *Description of the Coasts of North and South Guinea*, by John Barbot (1732), p. 354), but it was known to them at a later date as Onin.

ceremony. I passed by where her lifeless body still remained on the stake a few days afterwards. . . . At the eastern extremity of the town are a few large trees, which are covered with the heads of malefactors. The skulls are nailed to their trunks and large limbs and present a very appalling spectacle. The town swarms with water-rats from the lake, which burrow in the ground, and are so audacious that they not infrequently make their appearance under the dinner-table of Europeans before the cloth is removed. The population of the town of Lagos may amount to 5,000; but there are two or three populous villages on the north side of Cradoo Lake, over which the caboceer of Lagos has jurisdiction. This chief's power is absolute, and his disposition tyrannical to excess.[1]

It is not clear whether Akinshemoyin was succeeded by Kekere, the son of Gabaro, who in any case was of little importance. Ologun Kutere, a grandson of Ado, was the next king, and was succeeded by his second son, Adele, who was deposed in favour of his elder brother, Oshinlokun. This king was succeeded by his elder son, Idewu Ojulari, who was so unpopular that the King of Benin was appealed to by the Lagos people to order his deposition; on the order being given Idewu poisoned himself.[2]

The throne should now, in the ordinary way, have passed to Kosoko, the younger brother of Idewu, but this individual had fallen foul of a powerful chief, the Eletu, whose privilege it was to crown the Kings of Lagos. Taking advantage of his position as a member of the ruling house, Kosoko had carried off a young woman who was betrothed to the Eletu, and this was the beginning of a feud which brought to Lagos much suffering and bloodshed. The Eletu was determined that Kosoko should not succeed his brother, and by quick and determined action he secured the restoration of the deposed Adele. After a few years Adele died, and Kosoko made a vigorous effort to secure the throne, but the Eletu's party was too strong for him, and he was forced to fly to Whydah to save his life. Oluwole, the son of Adele, accordingly succeeded his father in the year 1836, but reigned only five years, being killed by an explosion of gunpowder in his palace, which was fired by lightning.

[1] *Sketches taken during Ten Voyages to Africa between the Years 1786 and 1800* (1822), by Captain John Adams, pp. 25-7.
[2] See Appendix B for genealogy of the King of Lagos.

During the reign of Oluwole the Eletu had the remains of Kosoko's mother disinterred and cast into the sea, and after this insult it was more than ever necessary to keep Kosoko out of Lagos. The Eletu's influence was therefore used in favour of Akitoye, the third son of Ologun Kutere and the uncle of Kosoko, who succeeded to the throne in 1841.

Akitoye was a weak and amiable king, with enlightened views and a great desire for peace with everyone, and he was anxious that the breach between his nephew and the Eletu should be healed. In spite of the advice of his councillors, who knew the character of Kosoko, and in spite of the entreaties of the Eletu, Akitoye insisted on inviting his nephew to return to Lagos, and on his arrival welcomed him kindly and loaded him with honours. Annoyed at the recall of his deadly enemy, and realizing that Lagos was not large enough to contain them both, the Eletu now left the island and went to live at Badagri. His departure was a serious loss to Akitoye, as the Eletu was the one man who might have saved him from Kosoko, but now that his personal enemy and the ablest of the king's advisers was away, Kosoko had no serious difficulty in satisfying his ambitions. Day by day his arrogance increased and more and more openly he worked for the overthrow of his uncle. The infatuated monarch refused to listen to any warnings about his nephew, his excesses were unrebuked, and Kosoko's followers were encouraged by the mistaken kindness of the king. At length even Akitoye could no longer be blind to the position. He saw that he had been deceived and that he himself was in grave peril; had he been a strong man and capable of rapid and decisive action all might yet have been well, but he hesitated and sent to Badagri for the Eletu, his strongest supporter. This gave Kosoko time to make his final preparations for the struggle that was now inevitable, and in July 1845 the fighting began. Akitoye had the support of the greater number of the people, but Kosoko's followers were better armed and fought with greater determination. In the midst of the battle the Eletu arrived and was welcomed by the king, but for some unexplained reason, probably in the hope that his departure might avert further bloodshed, the Eletu left again for Ikorodu; on his way thither he was captured by Kosoko's men and murdered with all his followers. The battle had now raged in Lagos for twenty-one days, most of the houses had been burnt to the ground, and the loss of life had been very heavy. Akitoye's position was hopeless, and he was at length persuaded to escape in a canoe and take refuge at Abeokuta,[1] from which place he was sent later, under escort, to Badagri.

Kosoko now established himself on the throne, after having massacred all of Akitoye's family and followers who were unable to escape. Writing in 1851, the British Consul at Fernando Po reported to the Foreign Secretary: 'I have been informed by a person that was at Lagos that the massacre in 1845 was awful; he exterminated the whole of his uncle's family, about 2,000, and the lagoon was a pest-house for weeks, owing to the dead carcasses in it.'[2] The time was, however, at hand when the British Government would be forced to intervene in the affairs of Lagos, and we shall see in Chapter X that retribution overcame Kosoko.

The other important offshoot of the Yoruba nation is the Edo (or Bini) people who inhabit the country to the east of Yorubaland proper. The Edos were certainly at one time under the rule or control of the Alafin of Oyo, but when the Portuguese visited Benin towards the end of the fifteenth century it had already become a powerful and independent kingdom.[3] The king was nominally absolute, but came in time completely under the power of a theocracy of fetish priests who retained their authority by the terror they created through wholesale human sacrifices. In spite of the barbarism of the people, and perhaps on account of the power of the priests, Benin was a well-organized kingdom and the government was thoroughly effective. Barbot gives some interesting information regarding it. He says that when he visited the city between the years 1678 and 1682, 'Oedo, the metropolis of Benin, was prodigious large, taking up about six leagues of ground in compass . . . there are . . . thirty very great streets, most of them prodigious both in length and breadth, being twenty fathom wide, and almost

---

[1] It was because his mother was an Egba that Akitoye received the support of the Abeokuta chiefs.

[2] *Papers relative to the Reduction of Lagos by Her Majesty's Forces on the West Coast of Africa* (1852), p. 96.

[3] For a list of Kings or Obas of Benin see Appendix I in *A Short History of Benin* by J. Egharevba (3rd ed., 1960).

two English miles long. . . . Europeans are so much honoured and respected at Benin, that the natives give them the emphatick name or title of . . . children of Gods.'[1] He notes also, that none of the natives of Benin was enslaved in his own country, though the highest counted it an honour to be styled the king's slaves; that human sacrifice was practised and that the king's servants were buried alive with their dead master, going willingly to their terrible doom; and that the king had a number of small horses. Towards the end of his book Barbot records that he was informed by one who visited Benin in 1702 that much of the glory of Benin had departed, Oedo being in a very 'mean state', and the greater part of it 'desolate'.[2]

The people were, and still remain for the greater part, pagan fetish-worshippers; efforts by the Portuguese to introduce Christianity were unsuccessful, or at any rate had no lasting effect. The condition of Benin City when it was captured by a British force in 1897 afforded terrible proof of the degradation of an intelligent people, who had been for centuries under the blight of a bloodthirsty priestly tyranny, and in late years had been forbidden even to trade with the Europeans in retaliation for the stoppage of the slave-traffic.

[1] Barbot, *op. cit.* See also Crow, *op. cit.*, p. 34, who visited Benin in 1791, and 'was much pleased with the gentle manners of the natives of Benin, who are truly a fine tractable race of people. When they meet an European they fall down on the right knee, clap their hands three times, and exclaim "We reverence you!" ' De Bry and Dapper, two Dutchmen who visited Benin in 1601 and 1668 respectively, also gave glowing accounts of the place.

[2] This is confirmed by Bosman: 'The Village of Benin, for it at present scarce deserves the Name of a City . . . is at least about four miles large. . . . Formerly this Village was very thick and close built, and in a manner over-charg'd with Inhabitants, which is yet visible from the Ruins of half-remaining Houses; but at present the Houses stand like poor Men's Corn, widely distant from each other.' See *A New and Accurate Description of the Coast of Guinea*, by William Bosman, p. 461. (Translated from the Dutch and printed in London, 1705.)

CHAPTER IV

POPULATION: (c)
HAUSALAND AND BORNU

O ye Unbelievers!
I worship not that which ye worship;
And ye do not worship that which I worship;
. . . To you be your religion; to me my religion.

The Koran (Sura cix)

Spread over a large area of northern Nigeria, and especially around Sokoto, Kano, Zaria, and Bauchi, are the Hausa-speaking tribes, all more or less of Negroid origin. For many years the Hausas were considered to be a distinct race, and the name was loosely applied to all the tribes that spoke the language; many tribes, notably the Kebbawa, now claim to be the descendants of the original Hausa stock, but it is generally accepted that no Hausa race exists today, although the language is spoken by a great many tribes as a mother tongue and as a supplementary language to their own by many more. A comparatively easy language to acquire, it has become the *lingua franca* of a large part of West Africa, and it is the only language of western Africa which has been reduced to writing by the Africans themselves, modified Arabic characters being used. There is hardly a place in the northern half of Africa where no one could be found who spoke or understood the Hausa language, and Mecca, of course, would see annually many Hausa-speaking pilgrims.

Owing to the systematic destruction of written records by their Fulani conquerors, we have little documentary evidence of early Hausa history.[1] There were, apparently, seven original states, the *Hausa Bakwai* (=seven), Kano, Rano, Zeg-Zeg (Zaria), Daura, Gobir, Katsena, and Zamfara, and to these were added later the *Hausa Banza* or *Banza Bakwai* (=unreal or

[1] Mr E. J. Arnett, CMG, formerly a Senior Resident in Nigeria and an authority on the subject, doubted whether this statement and that at page 51 relative to Sultan Bello's connection with the destructions of records are correct. The charges were certainly made by Bello's enemies.

illegitimate), which were probably 'not genuinely Hausa, but were penetrated by Hausa influences'.[1]

The establishment of the early Hausa states must have taken place at a very remote era, and prior to the spread of Muhammadanism the people were pagan; the new religion probably entered the country during the thirteenth century and made rapid progress, affecting profoundly the social as well as the religious life of the Hausas. A form of government grew up based on the doctrines of Islam, with a well-organized fiscal system and a highly trained and learned judiciary, administering Muhammadan law with ability and integrity. Each state was ruled over by its king, assisted by the usual ministers of oriental Governments, but we have little information of the actual rulers and their doings. In every instance the state took its name from that of its principal city, which was surrounded by a mud wall and a deep ditch of many miles in circumference; to these cities the people would fly for refuge from an invading army and as there was space within the walls for many farms the cities were well able to withstand prolonged sieges.

Although each state was independent of the others, they appear to have been bound together at intervals for mutual defence in a loose confederation, but there were constant internecine wars in which the fortunes of each rose and fell, none retaining for very long its precarious pre-eminence. Zaria conquered the pagan countries to the south and subdued Bauchi, Gobir fought and held at bay the nomad tribes of the northern desert, while Kano fought without much success against Bornu. From time to time Bornu armies overran Hausaland, while about the year 1513 Askia the Great, King of Songhay,[2] con-

---

[1] Temple, *op. cit.*, p. 406. In the above list I have followed Mr Temple, who states that some say Auyo (near Hadeija) should be substituted for Gobir. Lady Lugard, following Barth, substitutes Biram for Zamfara, and gives the seven *Hausa Banza* as Zamfara, Kebbi, Nupe, Gwari, Yauri, Yoruba, and Kororofa (see *A Tropical Dependency* (1905), by Flora L. Shaw (Lady Lugard), pp. 238 and 240). Sultan Bello of Sokoto substitutes 'Yareem' for Zamfara, and gives Zamfara, Kebbi, Nupe, Yauri, Yoruba, Borgu, and Ghoorma as the *Hausa Banza* (see Appendix to Denham and Clapperton, *op. cit.*).

[2] Songhay was a distinct state from the eighth to the sixteenth centuries. The Songhay people have occupied throughout historical times the country on both banks of the Middle Niger.

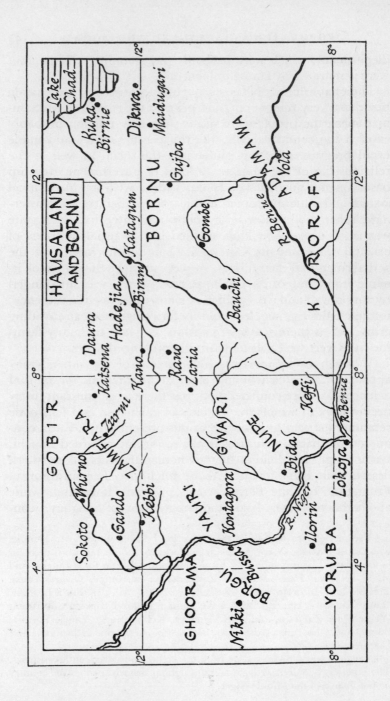

HAUSALAND AND BORNU

Lake Chad

Kuka •
Birnie •
Dikwa •
Maidugari •
Gujba •

BORNU

Gombe •
Gombe

R. Benue
A D A M A W A
Yola •

K O R O R O F A

Katagum •
Birni •

GOBIR
Daura •
Katsena •
Zurmi •
Wurno •
Sokoto •
Gando •
Kebbi •

Kano •
Rano •
Zaria •

Bauchi •

Keffi •

R. Benue

GWARI
NUPE

YAURI
Kontagora •
Bida •
Lokoja •
R. Benue

GHOORMA

BORGU
Bussa •
Nikki •

R. Niger
Ilorin •

YORUBA

quered Katsena, Zaria, and Kano, and made them provinces of his empire. The native dynasties were allowed to remain, but Songhay officials were left at their courts, and even after their departure the Hausa states could not for some time regain their former power. The Jukon, or Kororofa, pagans from the Benue valley, who had invaded Zaria as early as the fourteenth century, now ravaged the country as far as Kano and broke the spirit of its people. The *Kano Chronicle*[1] records that 'the people had to sit still and be afraid, and for twenty years they were not able to go to war'.

Hausaland now became the battleground of two great states, Bornu and Kebbi, which were struggling for the supremacy of that part of the western Sudan, but the life of the people flowed on in spite of everything. The Hausa had always been a trader, and a trader he continued to be, whether the country was distracted by civil wars or ruled by foreign conquerers, and Katsena, although brought into subjection by Bornu, rose into prominence as a place of learning.

Gobir was at last defeated and subdued by the desert tribes, and when it was eventually freed from their dominion its attention was directed to the subjection of its sister states. By the middle of the eighteenth century Zamfara had been conquered, and it was not long before Gobir was the paramount power in Hausaland. Its rulers were pagans, and Muhammadanism throughout the country was at its lowest ebb when the movement commenced which was to end with the establishment of a Fulani empire over the whole land.

While the Hausa states were yet powerful there had begun the peaceful immigration into the country of a race which was destined to become of the greatest importance in Nigeria. In spite of various theories, nothing definite is known of the origin of the Fulani.[2] They have been derived by various writers from Indian, Jewish, Malayan, and Phoenician stock. Mr C. L. Temple, formerly Lieutenant-Governor of the Northern Provinces of Nigeria, says that in their youth some of the Fulani bear a striking resemblance to the Egyptian portraits of

[1] A manuscript obtained in Kano by the Royal Niger Company containing what purports to be an authentic history of the city. This was probably written after the general destruction of Hausa records by the Fulani.

[2] Also known as the Fulas, Fulahs, Peuls, Puls, and Pulo.

the Hyksos shepherd kings of Egypt, while in old age they resemble the Jewish type.[1] Their language is supposed to be like that of the gipsies,[2] while Mr H. R. Palmer,[3] one of Mr Temple's successors in office, has traced a resemblance between the Fulani language and that of the aborigines of the Canary Islands.[4] The most generally accepted theory is that they came originally from Upper Egypt and migrated westwards across the north of Africa to the Atlantic coast, where a number settled, while others appear to have moved at a later date in an easterly direction and to have entered Nigeria during the thirteenth century. A portion of these immigrants drifted to the towns, mingling freely with the Hausa inhabitants, intermarrying with them and adopting the Muhammadan religion, and before very long their superior intelligence placed them in positions of importance. These people are known as the Fulanen Gidda (gidda=compound). The others held aloof, retaining their pastoral habits and their pagan beliefs, and keeping their blood pure; it is among these 'Cow Fulani' (Borroroje), as they are termed, that one finds the purest type, with the fine features, narrow nose and long, straight hair. For centuries the Fulani remained in Hausaland as a more or less subject race, but in the year 1804 Othman dan Fodio, a Fulani sheikh who had made the pilgrimage to Mecca, and whose reputed sanctity had given him great influence among the Faithful and even over the pagan King of Gobir, interfered with the king's servants on behalf of a party of Muhammadans who were being carried off into captivity. The king was angry and sent a message to Othman demanding his presence. As he failed to appear, troops were sent to fetch him, but these were easily defeated by Othman's devoted Fulani followers, who were, however, afterwards compelled to flee with their leader to escape the king's revenge. As a general massacre of the Fulani was now threatened, Othman raised the banner of revolt and defeated the king's forces in a decisive battle. The heads of the various Fulani clans now flocked to the successful sheikh, whom they recognized as the Sarkin Musulmi (Commander of the Faith-

[1] Temple, op. cit., p. 396.
[2] By the French authority, M. Delafosse.
[3] Later Sir Richmond Palmer, KCMG, CBE.
[4] Temple, op. cit., p. 396.

ful), asking his blessing and his authority to conquer the people among whom they had lived for so long on sufferance.

The *jihad* had commenced, Othman giving 'flags' to fourteen chiefs, who were authorized to wage war in the name of Allah and His Prophet, but it was not only against pagans that the *jihad* was directed. Those who were suspected of being lukewarm followers of the Prophet were as guilty in the eyes of Othman's fanatical adherents as those who were still in darkness, and their property, no less than the property of the unbelievers, was lawful spoil for triumphant virtue. Although Bornu was a Muhammadan country it was attacked and conquered in 1808, and only regained its independence by the military skill of a famous sheikh named El Kanemi. Nor were all of Othman's followers Fulani. Many of the natives of the country, who saw in the *jihad* only a struggle for the preservation of their religion, joined Othman's forces against their own people, and one at least of the 'Flag-bearers' was not a Fulani. The *jihad* was not at first entirely successful, but it was sufficiently so for Othman to hand over the cares of state to his brother Abdullahi and his son Bello, between whom he divided the country. He himself continued to preach and study until his death in the year 1817, at his son's capital, Sokoto. Abdullahi, in the meantime, had established himself at Gando, and on Othman's death he recognized Bello as Sarkin Musulmi, probably from necessity rather than from inclination.

Bello's reign was a troubled one, constant warfare being waged against the tribes which would not submit to Fulani rule, and it was not until the closing years of his life that he finally consolidated his dominions. The 'Flag-bearers' and their descendants continued to own allegiance to Sokoto, the empire including the emirates of Katsena, Kano, Zaria, Hadeija, Adamawa, Gombe, Katagum, Nupe, Ilorin, Daura, and Bauchi. In spite of his wars Bello found time to study and, like his father before him, was the author of several works on history, geography, and theology. He was visited, as we shall see, by Lieutenant Clapperton, at his newly-built town of Wurno, in 1824 and 1826, and sent a friendly letter by that traveller to the King of England. It is a curious fact that in spite of his devotion to learning it was Bello who ordered the destruction of the Hausa records. He died in 1837, and was succeeded by his brother Abubakr Atiku, in whose family and his own the Sultanate of Sokoto has continued ever since, carrying with it the title of Sarkin Musulmi.[1]

There is no doubt that the new rulers administered the country for some time with ability and justice. Gradually, however, as the 'Flag-bearers' passed away and the fine frenzy of the reformers had time to cool, corruption crept in and the administration went from bad to worse. 'The Governors or Emirs became slack, departed from the simplicity and austere mode of life of their forbears, adopted more and more the ostentatious habits of the pagan chiefs among whom they lived, and to whose power they succeeded, oppressed their own people, destroyed their subjects with the object of getting their women and children as slaves. Forgetting the words of their great leader " . . . Let no man think that I accept this office that I may be greater than another or that my slave may lord it over others", they became haughty, avaricious, and so greedy of power that some, notably the Emirs of Kano and Bauchi, questioned the authority of Sokoto itself. They became also effeminate, with the result that many of their pagan subjects threw off their yoke. Thus it was a diminished kingdom, from which the glory had departed, when the British arrived on the scene at the end of the nineteenth century.'[2] The fact, however, that the Fulani were able to maintain their rule for a hundred years, a comparatively small number of aliens governing a subject people, is a proof of their outstanding ability among the West African tribes.

Mr Temple says that 'The pure-blooded Fulani is an extremely reserved person, and the Emirs and better class Fulanen Gidda have retained this trait. Any manifestation of feeling, such as smiling or laughing, or showing great interest or sorrow or joy, is considered bad form amongst them. . . . Needless to say that the "purdah" in their household is very strict; also they never eat in public, or with their wives or children. A son is not supposed to look his father in the face, and the father never in public acknowledges the presence of his children—in better class families, that is to say.'[3]

[1] See Appendix A for genealogy.
[2] Temple, *op. cit.*, p. 398.
[3] *Ibid.*, p. 400.

The Fulanen Gidda are now so intermarried with the Hausa-speaking tribes that they are practically distinct from the Borroroje, and many of the so-called Hausa traders and Hausa soldiers are in reality as much Fulani as anything else. The Borroroje, on the other hand, are shy and exclusive, disdaining to mix their blood even with the Fulanen Gidda, and keeping with their herds as far from the haunts of men as they possibly can. Sir Hugh Clifford described them as 'the nomadic Fulani herdsmen—folks who converse with and are understood by their charges as though their mutual relations were those of parents and children rather than of man and beast and who, on occasion, to defeat the British tax-gatherers, call with frantic outcry upon the grazing herd to surround them, and running at high speed, protected and secure in the heart of the gallop-ing, plunging mob, vanish into the bush in a column of dust'.[1] In the past, Fulani youths were required to undergo a severe ordeal before they were permitted to marry or to receive any of the privileges of manhood, and some of the young married men voluntarily underwent the test a second time in a spirit of bravado. Posing in the middle of a circle of interested spec-tators, with both hands held high above the head, the youth was unmercifully thrashed with a whip or stick on his naked body, until the ordeal was stopped by the unmarried girls signifying that he had passed the test. Should he flinch or show in any way that he was sensible of the blows being inflicted, and the scars of this flogging were often visible throughout his life, the unfortunate youth became an object of derision and scorn, and was required to submit himself again to the ordeal in the following year. Some of the young men, holding a small mirror in one upraised hand, affected to arrange their hair with the other, with an appearance of utter unconcern in the severe punishment they were receiving at the same time.

When the Fulani became the rulers of Hausaland they found already in existence a well-organized system of law and govern-ment which they were wise enough to retain, and save for a change of rulers the Hausa states were little affected by the jihad. There was no change in the form of taxation, which

[1] *Address by the Governor, Sir Hugh Clifford, to the Nigerian Council* (1920), p. 26.

was based on the Koranic law, and included *zakat*, regarded in theory as alms paid by the Faithful and fixed in proportions relative to the nature and quantity of the property; when levied on crops it is termed *'ushr*, and the Hausa name for the tax on livestock is *jangali*. There was also a land tax, known as *kharaj*, in Hausa *kurdin kassa*, and a capitation tax, *jizyah*, Hausa *gandu*, generally levied on conquered tribes. In time there grew up a number of other imposts, and 'every form of handicraft had its special tax: smiths, dyers, weavers, leather-makers, salt-makers, canoe-men, hunters, fishermen, ferry-men, etc. In some places a liquor-tax was imposed, in others each date-palm or beehive paid its toll. Prostitutes, dancing-girls, gamblers, were taxed by one or another chief. Sellers in the market had for the most part to pay royalties on the wares they sold. Traders paid toll at every town which they passed. To all these and many other taxes were added the *gaisua*, or present, which every man had to bring when he came to see his immediate superior, more especially at the periodical festivals, together with arbitrary levies in cash or kind, irregular fines without trial, and forced labour for building the city walls or the houses of Chiefs.'[1] The *gaisua* was paid to the Sultan of Sokoto by the rulers of the other states in recognition of his position as head of the Muhammadans (Sarkin Musulmi), and there was a duty payable by officials on appointment which degenerated into a mere buying and selling of offices. The multiplicity of new taxes afforded the rulers and their satellites opportunities for the wholesale spoliation of the people, and these taxes were levied in disregard of the principles laid down in Muhammadan law.

The courts were at first, and always in theory, independent of the executive, and the judges, who were called *alkalai*,[2] administered the Muhammadan law of the Maliki school. This law is based on the doctrines of the Prophet, as handed down in the Koran and by tradition, and it includes both the religious or canon law and the social or civil code. The laws of temporal rulers and Governments are recognized only where they are not in conflict with the law of Allah as expressed through His

---

[1] *Political Memoranda* (1918), p. 173. An official publication written by Sir F. D. (later Lord) Lugard.

[2] Singular *Alkali*, Hausa rendering of *el Cadi*.

Prophet. Muhammadan judges are as a rule very learned in the law they administer, and frequently have access to considerable libraries containing the works of eminent jurists. The Emirs themselves exercised judicial powers in their own courts.

Succession to the throne is seldom directly from father to son. The principal officials are the *waziri*, i.e. the vizier or prime minister; the *maaji*, or *ajiya*, the treasurer; the *yari*, head gaoler; the *sarkin dogarai*, chief of police, etc.

To the east of Hausaland lies Bornu, at one time a great empire, the influence of which was felt throughout the greater part of the Sahara and the Sudan. The principal tribe is the Kanuri, which probably numbers about 1,300,000 persons, and is considered to be a mixture of Arab, Hamitic, and Negro tribes, established in Bornu for many centuries. Bornu was at first only a province of the empire of Kanem, a country lying to the east and north of Lake Chad, which was the first historical home of the Kanuri.

El Bekri, a Spanish Arab who wrote in 1067, refers to Kanem and says that it extended on the west as far as the River Niger, thus including the greater part of Hausaland. With the help of Tunis, the armies of Kanem appear to have subdued most of the Sahara by the end of the twelfth century, and a Kanem embassy is recorded as having visited Tunis about the year 1237. The power and influence of the country seem to have rapidly increased during the next hundred years, and before the thirteenth century had closed the empire stretched from the Niger to the Nile, and from Fezzan in the north to Adamawa in the south. Muhammadanism was introduced during the first great period of Kanem history. Towards the end of the fourteenth century the collapse of the empire was threatened by the repeated attacks of the Bulala tribe, and the king was compelled to vacate his capital in Kanem proper and retire into Bornu, where a new capital was built. In the course of the next century the empire was reorganized and increased once more in power, the nearness of its centre to the Hausa states involving it in constant struggles with them. In 1489 Bornu was shown on Portuguese maps as a country of some extent, and during the sixteenth century it was able to engage successfully the rising power of Kebbi, which had broken away from the Songhay empire to the west. The Bornu army at this time was partially armed with muskets,[1] and it is to this fact that the second period of Bornu prosperity was due. At any rate, the boundaries of the country were once again enlarged, and the zenith of power appeared to have been reached; but, like most of the states of tropical Africa, this power could not long be retained. Kanem and various other provinces declared their independence, and it was a weak and demoralized Bornu that had to face the Fulani invasion at the beginning of the nineteenth century.

The successful Fulani *jihad*, which began about the year 1804, had made that race the masters of Hausaland, and in 1808 the Fulani armies invaded Bornu, although it had been a Muhammadan country for centuries, and the *jihad* was supposed to be directed only against the infidel.[2] The Bornu army was defeated, the Sultan was forced to flee from his capital, and it looked as though Bornu would be added to the Fulani empire, when there came forward a remarkable man who was to save the country and re-establish its power. Muhamad el Kanemi was born in Fezzan, one of his parents being an Arab and the other a native of Kanem: he had been educated in Egypt, and had already gained a great reputation in Kanem for sanctity and learning when the Fulani invasion called him to the front. Claiming a divine inspiration, he raised a small number of fanatical followers, with whose aid he defeated the Fulani in a battle in which the Bornu force was at a serious numerical disadvantage. The people now flocked to his standard, and within a year he had defeated the Fulani in a series of battles and driven them from the country. Refusing the throne which his enthusiastic followers urged him to take, he restored the fugitive Sultan and did him homage, but retained all the real power in his own hands. The puppet Sultan continued to reign nominally in his newly-built capital at Birnie, but the Shehu (sheikh) as El Kanemi was called,

[1] 'Among the benefits which God [Most High] . . . conferred upon the Sultan was the acquisition of Turkish musketeers and numerous household slaves who became skilled in firing muskets.' See the translation by Mr H. R. Palmer of an Arabic manuscript by Ahmed ibn Fartua containing a history of the first twelve years of the reign of Mai Idris Alooma, 1571–83.

[2] The Fulani zealots who took part in the *jihad* treated as infidels all those Muslims who did not accept the puritanical reforms which were insisted on by the Wahhibi sect.

became the virtual ruler, and his town of Kuka (or Kukawa), built in 1814, was the real metropolis of the country. It was there that he was visited by Denham and Clapperton during the years 1822 to 1824, and they have left us a good description of the greatest of all the Bornu leaders. 'Compared to all around him he is an angel, and has subdued more by his generosity, mildness, and benevolent disposition than by the force of his arms.'[1] He was, however, severe in his punishments, and Denham records that a man was flogged to death, receiving 400 lashes with a thong of hippopotamus-hide, on a suspicion of his having been guilty of adultery during the month of Ramadan. At this time peace had been established with the Fulani, but when Clapperton visited Sokoto in 1826 he found that war had again broken out. El Kanemi died in 1835, and was succeeded by his son, Omar, who was visited by Barth in 1851. On El Kanemi's death the Sultan attempted to reassert himself and regain his lost power, but he was defeated and killed, and Omar became in theory as well as in practice the ruler of the country. His successors still retain the title of Shehu, which was assumed by the founder of their dynasty, in preference to that of Sultan.

The power of Bornu once more began to wane, and in 1893 Rabeh, who was formerly a slave of Zebehr Pasha, led an army from the Egyptian Sudan into Bornu. Rabeh's troops were part of the force with which Zebehr had held his military district before the overthrow of the Egyptian power in the Sudan by the Mahdi, and made a well-drilled and fairly well-equipped army which defeated the Shehu's troops and destroyed Kuka. The Bornu army was then reorganized and Rabeh was defeated, but he rallied his men and won a crushing and decisive victory, which was followed by a wholesale massacre of the inhabitants of the district. Rabeh was now the master of Bornu and he established his capital at Dikwa, while his army of 20,000 men, a quarter of whom were supplied with fire-arms, kept the people in subjection and enforced the payment of tribute. At last, in the year 1900, the French defeated and slew Rabeh in a battle on the banks of the Shari, and established the fugitive Shehu as ruler of Bornu. They demanded from him, however, an indemnity of 80,000 Maria Theresa

[1] Denham and Clapperton, op. cit., vol. ii, p. 181.

dollars,[1] and when this was refused they deposed him and installed another member of his family, Abubekr Garbai,[2] in his place. While this chief was endeavouring to raise the necessary money the country was being raided by Rabeh's son, who still led a remnant of his father's army, but he was at last defeated and killed by the French in a battle at Gujba, a place within the present limits of Nigeria, to which they had pursued him. This event hastened the effective occupation of Bornu by the British, an account of which will be given in Chapter XV.

After the adoption of the Muhammadan religion in Bornu the system of law and taxation closely approximated to that in force in Hausaland, but there existed in addition in Bornu a death duty, called *gado*, and a well-graduated income-tax, *haku bineram*; at no time does there seem to have been the multiplicity of taxes and illegal imposts which were so characteristic of the states under the rule of the later Fulani Emirs.

To the east of Bornu, and in the neighbourhood of Lake Chad, there is found a pastoral race of Shuwa Arabs, famous as cavalry in the armies of old Bornu, and now divided up into small clans under their own sheikhs. They speak a dialect of Arabic, in which many classical words, long disused by other Arabs, are retained, mixed with words of Negro origin. They possess large herds of cattle, which are moved from place to place in search of pasturage and water.

[1] These dollars, or thalers, were currency from the east to the west coast of Africa, and were in circulation in Abyssinia till the end of the nineteenth century. They have frequently been recoined, and those of the date 1780 were recoined specially for the purposes of the Abyssinian War of 1867. They have been demonetized in Nigeria.

[2] Died as Shehu in 1922.

CHAPTER V

POPULATION: (d) MISCELLANEOUS

Those who have a real faith need not be ashamed to look facts in the face.

J. H. OLDHAM: *Christianity and the Race Problem*

The less advanced and organized communities, the 'primitive tribes' of Lord Lugard's classification, are found principally among the hills of Bauchi and in that tract of country which lies east of the lower Niger and south of the Benue.

At the time that Lord Lugard wrote the most important of these was the large Ibo tribe, which with its various clans and offshoots numbers more than five million persons and occupies the greater part of the country between the Niger and Cross rivers, together with the Asaba district on the right bank of the Niger. Among these people there was no highly organized form of government and little tribal cohesion; practically every village was independent, and so great was the isolation of each small community that the inhabitants of neighbouring villages often speak in entirely different dialects. The Ibos were, and still are, almost entirely a pagan race, and they were much addicted to cannibalism. The Aros are held by some to be a clan of the Ibo tribe, and by others to be of an entirely different stock; however that may be, the fact remains that by their superior ability they acquired a complete ascendancy over the neighbouring Ibo clans.

In recent years the Ibos have made remarkable progress, educationally and otherwise, and the first African Governor-General of Nigeria, Dr Nnamdi Azikiwe, is an Ibo.

To the south-east of the Ibo country are the Ibibios, another tribe of pagans, and several smaller tribes, such as the Ekois, Efiks, Kwas, and Ogonis. In the Niger delta are found the Urhobos (or Sobos), Itsekiris (or Jekris) and Ijaws.[1] The last named are an almost amphibious people, who are largely

[1] For references to these tribes and their origins see Chapter II of *Trade and Politics in the Niger Delta, 1830–1885* (1956), by Dr K. O. Dike.

employed on river craft as sailors. The Itsekiris were formerly important as middlemen between the early European traders and the inhabitants of the hinterland. To the east and north of Benin are respectively the Ishans and the Kukurukus, who, together with the Urhobos, speak dialects of the Edo (or Bini) language. To the north-west of the Ibos, in the corner formed by the Rivers Niger and Benue, are the Igaras, who speak a language akin to Yoruba, and the Okpotos, and eastward of them is the large and important Tiv (or Munshi) tribe, an agricultural and at the same time warlike people. Intermixed with the Tivs and in small scattered communities is the remnant of the Jukon or Kororofa tribe, which was at one time the paramount race in this part of Nigeria; they are supposed to have come originally from Arabia and to have settled first close to Lake Chad. Moving southwards and westwards, they overran and conquered most of Hausaland, including Kano and Zaria, and a great deal of the country south of the Benue, but by the end of the eighteenth century their power had waned, and they are now of little political importance.

North of the River Benue, in the mountainous region of the Bauchi plateau, are a large number of primitive tribes addicted to cannibalism and other unpleasant practices, and wearing the scantiest of attire, in spite of the cold so often experienced in their mountainous country.[1] As a rule the women wear nothing more than two wisps of grass, in front and behind, suspended from a string around the waist, while in some cases the men wear even less than this. They are great agriculturists, and own some hardy ponies which they ride bareback. Their principal weapon is the bow, the poisoned arrows from which are effective up to a range of about 120 yards. Some are headhunters, and preserve the skulls of their vanquished enemies. Some eat anything from rats, mice, and bats to their own de-

---

[1] 'The condition of absolute nakedness is found among a certain number of the animistic tribes. Tangale, Longuda, Borok, and Pongo males, for example, are usually seen in a state of complete nudity, and so also are Keri-Keri, Koro, and Ngizim women. Unmarried girls of most pagan tribes wear only ornamental clothing. . . . The penis-sheath is worn. . . . The sheath is among the Plateau tribes, made of woven grass. . . . Men of importance are distinguished by the elaborate character of their penis-sheath.' See *The Northern Tribes of Nigeria* (1925), by C. K. Meek, pp. 40–1.

ceased relatives,[1] while others, more fastidious, will not eat their own people, but exchange corpses with neighbouring villages.[2] They are generally great drunkards, the whole tribe frequently drinking locally brewed beer until all are incapable. The largest of these tribes are the Angas and Tangale.

West of the Bauchi plateau are the Gwaris, who were never conquered by the Fulani, but suffered terribly from being constantly raided for slaves. South of the Gwaris are the Nupes, whose kingdom was a very ancient one. The people of Borgu claim to be of Coptic origin and to have been Christians at one time.

In addition to the tribes mentioned there are numerous others, speaking different languages and dialects, and giving other proofs of distinct origins. Some of the tribes consider the birth of twins to be lucky,[3] others kill both the twins and the mother, believing that where two children are born at one birth one must be the child of an evil spirit. Some firmly believe in the power of certain men to change themselves into animals;[4] some sacrifice human beings to their gods. In some tribes the men are circumcised; in others there are initiation ceremonies for boys and girls. Sometimes there are age groups, the members of which share each others' work and play. In the past, members of most of the tribes had facial and body marks, applied either during infancy or at puberty, by incisions or tattooing; the sight of an infant with deep gashes on either cheek, deliberately kept open that a permanent scar may be left, is peculiarly revolting but does not appear to affect the African mothers, who are in other respects most affectionate and kind to their children. It was, no doubt, essential in former years

[1] For example, the Longuda. Temple, *op. cit.*, p. 259.

[2] The Jarawa, *ibid.*, p. 169.

[3] The Igbira, *ibid.*, p. 155. Also the people of Benin, see Talbot, *op. cit.*, vol. iii, p. 723, and the map opposite p. 720 of the same volume, showing the distribution of the twin-birth tabu.

[4] 'I recollect the surprise of a Chief Justice new to Africa when an accused man pleaded guilty to having turned himself into a hyena by night and devoured children, because there was a consensus of village opinion that he had done so.' Lord Lugard, *The Dual Mandate*, p. 546. Mr C. K. Meek says that 'the belief in the ability of individuals to turn into animals is universal among the general mass of Muslims'. See Meek, *op. cit.*, vol. ii, p. 4.

that the members of each tribe should be easily identified, but the need for this has now departed, and it is to be hoped that the cruelties inseparable from the marking of children will soon entirely disappear.

Most of the tribes which have not been reached by Christianity or Muhammadanism believe in a multitude of evil spirits, ever on the look out for an opportunity to harm mankind, who have to be constantly placated. With many tribes the priests, or juju men, have to settle social and economic questions; in particular they have to decide when the yam[1] crop is fit to be eaten (for the yam eaten too young is unwholesome), and it is said that in some cases the date of the 'festival' is fixed by the position of certain stars, which shows an elementary knowledge of astronomy.

The physique of the Negro is generally very fine, though there is often combined with a well-developed, muscular body an extremely feeble constitution which succumbs easily to disease. The practice of carrying heavy loads on the head from the days of childhood gives an upright and graceful carriage and in most of the tribes the young women have particularly good figures, though in some parts of the country the deliberate fattening of girls before marriage[2] spoils their appearance to European eyes. Boys and girls come to puberty at a very early age, and grow old more rapidly than does the European, the women particularly being *passée* at an age when an Englishwoman would be at the prime of life.[3]

The Negro race has been the butt of much ill-informed abuse

[1] A large tuber (*Dioscorea*).

[2] In regular 'fatting houses', where special food, massage, and complete indolence has the desired effect.

[3] Sir Richard Burton speaks of 'the ugliest part of the old-womanhood in the East, long empty breasts like tobacco-pouches. In youth the bosom is beautifully high, arched and rounded, firm as stone to the touch, with the nipples erect and pointing outwards. But after the girl-mother's first child all changes. Nature and bodily power have been overtasked; then comes the long suckling at the mother's expense; the extension of the skin and the enlargement of its vessels are too sudden and rapid for the diminished ability of contraction, and the bad food aids in the continual consumption of vitality. Hence among Eastern women age and ugliness are synonymous. It is only in the highest civilization that we find the handsome old woman.' Note to Night 805 of *The Arabian Nights*. These remarks apply equally to some of the women of West Africa.

and contemptuous allusion, due probably in the first instance to an attempt by Europeans to justify the traffic in slaves. There does not appear to have been any strong colour prejudice until the seventeenth century,[1] although some of the earliest visitors to West Africa were most outspoken in their criticisms of the inhabitants. Thus Captain J. Welsh, who travelled as far as the Benin river in 1588, writes that the 'negroes [are] a people of beastly living, without a God, laws, religion or commonwealth'.[2] Again, Bosman, who was on the coast a century later, writes:

The Negroes are all without exception Crafty, Villanous, and Fraudulent, and very seldom to be trusted; being sure to slip no opportunity of cheating an European, nor indeed one another. A Man of integrity is as rare among them as a white Falcon, and their Fidelity seldom extends farther than to their Masters; and it would be very surprising if upon a scrutiny into their Lives we should find any of them whose perverse Nature would not break out sometimes; for they seem indeed to be born and bred Villains.[3]

Some of the white men of that period were, however, little better.

In more recent times Burton has asserted that the Negro is always a child, that he never develops, and that the race is an inferior one, which neither education nor anything else can raise to the level of the whites,[4] but in view of all the evidence to the contrary such an opinion would find few supporters today. To name only a few of those no longer living, such men as Booker Washington,[5] Professor Aggrey,[6] and Dr Henry Carr,[7] would have been a credit to any race. Even those who maintain that such men are exceptions, and not truly representative of

[1] *Islam at the Cross-Roads* (1923), by De Lacy O'Leary, D D, p. 88. See also *Christianity and the Race Problem* (1925) by J. H. Oldham, p. 34.

[2] Hakluyt's *Principall Navigations* (1599 edition), vol. ii, part ii, p. 19.

[3] Bosman, *op. cit.*, p. 117.

[4] *A Mission to Gelele, King of Dahome* (1864), by Sir Richard Burton, *passim*.

[5] Born 1859; died 1915. An American Negro teacher and reformer, chiefly famous for his work in connexion with the Tuskegee Institute.

[6] Born on the Gold Coast; died 1927. Was Vice-Principal of Achimota College.

[7] A Nigerian, born 1863, died 1945. Held high office in the Education Department and the Administrative Service of Nigeria. A man of great erudition and strong character.

their race, cannot deny that the number of exceptions is increasing, and that many of the Europeanized Africans, to use Lord Lugard's designation, are cultivated ladies and gentlemen of considerable attainments.

In 1920 Sir Hugh Clifford wrote of the Nigerians as having acquired 'an English education—in some instances wide, thorough, sound, and liberal, but more often it is to be feared, what, though it ranks locally as "scholarship", amounts to little more than a nodding acquaintance with the "three R's".'[1] At that time such an opinion was justified but the position has changed very considerably during the last forty years. There is still, however, a great difference between the educated Nigerians, mostly resident on the coast or in the large towns, and the more numerous illiterates and semi-illiterates who inhabit the less developed areas.

Among the non-native inhabitants of Nigeria are a number of West Indians, some of whom are descended from men formerly employed by the Government railway, and the descendants of liberated slaves from Brazil who returned to the country of their origin and settled in Lagos after it became a British colony. A number of people also came from Sierra Leone in 1842 and settled at Abeokuta.[2] There are some Tripoli Arabs resident in Kano and a number of Lebanese and Syrians who carry on an extensive trade. There are no European settlers in the country, and few Europeans remain in Nigeria for more than two years at a time; most of these are employed in the Government service, in banks and commercial companies, as contractors, or as missionaries. The total non-African population does not exceed 30,000.

[1] *Address by the Governor, Sir Hugh Clifford, to the Nigerian Council*, 1920, p. 52.
[2] English edition of *Iwe Irohin* of October 20, 1865. (A newspaper published for some years at Abeokuta.)

CHAPTER VI

THE PERIOD OF
UNRESTRICTED SLAVE-TRADE

Never can so much misery be found condensed into so small a space as in
a slave-ship.   WILBERFORCE

Remarkably little was known in Europe regarding western
Africa until comparatively modern times. Herodotus records
an expedition of Phoenician mariners, sent out by King Neco
of Egypt (about 612 BC), which sailed from the Red Sea and
returned to Egypt after passing through the Pillars of Hercules;
he relates what did not seem credible to him, but does, of
course, to us, that these men, in circumnavigating Africa, had
the sun on their right hand.[1] In another place[2] he refers to the
Carthaginian trade for gold with the natives of West Africa,
and there is a reputed voyage made by Hanno, the Carthaginian, for which there is separate evidence.[3]

From these early days there is a blank for nearly 2,000 years.
Some French writers have claimed that a flourishing trade was
established by the merchants of Dieppe and Rouen, in the
fourteenth century, along the coast from Cape Verde to the
Bight of Benin, and that a fort was built by them at Elmina in
1383; the trade was said to have been maintained for more
than fifty years, and was only abandoned on account of the
internal troubles of France. Villault, Sieur de Bellefond, who
is the chief authority for the French claim,[4] is supposed to have
got the story from the registers of the French Admiralty at
Dieppe, which were destroyed by a fire in 1694. In spite of
some support from a Dutch source,[5] the French claim is now

---

[1] *Herodotus*, iv. 42.
[2] *Ibid.*, iv. 196.
[3] *Periplus*.
[4] *Relation des Costes d'Afrique, appellés Guinée* . . . (Paris, 1669). See also
Les Navigations françaises . . . *d'aprés les Documents inédits*, by M. Pierre Margry
(Paris, 1867).
[5] See *The Dawn of Modern Geography* (1906), by C. Raymond Beazley,
vol. iii, p. 436.

generally admitted to be incapable of proof.[1] It is, however, remarkable that the Laurentian Portolano map of 1351 gives a more or less accurate idea of the coast-line of West Africa, and 'both the Guinea coasts as far as the Cameroons, and the southern projection of the continent, are herein presented with a comparative truth of outline which is, when we consider the date, among the confounding things of history'.[2]

It is not until the fifteenth century that we have any well-authenticated visits by Europeans to the coast of West Africa. The Portuguese were at this time an adventurous and seafaring people, and their merchants carried on an extensive trade with the states of northern Africa. Encouraged and helped by their prince, 'Henry the Navigator', their ships pushed farther and farther south along the African coast, in spite of the monsters and evil spirits that were reputed to haunt the unknown seas by the Equator. They sought the mythical kingdom of Prester John, which they did not find, and a sea route to India, which they did, and in their voyages they explored practically the whole coast-line of Africa and traded with the inhabitants. The first Negro slaves and the first gold dust were brought to Lisbon in 1441,[3] and in 1482 the Portuguese built a fort at Elmina on the Gold Coast, and laid claim to the whole country, a claim which was confirmed a few years later (in 1493) by the Papal Bull which, dividing the undeveloped parts of the earth between Spain and Portugal, allotted the greater part of Africa to the Portuguese.

By 1472 Portuguese vessels had got as far as the Bight of Benin, and here they found safe anchorages in the mouths of the many rivers which break the coast-line between Lagos and the Cameroons. In 1485 Benin City was visited by John Affonso d'Aveiro, and it was not very long before trade was established, ivory and pepper being taken in exchange for the products of Europe. The swampy land in the Niger delta and along the coast was inhabited by numerous small and savage tribes under petty chiefs who were hardly worth conciliating, but at Benin, which was within easy reach of the sea by means of a navigable river, there existed an organized kingdom ruled over by a monarch powerful enough to protect those whom he favoured.

[1] *The Dawn of Modern Geography*, vol. iii, p. 431.
[2] *Ibid*, p. 439.   [3] *Ibid.*, p. 567.

In this promising field Portuguese missionaries attempted to sow the seeds of Christianity, and King John II (1481–95) opened a friendly correspondence with the King of Benin, who showed signs of willingness to accept the new religion.[1] Churches and monasteries were established, but such conversions as were effected do not appear to have proved lasting, and after a while the efforts to spread the Faith in Benin were abandoned. But if the religious zeal of the Portuguese had little effect, in other directions their influence was more lasting. Many words of Portuguese origin remained in use in Benin until the end of the nineteenth century, and the King of Benin who reigned in 1553 could speak the language, which he had learned as a child.[2] Portuguese influence can also be seen in many of the brass figures, and carvings in other materials, which have been produced in Benin; specimens of this work, carried off from Benin when the city was captured by the British in 1897, may be seen today in the British Museum. At one time it was believed that the Portuguese had taught the Benin people the art of working in brass and carving in wood and ivory, but there are many indications which support the Benin tradition that metal-work had been known long before the coming of the Portuguese.[3] It is said, indeed, that brass casting was introduced into Benin, from Ife, before the end of the thirteenth century.[4]

The Portuguese were not long permitted to retain the West African trade as a monopoly. As early as 1481 the King of Portugal had found it necessary to send an embassy to Edward IV of England asking him to restrain his subjects from trading to the coast of Guinea, and particularly to prevent a fleet, which was then being prepared, from sailing to Africa.[5] In 1530 Mr William Hawkins, of Plymouth, called at the Sestos river[6] and traded for elephants' teeth.[7] In 1553 the first English ships reached the Benin river, and the long British connexion with Nigeria was begun.

The ships were under the command of Captain Windham,

---

[1] Barbot, op. cit.
[2] The First Voyage to Guinea and Benin (1553), Hakluyt, vol. ii, part ii, p. 12.
[3] See Talbot, op. cit., vol. i, p. 29.   [4] Egharevba, op. cit., p. 12.
[5] Hakluyt, op. cit., vol. ii, part ii, p. 12.
[6] Situated in what is now Liberia.   [7] Hakluyt, op. cit., vol. ii, part ii, p. 16.

and were piloted by a Portuguese named Pinteado, who from the first appears to have been most unfairly treated by Windham and the other Englishmen. The squadron was anchored at the mouth of the river, while Pinteado and some English merchants went up by boat for about 150 miles and then overland to the city of Benin. They were well received by the king, and within thirty days they had collected 80 tons of pepper, the king offering credit in case their merchandise was not sufficient to balance the cost of the pepper. In the meantime the crews of the vessels were dying rapidly,[1] and Windham sent up to Benin to recall the others; there was more pepper coming in, and Pinteado went down to the ships to prevail on Windham to wait a little longer, but when he arrived he found Windham already dead and the others in no mood for further delay. He then offered to go back to Benin to fetch the merchants left there, but this was refused, and he then wrote to them, promising to return and rescue them if he lived; he died, however, a week later. The ships returned to England, having lost 100 men out of 140 who had sailed. There is no record of the fate of the merchants who were left at Benin, and it must be presumed that they perished there. In 1561 the Company of Merchant Adventurers for Guinea proposed to send Mr John Lok[2] on a mission to West Africa, and instructed him to make inquiries regarding the missing merchants, but Mr Lok declined the mission and no further effort was made.

In 1588 Captain Welsh sailed with two ships to the Benin river, where he anchored and, as before, the merchants went up by boat to Gwato, and thence overland to Benin. They were there two months, and brought home a cargo of 'pepper and Elephants' teeth, oyle of palm, cloth made of Cotton wool very curiously woven, and cloth made of the barke of palm trees'.[3]

---

[1] '. . . our men partly having no rule of themselves, but eating without measure of the fruits of the country and drinking the wine of the Palme trees that droppeth in the night from the cut of the branches of the same, and in such extreme heate running continually into the water, not used before to such sudden and vehement alterations (than the which nothing is more dangerous), were thereby brought into swellings and agues; inasmuch that the later time of the yeere comming on, caused them to die sometimes three & sometimes 4 or 5 in a day.' *Ibid.*, p. 13.

[2] John Lok had already (in 1554) made a voyage to the Gold Coast.

[3] Hakluyt, *op. cit.*, vol. ii, part ii, p. 128.

The same captain visited Benin in 1591, and brought back 589 sacks of pepper, 150 tusks, and 32 barrels of palm oil.[1] These are the first references to the oil which later was exported in such quantities as to give its name to the rivers from which it was obtained.

With the discovery of America and the establishment of Spanish colonies in the West Indies there arose a demand for African slaves[2] and, as the Spaniards were prevented by the Papal Bull from going to Africa for their slaves, they were obliged to obtain them through the Portuguese, who for over fifty years enjoyed a monopoly in this lucrative traffic. The Reformation, however, lessened the influence of the Papal Bull, and in the sixteenth century the merchant adventurers of all the Protestant nations of Europe swarmed to the West African coast to get their share of the trade. In 1562 Sir John Hawkins, the son of William Hawkins, took 300 slaves from Sierra Leone to Hayti, being the first Englishman to engage in this traffic; his example was, unfortunately, followed by many others. Owing to the success of this first venture, Hawkins was in the following year given command of a squadron of seven ships, the flagship of which was named the *Jesus*,[3] which sailed to Africa to carry slaves to the West Indies.

[1] Hakluyt, *ibid.*, p. 132.

[2] The Spaniards had practically exterminated the natives of the West Indies by the cruelties inflicted on these gentle people, who were unable to carry on the arduous work in the mines to which they were driven by their conquerors. In order to save the survivors, Bishop Las Casas, a good and humane man, petitioned the Emperor, Charles V, to allow the importation of more Negroes into the West Indies to do the work which was proving too much for the aborigines. In later years the bishop declared that, if he could have foreseen the evil results of his proposal, he would never have made it. There were already Negro slaves in the West Indies at the time, and Las Casas was not responsible for starting the slave-trade.

[3] The people of those days saw nothing incongruous in the use of such a name for a slave-ship, and were nothing if not inconsistent. Queen Elizabeth called the slave-trade 'a detestable act which would call down the vengeance of heaven upon the undertakers'—and knighted Sir John Hawkins. A synod of Protestant Churches held in France in the year 1637 decided that slavery was not condemned 'in the Word of God' and was of the right of nations, while the following appears in a bill of lading of the American slaver *Sierra Leone*, which was carrying on business in the middle of the eighteenth century: 'Shipped by the Grace of God in good order and well conditioned by William Johnson & Co., owners of the said schooner, whereof is master

The value of the trade was now recognized in England, and in 1618 a Charter was granted by King James I to 'the Company of the Adventurers of London trading into Africa'; this company built 'Fort James' on a small island in the River Gambia, not far from the present site of Bathurst. Another company, formed in 1631 to supply slaves to the West Indian Colonies, established a fort at Kormantin, on the Gold Coast, and more British forts were built later along that coast from time to time. Meanwhile, the Dutch had become serious rivals to the Portuguese, from whom they captured the fort at Elmina in 1637; in 1642, the Dutch having withdrawn their claim to certain territory in Brazil, the Portuguese retired altogether from the Gold Coast, surrendering all their property there to Holland. The Dutch then attempted to drive the English out, and succeeded in capturing all their forts except Cape Coast Castle, but new forts were built, and in spite of many vicissitudes British influence in West Africa steadily grew.

Other nations also attempted to gain a footing and forts were erected wherever opportunity offered, to serve as depots for the slaves awaiting shipment and to protect the European merchants from attack. These forts changed hands from time to time as a result of war or purchase, and were in many cases the property rather of the merchants of a nation than of their Government. Portuguese and Frenchmen, Dutchmen and Danes, Brandenburgers and British, Swedes and Spaniards, were all at different times trading along the coast, preying upon the unhappy Africans and themselves being preyed upon by pirates and privateers. It was a lawless period, when a man owned only what he was able to defend. Life was cheap, and the garrisons of the forts and the crews of slave-ships were decimated by disease. Arms and spirits were given to the Africans in exchange for slaves, and the petty chiefs along the coast, who were encouraged by the slave-dealers to raid their neighbours, became gradually more powerful and wealthy by means of the traffic in human flesh and blood.

It is difficult for us to conceive the amount of misery caused

under God for this present voyage, David Lindsay, & now riding at Anchor in the harbor of Newport, & by God's grace bound for the coast of Africa. . . . And so God send the good Schooner to her desired port in safety. Amen.' See *The American Slave Trade* (1907), by John R. Spears, p. 40.

by the slave-trade during the three centuries that it flourished in West Africa, or the degrading effect it had both on the Negroes and on the scarcely more civilized whites who enriched themselves at the expense of their fellow-men. The numbers that suffered and died in the barracoons and slave-ships formed only a part of those affected by the constant raids and the inter-tribal wars which were waged for the purpose of making slaves. The chiefs were not averse from raiding even villages belonging to their own tribes if it was necessary to obtain slaves at once for some impatient dealer. Villages were sometimes surrounded at night and set on fire, the wretched inhabitants being seized as they escaped from the flames, those useless as slaves being often butchered in cold blood to satisfy the lust for cruelty. It is true that slavery has been an institution in Africa from immemorial times, and that slaves were bought and sold on the West African coast before the first European arrived there, but owing to the enormous demand caused by the establishment of plantations in the New World, and the greater facilities provided by fire-arms for the slave-raiding chiefs, the trade increased by leaps and bounds under European management.

The cruelties practised by white men in this trade are almost unbelievable. The condition of the crowded hold of a slave-ship during the long 'middle passage'[1] in tropical weather across the Atlantic would explain the reason why scores of slaves died on every voyage, and why others would, when the opportunity offered, leap overboard to escape sufferings worse than death.[2] Men and women were flogged to compel them to eat, and hot irons were occasionally used to force them to open their mouths and swallow the food which they were too sick at heart to eat willingly. They were flogged again to make them dance and sing in order that they should not brood over their misfortunes. Unbounded licence was given to the officers and crews of slavers as regards the women. The men slaves were fastened together in pairs by handcuffs and leg-irons, and frequently were stowed so close together as to admit of no other

[1] Each slaving voyage was made up of three passages, one from the home port to West Africa, the 'middle passage' from West Africa to America or the West Indies, and the passage back to the home port.
[2] Most slave-ships had a high netting around the bulwarks to prevent this.

posture than lying on their sides. The height between decks
was sometimes only eighteen inches, so that the slaves could
not turn round or even on their sides. In about the year 1785
one ship took on board 700 slaves, who were

so crowded that they were obliged to lie one upon another. This
occasioned such a mortality among them that, without meeting with
unusual bad weather, or having a longer voyage than common, nearly
one-half of them died before the ship arrived in the West Indies.[1]

Their sufferings before they embarked were almost as great.
After a long and painful march to the coast, weighted down
with chains and remorselessly driven on by their cruel captors,
they were crowded into barracoons until they could be sold.[2]
William Bosman, a Dutch slave-dealer who was on the West
Coast at the end of the seventeenth century, wrote as follows:

When these Slaves come . . . they are put in Prison all together,
and when we treat concerning buying them, they are brought out
together into a large Plain; where, by our Chirurgeons, whose Province it is, they are thoroughly examined, even to the smallest
Member, and that naked too both Men and Women, without the
least Distinction or Modesty. . . . In the mean while a burning Iron,
with the Arms or Name of the Companies, lyes in the Fire; with
which ours are marked on the Breast. This is done that we may distinguish them from the Slaves of the English, French or others
(which are also marked with their Mark); and to prevent the
Negroes exchanging them for worse; at which they have a good
Hand. I doubt not that this Trade seems very barbarous to you, but
since it is followed by meer necessity it must go on; but we yet take
all possible care that they are not burned too hard, especially the
Women, who are more tender than the Men.[3]

[1] *The Slave Trade and its Remedy* (1840), by T. F. Buxton, p. 128.

[2] It was estimated that for every 300 slaves who remained alive after a
year in the West Indies or America, 700 Negroes had perished. Of these 500
died at the time of the raid by which the slaves were secured, or during the
long march to the coast and while awaiting shipment, 125 more died on the
voyage, and 75 after landing. *Ibid.*, p. 199.

[3] Bosman, *op. cit.*, p. 364 (English translation published in London,
1705). See also Bryan Edwards: 'It is the custom among some of the planters
in Jamaica to mark the initials of their name on the shoulder or breast of
each newly purchased negro, by means of a small silver brand heated in the
flame of spirits . . . but it is growing into disuse.' *The History of . . . the West
Indies* (second edition, 1794), vol. ii, p. 130. Slaves continued to be branded
until the nineteenth century.

One wonders whether the care exercised was to save the Negroes from unnecessary pain or to avoid injury to valuable property.

In another place Bosman says of the slaves:

They come aboard stark-naked, as well Women as Men: In which condition they are obliged to continue, if the Master of the Ship is not so Charitable (which he commonly is) as to bestow something on them to cover their Nakedness. You would really wonder to see how these Slaves live on Board; for though their number sometimes amounts to six or seven Hundred, yet by the careful Management of our Masters of Ships, they are so regulated that it seems incredible: And in this particular our Nation exceeds all other Europeans; for as the French, Portuguese and English Slave-Ships are always foul and stinking; on the contrary ours are for the most part clean and neat.[1]

In the year 1712, by the Treaty of Utrecht, the British secured a thirty-year monopoly of the slave-trade to the Spanish colonies, which was of great value. British influence on the West Coast of Africa steadily increased, and from this time the British took a leading part in the traffic.[2] It would be pleasing to think that this resulted in some amelioration of the unhappy lot of the slave, but this, unfortunately, was not the case.[3] In 1781 the British slave-ship *Zong* was on a voyage across the Atlantic with a full load of slaves, when it was discovered that the water supply was short and would prove insufficient for the numbers on board. If the slaves died a natural death (which presumably included death from thirst), the loss would fall on the owners, but if they were thrown over-

[1] Bosman, *op. cit.*, p. 365.

[2] In 1771 sixty-three British ships took 23,301 slaves from the Bight of Benin alone. The total export of slaves at that time was 74,000 a year, of which British ships were responsible for 38,000; French for 20,000; Portuguese for 10,000; Dutch for 4,000; and Danish for 2,000. Of this total 14,500 slaves came from the Bonny and New Calabar rivers. See Bryan Edwards, *op. cit.*, vol. ii, pp. 56–7.

[3] An anonymous writer in 1799 thought that the Portuguese ships were better, as they were 'navigated chiefly by black mariners, who sympathized more with the sufferings of their countrymen than the whites. Before the slaves are shipped they are catechized and receive the rite of baptism.' See *A Historical and Philosophical Sketch of the Discoveries and Settlements of the Europeans in Northern and Western Africa at the Close of the Eighteenth Century*, printed by J. Moir, Edinburgh, 1799.

board the loss would be covered by insurance; so 132 slaves were cast into the sea to drown, and the underwriters were compelled by the courts to pay to the owners £30 for each slave lost. There were, however, even then some squeamish persons (or perhaps it was only the unfortunate underwriters) who suggested that the master of the *Zong* should be prosecuted for murder, but this was ridiculed because the 'blacks were property'.[1]

Throughout this period no attempt was made to establish forts along the Nigerian coast similar to those on the Gold Coast,[2] the reason being that the river estuaries provided safe harbours for the slave-ships which were lacking elsewhere in the Gulf of Guinea. As a rule a vessel would enter a river and, after a preliminary present to the local chief to secure the right of trade, the crew would erect an awning of matting and thatch from bow to stern to afford protection from the sun to the slaves and to themselves. This was done because the ship might remain for months in the river waiting for her full cargo of slaves. As the power of the chiefs increased so did their demands from the European slave-dealers, and the custom of making presents to the chiefs prevailed long after the disappearance of the slave-trade. These presents, or 'dashes', were known by different names in the several rivers, and varied in amount, but they were always necessary before any trading could be attempted, and served moreover as payment for protection while in the power of the chiefs. In some places a gift known as 'shake-hands' had to be made, in others a 'topping' proportionate to the amount of trade, or a tax known as 'comey', payable on every slave or ton of cargo exported. In Bosman's day, the late seventeenth century, the charges for each ship at Benin amounted to about £6; in 1817 a 'dash' of £2 had to be paid to the King of Benin before a vessel of under 400 tons could trade within his territories, and as late as 1888 'comey' was being paid by the merchants in the different rivers at rates varying from 1s. 6d. to 2s. 6d. for each ton of palm oil exported.

Barbot, who visited the coast between the years 1678 and

---

[1] *The English People Overseas*, vol. iv, *Britain in the Tropics*, by A. Wyatt Tilby (1912), p. 98.

[2] There was a French fort at Lagos for a short while.

1682, gives some interesting details of the trade and of the people. He had a poor opinion of the Negroes, and thought still less of the Portuguese. At Warri, or, as he calls it, Ouwere, the Dutch and the Portuguese were trading largely, and the Dutch had actually made an attempt to cultivate cotton. 'The Portuguese missions', he says, 'seem to have made a deeper impression on the people of Ouwere than in other parts of Guinea, for many of them still seem to retain some principles of Christianity; and to this day they have a chapel in the town of Ouwere, in which is a crucifix, or an altar, and on the sides of it the figures of the blessed Virgin Mary and of all the apostles, with two candlesticks by them; to which the natives resort from all parts, and there mutter some words in their language before the crucifix, every one of them carrying beads in their hands as is used by the Portuguese'.[1] He also reports that the King of Warri who was reigning in 1644 was 'a Mulatto, born of a Portuguese woman married to King Mingo; and the said Prince was called Don Antonio Mingo. He always wore the Portuguese habit and a sword by his side'.[2] How this came about is explained in a story which Barbot heard and which he repeats in his book. It appears that two Portuguese priests came to Warri and endeavoured to convert the king and his people, urging them to wear clothes and to restrict themselves to one wife each. Mingo, who probably rejoiced in a large *harem*, refused to adopt a religion which would leave him only a single wife, unless the one wife could be a white woman, possibly thinking that the proviso was a safe one. Not to be beaten, however, the priests went to the island of St Thomé, and there persuaded a Portuguese woman that it was her duty to marry

[1] Barbot, *op. cit.*, p. 378. See also Adams, *op. cit.*, who says: 'On entering the first apartment of the palace (at Warri) we were much surprised to see placed on a rude kind of table several emblems of the Catholic religion, consisting of crucifixes, mutilated saints, and other trumpery. Some of these articles were manufactured of brass, and others of wood. On inquiring how they came into their present situation, we were informed that several black Portuguese missionaries had been at Warre, many years since, endeavouring to convert the natives into Christians; and the building in which they preformed their mysteries we found still standing. A large wooden cross, which had withstood the tooth of time, was remaining in a very perfect state in one of the angles formed by two roads intersecting each other. We could not learn that the Portuguese had been successful in making proselytes' (p. 97).

[2] Barbot, *op. cit.*, p. 377.

King Mingo and thus ensure that he and his people should receive the blessings of Christianity.

The Dutch maintained slave depots at Benin for some time, and for a few years, from 1788 to 1792, the French also had an establishment there, but British ships kept the bulk of the trade, and it is estimated that during the palmy days of the slave-trade[1] more than half the slaves exported from the West Coast of Africa were shipped in British bottoms from the rivers between Calabar and Bonny. Public opinion in Great Britain was, however, slowly hardening against the trade.

In England there had always been a few who thought the traffic criminal, but it was not until 1727 that slavery was publicly denounced by the Quakers.[2] During the reign of William III, Sir John Holt, the then Lord Chief Justice, had decided that any slave who entered England became a free man, as 'one may be a villein in England but not a slave'. This judgment, however, had little effect, and runaway slaves were publicly advertised for and recovered by their owners. In 1739 the Courts reversed an opinion given by the Law Officers of the Crown that slaves became free by being in England or being baptized, but in 1772 Lord Mansfield ruled, in the case of the slave James Somersett, that 'as soon as any slave sets his foot on English ground he becomes free'. In spite of this celebrated judgement, a Resolution to the effect that 'the slave-trade is contrary to the laws of God and the rights of men' was lost in Parliament in 1776, and no less than twelve Resolutions presented by Wilberforce[3] in 1789, condemning the slave-trade, were lost by large majorities. However, in 1787[4] a powerful Society for the Abolition of the Slave-Trade was formed,[5] and several Bills were presented to Parliament between 1788 and 1796 to prohibit the further importation of slaves into the West Indies; these Bills were all rejected, but

[1] A slave could be purchased on the African coast in 1786 for £22 and sold in the West Indies for £65.

[2] The Pennsylvania Quakers followed the example of their English co-religionists in 1754, and actually set free some of their slaves.

[3] William Wilberforce (1759–1833) was a Member of Parliament and an earnest advocate of the abolition of slavery.

[4] An informal society was formed in 1783.

[5] Granville Sharp and Thomas Clarkson were the most active members, the former being Chairman.

something was accomplished by the grant of bounties to the masters and surgeons of slavers whose human cargoes escaped excessive mortality and disease.

In 1802 the Danish Government declared the slave-trade illegal, and in 1804 the importation of slaves was prohibited by the United States of America.[1] In 1805 the British Government took the first definite steps to put a stop to the trade, and in 1807 an Act was passed prohibiting, as from March 1, 1808, any slaves being carried in a British ship or landed in a British colony.[2] It had taken twenty years for the Society to persuade Parliament to legislate against the slave-trade, but another century was to elapse before slave-raiding was stamped out in Nigeria. It was thought at first that the suppression of the trade, once it had been made illegal, would not be difficult, but events proved otherwise, and after some time it was realized that the traffic must continue until it was attacked at the source. To get into touch with the powerful chiefs of the interior then became the object of the Government and philanthropists alike, and it was fortunate that at this time the interest of geographers was centred on the problem of the Niger and the exploration of Africa generally. The explorers as well as the philanthropists did their share in the abolition of the slave-trade.

[1] In spite of this, slaves were being brought from Africa to American ports as late as 1860. Slavery was not abolished in the United States until 1865.

[2] In 1811 slave-dealing was made a felony, and in 1824 it was declared to be piracy. Slavery was abolished in British colonies in 1834, Parliament voting a sum of £20,000,000 to compensate the slave-owners. Slavery continued in the French colonies until 1848, in Cuba till 1886, and in Brazil till 1888. A form of slavery continued in the Portuguese colonies of St Thomé, Principe, and Angola as late as 1908.

CHAPTER VII

THE EXPLORATION
OF THE INTERIOR

Follow after—we are waiting, by the trails that we lost,
For the sounds of many footsteps, for the tread of a host.
Follow after—follow after—for the harvest is sown:
By the bones about the wayside ye shall come to your own.

R. KIPLING: *A Song of the English*

Although the Portuguese explorers had reached the Bight of
Benin as early as 1485, and the slave-ships of all nations had
been visiting the river mouths between Lagos and Calabar for
over 300 years, yet little was known of the interior of Nigeria
at the beginning of the nineteenth century. It is true that a few
merchants had visited Benin and that, soon after its discovery,
Portuguese missionaries and officials had had dealings with the
king of that city, but it is probable that the Binis themselves
knew very little of the hinterland and could give only vague
accounts of the people who lived there. No other attempt to
visit the inland districts has been recorded, and this is not
remarkable. The slave-dealers had no incentive to exploration
and, in any case, it was almost impossible for them, as their
sailing-ships could hardly have ascended the rivers very far,
and boat expeditions would have been at the mercy of the
savage tribes along the banks. In these circumstances it is easy
to understand why they did not discover the existence of so
great a river as the Niger, or realize that the many openings
which they regarded as separate rivers were but the different
channels of its delta. All that was known was that large and
powerful states lay behind the mangrove swamps that bordered the coast, and somewhere in the interior there was
believed to be a great river, but where it rose and whither it
flowed remained a mystery.

The existence of the Niger had been known vaguely to the
ancients. Herodotus records[1] an expedition of some Nasa-
monian youths who, travelling in a westerly direction from

[1] *Herodotus*, ii. 32.

Egypt, came at length to a large river flowing eastwards, and attempts have been made to identity this river with the Niger. Strabo[1] and Pliny[2] allude to the Niger; Mela[3] asserts that it flows from west to east, but acknowledges ignorance of its destination, deprecating the suggestion of the earlier writers that it flowed under the sands of the deserts; Ptolemy[4] is extremely vague as to its course, but he breaks away from the tradition that the Niger was a tributary of the Nile. Even the Arabs, whose knowledge of the geography of northern Africa was considerable, found the problem of the Niger too much for them. El Edrisi (*circa* 1153) states that the Niger, which he calls the 'Nile of the Negroes', rises at the same place as the Nile and flows west across Africa into the Atlantic; Abulfeda (1274–1331) follows this theory. El Bekri, a Spanish Arab, who wrote in 1067, mentions the Niger and refers to Kanem (Bornu) as a 'country of idolaters'. About 1237 an embassy from the King of Bornu visited Tunis, and in 1355 a book was completed which recorded the travels in the Sudan of Ibn Batuta, who was sent by the King of Morocco on a mission of discovery. Ibn Batuta did not reach the country which is now known as Nigeria, but he mentions the existence of the Niger and states that it flowed to the east. Leo Africanus (1526), who besides being a great traveller had a knowledge of Arabian literature, agreed with the general Arab theory that the Niger flowed to the west, and this error was repeated by the Portuguese cartographers, who evidently considered the Senegal and the Gambia to be the mouths of the Niger. The French geographers at first repeated the mistake, and in a map published by De Lisle as late as 1700 the Niger is shown as flowing to the west, though the same gentleman in 1714 published a map showing its true direction and treating the Senegal as a separate river. D'Anville, who issued a map in 1749, gave the Niger an easterly course, and made it meet another stream flowing west at a place he calls Wangara.[5] The same map shows the Arab 'Nile of the Negroes' as a distinct river flowing north-west into the 'Lake of Bornu'.

The general uncertainty as to the direction of the Niger was

---

[1] *Geography*, Book 17 (*circa* AD 19).   [2] *Naturalis Historia* (*circa* AD 77).
[3] *De situ orbis* (*circa* AD 47).   [4] *Geography* (*circa* AD 150).
[5] Not to be confused with the place now bearing that name.

probably caused by the confusion of that river with others. The Shari flows to the north-west into Lake Chad, and the Benue flows from east to west, and was perhaps at one time connected with Chad; the Senegal, the Gambia, and the Rio Grande are large rivers flowing westward into the Atlantic, and it is not perhaps very strange, with the vague information available, that geographers should have considered all of these as one continuous waterway crossing Africa from east to west. As we shall see later, even at the beginning of the nineteenth century, although the true direction of the Niger was known, its termination formed the subject of the most fanciful conjectures, the mythical Kong Mountains[1] forming an apparently impassable barrier to what was, in fact, its true course to the sea.

As the coast of Africa became better known, increasing interest was taken in the problem of the interior, and this was given definite shape in 1788, when the African Association was formed in Great Britain for the purpose of the exploration of Africa and, more particularly, the discovery of the route of the Niger. At this time the existence of various states in the western Sudan was more or less known, and the importance and wealth of Hausaland and Bornu were freely rumoured, but the course of the Niger remained a fascinating mystery, which was only to be revealed at the cost of many lives. The Association offered to defray the expenses of explorers, and there were not lacking men who 'yearned beyond the skyline where the strange roads go down'. The first was John Ledyard, who intended to cross Africa from Egypt to the Niger, but died in Cairo in 1788 before his expedition could start. In 1789 a party from Tripoli, led by a Mr Lucas, was driven back by the Arabs without gathering any reliable information of the Niger. In 1791 Major Houghton[2] travelled with some Moorish merchants from the Gambia, but was plundered and deserted by them and, after wandering alone for some days, died in the desert. A party which started from Sierra Leone was forced to retire without accomplishing anything, but the man was now forthcoming who was to succeed in reaching the Niger.

This was Mungo Park,[3] a young Scottish doctor, who had travelled in the East as a surgeon in the employ of the East

---

[1] The real Kong Mountains are on the Ivory Coast.
[2] Formerly British Consul in Morocco.   [3] Born 1771.

India Company, and whose love of adventure prompted him to offer his services to the Association. His offer was accepted, and in 1795 he started on his first expedition. Following the lead of Major Houghton, he ascended the Gambia, and passing Jarra, where that unfortunate officer had died, pushed on to his objective. Ill-treated and robbed of his effects by Negro chiefs, plundered and insulted by Moorish merchants, captured and kept a prisoner by a Moorish chieftain, the intrepid explorer never lost heart and, escaping from one difficulty after another, insisted on pressing on in spite of the entreaties of his African servants. After intense sufferings from the want of food and water, he was rewarded on July 20, 1796, with the sight of 'the long sought for, majestic Niger, glittering to the morning sun, as broad as the Thames at Westminster, and flowing slowly *to the eastward*'.[1] The problem of the direction of the Niger was now solved, and Park notes in his journal: 'The circumstances of the Niger's flowing towards the east, and its collateral points, did not, however, excite my surprise; for although I had left Europe in great hesitation on this subject, and rather believed that it ran in the contrary direction, I had made such frequent inquiries during my progress concerning this river and had received from Negroes of different nations such clear and decisive assurances that its general course was *towards the rising sun*, as scarce left any doubt on my mind.'[2] After following the Niger eastwards for a short distance, the traveller turned and began his journey back to the coast. This proved no less dangerous and arduous than the outward journey; he was stripped and robbed by bandits, and his position seemed hopeless. 'I saw myself in the midst of a vast wilderness, in the depth of the rainy season; naked and alone; surrounded by savage animals, and men still more savage. I was five hundred miles from the nearest European settlement.'[3] He was now without followers, and even his horse was gone, but he struggled on on foot, and at last reached a village where he received kind treatment. Here the fever which had been troubling him ever since the beginning

---

[1] *Travels in the Interior Districts of Africa* . . . *in the Years 1795, 1796, and 1797* (London, 1798), by Mungo Park, p. 194.
[2] *Ibid.*, p. 195.
[3] *Ibid.*, p. 243.

of the rainy season, and for which he had no medicine, finally prostrated him, and for five weeks he was unable to move. When he was convalescent he managed to attach himself to a slave-caravan which was travelling to the Gambia, and in spite of the hardships of the journey he arrived safely on June 10, 1797, at the place he had started from eighteen months earlier. Park left the Gambia in a slave-ship for the West Indies, and in December reached England, where his discoveries aroused the greatest interest. The celebrated geographer, Major Rennell,[1] collated the information obtained by Park with that supplied by the Arab writers and embodied the results, with theories of his own derived from them, in a *Geographical Illustration*, which was published as an appendix to Park's journal. The general conclusion was that the Niger flowed eastward and ended in a lake or swamp called Wangara, into which another river flowed from the east, and Major Rennell's reputation was sufficient to cause his opinion to prevail generally. Reichard (1802) was the only theorist who was dissatisfied with the general belief in the abrupt termination of the river in the Wangara swamp, and he maintained[2] that it flowed southward from Wangara into the Gulf of Guinea; his theory, however, attracted little attention.

In 1798 two Germans, Frendenburg and Horneman, were sent out by the Association; the former died before starting, but Horneman left Cairo, and in April 1800 he wrote that he was about to start for Bornu. Nothing more was heard from him, but it is known that he crossed the desert and died in the Nupe country.[3] Another German, Roentgen, was sent out, but he was murdered by his African servant; and the travels of the Swiss explorer Burckhardt[4] in northern Africa were valueless from the point of view of discovery.

The British Government, however, was now interested in the problem of the Niger, and it was decided that an expedition should be sent out for the discovery of its course and termination. The command of the expedition was entrusted to Park, on whom a Captain's commission was betowed, and in January

[1] 1743–1830.
[2] See *Ephemerides Geographique* (Weimar, 1803), vol. xii.
[3] See Denham and Clapperton, *op. cit.*, vol. ii, p. 296.
[4] 1784–1817.

1805 he sailed for Goree[1] with a small party of officers and artificers. At Goree volunteers were asked for from the garrison, and one officer and thirty-four men were selected from those who offered their services. On April 27th the expedition started. It consisted of Park, his brother-in-law Anderson, Mr Scott, Lieutenant Martyn of the Goree garrison, and forty other Europeans, with Isaaco, a Mandingo priest and merchant, as a guide. That the expedition started so late in the season was due to delays and procrastinations in England for which Park was not responsible, but it is strange that a man of his experience should have thought it advisable to start with so large a party of Europeans and without a proportionate number of Africans to carry out the arduous duties, which in that climate prove a severe strain on the health of white men. From the beginning there were difficulties. The donkeys used for carrying the stores proved unmanageable or broke down under the heavy loads; the caravan was attacked and temporarily scattered by swarms of bees;[2] the rains commenced, and the men sickened and died; Anderson and Scott, the only members of the party on whom Park could rely, became too ill to assist him; and the local people stole openly from the enfeebled soldiers. Only Park's indomitable will enabled him to press on. He was ill himself, but he seems to have done most of the work, driving the donkeys, replacing fallen loads, doctoring the sick, taking observations, and keeping watch at night. At length, on August 19th, the Niger was reached by the remnant of the party, Park, Anderson, Martyn, and seven other Europeans; the rest had died or been murdered by robbers. With the assistance of the only other man capable of exertion, Park now set to work to convert two old canoes which he bought into a 'schooner', in which he proposed to sail down the Niger and emerge by the mouth of the Congo, which river he now believed to be identical with the Niger. Before he could embark, however, more of his followers, including his brother-in-

[1] A small island off Dakar, included in the republic of Senegal. It was held in turn by the Dutch, French, and English, who garrisoned it during the Napoleonic wars. It was finally handed over to France in 1817.

[2] This happens not infrequently in Africa. The British troops attacking Tanga in November 1914 were much harassed by bees, disturbed by their advance.

law, had died, and those who actually started on the voyage downstream were Park, Martyn, and three of the soldiers, of whom one was mad and the others ill. From Sansandig, where the voyage started, Park sent back his faithful guide Isaaco with his journal[1] and letters to his friends and relatives. His letter to Lord Camden, dated from 'On board of His Majesty's Schooner *Joliba*', November 17, 1805, breathes the spirit of the man: ' . . . I am sorry to say that of forty-four Europeans who left the Gambia in perfect health, five only are at present alive . . . but I assure you I am far from desponding . . . and shall set sail to the east with the fixed resolution to discover the termination of the Niger or perish in the attempt. I have heard nothing that I can depend on respecting the remote course of this mighty stream; but I am more and more inclined to think that it can end nowhere but in the sea. My dear friend Mr Anderson and likewise Mr Scott are both dead; but though all the Europeans who are with me should die, and though I were myself half dead, I would still persevere; and if I could not succeed in the object of my journey, I would at last die on the Niger. . . .'[2] To his wife he wrote: ' . . . I think it not unlikely but I shall be in England before you receive this. . . . We this morning have done with all intercourse with the natives; and the sails are now hoisting for our departure for the coast.'[3]

The *Joliba* started on her journey downstream on November 19th, manned by the five Europeans, Amadi, a guide engaged in place of Isaaco, and three slaves. Nothing more was ever heard from Park, and there is no doubt that he perished, with his remaining followers, in the rapids at Bussa. Rumours of a disastrous end to the expedition filtered through to the coast, and in 1810 Isaaco was engaged by the Government to investigate the matter. He travelled to Sansandig, and there met Amadi, who informed him that the *Joliba* was attacked at several points of the river by the local people, but that the attacks had been repulsed. At Yauri Amadi was paid off, and a few days later the *Joliba* struck a rock in one of the narrow gorges

---

[1] *The Journal of a Mission to the Interior of Africa in the Year 1805, by Mungo Park, together with other Documents, Official and Private, relating to the Same Mission* (London, 1815).

[2] *Ibid.*, p. lxxx.   [3] *Ibid.*, p. lxxxii.

through which the Niger runs at Bussa, the white men and their slaves perishing in the water or at the hands of the hostile tribesmen on the bank. There is no reason why Amadi's story should not have been the true one, and Isaaco, a reliable man, believed him. An almost identical story was told to Clapperton at Sokoto in 1824,[1] and some of Park's belongings were seen by Lander at Bussa in 1830,[2] but there were several, especially of Park's immediate family, who refused to believe in his death, and from time to time rumours were published of white men being alive somewhere in the interior. Park's son, Thomas, firmly believed his father to be alive, and in 1827 he made an attempt to penetrate into the country from Accra, but was murdered or died before he had gone very far.[3]

The fate of Mungo Park and the Napoleonic wars combined to stop any further exploration for some years, but Park's theory of the identity of the Niger and Congo was not forgotten. In 1816 the Government authorized another expedition to test the correctness of this theory. Major Peddie, with a large and well-equipped party, was to cross from the Atlantic coast to the Niger, which they would descend, to meet, it was hoped, a party led by Captain Tuckey, which was to ascend the Congo. Major Peddie died soon after landing, and his successor, Captain Campbell, did not very long survive him, the remainder of the party being compelled to return, baffled, to the coast. Tuckey's party was no more successful; the cataracts of the Congo barred the passage of their boats, and attempts to push on by land were frustrated by disease. Tuckey and most of his officers died, and the expedition was forced to return after an advance of less than 300 miles.

In the same year as Peddie and Tuckey started on their disastrous expeditions there was published by James M'Queen a

[1] See Denham and Clapperton, op. cit., vol. ii, p. 343, and Appendix VIII.

[2] See Journal of an Expedition to Explore the Course and Termination of the Niger (1832), by R. and J. Lander, vol. ii, pp. 6, 12, and 36.

[3] Sir James Alexander, in his Excursions in Western Africa, and Narrative of a Campaign in Kaffir-land (1840), states that Thomas Park was a midshipman, aged nineteen, and was given three years' leave of absence to search for his father. He lived at Accra for three months with the local people, refusing to live with Europeans, and 'allied himself with an Accra female by way of learning the language.' p. 182.

pamphlet supporting the theory of Reichard that the Niger flowed into the Gulf of Guinea, and in 1821 he published a book[1] setting out in full the results of his inquiries and studies, and his reasons for believing that the Niger found its outlet where, in fact, it did. M'Queen was a resident in the West Indian island of Grenada and, being interested in geography and the explorations of Mungo Park, he took the opportunity of questioning the slaves from the part of Africa through which the Niger runs. Their answers, and his own study of the Arab geographers, convinced him that no other outlet was possible, and he laid down from deduction what has been found to be a very accurate description of the general course of the Niger and the relative position of the Benue.

M'Queen's theories, however, received little attention, and attempts were still made to reach the Niger from the Atlantic or Mediterranean coasts. Captain Gray, a survivor of Peddie's expedition, made a further attempt to follow in Park's foot-steps, but was compelled to return unsuccessful, after being detained for a year in the interior. In 1818 Mollien, a French-man, failed in the quest, and the following year Lyon and Ritchie started from Tripoli, but did not succeed in crossing the desert, and Ritchie died at Murzuk.

In 1821 the British Government, at that time on the best of terms with the Basha of Tripoli, determined to send a party across the desert from that place, and an Arab escort was arranged for. Major Denham,[2] Lieutenant Clapperton,[3] and Doctor Oudney,[4] with a carpenter named Hillman,[5] formed

[1] *Geographical and Commercial View of Northern Central Africa, containing a Particular Account of the Course and Termination of the Great River Niger in the Atlantic Ocean* (Edinburgh, 1821), by James M'Queen.

[2] Born 1786; appointed Superintendent of Liberated Slaves, Sierra Leone, 1826; appointed Governor of Sierra Leone 1828; died there the same year.

[3] Born 1788; died near Sokoto on a second expedition in 1827.

[4] Appointed Political Agent to Bornu before leaving England.

[5] In 1834 Sir James Alexander saw Hillman at the Gambia, and heard from him that on his return from the expedition all that he was offered was £24 a year, the superannuation pay of a retired carpenter, so he sailed for Fernando Po with Captain Owen and helped with the clearing and building there, and was then sent to the Gambia, where he was earning six shillings a day. He referred to 'the unfortunate jealousies' that existed between Denham and Clapperton. Alexander, *op. cit.*

the party, which arrived at Tripoli in November 1821, but the
usual Oriental delays prevented the expedition from starting
across the desert till the following November. They followed
one of the usual caravan routes marked out by the skeletons
of the unhappy slaves who had perished in their terrible journeys to the Tripoli markets. Major Denham notes in his journal[1]
on December 22nd: 'During the last two days we had passed
on an average from sixty to eighty or ninety skeletons each
day; but the numbers that lay about the wells at El-Hammar
were countless'; and in another place: 'Round this spot were
lying more than one hundred skeletons. . . . The Arabs laughed
heartily at my expression of horror and said, "they were only
blacks, *nam boo!*" (damn their fathers).' At last, after suffering
from thirst and fatigue, and from the intense heat of the
sun and the scorching wind, they reached, on February 4,
1823, their first objective, Lake Chad, and on the 17th they
arrived at Kuka, the capital of Bornu. Here they were received by Muhammad el Kanemi, the famous Shehu (sheikh),
to whom they presented a letter of introduction from the
Basha of Tripoli. As stated above, El Kanemi had forced the
Fulani invaders to withdraw from Bornu and, while leaving to the
Sultan of Bornu his title and the outward appearances of royalty,
retained in his own more capable hands the government
of the country.[2] He was an enlightened ruler, and treated
his British visitors with honour and consideration. The
puppet Sultan was also visited, and after a delay of over
two months arrangements were made for further journeys
of exploration. Denham accompanied the Arabs of his escort
and a contingent of Bornu troops on a slave-raiding expedition
into the Mandara country, but the expedition was defeated
by the people whom they intended to raid, and Denham himself narrowly escaped with his life. In December the party was
strengthened by the arrival of Ensign Toole, who crossed the
desert with a caravan, and in January 1824 Denham and
Toole started off to explore the Shari river and the shores of
Lake Chad; but on February 26th Toole died at Angala.
On May 19th Mr Tyrwhitt joined Denham with fresh presents

[1] Denham and Clapperton, *op. cit.*
[2] On the death of El Kanemi he was succeeded as Shehu by his son, who
deposed the Sultan and ruled in name as well as in fact.

88   HISTORY OF NIGERIA

for the Shehu from the British Government, in return for the
kindness he had shown to the travellers.

In the meantime Clapperton and Oudney had set out to
explore the Hausa states, and if possible to reach the Niger.
They left Kuka on December 14, 1823, but Oudney died
at Murmur, between Katagum and Kano, on January 12th,
and Clapperton was compelled to push on alone, reaching
Kano on the 20th. He was not impressed with what he saw.
'Arrayed in naval uniform, I made myself as smart as circumstances would permit. . . . At eleven o'clock we entered Kano,
the great emporium of the kingdom of Hausa; but I had no
sooner passed the gates than I felt grievously disappointed, for
from the flourishing description of it given by the Arabs, I
expected to see a city of surprising grandeur: I found, on the
contrary, the houses nearly a quarter of a mile from the walls,
and in many parts scattered into detached groups, between
large stagnant pools of water. I might have spared all the pains
I had taken with my toilet, for not an individual turned his
head round to gaze at me, but all, intent on their own business,
allowed me to pass by without notice or remark.' At Kano he
stayed awhile, waiting for an escort, and there he heard vague
reports of the Niger, and of the death of Horneman at Nupe
twenty years before.   On March 16th he arrived at Sokoto,
and was received by Sultan Bello, the son and successor of
Othman dan Fodio, who had led the Fulani *jihad* and established his empire. Promises were made that Clapperton should
be allowed to go to Yauri and Nupe, and there see the Niger
for himself, but the Sultan finally refused to let him go, on
the grounds of the dangers involved. He was, however, extremely friendly, gave Clapperton an account of the death of
Mungo Park, and told him what he knew (very little) of the
course of the Niger; he also gave him an extract from a book
written by himself on the history and geography of the country, and a map[1] of Sokoto and the neighbouring territory. He
was anxious that the King of England should send a physician
and a Consul to reside at Sokoto, and promised to send an
escort to the coast to convoy some guns, which he requested
as a present, and the British mission which would accompany

[1] Reproduced in the *Narrative* of Denham and Clapperton, *op. cit.*, and in
The Making of Northern Nigeria (1911), by Captain (later Sir) C. W. J. Orr.

them. On May 4th Clapperton left Sokoto, bearing with him a letter from the Sultan to King George IV, and on July 8th he arrived at Kuka.

Some days later Denham returned from an expedition to Lake Chad, and on August 16th Denham, Clapperton, and Hillman left Kuka to return to Tripoli, which they reached on January 26, 1825. Mr Tyrwhitt remained at Kuka as British Consul, but letters received by Major Denham and the Consul at Tripoli, from El Kanemi, gave particulars of his death on October 22, 1824, and transmitted a list of his effects.[1]

In the meantime Giovanni Belzoni, the Italian explorer and Egyptologist (born 1778), had attempted to reach Timbuktu from the Guinea Coast, but died at Gwato, in the Benin country, in 1823. Major Laing had attempted to reach the Niger from the Gold Coast, and had failed; he tried again from Tripoli in 1826, and reached Timbuktu, but was murdered on the return journey. A Frenchman, Caillié, started in 1827, and reached Timbuktu the following year, returning safely across the desert to Tangiers.

Encouraged by the friendly reception of Denham and Clapperton, the British Government determined on another attempt at exploration, and a party was sent to the coast of the Gulf of Guinea for that purpose. The party consisted of Clapperton and his personal servant, Richard Lander,[2] Captain Pearce, and Surgeon Morrison, and a start was made from Badagri on December 7, 1825. Morrison became very ill and attempted to retrace his way to the coast, but died before he reached it; Pearce died soon after, and Clapperton and Lander went on alone. No difficulty, save that of importunate hospitality, was placed in their way, and they passed safely through the Yoruba country and crossed the river close to Bussa, where confirmation was obtained of Park's fate. Proceeding first to Kano, the two Englishmen went on to Sokoto, where Clapperton presented himself to the Sultan. His reception, however, was by no means as cordial as he had expected. Bello was distracted by civil wars and rebellion, and lent a ready ear to

---

[1] This list included 'two scrapers of pig's hair' (toothbrushes) and 'three looking-glasses for the nose' (spectacles).

[2] Born 1804; died 1834.

the insinuations of the Arabs, anxious to keep Europeans from
what they regarded as their own preserves, that Clapperton
was in reality an enemy and a spy. The friendly feeling that
had existed between Sokoto and Bornu at the time of Clapperton's last visit had disappeared, and Bello strongly resented
the fact that the British officer had brought muskets for the
Shehu as well as for himself. The worries caused by the treatment he received and the apparent impossibility of accomplishing his mission so aggravated the fever from which Clapperton was suffering that he died on April 13, 1827, at Jungavie,
a small village five miles east of Sokoto.

After Lander had buried his master's remains, he proceeded
to Kano, and travelled southwards from there, hoping to reach
the Niger and complete the task which Clapperton's death had
left unfinished. He got as far as Dunroro, a place not very far
from the Benue, where he was compelled to turn back, and
after some delay and trouble at Zaria was only able to return
to Badagri by the route he had followed with Clapperton. He
reached Badagri on November 21st, but his troubles were
not yet over. The Portuguese slave-merchants persuaded the
inhabitants that he was a spy and to prove his innocence he
had to submit to an ordeal by poison, which would have killed
him had he not taken a powerful emetic at once. He got on
board a ship on January 20, 1828, and reached England
at the end of April, bringing with him Clapperton's journal[1]
and his own.[2]

It was now becoming more or less generally accepted that
the theories of Reichard and M'Queen as to the termination
of the Niger were correct, and several naval officers and traders
to the coast believed that the estuaries between the Benin
river and Old Calabar were in fact the outlets of the great
river. In these circumstances it seems strange that no attempt
was made to ascend the supposed outlets from the sea, and
that the attempt of a Mr Nicholls in 1805 to ascend the Old
Calabar river in the hope of proving it to be the estuary of the
Niger was not repeated in one of the other rivers. But even at

[1] Published as *Clapperton's Journal of a Second Expedition into the Interior
of Africa* (Philadelphia, 1829).
[2] Published by Lander as *Records of Captain Clapperton's Last Expedition
to Africa . . . with the Subsequent Adventures of the Author* (London, 1830).

this late period there were still many fanciful theories as to the course of the Niger, and General Donkin attempted in 1829 to prove that the river flowed north, across (and under) the sands of the Sahara desert to the Mediterranean![1]

[1] *A Dissertation on the Course and Probable Termination of the Niger* (London, 1829), by Lieutenant-General Sir Rufane Donkin.

CHAPTER VIII

THE EXPLORATION
OF THE INTERIOR (*continued*)

Follow after—follow after! We have watered the root,
And the bud has come to blossom that ripens for fruit!

R. KIPLING: *A Song of the English*

It remained for Richard Lander to succeed where others had
failed, and by his success to settle the Niger mystery for ever.
He possessed no advantages of birth or education, but his
imagination had been fired during his travels with Clapperton,
and he was eager to return to Africa and solve the great problem of the Niger. He accordingly offered his services to the
British Government for this purpose and his offer was accepted, the Government undertaking to pay to his wife the
sum of £25 quarterly for one year, and to give him a gratuity
of £100 on his return! Lander's brother John,[1] who volunteered
to accompany him, was refused either salary or reward. The
instructions given to Lander showed that the Government had
no definite idea as to the course of the Niger below Bussa; he
was to follow it to Funda, where he was to see whether there
was any lake or swamp into which the river flowed. If at Funda
he found that the river still flowed to the southward he was
to follow it to the sea, 'where, in this case, it may be presumed to empty its waters; but if it should be found to turn
off to the eastward, in which case it will most probably fall into
Lake Tshad . . . ' he was to follow its course 'even to Bornou'.

The brothers left England in January 1830 and landed at
Badagri on March 22nd. On June 17th they reached Bussa, but
it was not until September 20th that they were able to depart
in two canoes, on their journey down the Niger. They met
with no opposition from the inhabitants during the first
part of the voyage, and on October 25th they passed the confluence with the Benue, but near Asaba they fell in with
fifty large armed canoes, manned by a number of Africans

[1] Born 1807; died 1839.

dressed, more or less, in European fashion, and flying flags
which were passable imitations of the British ensign. The first
hope that these might be friends was not realized. The men
in the canoes were Ibos, who were up the river to trade only
with those who were too strong for them to plunder, and the
travellers were soon overpowered, most of their papers and
possessions being lost in the struggle or retained by their captors. The following day, November 6th, they were carried
off to Abo and presented to the Ibo chief, Obie, and here also
they met men from the Brass river, who told them that an English brig was even then at Brass. After a few days they were
ransomed by 'King Boy' of Brass, to whom they gave a bill on
the master of the English brig both for the amount he paid as
ransom to Obie and for his own remuneration. They were then
carried to Boy's town and, while John Lander was detained
there as a hostage, Richard was permitted to go in a canoe
with Boy to the River Nun ('the first Brass river'), where the
brig *Thomas* of Liverpool was lying. His reception on board
was not encouraging. Four of the crew had just died of fever
and the rest were ill; the master, Thomas Lake, was not only
ill, but was a thoroughly unpleasant person, and with the most
offensive oaths refused to honour Lander's bill or to pay anything at all for him. In despair Lander asked Boy to take him
to the Bonny river, where other British ships were lying, but
this was, perhaps not unnaturally, refused on the ground that
if one captain would not pay there was no reason to think that
others would. At last Lake promised that if Lander could get
his brother on board he would take them away, but he flatly
refused to pay anything by way of ransom. Boy was at length
persuaded to go for John Lander in the hope of getting some
payment in return, and brought him on board, but Lake had
no intention of redeeming the promises of the brothers and
they themselves were powerless to do anything. Boy returned
to the shore in disgust to reflect on the perfidy of white men,
but the Landers were not yet out of danger. Lake had refused
to pay the African pilot who had brought the ship into the
river, and this individual had a battery of guns mounted in
such a position as to cover the passage. Boy was suspected to
be gathering his forces for an attack upon the brig, and the
heavy seas on the bar, coupled with an adverse wind, pre-

vented their leaving the river for some days. However, on November 27th, after narrowly escaping being wrecked among the breakers, the ship escaped from the river and the brothers were landed at Fernando Po.[1] Here they obtained a passage home and, after a long and tedious voyage, arrived in England on June 9, 1831.[2] In the seventeen months during which they had been away they had solved the mystery which had puzzled the world for centuries. From the inhabitants of the countries through which they had passed they had received, on the whole, kind and hospitable treatment, and it was reserved to a savage of their own race to form the exception. It is satisfactory to know that the British Government at once made arrangements to pay to King Boy the sum promised him by the Landers, a small sum in comparison with the results obtained by the successful termination of their journey.

The first attempt to put the discovery of the Landers to practical use was made by Mr Macgregor Laird,[3] a Liverpool merchant, who at once set about the formation of a company to trade on the Niger. In 1832 two small steamers, the *Quorra* and the *Alburkah*,[4] entered the delta and commenced to explore the various channels. On board were Laird, Richard Lander, Dr Oldfield, and Lieutenant Allen,[5] who was sent by the Government to survey the river. In the six weeks during which the delta was being explored eighteen men died, but the vessels at last got into the main river, where the conditions were not so bad; the season, however, was far advanced, and the river was falling, so they were unable to ascend much above Lokoja, where disease again took a heavy toll. Although him-

[1] While the Landers were waiting at Fernando Po for a homeward-bound vessel, Captain Lake called there again in the *Thomas* and offered them a passage, which they refused. The *Thomas* left, and within sight of the island was attacked by a pirate vessel, and nothing more was ever heard of the brig or her commander.

[2] On their return they published a *Journal of an Expedition to explore the Course and Termination of the Niger* (1832), 3 vols.

[3] Born 1808; died 1861. A member of the family which started the famous shipbuilding firm.

[4] This vessel, designed and built by Mr Laird, was the first iron ship that performed a sea voyage. The two vessels were seen 'decaying' at Fernando Po by the members of the Niger Expedition of 1841.

[5] Allen was a fair artist, and published a volume of *Views on the Niger* (1840).

self very ill, Laird managed to visit Funda[1] (on the Benue) by boat; at first he was well received by the king, but soon found himself under restraint, obtaining his release after some time by a stratagem which he describes:

. . . Everything being ready, I fired my pistol, and up flew four beautiful rockets, the discharge of which was immediately followed by the blaze of six blue lights, throwing a ghastly glare over the whole scene. The effect was electric, the natives fled in all directions, and the king, throwing himelf to the ground, and placing one of my feet on his head, entreated me to preserve him from harm, and inform him what was the decision of the fates. . . . I then took from my pocket a little compass, and explained that if the needle pointed towards me when placed on the ground I was to go, if towards him I was to stay. . . .[2]

The result may easily be guessed, and Laird was soon able to rejoin his friends. The ships at once descended the Niger and proceeded to Fernando Po, whence Laird returned to England.

During the next season Oldfield and Lander again ascended the river. Rabba, at that time the capital of Nupe, was reached, and the Benue was navigated for over 100 miles, the ships then returning to Fernando Po. Determined to persevere, Lander again dispatched the *Alburkah* up-river, and was following in a boat with supplies, when he was attacked by armed canoes at Angiama in the delta and driven back, three of his African crew being killed and himself fatally wounded; he died at Fernando Po on February 2, 1834. This was the end of the expedition, which from the explorer's point of view had accomplished little, as a trading venture had been a complete failure, and had resulted in the deaths of all but nine of the forty-eight Europeans who had entered the river. Macgregor Laird never returned to West Africa, but he continued to take a lively interest in the question of the development of trade on the Niger, which was for the moment held up by the frightful mortality which appeared inevitable.

In 1835 Mr John Beecroft[3] ascended the Niger as far as

[1] Destroyed by the Fulani in 1853.

[2] *Narrative of an Expedition into the Interior of Africa by the River Niger in 1832–34* (1837), by Macgregor Laird and R. A. K. Oldfield, 2 vols.

[3] John Beecroft was born in 1790, and, while an apprentice on a coasting vessel, was captured by a French privateer in 1805 and kept a prisoner in France till 1814. He then entered the merchant service, served with Sir

Lokoja in the *Quorra*, and again in 1840 he got within 40 miles of Bussa in the *Ethiope*, the property of a West African merchant, Mr Jamieson.[1] In another expedition in the *Ethiope* in 1845 he reached Rabba. Beecroft also explored the Benin river in 1840[2] and the Old Calabar river in 1842.

In 1841 a large expedition was sent out to the Niger by the Government, against the advice of Macgregor Laird and Jamieson. It consisted of three steamers, the *Albert*, *Wilberforce*, and *Soudan*, and the schooner *Amelia*, and no trouble or expense was spared to make it a success. The ships were under the command of naval officers, Captain (afterwards Admiral) Trotter, Commander (afterwards Admiral) W. Allen,[3] and Commander Bird Allen, who were empowered to make treaties with the chiefs for the stoppage of the slave-trade. Missionaries accompanied the expedition, and among them was an African, Samuel Crowther,[4] who twenty-three years later was to be consecrated Bishop of the Niger Territories. Materials were taken out for the establishment of a model farm, and everything was done that medical science of the day could suggest for the preservation of the health of the European crews. Fever, however, was to prove too much for them. The ships ascended as far as Lokoja with little difficulty, and there the model farm was started on land purchased from the local chiefs,[5] but now sickness broke out, and in a short while there were hardly

Edward Parry in the Davis Straits, and joined the naval settlement at Fernando Po in 1829. When this settlement was broken up in 1834 Beecroft remained on the island, governing the freed slaves and other Africans who had drifted there, without authority, but with their full consent. In 1843 he was appointed Governor of the Island by the Queen of Spain (without salary), and in 1849 he was appointed British Consul at Fernando Po, his jurisdiction including the coasts of what is now Nigeria. He died in 1854.

[1] Author of *An Appeal against the Niger Expedition* (of 1841), *Commerce with Africa*, and other pamphlets.

[2] An account of Beecroft's journey is given in the *Journal of the Royal Geographical Society for 1841*.

[3] Surveyor with the 1832 expedition.

[4] Samuel Adjai Crowther was a Yoruba, born about 1809. He was sold into slavery while a youth, but the slave-ship in which he was being carried to America was captured by a British cruiser, and he was taken to Sierra Leone, where he was educated. He died in 1891.

[5] 700,000 cowries (= £45) was paid for 16 miles of land along the right bank of the Niger, the property being about 4 miles deep.

enough men left fit to work the ships.[1] The *Soudan* was sent down the river with the sick, and reached Fernando Po with difficulty, being worked almost single-handed by Lieutenant Fishbourne, the rest of the crew being overcome by fever. In a few days the sick-list on the remaining ships had increased considerably, and the *Wilberforce* was sent down the river. The *Albert* ascended as far as Egga, and then, with almost every man dead or dying, succeeded in reaching the delta, where she was met by Mr Beecroft in the *Ethiope* and escorted safely to Fernando Po. In two months there had been forty-eight deaths from fever out of a total of 145 Europeans who had entered the river. Trotter had been invalided, Bird Allen was dead, but the survivors were about to ascend the river again when orders were received to abandon the attempt. Carr, a coloured West Indian, who had been employed for the model farm, tried to reach Lokoja by canoe, but was murdered in the delta. The *Wilberforce* re-ascended the river with a few officers and an African crew, the people who had been left at the model farm at Lokoja were removed, and the expedition was abandoned.[2]

This disaster made both the philanthropists and the trading community pause in their attempts to open up the Niger, but the Government was determined to find out all that was to be known of this baffling country, and in 1850 another expedition set out from Tripoli to cross the desert. It was commanded by Mr James Richardson, who was accompanied by two Germans, Dr Heinrich Barth and Dr Adolf Overweg. Leaving Tripoli on March 24, 1850, the travellers passed through Murzuk, Asben, Air, and Agades, where they separated, Richardson proceeding towards Bornu and the others to Kat-

---

[1] It is recorded that the first man to die was a total abstainer. 'Indeed, we had a case of one confirmed drunkard escaping entirely. The middle course, of moderation in all things, appears to be the safest.' *Narrative of the Expedition . . . to the River Niger in 1841* (1848), by Captain W. Allen, vol. ii, p. 16.

[2] For accounts of this expedition see *Journals of the Rev. James Frederick Schon and Mr Samuel Crowther, who with the Sanction of Her Majesty's Government accompanied the Expedition up the Niger in 1841* (1842); *Medical History of the Expedition to the Niger during the years 1841–2, comprising an account of the Fever which led to its Abrupt Termination* (1843), by Dr J. O. M'William; and the *Private Journal kept during the Niger Expedition* (1843), by W. Simpson.

D

sena. Already the members of the expedition had suffered much from robbery and had narrowly escaped with their lives at the hands of the fanatical nomads of the desert. At Katsena Barth was detained for some while and relieved of most of his belongings, and throughout his stay in the country his property was systematically plundered by bandits on the one hand and the officials of the various towns on the other. He succeeded at length in getting away from Katsena and, passing through Kano, entered the territories of Bornu. Here he learnt of Richardson's death and saw his grave (at Ngurutuwa, two miles north-east of Bangego), and on April 2, 1851, reached Kuka. He was hospitably received by the Shehu, son of El Kanemi, who had befriended Denham and Clapperton, and obtained from him Richardson's journal, which was dispatched by a slave-caravan to Tripoli, and reached England safely.[1] In May Overweg, who had visited Zinder in the interval, joined Barth, and soon afterwards the two again separated, Overweg exploring Lake Chad in the collapsible boat which they had brought with them across the desert, while Barth proceeded to Adamawa. On June 18th he saw the Benue for the first time and crossed it close to its confluence with the Faro; next day he entered Yola, but was forced to leave within a week after being subjected to many insults. Overweg and Barth met again in September, and then once more separated to carry out independent explorations. In August of the next year they met for the last time on the shores of Lake Chad, and there Overweg died on August 23, 1852.[2]

Barth was now alone, but having by this time received letters from the British Government authorizing him to carry on with the duties originally allotted to Richardson, he determined to persevere in the attempt to reach Sokoto and the Niger. He accordingly travelled through Zinder and Katsena to Wurno, where he met the Fulani Sultan of Sokoto, son of Bello, at first the friend and later the persecutor of Clapperton. After visiting Sokoto and Gando, he reached the Niger at Say

[1] Published as *Narrative of a Mission to Central Africa Performed in the Years 1850–1 under the Orders and at the Expense of Her Majesty's Government* (1853), by the late James Richardson, 2 vols.

[2] His grave was discovered some years ago, and his remains were transferred to the cemetery at Maidugari.

on June 20, 1853, and then proceeded to Timbuktu, which he reached on September 7, 1853; here he remained until May 1854, when he retraced his steps through Say, Gando, and Sokoto to Kano, and later to Bornu. On November 29, 1854, he met Dr Eduard Vogel, who had been sent out to assist him, and learnt from him that an expedition had been sent up the Benue to try to get into touch with him.[1] He got back to Kuka on December 11, 1854, where he met two sappers, Corporal Church and Private Macguire, who had accompanied Vogel across the desert. On May 4, 1855, Barth and Church left Kuka with a caravan for Tripoli, where they arrived safely in August, Barth reaching England on September 6, 1855, after an absence of nearly six years, during which time he had covered an immense amount of country and acquired a great deal of useful information. His great book, published in 1857 in German and English, still remains the most important work ever written on the districts of which he treats.[2]

Before Barth left Kuka, Vogel and Macguire had started off to explore the country lying between Bornu and the Nile valley, but nothing more was ever heard from them. Later it was reported that Vogel had been murdered in the Wadai country about February 1856 and Macguire not long after.

The news that Barth had crossed the Benue was received in England in 1852, and it was considered necessary to prove that this was the same river that had been explored by Lander and Oldfield in 1833, which at that time was known as the Chadda. The Government accordingly entered into a contract with Mr Macgregor Laird to build and equip a suitable vessel, on which as few white men as possible were to be employed; naval officers were to be supplied to navigate the vessel and survey the river, and Mr Laird was to send out representatives for trading purposes, the whole expedition being placed under the command of Mr Beecroft, who was now the British Consul at Fernando Po. It was hoped that the expedition would meet and be of assistance to Drs Barth and Vogel. Before the *Pleiad*,

---

[1] The *Pleiad* expedition of 1854, *infra*.

[2] *Travels and Discoveries in North and Central Africa* (1857–58), by Dr H. Barth, 5 vols. A two-volume condensed edition was also published in 1890. Barth was made a CB. He died in 1864 at the early age of forty-four.

the steamer supplied by Laird, could reach the coast Beecroft had died, and the command of the expedition devolved upon Dr Baikie, RN.[1] The ship was in the Niger and Benue for four months in 1854, and although it was impossible to get into touch with Barth or Vogel[2] the identity of the Benue and Chadda were established, careful surveys were made, and there was for the first time a certain amount of successful trading.

Of far greater importance, however, was the fact that not a single member of the crew, which consisted of twelve Europeans and fifty-four Africans, had died, probably on account of the prophylactic use of quinine. It had at last been proved that ships could remain in the river to trade, if not with impunity, at any rate with a reasonable amount of security to life and some chance of commercial success. This was the first tangible result of the discoveries that had been so slowly and so painfully made, and with the successful return of the *Pleiad* the pioneer exploration of Nigeria may be said to have closed. There yet remained many gaps to be filled up in the map of the country, but this was done by degrees by Dr Baikie and others.

Assisted by a subsidy from the Government, Mr Laird dispatched another steamer, the *Dayspring*, to the Niger in 1857, with Dr Baikie in command and Lieutenant J. H. Glover, RN.,[3] as Surveying Officer and second-in-command. The steamer ascended the Niger as far as Jebba, but the engines were not powerful enough for the strong current met there, and she was wrecked on the 'Juju rock'.[4] After the disaster Lieutenant Glover explored the river as far as Bussa, and then

---

[1] Born 1824, died 1864. Dr Baikie's subsequent career in Nigeria is described in Chapter XII.

[2] Vogel stated in a letter that he had crossed the Benue on April 30, 1855, 'exactly on the spot from where the steamer *Pleiad* had returned, numerous empty pickle and brandy bottles giving sure evidence that Englishmen had been there'. See *Notes on Some Languages of the Western Sudan* (1912), by P. A. Benton, p. 282.

[3] Afterwards Sir John Glover, Administrator of Lagos. Born 1829; died 1885. See Chapter XI.

[4] A part of the engines of the *Dayspring* was found by the engineers who were constructing the railway bridge at Jebba (completed 1916), and can now be seen on the platform of the station there.

proceeded overland to Lagos, through the Yoruba country, returning by the same route to his shipwrecked companions with some much-needed food and stores.[1] The party was eventually rescued by another of Laird's vessels, the *Sunbeam*, in 1858.

In 1862 Sir Richard Burton, at that time a Vice-Consul at Fernando Po, visited Benin.[2] Mr Joseph Thomson[3] in 1885 travelled to Sokoto and Gando, and concluded treaties there on behalf of the Royal Niger Company.[4] Captain Lugard,[5] later Governor-General of Nigeria, concluded similar treaties in Borgu in 1894.[6] Sir Claude Macdonald[7] explored the upper Benue in 1889. Captain Claude Alexander died in 1904 while exploring the country between the Benue and Lake Chad,[8] in company with his brother, Lieutenant Boyd Alexander, and Mr P. A. Talbot.[9] In 1910 Boyd Alexander was murdered while travelling through Wadai.[10] In the coastal region much exploratory work was accomplished by Sir Harry Johnston,[11] while serving as a Vice-Consul in the Oil Rivers, and Roger Casement, when in the same service, narrowly

[1] Several slaves escaped from Lagos and attached themselves to Glover's party on the return journey in the hope of reaching their own country: the result was that the party was attacked by the slave-owners and suffered some casualties.

[2] See *My Wanderings in West Africa, a Visit to the Renowned Cities of Wari and Benin* (1863), by a FRGS, and articles in *Fraser's Magazine for Town and Country*, vol. lxvii.

[3] Born 1858; died 1895. A brief account of this journey is given in *Mungo Park and the Niger* (1890), by Joseph Thomson.

[4] See Chapter XII.

[5] Afterwards Sir Frederick, and later Lord, Lugard, PC, GCMG, CB, DSO.

[6] Accounts of Captain Lugard's journeys in Borgu were published in the *Journal of the Royal Geographical Society* in 1895. See also *Lugard. The Years of Adventure, 1858–1898* (1956), by Margery Perham.

[7] Commissioner and Consul-General, Niger Coast Protectorate, 1891–96. Afterwards Ambassador at Pekin and Tokio. Born 1852; died 1915.

[8] See *From the Niger by Lake Chad to the Nile* (1907), by Boyd Alexander.

[9] Later a Resident in the Southern Provinces of Nigeria, and author of several ethnographical and other works on the country.

[10] See *Boyd Alexander's Last Journey* (1912), by H. Alexander.

[11] Born 1858; died 1927. Carried out extensive exploration in East and West Africa, and served for many years in the Consular Service. Was the author of many works on Africa and African languages. See Chapters XII and XIV.

escaped an explorer's death only to meet later with a less honourable end.

The discovery of the Niger and the exploration of Nigeria were accomplished, as we have seen, at a very heavy cost. Death and suffering were too often the fate of the explorer, who had to undergo dangers from a hostile and fanatical population and from diseases for which there was then neither explanation nor remedy. The numerous expeditions that were sent out had as their object the spread of the Christian religion and the interests of science and trade, but above all were designed to further the great aim of successive British Governments throughout the nineteenth century, the abolition of slavery and the attendant horrors of the slave-trade. The result was achieved by the lavish expenditure of British money and British lives.

CHAPTER IX

THE PERIOD OF RESTRICTED SLAVE-TRADE

The woof of farce together bound
By warp of grimmest tragedy.

E. C. ADAMS: Preface to *Lyra Nigeriæ*

We have seen, at the end of Chapter VI, that the slave-trade was made illegal for British subjects in 1808. There had existed for some time previously a small legitimate traffic in the products of the country, particularly palm oil, and this traffic was now taken up seriously by British merchants and grew steadily in importance. As no action was taken by other nations against the slave-trade, the immediate result of the British Government's action was merely the transfer of the profits of the trade to aliens, the Portuguese and Spaniards particularly taking up the evil traffic which British merchants were forbidden to pursue.

A British naval squadron was stationed on the West African coast to intercept the slave-ships,[1] and many captures were made, but, if anything, this interference with the trade involved more suffering to the slaves. They were collected in concealed barracoons ashore, miserably fed, and often short of water, and, when a favourable chance presented itself, hurriedly embarked on small and unsuitable vessels.[2] An English captain named Crow, who had himself commanded slave-ships when the trade was legal, and had on at least two occa-

---

[1] Slaves rescued from slave-ships were landed as a rule at Sierra Leone (and, later, at Fernando Po). The settlement at Sierra Leone had been established in 1788, when some land was bought from the local chief and a number of destitute Africans, who had somehow drifted to England, were settled there. The settlement grew in importance, and was at one time the headquarters of all the British West African Colonies, from the Gambia to Lagos.

[2] Richard Lander saw at Badagri, in 1828, barracoons containing more than 1,000 slaves, and 400 were embarked in a small schooner of 80 tons. *Records of Captain Clapperton's Last Expedition . . .*, p. 326.

sions received the Government bounty of £100 awarded to the masters of ships who landed their human cargoes in good condition and without an undue number of deaths on the voyage, wrote as follows in his memoirs:

One thing is clear: instead of saving any of the poor Africans from slavery, these pretended philanthropists have, through the abolition, been the (I admit *indirect*) cause of the death of thousands: for they have caused the trade to be transferred to other nations who, in defiance of all that our cruisers can do to prevent them, carry it on with a cruelty to the slaves, and a disregard of their comfort and even of their lives, to which Englishmen could never bring themselves to resort.[1]

The more humane tratment of the slaves during the period when the traffic was lawful was probably due, however, rather to competition than to the superior humanity of the English traders. As Crow himself says, 'could any one in his senses suppose that, after paying perhaps £35 for a negro, their owners would not take especial care of them, and give them those comforts which would conduce to their health?'[2] and he admits, while defending the characters of the masters of British slavers, that the crews were of the very dregs of the community, jail-birds and fugitives from justice.[3]

At length, in 1817, treaties were signed with the Spanish and Portuguese Governments which, it was hoped, would drive the slave-ships of those nations from the seas. Spain received a sum of £400,000 from the British Government as the price of her agreeing to permit British cruisers to search and detain Spanish ships with slaves on board; for a similar privilege as regards Portuguese ships north of the Equator Portugal received £300,000, besides the cancellation of a debt of £600,000. These bribes were wasted, as the treaties had little practical effect. Portuguese ships south of the Line could not be touched, while no ship could be detained unless she actually had slaves on board. The slavers, fitted quite obviously to carry no other cargo than human beings, sailed boldly along the coast or anchored in rivers, watching their opportunity to embark their slaves and be off to sea.

[1] *Memoirs of Captain Crow*, p. 133.
[2] *Ibid.*, p. 42.   [3] *Ibid.*, p. 169.

To meet this difficulty the so-called 'Equipment Article Treaty' was entered into with Spain in 1835, by which the mutual right of search of merchant vessels, and detention if the necessary equipment of a slaver were found on board, was agreed to, Courts of Mixed Commission at Sierra Leone adjudicating in each case. The Portuguese would not at first sign a similar treaty, and the Spanish traders, by substituting the Portuguese flag for their own, carried on as before in practical safety. Disregarding the treaty of 1817, by which the right of the Portuguese to trade in slaves south of the Equator was recognized, the British Parliament passed an Act assuming the power to search and seize all Portuguese slave-ships, and the Portuguese Government at last, in 1842, signed an 'Equipment' treaty.

Most of the slavers now began to sail under the American flag on their voyage to the coast, changing to Spanish, Portuguese, or Brazilian colours after the slaves were taken aboard. By so doing they escaped capture outward bound as the American Government did not recognize the 'Equipment' treaties, and when loaded they were liable only to confiscation of their ships if captured under the other colours. So great were the profits of the trade that it was considered a paying concern if one out of every three slavers could escape the vigilance of the preventive squadron and land its human cargo in the New World. British subjects were liable to severe punishment if caught in slave-ships, but foreigners could not be punished otherwise than by the confiscation of their ships and the slaves on board. Moreover, the ship could not even be detained if no slaves were found in her, even though there was unmistakable evidence that they had recently been aboard, and this led to hundreds of slaves being thrown overboard from slavers chased by men-of-war.[1] For example, the following incident is recorded in the *Sunday Times* of April 1, 1832:

The *Black Joke* and *Fair Rosamond* tenders, in the River Bonny, captured, in September, two Spanish armed brigs the *Regulus* and *Rapido*. They each sailed with 400 slaves on board: but being chased, the miscreants in the *Rapido*, not being enabled to land their slaves in the canoes quick enough, threw overboard 125

---

[1] Sickly slaves were also thrown overboard before entering a Brazilian port to escape customs duty.

shackled together, only two of whom were saved. Both vessels were taken to Sierra Leone and condemned.[1]

It is true that on some occasions the captains of British cruisers took the law into their own hands by landing the crews of captured slavers at the nearest convenient point on the coast, leaving them there to the mercy of the climate and the inhabitants. It was stated before a House of Commons Committee that in February 1841 there were over fifty white men landed from captured slave-ships in the neighbourhood of Bonny, and that by the end of May not ten remained alive, the rest having died of starvation and fever.[2]

Even in the preventive squadron the loss of life from disease was very high. Quinine and mosquito nets were unknown, and the common treatment of fever was by bleeding. As late as 1859 H.M.S. *Trident* lost eight officers and thirty-six men from yellow fever in two months, and such a death-roll was by no means uncommon. From 1820 United States warships paid intermittent visits to the West Coast of Africa, and in 1842 the American Government bound itself by treaty with Great Britain to maintain a sufficient and adequate squadron on the coast for the suppression of the slave-trade. This obligation was never properly fulfilled,[3] and the few ships were withdrawn at the beginning of the civil war. However, the British squadron persevered in its work and effected many captures.

[1] It was only possible to secure the condemnation of these vessels on account of the two men who were rescued. Had no one been rescued the vessels would have escaped.

[2] *Report from the Select Committee on the West Coast of Africa*, 1842, Minutes of Evidence, p. 92.

[3] See *The American Slave Trade* (1907), by John R. Spears, p. 151. This book, written by an American, makes it quite clear that it was the attitude of the United States people and Government which prevented the slave-trade being put a stop to earlier than it actually was. 'At Vicksburg, in 1859, a convention of commercial men resolved by a vote of forty to nineteen that "all laws, State or Federal, prohibiting the African slave-trade ought to be repealed"; also that "the convention raise a fund to be dispensed in premiums for the best sermons in favour of reopening the African slave-trade".' *Ibid.*, p. 211. We have seen that the American Government would not recognize the 'equipment' treaties, and so jealous were they of British interference with the slave-ships of a 'free' people that American slavers could safely pass through the cordon of British cruisers with their cargoes of human beings on board.

In 1822 the boats of two British cruisers boarded and captured six French and Spanish slavers in the Bonny river after a desperate fight. Resistance was not uncommon, and in 1845 a prize-crew placed by H.M.S. *Wasp* on a captured slave-ship was massacred by the slavers. From 1829 to 1849 British warships captured 1,077 slavers[1] and set free their cargoes, but in spite of everything the trade still flourished.

It was estimated by Bryan Edwards[2] that an average of 20,000 African slaves was imported annually into the British colonies in America and the West Indies between the years 1680 and 1786, during which period the trade was legal. A memorandum attached to the *Report of the House of Commons Select Committee on the Slave Trade* in 1848 gives the following estimated figures of the annual export of slaves from Africa, to all destinations, between the years 1788 and 1847:

In 1788	.	.	100,000	
From 1798 to 1810	.	.	85,000	yearly average
,, 1810 ,, 1815	.	.	93,000	,,
,, 1815 ,, 1819	.	.	106,000	,,
,, 1819 ,, 1825	.	.	103,000	,,
,, 1825 ,, 1830	.	.	125,000	,,
,, 1830 ,, 1835	.	.	78,500	,,
,, 1835 ,, 1840	.	.	135,800	,,
In 1840	.	.	64,114	
,, 1841	.	.	45,097	
,, 1842	.	.	28,400	
,, 1843	.	.	55,062	
,, 1844	.	.	54,102	
,, 1845	.	.	36,785	
,, 1846	.	.	76,117	
,, 1847	.	.	84,356	

'During the nine months from October 1820 to July 1821, 190 cargoes of slaves were taken out of the River Bonny, and 163 out of the Old Calabar.'[3]

All this time the legitimate trade was growing, and in 1826 it was reported that twelve sail of British merchant vessels and

[1] Wyatt Tilby, *op. cit.*, p. 127.

[2] Bryan Edwards, *op. cit.*, vol. ii, p. 55.

[3] Dispatch from Sir Charles MacCarthy, presented to Parliament in 1822, and quoted by Captain Denham before a House of Lords Committee of 1849–50. See *Commerce with Africa* (1859), by Robert Jamieson, p. 21.

twelve sail of foreign slavers were in the Bonny river at the same time.[1] It was not, however, till 1842 that a British naval officer was able to state that 'the slave-trade at Bonny and at Calabar has been done up these three years; it is not carried on at all',[2] while another witness before the House of Commons Committee declared that the Africans 'scarcely take the trouble of buying slaves in Bonny now, they get so well remunerated by palm oil'.[3] It is estimated that the amount of palm oil imported into Liverpool from the Oil Rivers[4] in 1806 was 150 tons, in 1819 over 3,000 tons, and in 1839 about 13,600 tons.[5] The trade was carried on entirely from ships. Merchants would put on board of a vessel, in the charge of the master or a supercargo, a certain quantity of merchandise, and the ship would move from place to place until the cargo had been disposed of, palm oil, ivory, and other produce being taken in exchange for the manufactured articles brought from England. When a regular trade had been established with any particular locality, the ship would enter the river and anchor, an awning of matting being put up to keep off the sun and rain. The African merchants would then bring their produce to the ship and barter it for their requirements,[6] the ship remaining in the river sometimes for several months. As a result the crews suffered severely from fever, and there was a high death-rate, vessels sometimes being unable to sail owing to the lack of sufficient men to work the ship.[7]

As the value of the trade increased, rival merchants and supercargoes exercised unceasing vigilance in order to outmanœuvre one another, and disputes of all kinds were rife,

[1] *Report from the House of Commons Select Committee on the West Coast of Africa* (1842), p. 24.

[2] *Ibid.*, p. 132.

[3] *Ibid.*, p. 92.

[4] The Oil Rivers were those between the Benin river and the Cameroons.

[5] *Commerce with Africa*, by Robert Jamieson, p. 21. 183,000 tons of palm oil were exported from Nigeria in 1960, in addition to 418,000 tons of palm kernels.

[6] See evidence of Sir Richard Burton before the Select Committee of the House of Commons, 1865, p. 90 of *Report*.

[7] In order to reduce the amount of sickness in his ships, Mr Robert Jamieson kept them at Fernando Po, where they were loaded by tenders which entered the Oil Rivers with reduced crews.

to the detriment and occasionally to the stoppage of trade. The masters of the vessels trading to the coast were as a rule ruffians of the worst kind, guilty of the most brutal treatment to the Africans with whom they dealt and to the crews of their own vessels. A typical ruffian of the period was Captain Lake of the brig *Thomas*, who refused to ransom the Lander brothers after their descent of the Niger in 1830. On the day of his arrival at Fernando Po, Richard Lander noted in his journal:

We were glad to get out of this vessel, for the unfeeling commander . . . employed every means he could think of to annoy us and make us uncomfortable while we were with him. At night, while the people were sleeping, he would make his men draw water and throw it over them for mere amusement. There are many commanders as bad as he is on the coast, who seem to vie with each other in acts of cruelty and oppression. The captain of the palm-oil brig *Elizabeth*, now in the Calabar river, actually whitewashed his crew from head to foot while they were sick with fever and unable to protect themselves; his cook suffered so much in the operation that the lime totally deprived him of the sight of one of his eyes, and rendered the other of little service to him.[1]

Dr Madden, who was sent out to West Africa by the British Government in 1841 to report on the situation, stated that

the manner in which the trade is carried on in the Bonny, and in which the natives and the crews of these ships are occasionally treated by the masters, calls for immediate attention. The commanding naval officer on this station has been frequently obliged to visit the Bonny and take cognizance of cases of violence and injustice on the part of these persons either against the natives or their own people. . . . When I was in the Bight of Benin . . . the master of a vessel was then in the Bonny who had been recently tried in England for the murder of one of his sailors by flogging him so severely that he died, and been sentenced to imprisonment for several months, and yet had no sooner got out than he was re-appointed to the command of one of the largest vessels in the trade. . . . In the year 1838 a number of Kroomen[2] were sold by the orders of one of our merchant vessels . . . one of the Kroomen had been

---

[1] *Journal of an Expedition to Explore the Course and Termination of the Niger*, by R. and J. Lander, p. 286.

[2] Kroomen, Kruboys, or Krooboys inhabit the coast of what is now Liberia. They have worked as deck-hands on European vessels for centuries, and many have been employed on British warships on the African

ordered to keep watch over the store house, which duty it was alleged was neglected; in consequence of which the master induced the chief or king of the town, off which the *Protector* was moored in the Benin, to send the whole of the Kroomen on board a Portuguese slaver.[1]

Dr Madden adds that in his day the people of Bonny had not improved as a result of their long connexion with Europeans, as 'the generality of the traders who frequent that river are not calculated to leave many germs of civilization in any barbarous soil'.

Writing as late as 1854, Dr Baikie says:

As an example of the conduct at times of civilized people, I will here relate what had occurred in the Brass river very shortly before this period. A white trader, then agent for an English house, had, out of a mere freak, ordered a native who came on board his ship one day to be seized and flogged. This lad's father, however, was a man of consequence on shore, and, on hearing of this outrage, he summoned his friends, and in two large canoes attacked and boarded the ship. The white captain armed his Kruboys with muskets, but they, unwilling to quarrel with the natives or to fight in a bad cause, gave way; the captain . . . was put into a canoe, taken ashore, and fastened to a tree, where he was left for twelve hours, and the natives said openly they would have killed him, but that they feared a visit from an English man-of-war. The same individual trained his Krumen to fight with the Krumen of other trading ships in the river, and, in short, endeavoured to carry on his trading by brute force. Such transactions as these were formerly of daily occurrence, but now fortunately they occur but rarely; but what can be expected of native tribes, who see before them, acted by so-called civilized men, deeds which would disgrace a very savage?[2]

How little the British traders were interested in the spread of civilization may be gathered from the fact that in 1840 a young girl was sacrificed at Bonny without a single protest being

station. They are quarrelsome and not very honest, but are generally loyal to their employers. They have never sold slaves or allowed themselves to be enslaved.

[1] *Report of Dr R. R. Madden, Commissioner of Inquiry on the State of the British Settlements . . . and the Foreign Slave-Trading Factories along the Western Coast of Africa in the Year 1841*, p. 34.

[2] *Narrative of an Exploring Voyage up the Rivers Kwora and Binue in 1854* (1856), by W. B. Baikie, p. 326.

registered by the masters or supercargoes of the vessels then in the river, although they knew well the fate to which she was doomed;[1] yet two years before they had appealed to the captain of a ship-of-war on account of the illegal exactions made by King Pepple of Bonny, who was forced to sign a treaty binding himself to abstain from such acts in the future.

In these circumstances it is not remarkable that the chiefs and people remained in a state of savagery to so late a period, in spite of the considerable wealth they acquired as middlemen in the palm-oil trade. Dr Madden stated that

the people of Bonny do not suffer the inland natives to bring down oil to the coast. They keep a great number of armed boats, many of them with a carronade or brass swivel mounted on the bow. These boats they send up the river for the oil as far as Eboe, and purchase it from the country people. The price they pay for it is extremely small; in fact, so trifling as hardly to remunerate the sellers for the trouble and expense of gathering the nuts and extracting the oil from them. . . . The people of Bonny, who have managed to get this trade into their hands, are one of the most barbarous, dishonest, and treacherous races in this part of Africa. Our extensive commercial relations with them for nearly thirty years have not produced any change in their savage customs and superstitions.[2]

No attempt had yet been made to interfere with the native administration in any part of Nigeria. Slave-ships were attacked in the rivers and occasionally some gross outrage by the Africans on a British merchant-ship was punished by a naval force but the chiefs were invariably treated as ruling potentates,[3]

---

[1] Report of Dr R. R. Madden, Commissioner of Inquiry on the State of the British Settlements . . . and the Foreign Slave-Trading Factories along the Western Coast of Africa in the Year 1841, p. 32. Captain Crow, who was at Bonny in 1804, endeavoured without success to save a girl who was being sacrificed. He tells us that 'it was the custom there, once in seven years, to sacrifice a virgin, of fifteen or sixteen years of age, as a propitiatory offering . . . she is thrown into the sea by the priests, and is instantly devoured by the sharks'. Memoirs, p. 83. It is said that until quite recently a man was killed every year in Lagos and thrown into the lagoon as a sacrifice to the local deity.

[2] Report of Dr R. R. Madden, Commissioner of Inquiry on the State of the British Settlements . . . and the Foreign Slave-Trading Factories along the Western Coast of Africa in the Year 1841, p. 32.

[3] As lately as 1879 the chief of Itebu was saluted by the yacht of the Governor of Lagos with seven guns.

and governed or misgoverned their people without let or hindrance. It is said that 'Delta society in the nineteenth century rested on a foundation of slavery; terror and despotism were normal features of a system that had to keep the masses in subjection'.[1]

King Pepple, as we have seen, signed a treaty binding himself to abstain from acts of aggression, and he also undertook to put a stop to the slave-trade in his dominions and gave other indications of his friendship for the British, or at any rate his respect for their power. Yet this monarch did not scruple to celebrate the anniversary of his father's death with a cannibal feast, justifying himself to a British supercargo by saying that 'it was the custom of his country; that his father did it, and his forefathers also'.[2]

Mr. Macgregor Laird, who visited the country in 1832, stated to a House of Commons Committee:

I have seen the chiefs of Old Calabar and Cameroon, men who annually do business with English ships to the extent of a quarter of a million, strutting about with nothing on but the 'clout', now changed from the 'bark of trees' to a bandana handkerchief, and their heads covered with a gold or a silver-laced footman's hat, which the palm-oil captains had persuaded them was the distinguishing mark of a nobleman in Great Britain.[3]

In spite of the savagery of the inhabitants and the ill-conduct of the majority of the British traders, in spite of the evil effects of the climate and the machinations of the Spanish and Portuguese slave-dealers, who were bitterly hostile to the nation that was ruining their inhuman business, legitimate trade continued

[1] Dike, op. cit., p. 36.

[2] Report from the Select Committee on the West Coast of Africa (1842), p. 100. Captain Crow reports the eating of a Kwa chief taken in battle by another king of the Pepple family in 1804. Memoirs, p. 84.

[3] Ibid., p. 577. Even as late as 1880 some of the chiefs had rather primitive ideas regarding dress, and of one of them the Consul reported in a dispatch to the Foreign Office: ' . . . only recently he had to be reproved for coming to the Consulate on business with simply a hat on and otherwise in a state of nudity. Ever since he has renounced this paradisiac condition of unclothedness when he attends at the Consular Court, the costume he at present assumes at these official meetings is disturbing to one's gravity of countenance. The last time I saw him, when he came to bid me adieu, he wore pink tights, a cabman's many-caped coat, a red chimney-pot hat, and blue spectacles.'

to prosper and grow. At Calabar, for example, the Africans did a large trade in palm oil, and Captain Adams, writing in 1822, reported that 'many of the natives write English, an art first acquired by some of the traders' sons, who had visited England, and which they have had the sagacity to retain up to the present period. They have established schools and schoolmasters for the purpose of instructing in this art the youths belonging to families of consequence.'[1] No European merchants ventured to establish themselves ashore, but as the chiefs in the rivers became more powerful through increased wealth, and able at a price to protect them, some of the more adventurous spirits took up their residence in hulks anchored in the rivers or moored to the banks. These hulks were at once the homes and the warehouses of the merchants; many were armed, and for a very long period represented the only permanent trading establishments. Long after the hulks had been abandoned the people of the Oil Rivers spoke of the head agent of a firm as the 'captain', of the floor of a house as the 'deck', and of the kitchen as the 'galley'. After a while some of the land on the banks of the rivers was acquired by the merchants on which to store their produce or to cooper their casks, but it was not until comparatively recent times, the late 'seventies or early 'eighties of the nineteenth century, that stores and dwelling-houses were built ashore, land being granted to the merchants by the chiefs free of rent, but subject to the payment of 'comey' on goods exported.

The position of the merchants trading in the rivers in these early days was a peculiar and dangerous one. They were completely at the mercy of the African chiefs, and had no means of enforcing the payment of debts due to them. There was no law and no authority other than that exercised by the captains of Her Majesty's ships on the station. The British had acquired a certain prestige by reason of their campaign against the slave-trade and the presence of the naval squadron, which was at this time based on Fernando Po. This island had been discovered[2] by the Portuguese before the end of the fifteenth century, but no permanent settlement was made on it, and in

---

[1] Quoted in *Nigerian Perspectives* (1960), by T. Hodgkin, p. 181.
[2] At first called Formosa; it was later given its present name in honour of its discoverer, Fernando Povo.

1778 it was ceded to Spain. An attempt by the Spaniards to develop it ended disastrously, and it was abandoned till 1827 when, with permission from Spain, Great Britain took over the administration of the island and used it as a landing-place for rescued slaves and as a base for the ships engaged in that locality in the suppression of the slave-trade, the British 'superintendent' being granted a Spanish commission as Governor. In 1834 the naval establishment at Fernando Po was discontinued, but Mr Beecroft, who had previously served as superintendent, remained on the island, governing the freed slaves and other Africans who had drifted there, without authority but with their full consent. In 1843 Beecroft was appointed Governor of Fernando Po by the Queen of Spain, no Spanish Governor being sent out till 1858.

In spite of the frequent visits of naval ships to the rivers, the lack of adequate and continuous supervision over the trade became more and more unsatisfactory, and representations were made to the British Government 'from time to time by persons engaged in legal trade in the Bights of Benin and Biafra, stating that it would be desirable that a person should be appointed to reside in that part of Africa as agent on the part of Her Majesty's Government, for the purpose of regulating the legal trade between British merchants and the ports of Benin, Brass, New and Old Calabar, Bonny, Bimbia, the Cameroon, and the ports in the territories of the King of Dahomey'.[1] The Government at last decided to make such an appointment, and Mr Beecroft was selected as the first Consul for the Bights of Biafra and Benin,[2] with his headquarters at Fernando Po. In his letter of appointment he was informed that he had been chosen 'in consideration of your general knowledge of African affairs and of the habits of the Blacks, and because of the influence which you appear to have acquired over the native chiefs of the places to which your Consular jurisdiction will extend'.[3] Mr Beecroft took up his duties in the latter part of 1849, and from this date direct British influence in Nigeria may be said to have begun.

[1] Dispatch from Viscount Palmerston to Mr Beecroft, dated June 30, 1849.
[2] The limits were Cape St Paul on the west and Cape St John on the east.
[3] Dispatch from Viscount Palmerston to Mr Beecroft, dated June 30, 1849.

CHAPTER X

THE CONQUEST OF LAGOS

Such as were those, dogs of an elder day,
Who sacked the golden ports,
And those later who dared grapple their prey
Beneath the harbour forts.

H. NEWBOLT: *Minora Sidera*

Within a few months of his appointment as Consul for the Bights of Benin and Biafra, Mr Beecroft was employed on an important mission to the King of Dahomey,[1] in the hope of persuading that monarch to put a stop to the slave-trade. This powerful and bloodthirsty tyrant had made his country wealthy through the immense profits of the traffic, and the people had practically abandoned agriculture and industry. With a large and well-disciplined army, which included 18,000 Amazons, those terrible women-fighters who gave such trouble to the French in later years, the King of Dahomey overran the neighbouring countries and carried off thousands of captives for sale as slaves and for human sacrifice. He was offered by the British Government a subsidy for three years, equivalent to his annual profit from the sale of slaves, if he would give up his evil ways and encourage agriculture and legitimate trade; in reply he professed the greatest friendship and respect for the British, but regretted that he could not give up a traffic on which he entirely depended.

It was the opinion of Mr Beecroft that the king was disposed to listen to the remonstrances of the British Government, but was unable to go against the wishes of his military advisers. It was, however, probably the increase of the trade in Lagos that influenced his decision. The vigilance of the British cruisers on the coast was reducing the profits of the slave-trade, and the close watch kept on his port of Whydah would no doubt in time have compelled him to accept the subsidy offered in lieu of a traffic that no longer paid. How-

[1] Dahomey, which became a French colony, is now a republic; it bounds Nigeria on the west.

ever, just as things were beginning to look dark for the slave-trade the energy of Kosoko, King of Lagos, gave it a last fillip. But it was Lagos and not Dahomey that benefited. The effect of this on the mind of the King of Dahomey is explained in a letter from Mr Thomas Hutton, a merchant who visited Whydah in 1850:

... The King of Dahomey sent to me several times when I was at Whydah, to go up to him (at his capital, Abomey), as he had something to say to me. With much difficulty I got myself excused; ... and he then sent me a private and friendly message, and one of his confidential friends told me what I have stated above, that unless the Slave Trade is first put a stop to at Lagos, it will be useless for the British Government to send to him treaties for his agreement, as he considers it would be derogatory to his dignity, and would lower him in the eyes of his subjects and the nations around, who would not be able to understand the reason that an interior King should be the first that is made to stop the Slave-Trade, while the sea-side King of Lagos, so near to come at, is not even spoken to on the subject and carries on the trade as if he was sanctioned in it.[1]

Mr Hutton concluded his letter by pointing out that the occupation of Lagos would be a severe blow to the slave-trade.

When in 1851 the Reverend (afterwards Bishop) Samuel Crowther was received in audience by Queen Victoria, he told Her Majesty that 'the slave trade on that part of the African coast would be at an end if Lagos, the stronghold of its greatest supporter, was destroyed'.[2]

Mr Beecroft also, in an official letter to Viscount Palmerston, dated July 22, 1850, says of the King of Dahomey: 'I am perfectly satisfied that he is under the control and opinion of several of his principal officers', and in the same letter:

Lagos is another point. If the legitimate chief[3] could be seen and communicated with, so as to make a treaty with him for the suppression of the foreign Slave-Trade, and place him at Lagos, his former seat of Government, it would release the people of Abbeokuta from the jeopardy that they are continually in, from the fear of the King

---

[1] *Papers Relative to the Reduction of Lagos by Her Majesty's Forces on the West Coast of Africa* (1852) p. 40.

[2] *The Letters of Queen Victoria, 1837–1861* (1907), edited by A. C. Benson and Viscount Esher, vol. ii, p. 443.

[3] Akitoye, see Chapter III.

of Dahomey. Her Majesty's steamer *Gladiator* has captured two empty slavers. Her Majesty's steamer *Hecla* two with slaves, lately from Lagos. I believe they have been trying it hard there latterly.[1]

King Kosoko of Lagos was doing more than merely dealing in slaves. He was trying by every means in his power to annoy and damage the British and their friends. While in exile at Whydah he had seen and envied the huge profits that were being made there in the trade and, on his return to power in Lagos, he joined with the slave-dealers to make his town the most notorious slave-depot in West Africa. He realized that British influence was being used to put a stop to the traffic, and he spared no pains to destroy this influence among his neighbours. British merchants and a number of liberated slaves were residing at Badagri, and Kosoko endeavoured to secure the friendship of the Badagri chiefs and have the British driven out. Badagri, however, was not sympathetic, and it was, moreover, largely under the influence of Abeokuta, where European missionaries were established and the chiefs were particularly well disposed to the British. Kosoko was, however, successful in forming an alliance with the chief of Porto Novo and the King of Dahomey. He gave, if not material, at any rate moral support to Dahomey in its war with Abeokuta, and it is said that when he heard that Abeokuta had actually been attacked he had salutes fired in honour of the victory which he considered certain. As a matter of fact, the army of the King of Dahomey was driven back, losing thousands in the unsuccessful assault on the town and during the retreat, largely as a result of the warning which Mr Beecroft had been able to give of the impending attack when he visited Abeokuta in February 1851. The Dahomey army arrived in front of the town in March, and the walls were stormed by the Amazons, who actually effected an entrance at several points; the shame of being defeated by women, however, spurred the Egba warriors to a desperate resistance and final victory.[2]

In June of the same year Kosoko's intrigues began to affect the situation at Badagri. To this place the ex-King of Lagos, Akitoye, had been sent by the Abeokuta chiefs soon after he had fled to them for refuge in 1845, and there his adherents

[1] *Papers Relative to the Reduction of Lagos by Her Majesty's Forces on the West Coast of Africa* (1852), p. 43. [2] *Ibid.*

had rallied to him. Not strong enough to attack Lagos, his position at Badagri enabled him to stop any communication by the
creeks between Kosoko and his allies at Porto Novo. Akitoye's
position, however, was very precarious. Enemies were on
either side of him, some of the inhabitants of Badagri were
hostile, and Kosoko had offered a premium for his head. He
pointed out the danger of his position to Mr Beecroft when
the Consul was passing through Badagri on his way to Abeokuta at the beginning of the year. On Mr Beecroft's return
from Abeokuta he received the following letter[1] from Akitoye:

I, KING AKITOYE, of Lagos, salute you and your great Queen and
Government, and I wish you all happiness, peace and prosperity,
May God bless your great Queen, and grant her a long and happy
reign.

I rejoice very much to see the day which has brought you, the
Representative of England, to this town, particularly at this time
when I am surrounded by dangers. Indeed, I very much need your
protection, as my life is every moment at stake.

I humbly beg to bring my case before you, and trust you will
condescend to listen patiently to what I have to say.

In order that you may better understand the whole affair, allow
me at the commencement to inform you that the King of Benin has
the undisputed right to crown or confirm the individual whom the
people of Lagos elect to be their King.

After the death of the late King, which happened about nine years
ago, I was unanimously chosen by the people of Lagos to be their
King, and was lawfully crowned or confirmed by the King of Benin.

As a King who delights in peace, and wishes for nothing so much
as the welfare and prosperity of his people, I endeavoured to promote peace among all classes of people. To this end I recalled home
many exiles who had been sent away from the kingdom in the preceding reign. I chartered a vessel to go to Whydah, and to bring
back my nephew, Kosoko, although it was at a great expense. I
admonished him to put away all former hostilities, and begged that
we should all live together in peace. After three years' peaceful
reign, I thought of inviting the English to Lagos; but knowing that
they are much against the Slave-Trade, and that no friendly intercourse can exist between us without giving it up, I, after much
consideration, determined to abolish it from my dominions, if the
English will agree to carry on lawful trade with me.

[1] *Papers Relative to the Reduction of Lagos by Her Majesty's Forces on the West
Coast of Africa* (1852), p. 97.

Accordingly I wrote two letters, one to the ships of war and the other to the Governor of Cape Coast, but which letters I sent to Badagry to be forwarded; but, I am sorry to say, were delayed for a long time. This was at the year 1845.

While I was thinking of nothing but how to regulate the affairs of my kingdom in peace and quietness, Kosoko, my nephew, whom I have mentioned above, without any regard to the obligations he was under, breaking through all ties of gratitude and common humanity, made preparations for entering into animosities with me.

He, in the preceding reign, had been found guilty of an attempt of usurpation, in consequence of which he was banished. A few days after I wrote the letters to the English Government, he (Kosoko) collected a large number of his wicked boys together and waged war upon me. This war lasted twenty-one days, during which time more than thousand of lives were lost, and which terminated in my being expelled from Lagos—bribery and treachery leaving me no alternative.

Kosoko, having thus set himself upon a blood-stained throne, has maintained his position by his daring wickedness, though the King of Benin never acknowledged nor confirmed him, and though thousands of people are against him.

Bching thus turned away, I took refuge among my own friends and relatives at Abbeokuta, who kindly took me up and protected me against Kosoko's inhuman attempt to seek my life. But thinking that I should have better chance to communicate with the English, and that I might be nearer Lagos to watch the movements of Kosoko and the affairs of my kingdom, I took my residence at Badagry.

I need not tell you, Sir, what a calamity it is for a King to be reduced to my distressful circumstances. I find myself obliged to solicit your assistance, and I am reduced to the necessity of begging your aid against an enemy who has seized my throne and kingdom.

My humble prayer to you, Sir, the Representative of the English Government, who, it is well known, is ever ready and desirous to protect the defenceless, to obtain redress for the grievance of the injured, and to check the triumphs of wickedness, is, that you would take Lagos under your protection, that you would plant the English flag there, and that you would re-establish me on my rightful throne at Lagos, and protect me under my flag: and with your help I promise to enter into a Treaty with England to abolish the Slave Trade at Lagos, and to establish and carry on lawful trade, especially with the English merchants.

Trusting my petition will meet with a favourable reception, I remain, &c.

(Signed) AKITOYE.

So real was the danger in Badagri that the Consul advised
Akitoye to embark with him and proceed to Fernando Po, and
after some natural reluctance to go to an unknown country,
Akitoye agreed and departed with Mr Beecroft. Some months
later fighting broke out at Badagri between Akitoye's followers
and the people of Porto Novo. The former were victorious, and
a little later succeeded in beating off an expedition sent by
Kosoko to the assistance of his friends. In the fighting, however,
much damage was done to the town, and an English merchant was killed, further hostilities being prevented only by
the arrival of a thousand men from Abeokuta, who had been
sent to assist in the defence of the place. The commander of
this force addressed the following letter[1] to Captain Jones, the
senior naval officer then in the neighbourhood:

OBBA SHORON, second to the King, and Commander-in-chief of
the Forces of all Abbeokuta, salute you and hope you are in peace.

I beg to send you the following words, and hope they will meet
with a kind consideration.

I doubt not you have heard of the affairs of Lagos, the expulsion
of Akitoye, the lawful King, and the usurpation of the throne of
Lagos by his nephew, Kosoko. I therefore omit repeating anything
more about it here, but merely to represent to you the condition
we are in and the assistance we need. I assure you, Sir, our situation is such, that should you delay us speedy relief, or delay the
execution of the affair any longer, it would be very dangerous for us.
Delay, indeed, is wholesome in some cases; but in circumstances
like this in which we are placed, delay would be defeat—it would
be loss to us.

I have stated the difference between Akitoye and Kosoko to Her
Majesty's Consul, John Beecroft, Esq., upon his last visit to Abbeokuta, and have begged him to take Akitoye under British protection, as Kosoko does not desist from seeking to kill him.

As a sure means of safety, that excellent personage advised Akitoye to go on board with him; Akitoye listened to the advice, and
gratefully accepted the offer.

Kosoko, that you may know, has influence enough (through
bribes) to gain over the different tribes of Africans to his interests.

Thus, a short time ago, he encouraged and aided the Dahomians
to make war upon Abbeokuta, concerning which the Consul fore-
warned us.

[1] *Papers relative to the Reduction of Lagos by Her Majesty's Forces on the West
Coast of Africa* (1852), p. 130.

They indeed came; a desperate battle was fought, and many lives lost; but, by the help of God, we have been enabled to repulse them; and but twenty days since, Kosoko's party here at Badagry has raised war against the people of Akitoye; many were also killed, but thank God, Akitoye's party gained the day. At present Badagry is the only medium of communication between the English and Abbeokuta, as Lagos is still under the administration of Kosoko, who is an enemy both to Abbeokuta and the English.

Ammunition and other useful articles are purchased by us at Badagry. Kosoko is too penetrating as not to perceive such advantages; he therefore is labouring to cut off all intercourse between the English and Abbeokuta.

He is endeavouring to raise a very large army, composed of the different tribes of Dahomians—Isos, Jebos, Porto Novians, Ottas, and the people of Ado and Pokra, against Badagry and Abbeokuta.

Being apprised of this, I left Abbeokuta for Badagry, with a view to secure our interests here—our only seaport town; and also with a view to communicate these matters to you, and ask your assistance; for we fear, should Kosoko succeed in causing all these people to rise against us, we cannot encounter them without destruction.

I humbly and earnestly beseech you, therefore, to interfere in our behalf, to save our lives from the impending storm, and to prevent our being cut off as a nation, which you can easily do by overthrowing Kosoko and his slave-town Lagos, and reinstating Akitoye on his lawful throne there, and that before Kosoko should be able to carry his designs into execution, i.e. within the next two or three months.

If Lagos is destroyed and Akitoye restored, we should have little to fear, as it is the mainspring by which all other parts are put in motion.

I would also humbly request that the Queen should take possession of this town, and that she should place some person of authority here, which would greatly contribute to our safety and the welfare of this country at large.

I would again pray you, in conclusion, to take the welfare of this whole country and thousands of people into your consideration. If you please to send me word what we may expect, I shall be much obliged to you. Wishing you well,

I have, &c.

(Signed) OBBA SHORON.

P.S.—I have mentioned all the above words to Captain Heath, who promised to tell you all about it, and I thought I had better put my words on paper also, and send it to you that you may read them.

The time had come when Kosoko would have to be attacked. Letters addressed to him with warnings against molesting British subjects at Badagri were returned unopened, with a verbal message to the effect that he desired no communication with the British. Mr Beecroft had received instructions from the Foreign Secretary to conclude a treaty with Kosoko for the abolition of the slave-trade and, should such a treaty be refused, to remind him 'that Lagos is near to the sea, and that on the sea are the ships and the cannon of England; and also to bear in mind that he does not hold his authority without a competitor, and that the chiefs of the African tribes do not always retain their authority to the end of their lives'. In pursuance of these orders the Consul left Fernando Po in H.M.S. *Bloodhound* in November 1851 accompanied by Akitoye and a few of his followers. Off Lagos he met Commander Wilmot, of H.M.S. *Harlequin*, who reported that he had found a safe channel for boats into the lagoon, and that he had had a personal interview with Kosoko, who seemed disposed to be friendly. On November 20th ten boats left the squadron which had assembled off Lagos and, flying the white flag, approached the entrance of the lagoon, the crews landing on a sandy spit at the eastern side. While there, a messenger arrived from Kosoko and stated that if the ten boats advanced towards the town they would be fired on, but that one boat would be peaceably received. A party of about a hundred armed men watched the movements of the British party, and two Brazilian merchants came forward and urged the Consul not to proceed any farther, except under the conditions laid down by Kosoko. After some discussion, Mr Beecroft consented to go with two boats, and permission for this being granted by Kosoko, the Consul and three naval officers proceeded to the town in two gigs. After a delay of two hours they were ushered into the presence of Kosoko, who was surrounded by armed men, and a fruitless conference ensued, Kosoko endeavouring to evade the issue by stating that he was not his own master and could take no action without the approval of the King of Benin, who was his suzerain. Finally, however, on being pressed, he definitely refused to sign any form of treaty, with a plain intimation that the friendship of England was not wanted. The party accordingly re-embarked and returned to the ships.

The Consul now called upon Commander Forbes, the senior officer of the Bights Squadron, for a proper escort under which he could again approach Lagos, and perhaps, by a show of force, persuade Kosoko to sign the treaty. Accordingly, on November 25th H.M.S. *Bloodhound* entered the lagoon with twenty-one armed and manned boats in tow, the force consisting of 306 officers and men. The ship flew a flag of truce, and a similar flag was carried on a gig, containing a naval officer and the Consul, which advanced 200 yards ahead of the *Bloodhound*. Ignoring a harassing fire of musketry from the shore the force advanced to within a mile of the town, when the *Bloodhound* went aground, and shortly afterwards fire was opened on the ship with cannon of various calibres. After twenty minutes of this the flags of truce were hauled down and the fire was returned, but the force available was insufficient to reduce the town, and a landing-party succeeded only in setting fire to a few houses. As nothing more could be accomplished without great sacrifice of life, the flotilla retired, the casualties having amounted to two officers killed and two officers and fourteen men wounded.

Both Mr Beecroft and Commander Forbes were reprimanded for having attacked Lagos without first communicating with Commodore Bruce, the Commander-in-Chief of the naval forces on the Coast, but steps were immediately taken to send a sufficiently strong expedition against Kosoko. On the night of November 30th a naval party landed, in bright moonlight, on the eastern side of the entrance to the lagoon, and burnt a village and large barracoons belonging to the Portuguese slave-dealers, capable of accommodating over 5,000 slaves. The party met with but slight resistance and suffered no casualties. On December 18th Mr Beecroft met Commodore Bruce off Lagos, and arrangements were made to attack and depose Kosoko and place Akitoye on the throne. The Consul accordingly proceeded to Badagri, where he had left Akitoye after the abortive attack on Lagos, and re-embarked him; his followers were instructed to march along the beach to Lagos.

On December 23rd the boats crossed the bar and met Akitoye's men at the agreed rendezvous, a white necktie being given to each man as a distinguishing mark. It was arranged that these auxiliaries should advance along the west bank of

the lagoon parallel with the naval boats, and be ready for transportation to Lagos island when required. The complete force
consisted of H.M.S. *Bloodhound*, H.M.S. *Teazer*, the Consul's
iron galley fitted as a rocket boat, and the armed boats of the

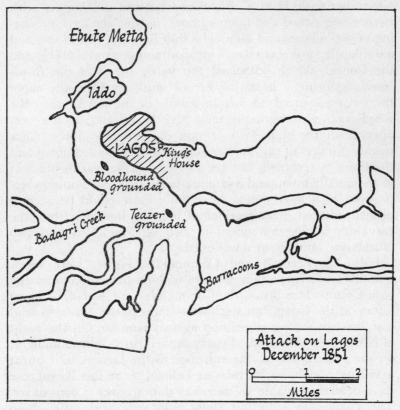

Ebute Metta

Iddo

LAGOS
King's House

Bloodhound
grounded

Badagri Creek

Teazer
grounded

Barracoons

Attack on Lagos
December 1851

0   1   2

Miles

squadron, with about 400 officers and men under the command of Captain L. T. Jones. The larger ships were unable to
cross the bar.

On Christmas Day an ineffective fire was opened from the
town, and the following day an advance was made, the *Bloodhound* leading, with the boats of H.M.S. *Sampson*, followed
by the *Teazer* with the galley, and the boats of H.M.S. *Penelope*. The defence of Lagos consisted of an embankment and
ditch from the southern point of the island to the northern
point, along the whole length of what is now the Marina, a

distance of about two miles. This afforded excellent cover for Kosoko's musketeers, and at chosen points stockades of stout coconut trees were provided for cannon, which were so laid as to cover all the most difficult parts of the channel. At places where the water was deep enough for boats to approach the shore double rows of stakes were placed in the water.

No sooner did the flotilla begin to move than a heavy fire of guns and musketry was opened from the town. The return fire was not very effective against the carefully prepared fortifications, but the *Bloodhound* and the boats with her continued to advance until the *Bloodhound* grounded close to the north-west point of the island. A heavy fire was then opened on the stockade and the town, and an attempt was made to land and spike some guns which were being brought to bear on the ship. The heavy fire of musketry and the stakes in the water prevented the landing-party from carrying out this plan, in spite of the gallantry of the carpenter of the *Sampson* who, neck deep in water, hewed away at the stakes with an axe to make a passage for the boats. Firing was carried on intermittently for the rest of the day, but nothing more could be accomplished until the *Teazer* and the remainder of the boats joined. The *Teazer* had grounded early in the morning, close under the guns of the enemy at the southern point of the island, and it was found impossible to move her for the rest of the day. At first the *Teazer's* 32-pounder bore on the enemy battery and kept it in check, but two guns were brought to a stockade which could not be fired at by the *Teazer* as she lay aground, and a heavy and well-directed fire was opened on the ship. It was obvious that unless those guns were silenced they would destroy the *Teazer* before she could be floated, and in spite of the odds Captain Lyster, who was in command, decided to land and spike them. Eight boats, therefore, pulled for the stockade, and the landing-party forced their way in and spiked the guns, but in retreating to their boats they were attacked by large numbers and lost heavily. One lifeboat was actually captured by the enemy, and her crew had to embark in the others, crowding them to such an extent that they were difficult to handle. The anchor of the rocket-boat had been let go by an excited Kruboy without orders, and it was impossible to move her until Lieutenant Corbett, who had already been severely wounded on shore, cut away the chain cable with a chisel, being wounded five times in doing so. The *Teazer* was saved, but the cost was heavy, one officer and thirteen men being killed and four officers and over sixty men wounded.

Next morning, December 27th, the *Teazer* and her flotilla of boats joined the *Bloodhound* and firing was recommenced, a rocket exploding a magazine and starting a fire which destroyed most of the town.[1] More boats now arrived from the squadron in the roadstead, but it was obvious that no further resistance would be offered by the enemy. A summons was sent to Kosoko to surrender, but no reply was received, and although fugitives could be seen crossing to the mainland in canoes, no further hostile action was taken by the British. On the afternoon of December 28th it was ascertained that Kosoko and his supporters had abandoned the island, and Akitoye was invited to land and take possession. Over fifty cannon were found in the different stockades and the defences as a whole were excellently planned, bearing unmistakable evidence of their foreign design. The total British casualties amounted to two officers and thirteen men killed and five officers and seventy men wounded. A thousand warriors sent by the King of Dahomey to assist Kosoko did not arrive in time, and returned quietly when they found that they were too late. A small detachment of Egbas arrived to assist the British, but they also were too late.

[1] The burning of a native-built town in Nigeria is not as serious a disaster as it sounds. The houses are generally built of mud, and the thatched roofs, the only inflammable parts, can easily be repaired.

CHAPTER XI

THE COLONY OF LAGOS

So give them a passing thought sometimes,
Those men of the earlier day;
The men who have founded the track we tread,
The men who have 'paved the way'.

E. C. ADAMS: *Juggernaut*

On January 1, 1852, King Akitoye of Lagos went off to H.M.S. *Penelope* and signed a treaty with Commodore Bruce and Mr Beecroft for the abolition of the traffic in slaves, the encouragement of legitimate trade, and the protection of missionaries.[1] A Vice-Consul was appointed to Lagos to watch over British interests and to see that the terms of the treaty were duly carried out and, with the appointment of a special Consul for Lagos and the Bight of Benin in 1853, the separation of Lagos from the Oil Rivers began and lasted until 1906. The Portuguese slave-dealers were expelled from the town, but in a few months they were back again, and an attempt was made quietly to reopen the traffic in slaves. Akitoye was true to his word and the miscreants were at once arrested, but there was still a very large party in favour of renewing the trade, and they were liberally supplied with arms and ammunition by the Portuguese dealers. Hostilities broke out in August 1853 in spite of the efforts made by the Consul, Mr Campbell, and a force of marines was landed to protect the consulate and the missions. Further efforts were made by the Consul and the naval officers to reconcile the rebels to the king, but on August 13th Kosoko landed on Lagos island and put himself at the head of the revolt. A larger force was now landed from the naval ships at anchor off the town and Kosoko's party was attacked and driven out.

Three weeks later Akitoye died suddenly,[2] and it is thought

[1] See Appendix C. Akitoye continued to receive the revenues, which were mainly derived from import and, later, export duties. The customs duties were 'farmed' to British and foreign merchants.

[2] Contrary to custom, his son Dosumu did not sacrifice slaves at his father's funeral.

that he was poisoned. His son Dosumu[1] was at once installed as king, but for the first few months of his reign there were constant alarms, as the war canoes of Kosoko were frequently in the neighbourhood of Lagos. In January 1854 the Consul presided at a 'palaver' between the two parties, and an agreement was come to by which Kosoko was recognized as King of Palma and Lekki as a condition of his relinquishing all claim to the throne of Lagos.

The slave party, however, was not entirely crushed, and it was found that Dosumu had not the power necessary to keep them under control or to ensure good government. Writing to the Secretary of State for Foreign Affairs on April 9, 1860, Consul Brand says:

. . . There is a measure which, if adopted, would tend to put an end to the Slave-Trade, and increase the legal commerce and industrial prosperity of this line of coast to an unlimited extent, the occupation of Lagos, either as a possession or by way of Protectorate. . . . Lagos, at present, may be said to have no Government; there is no effective protection to property, no mode of enforcing the payment of debts applicable to Europeans; and the wonder is that in such a state of things there are so few disturbances. The presence of the *Brune*, inefficiently manned as she is by twenty-five Kroomen, if not a source of security, is at least the symbol of protection; . . . this Consulate exercises at present a feeble, irregular, and irresponsible jurisdiction over a variety of judicial, police, and even administrative matters, which have gradually been pressed within the range of its action, which occupy nearly the whole of the Consular Officer's time, but which have no relation whatever to a Consul's ordinary duties. This jurisdiction has been acquiesced in by the various sections as matter of necessity, knowing that the Consulate is the only place where their cases will be heard with impartiality; but, in a large and increasing commercial community, there

---

[1] Also spelt 'Docemo'. Sir John Glover, when administering the Government of Lagos in 1863, after Dosumu had been deposed, wrote of him to the Duke of Newcastle as follows: ' . . . The ex-king is both rogue and fool, but would not be badly disposed, were it not for the evil councillors who are about him. I would venture with all respect to suggest to Your Grace that Her Majesty's Government impress upon him the fact that he was not King of Lagos by his own right or might, and that the same power which placed his father as King of Lagos, and who at his father's death took him out of a fishing-canoe and made him King against the wishes of his Chiefs, had the full right to unking him, when he failed in keeping his treaty.'

are questions of great importance affecting trade and property frequently arising, which the Consul has not the means, even if he had the authority, of dealing with in a satisfactory manner . . . I believe such a measure would be hailed with delight by the people here; and, by ensuring protection to property, and a regular administration of justice, it would give a great impulse to the prosperity of Lagos and the surrounding country.[1]

In June 1861 the Foreign Secretary instructed the Consul to arrange for the occupation of Lagos in a dispatch containing the following:

It is not without some reluctance that Her Majesty's Government have determined, by the occupation of Lagos, to extend the number of British Dependencies on the African coast; but they have been induced to come to this determination because they are convinced that the permanent occupation of this important point in the Bight of Benin is indispensable to the complete suppression of the Slave-Trade in the Bight, whilst it will give great aid and support to the development of lawful commerce, and will check the aggressive spirit of the King of Dahomey, whose barbarous wars, and encouragement to slave-trading, are the chief cause of disorder in that part of Africa. Her Majesty's Government would be most unwilling that the establishment of British sovereignty at Lagos should be attended with any injustice to Dosumu, the present Chief of the island; but they conceive that as his tenure of the island in point of fact depends entirely upon the continuance of the protection which has been afforded to him by the British naval authorities since the expulsion of Kosoko, no injustice will be inflicted upon him by changing this anomalous protectorate into an avowed occupation, provided his material interests are secured. It will be right, therefore, to assign him an adequate pension, to be paid out of the revenue of the island.[2]

On July 30, 1861, Mr McCoskry, the acting Consul,[3] and Commander Bedingfield, the senior naval officer of the Bights Division, summoned Dosumu to a secret conference on

[1] *Papers Relating to the Occupation of Lagos* (1862), p. 4.
[2] *Ibid.*, p. 5.
[3] Mr McCoskry was a merchant who lived for many years in Lagos, and, later, at Lokoja. He acted as Consul after the death of Mr Foote in 1861. In 1861 he offered to 'farm' the customs revenue of Lagos for 2,000 bags of cowries a year.

E

board H.M.S. *Prometheus*, which had been brought into the lagoon. The intentions of the British Government were explained to him, and he promised to lay the matter before his chiefs. On August 1st Commander Bedingfield and the Consul went to the king's house to receive his answer, but found that the party opposed to the cession had influenced him to refuse; this he did on the ground that as the treaty of cession had been drawn up in Lagos, he did not believe it was done in accordance with the instructions of the British Government and, all arguments failing to convince him to the contrary, the British representatives departed. Dosumu was, however, informed that unless he could make up his mind by August 6th formal possession would be taken of the island in the name of the Queen of England. Threats against the British and the avowed intention of opposing any occupation by force were met by the necessary dispositions, and the presence of H.M.S. *Prometheus* within gunshot of the town had a sobering effect on the malcontents. It was necessary, however, for a party of armed marines to accompany the Consul and Commander Bedingfield to a second conference, to which they had been invited by the king, but in spite of much excitement the meeting ended satisfactorily. The next day, August 6, 1861, the king and four of his principal chiefs signed the treaty[1] at the Consulate, a proclamation was read declaring that Lagos was taken possession of in the name of the Queen, and the British flag was unfurled. The ceremony concluded with a salute of twenty-one guns and the singing of the national anthem by the children of the mission schools. In the evening a dinner was given on board of the *Prometheus*, which was attended by most of the principal residents in Lagos. Dosumu was invited but was not present.

Although the annexation of Lagos resulted in the suppression of the slave-trade and the establishment of an effective and civilized government, there was considerable opposition and criticism from various quarters. Dosumu and his chiefs protested that they had not understood the terms of the treaty, which had in any case been forced upon them. The liberated Africans, most of them from Sierra Leone, intrigued against the Government and frightened the chiefs with a tale that the

[1] See Appendix D.

cession involved the loss of their lands. The reason given by Sir Richard Burton for this attitude of the Sierra Leone merchants was that 'they were in debt to the natives, and debt under English is a very different thing from debt under native rule. Besides which, all of them had slaves, and most of them, when occasion served, were slave-dealers.'[1] The British merchants, glad enough at first of the security of the new régime, soon blamed the British rule for the slump in trade which immediately followed the annexation, owing to the civil war which began at the same time in Yorubaland. Even the missionaries did not look with favour on a policy which threatened to rob them of their prestige among the people. Petitions were addressed to Queen Victoria by Dosumu and his chiefs, but the former was satisfied by the fixing of his annual pension at 1,200 bags of cowries,[2] equal at that time to about £1,030,[3] and the latter withdrew their opposition when it was pointed out that private rights to property were not affected by the change of government.

In 1862 Lagos was created a Colony or 'Settlement', and for a few years the Governor was also Consul for the Bight of Benin, an arrangement which proved thoroughly unsatisfactory, and had to be discontinued in 1867, the Consul at Fernando Po again taking charge of all the territory from the eastern borders of Lagos to the Cameroons. At this time there were about sixteen British traders in Lagos, in addition to one French, two Italian, three Hamburg, and five Brazilian. Sir Richard Burton, who visited Lagos in 1862, said that 'the streets want only straightening, widening, draining, and cleaning . . . the town is filled with deep holes, from which the sand mixed with swish for walls has been dug . . . these become

[1] *My Wanderings in West Africa* (1863), by Sir Richard Burton, vol. ii, p. 215.

[2] Small shells (*Cypraea moneta*), about half an inch in length, fastened together, as a rule, in strings of 40 or 100 each. These shells were imported from the East Indies.

[3] Dosumu's pension was continued after his death (in 1885) to his successors as an act of grace. His son Oyekan was recognized as King of Lagos in 1885, and was succeeded by his younger brother, Eshugbayi Eleko, after his death in 1900. Eshugbayi received an allowance of £300 a year until the end of 1920, when he was deposed; he was reinstated in 1931. See Appendix B for the genealogy of the later Kings (or Obas) of Lagos.

favourite stores for offal and rubbish, and the hot weather fills them with putrefaction. . . . Everything has the squalid, unclean look of an idle people.'[1] Work had, however, been begun on the Marina, which is now the main street of a town which compares not unfavourably with other tropical cities. The Governor lived in a house with four small rooms, the lower part of which was used as an armoury, the same building that was referred to by Burton as a 'corrugated iron coffin or plank-lined morgue, containing a dead consul once a year'.[2] In this house the Governor would receive the people, listen to their grievances and settle their disputes. To this sanctuary would repair the fugitive slaves who had escaped from their masters on the mainland, crossing the lagoon in canoes to seek freedom under the British flag. In the words of Mr McCoskry, the former acting Consul, 'the Governor would probably find a fugitive at the foot of the stairs on his knees when he came down in the morning'.[3] Lagos was garrisoned at first by two companies of the West India Regiment and a force of 'Hausas', raised by Captain J. H. Glover,[4] the Lieutenant-Governor; these Hausas performed both military and police duties. Two small gunboats were lent for a while by the Admiralty to the Lagos Government.

Very much against the will of Dosumu, Kosoko and his principal lieutenant, Tappa, were now allowed to return to Lagos, and in 1863 Kosoko ceded Palma and Lekki to the Government in return for a pension, which he drew until his death in 1872. Badagri, Palma, and Lekki were the first additions to the Colony; in 1863 Ado and Oke-Odan, to the west of Lagos, were added, and between 1883 and 1895 Appa, the Itsekiri country as far as Mollume, Ogbo Mahin, Ijebu-Ro, Itebu,

[1] *My Wanderings in West Africa*, by Sir Richard Burton, vol. ii, pp. 223–40.

[2] *Ibid.*, p. 213. Consul Campbell died in 1859; his successor, Mr Brand, died in 1860; and Mr Foote died in 1861.

[3] *Report from the Select Committee of the House of Commons on Africa (Western Coast)* (1865,) p. 72.

[4] Afterwards Sir John Glover, and affectionately remembered by the Africans as 'Golobar'. In 1873 he led a force of Hausas and local allies from the Volta to Kumasi, materially assisting in the defeat of the Ashantis by his loyal co-operation with the main force under Sir Garnet Wolseley. For his adventures on the Niger see Chapter VIII.

Aiyesan, Igbessa, Ilaro, and Kotonu were included in the Lagos territories. Kotonu was, however, exchanged with the French in 1889 for Pokra, a district north of Badagri.

In 1863, owing to several hostile acts by Possoo, a chief who had established himself at Epe with the irreconcilable portion of Kosoko's warriors, it was necessary for the Lagos Government to take action. A parley being refused, a force of Hausas, supported by a few marines and bluejackets from H.M.S. *Investigator*, advanced against the town, but after some indecisive fighting retired to the gunboat, which then shelled and set fire to a portion of Epe. This had little effect on Possoo, who retaliated by attacking Government canoes and, suspecting one of his prisoners to have belonged to the Hausa force which had attacked him, sent the unfortunate man to the King of Ijebu to be sacrificed. A larger force, including a detachment of the West India Regiment, was then sent to Epe, and the people being taken by surprise, the town was entered without fighting. The advantage gained, however, was abandoned in the hope that Possoo might be persuaded to adopt a peaceful attitude, the chiefs promising that he would come to a meeting if the troops withdrew, and the Muhammadan chiefs swearing on the Koran that he would do so. The force re-embarked, but Possoo did not appear, and after waiting for two hours longer than the time agreed a second landing was made. The interval had been employed in strengthening the defences, and stubborn resistance was made, but the part of the town which had not been destroyed at the first attack was burnt, and the force returned to the ship under cover of her guns. The casualties amounted to four men killed and four officers and thirty-three men wounded. After the destruction of Epe the gunboat *Handy* was sent to effect a blockade, but Possoo was now inclined to peace, and readily signed a treaty by which he bound himself to stop the slave-trade and recognize the Lagos Government.

The young Administration was now faced with the open hostility of the Egbas. We have seen that in 1851 Mr Beecroft was able to give timely warning of the proposed attack on Abeokuta by the Dahomey army, and as further attacks were threatened the British Government sent cannon to Abeokuta, and a naval officer went there to teach the Egbas how to use them. British missionaries had been established at Abeokuta since 1843, and the Egbas entertained the most friendly feelings for the British until the time when Lagos became a Colony, when their feelings seem to have undergone a complete change. This they attributed to the fear that their independence would be lost as the independence of Lagos had been, and they refused to allow a Consul, who had been sent to look after British interests in Abeokuta, to enter the town, pointing out that the establishment of a Consulate at Lagos had been the first step towards occupation. It is probable, however, that the severe blow to the slave-trade involved in the establishment of the British Colony was the chief cause of their hostility, and it was suggested that they were prejudiced against the Lagos Government by the Sierra Leone people resident there, and by the European missionaries at Abeokuta. Giving evidence before a Parliamentary Committee in 1865, Mr Wilde, the Superintendent of the Slave-Trade Department of the Foreign Office, made the following remarks: 'It is with regret I say that I think the missionaries like to be thoroughly independent, and to be the advisers of the native powers; they do not like any interference with their policy.'[1] This opinion was shared by other witnesses.

At first the Egbas were too busy with other enemies to give trouble to Lagos. In 1864 the Dahomey army made another attack on Abeokuta, but was repulsed, the town walls having been repaired, trenches dug, and the guns presented by the British Government some years before mounted on the ramparts. The Christian community provided a separate corps, under their own leader, and this corps took a conspicuous share in the defence. The Dahomey troops never again reached the walls of Abeokuta, but annual raids into Egba territory continued,[2] and the Egbas dared not meet their foes in the field, being almost continuously confined to their towns until the rising of the rivers in the rainy season put a safe barrier be-

---

[1] *Report from the Select Committee on Africa (Western Coast)* (1865), p. 119. More than ten years before this Consul Campbell (and others) had to complain of the interference of the Rev. Mr Gollmer in the political affairs of Lagos.

[2] In 1865 the King of Dahomey wrote to the Governor of Lagos inviting his co-operation in an attack on Abeokuta, and promising to hand over the town to the British after its capture.

tween them and Dahomey. Mr Johnson, himself a Yoruba, says that:

> During these periods . . . there were some desperadoes among the Egbas who would venture across the river to within two miles . . . to spy out the enemy, and sometimes to scare them by letting off firearms. In order to capture such men the Dahomians would come down unseen as near as possible to the river . . . setting scouts to apprise them of the approach of Egba spies. After these had passed on towards the Dahomian camp, they would emerge from their hiding-places and cut off their retreat. . . . In this way several were caught, and some of those who escaped died of fright, or of exhaustion and thirst.[1]

In the meantime the power of Ibadan was steadily growing, while that of the Alafin of Oyo became more and more shadowy and his influence in Yorubaland practically vanished. Ibadan had fought and subdued the Ijeshas and Ekitis, and Ijaye was attacked, ostensibly to avenge an insult offered to the Alafin. The Egbas, jealous of the increasing power of Ibadan, joined with the Ijebus to assist Ijaye, and the Fulani of Ilorin took the opportunity to attack the Ibadans who, however, defeated all their enemies in turn and captured Ijaye after a long siege. Among the prisoners taken at Ijaye was a Mr Roper, an English missionary, who was only released by the direct order of the Alafin, to whom the other missionaries appealed; he was at first mistaken for a coloured American sharpshooter who had joined in the defence of the town. Captain Glover, then in command of H.M.S. *Handy*, was sent to Ibadan to try to negotiate a truce, as the hostilities were seriously affecting the trade of Lagos, but he was not successful. At length, towards the end of 1864, the Alafin intervened between the parties and a peace was patched up, marred, however, by a treacherous attack of the Egbas on the Ibadans after the cessation of hostilities.

The dispute between Ibadan and the Egbas was mainly an economic one. The Ibadans wished to secure a direct road to the Lagos lagoon in order that their trade with the European merchants there should not be handicapped by having to pass through the Egba territory, where heavy tolls were levied. The obvious road was one terminating at Ikorodu, and the people

[1] Johnson, *op. cit.*, p. 362.

of that town were more than willing to allow the Ibadan traders
to pass, as they would benefit from the traffic. This the Egbas
were not prepared to allow, and no sooner had the peace with
Ibadan been concluded than they persuaded their allies to join
with them in an attack on Ikorodu. In their extremity the
Ikorodu chiefs looked to Ibadan for aid, but Ibadan was in no
position to help them, and they then turned for help to the
Lagos Government. The trade of Lagos had already suffered
considerably, and the Government was more than ever concerned when Ikorodu was attacked, as this brought the fighting
to within a few miles of the Colony.[1] Captain Glover, who
was now administering the Government, appealed to the Egba
chiefs to raise the siege, but without result. A formal ultimatum was then sent, but was disregarded, so a company of the
West India Regiment was dispatched from Lagos to Ikorodu
in March 1865 and the Egbas were driven off with heavy loss.[2]
In 1867 the Egbas expelled all the European missionaries and
traders, and they were not allowed to return to Abeokuta for
about twelve years.

In 1870, and again in 1871, there were disastrous fires which
destroyed large sections of the town of Lagos, the bamboo and
thatch with which most of the houses were built burning
fiercely. Rumours that the British intended to abandon Lagos
unsettled the inhabitants at this period, and this belief was
fostered by the old slave-dealing faction which did everything
possible to discredit the administration. The ignorant people
were easily persuaded that the Franco-German War was a conflict between Great Britain and Portugal, and every German
victory was hailed as a Portuguese success. The report of the

[1] 'In an interview with the acting Governor in 1863 the head chief of
the Abeokutans not only admitted that robbery and destruction of property
were the natural results of war, but stated that it was their custom under such
circumstances to destroy trade and property in order to recruit the army and
to drive the people to war, and that if they allowed trading there would be
no soldiers.' *Report of Colonel H. St George Ord, the Commissioner appointed to
inquire into the Condition of the British Settlements on the West Coast of Africa* (1865).

[2] 'Within an hour of the engagement the Egbas had taken to their heels;
large numbers perished in the fight. It was ascertained afterwards that those
who fell from bullets were very few indeed, but the majority died from fright
and thirst induced by exhaustion in the flight; for as the rockets flew overhead with hideous noise and streaming fiery tails, a thing unseen before, they
were panic-stricken.' Johnson, *op. cit.*, p. 360.

surrender of the French Emperor at Sedan was actually distorted into the capture of Queen Victoria! In these circumstances it was necessary to garrison Lagos with three companies of the West India Regiment during the absence, at the Ashanti War of 1873, of the Hausa force from Lagos.

In 1877 another war broke out in Yorubaland. The Egbas and the Ijebus were attacked by the Ibadans, and while the latter were fully occupied with these enemies, the Ekitis, who had never accepted the yoke of Ibadan with a good grace, revolted and marched against them, and a little later the Fulani advanced from Ilorin to avenge their previous defeats. In 1878 the Ibadans gained a notable victory over the Fulani at Ikirun, and minor sucesses against their other enemies made them momentarily safe. In spite of this they were in a very critical position. They had no friends, and enemies hemmed them in on every side, on the north the Fulani, to the east a confederation of Ekiti and Ijesha, to the west the Egbas, and to the south the Ijebus. They were cut off from the sea and could get no ammunition, while their opponents were obtaining modern rifles from merchants in Lagos. An attempt to detach the Ijebus from the hostile alliance was unsuccessful, and the war dragged on, neither side being able to obtain any decided advantage owing to their methods of fighting, a description of which was given by Sir Richard Burton in his evidence before a Parliamentary Committee:

They build a solid wall and a deep ditch, behind which they encamp; they go out to fight, and as soon as a man is killed they retire for the day.[1]

The war degenerated into a series of raids, but the trade of the country was brought to a complete standstill and there was no security for life or property.

At last, in 1881, the Alafin of Oyo made an attempt to reconcile the two parties. The Dahomey armies, which had found Abeokuta too tough a nut to crack, were now directing their annual slave-raids against the frontier towns of Yoruba proper, which owed allegiance to Oyo, and threats were made against the metropolis itself. The Alafin was unable to protect his people without assistance from Ibadan, and so long as the civil

[1] *Report from the Select Committee on Africa (Western Coast)* (1865), p. 98.

war lasted it was useless to look for aid from that quarter. It was in these circumstances that he applied to the Lagos Government for assistance in bringing the disastrous inter-necine wars to a close, his letter to the Governor being con-veyed to Lagos by the Rev. Samuel Johnson,[1] an African clergyman, who acted later on several occasions as the Govern-ment's intermediary in the peace negotiations. In response to the Alafin's appeal the Government of Lagos sent messengers to the combatants and invited to Lagos representatives of the warring Yoruba tribes, but the meeting was without result and the war continued. The following year, however, the Ijebus sent representatives to Ibadan to treat for peace, and messen-gers arrived from the Emir of Gando, overlord of Ilorin, to en-deavour to arrange matters between the Fulani and Ibadan; mutual suspicion did not admit of any definite reconciliation, although both parties were manifestly eager to put an end to a conflict which was barren of results and ruinous to the country. The Government and the missionaries, however, continued their attempts to bring about a peace and in 1884 the Rev. J. B. Wood,[2] a European missionary resident at Abeokuta, visited the armed camps of the Ibadans and the Ekitis in an endeavour to reconcile them, but without success, a visit by the same gentleman the next year being equally fruitless. In 1886 the Governor of Lagos sent the Rev. S. Johnson and the Rev. C. Phillips, another African clergyman, with letters to the rival camps, urging the necessity for peace and offering the services of the Government as arbitrator. This offer was gratefully accepted, and three European officials, with an escort of fifty Hausas and a gun, proceeded to the rival camps, a treaty was signed on the battlefield, and both armies withdrew, the camps being burnt by the arbitrators.

The Colony of Lagos was now firmly established. Its boun-daries had been extended to the east and west, and in the Yoruba country its influence was steadily growing. When first created a 'Settlement' in 1862 Lagos was a separate administra-tion under a Governor. In 1866 it was included in the 'West African Settlements' under a Governor-in-Chief resident at Sierra Leone, but a separate Legislative Council was retained

[1] Author of *History of the Yorubas*.
[2] Author of *Historical Notices of Lagos, West Africa,* and other works.

and an Administrator was immediately responsible for its government. In 1874 it was brought under the Governor of the Gold Coast, with a Lieutenant-Governor or a Deputy Governor in charge locally. At last, in 1886, it was set up again as a separate Colony under its own Governor, and its history from this date will be dealt with in Chapter XVII.

CHAPTER XII

THE BEGINNINGS OF ADMINISTRATION IN THE OIL RIVERS

And some we got by purchase,
And some we had by trade,
And some we found by courtesy
Of pike and carronade.

R. KIPLING: *The Merchantmen*

We must now return to the situation in the rivers to the east of Lagos. In 1849, as we have seen, Mr Beecroft was appointed Consul for the Bights of Benin and Biafra, his jurisdiction extending from Dahomey to the Cameroons. The first few years of his Consulate were fully occupied in the affairs of Dahomey and Lagos, but in 1853 the appointment of a separate Consul for Lagos relieved him of this important section and gave him more time for the supervision of the Niger and the Oil Rivers. Even then his time was very fully occupied, and it was impossible for him to visit all the rivers as often as was desirable, as he was almost entirely dependent on ships-of-war for transport from one place to another.

Soon after the establishment of the Consulate, owing to the inability of Mr Beecroft to render assistance appealed for, the merchants and supercargoes of the ships in the rivers themselves fitted out some armed canoes to attack and punish a party of river pirates in the delta of the Niger, whose outrages were hampering trade. It was recognized that some local assistance would have to be given to the Consul if order was to be maintained in the rivers, and writing in 1854 Dr Baikie describes 'a commercial or mercantile association' organized by some of the merchants at Bonny, 'the members being the chief white and black traders in the place, and the chair occupied by the white supercargoes in monthly rotation. All disputes were brought before this court, . . . and with the consent of the King, fines are levied on defaulters. If any one refuses to submit to the decision of the court, or ignores its jurisdiction, he is tabooed, and no one trades with him. The natives stand in much awe of it, and readily pay their debts when threatened with it.'[1] The success of this unofficial court was so remarkable that, with the sanction of the Consul and the naval authorities, similar 'Courts of Equity' were established on the different rivers.

These courts, which by 1870 were working at Old Calabar (now Calabar), Bonny, New Calabar (now Degema), Brass, Opobo,[2] Akassa, and the Benin river, were composed of the agents of the various firms, and were presided over in turn by each of the members, in order that no one should obtain, as President, undue influence among the inhabitants to the detriment of his rivals in trade, or should incur the displeasure of the powerful chiefs by being the regular mouthpiece of the court, which did not always decide in favour of the African litigant. In their early years the Courts of Equity possessed no legal status, being formed by agreement between the merchants and the chiefs, although the rules laid down by the courts were referred to the British Government for approval and were in some cases disallowed. The courts, however, did very useful work in regulating the payment of 'comey', pilotage fees, and the settlement of debts, and in the absence of any effective administration they supplied a long-felt want, although, even at their best, they required constant supervision by the Consul.

In 1854, at the request of the Court of Equity,[3] Mr Beecroft deposed King Pepple of Bonny, who was ruining the country by his crimes and the constant tribal warfare for which he was responsible. He was sent first to Fernando Po, and then to Ascension, and at length was permitted to visit England, where he was received with open arms by the heads of the missionary societies and leading members of the Government. In 1861 he returned to Bonny with, we are told, 'exaggerated notions of his own importance'. He was accompanied by several English men and women who had accepted positions at his 'Court', but these unfortunate people received no part

---

[1] Baikie, op. cit., p. 356.   [2] Or 'Egwanga'.

[3] Dr K. O. Dike maintains that only the European members of the Court of Equity were in favour of this and that the chiefs, in spite of their hostility to the King, were opposed to his exile and deposition. Dike, op. cit., pp. 142–3.

of the large salaries they had been led to expect, and were glad to return to England by the first opportunity.

Trade in the meanwhile had begun on the Niger. The successful voyage of the *Pleiad* up the Niger and Benue in 1854, an account of which is given in Chapter VIII, had proved that it was possible for vessels to navigate these rivers without losing a large proportion of their crews from fever and other tropical diseases. It was disease that had caused Mr Macgregor Laird's first attempt at trade in 1832 to be a failure, but now there seemed no reason why he should not succeed in establishing successful commercial traffic with the people of the interior. In 1857 he entered into a contract with the British Government for the yearly visit of a trading steamer to the rivers at the time of high water, the enterprise being assisted by a subsidy for five years, beginning with £8,000 and decreasing annually at the rate of £500 a year.[1] Hulks were moored at Onitsha, Abo, and Lokoja,[2] where the produce purchased could be stored pending the arrival of the annual steamer; these hulks were the first stations established, and had the advantage of being removable from one place to another and of being more easily defended than a station on shore. They were as a rule in the charge of educated Africans, the number of Europeans employed being deliberately kept as low as possible. Salt, beads, cotton goods, and, at stations near the coast, spirits, guns, and gunpowder were the articles in chief demand by the people, and they brought in exchange palm oil, benniseed, and ivory.

The first steamer to visit the river under the contract was the *Dayspring*, which, as we have seen in Chapter VIII, was wrecked at Jebba in 1857. The crew was rescued in the following year by the *Sunbeam*, and in 1859 the *Rainbow* ascended the river with Dr Baikie in charge. As the attempt on this occasion was made too early in the season, the steamer went aground before she had gone far, and Baikie therefore returned to Lagos and travelled overland to Rabba, where he had

---

[1] In 1858 Mr Laird issued a small copper coin, of the value of one-eighth of a penny, as a substitute for the strings of cowrie-shells, which were at that time the only currency on the upper river. The coin became very popular with the people, but, as its issue was held to be an infringement of the royal prerogative, it had to be withdrawn.

[2] Called at first 'Laird's Town'.

already made friends with Masaba,[1] the King of Nupe. The slave-dealing party in the Lagos territories, however, resenting Baikie's influence, intrigued against him, with the result that Masaba requested him to leave Rabba. He accordingly moved to Lokoja, which became the headquarters of British trade and influence in the interior; but Masaba continued to afford him a measure of protection and even advanced him money when he was temporarily embarrassed. The *Rainbow* got up the river in due course, and was returning fully laden with produce when she was attacked, about seventy miles from the sea, by armed tribesmen, two members of the crew being killed.

Laird appealed to the Government for adequate protection for his vessels, and orders were issued for a ship-of-war to escort the annual steamer up the river; through a misunderstanding, however, no escort was provided in 1860 and no vessel ascended the river that year. Dr Baikie, who had remained at Lokoja, was completely isolated there for over eighteen months, and Laird's trading station at Abo was looted. In 1861 H.M.S. *Espoir* entered the Niger and, after a fruitless attempt to secure a peaceful understanding, some of the villages which were responsible for the attack on the *Rainbow* in 1859 were shelled and destroyed, the inhabitants returning the fire with spirit. Each year thereafter, until 1871, a man-of-war was sent up the river to show the flag and protect the growing trade.

By the *Sunbeam* in 1861 Dr Baikie received orders from the Foreign Office to return to England, but he pointed out that he was in debt to Masaba and could not leave without paying him; that he had opened a market to which all the neighbouring people resorted; and that he could not desert those who had placed themselves voluntarily under his protection. Baikie's position was a curious one. He was never appointed Consul at Lokoja and, indeed, the Consulate there was not established until after his death, but he held an official position 'in command of the Niger expedition', receiving a small salary from the Government, but maintaining and improving the Lokoja settlement out of trading profits. In 1862 he visited Bida, Zaria, and Kano, being well received everywhere and doing a great deal, through the high regard in which he was held by the

[1] Died 1872. His successors were hostile to the British. See Chapter XIII.

Africans, to improve the possibilities of trade and the prestige of Great Britain. In 1864, his health failing, he asked permission to return to England, but died at Sierra Leone on the way home.

Macgregor Laird had died in 1861, but the work which he and Baikie had successfully started was not allowed to perish. Various firms established stations on the river and sent up their steamers every year, and the trade prospered and grew. This was, however, by no means to the liking of the inhabitants of the delta, who saw themselves being ousted from their valuable position as middlemen, and the Brassmen[1] particularly were unsparing in their efforts to prevent the European merchants from reaching the interior markets.[2] They complained bitterly to the British Consul at Fernando Po when he visited them of this encroachment on their rights, they mounted cannon on the banks of the river to fire on passing steamers, and they urged the up-country tribes to attack and plunder the trading stations. In 1866 the British Government decided to establish a Consulate at Lokoja, and Mr J. L. McLeod, an ex-naval officer, was appointed Consul. He proceeded up the river in H.M.S. *Investigator* in August 1867, and on the way up the ship was attacked with great determination by the Africans, who were well armed with rifles. The ship went aground, and was for a few days in great danger, but some of the stores were thrown overboard and, driving off the canoes which surrounded them in an attempt to board, the crew managed to get the ship across a sandbar and safely up to Lokoja. The whole of the river was now in a ferment. Bishop Crowther was arrested by a chief, who demanded £1,000 ransom for him, but the Bishop was rescued by Mr Fell, the Consul's assistant, who was, however, killed by a poisoned arrow during the fighting. The *Investigator* left the river soon afterwards, and the settlement at Lokoja was blockaded by hostile tribes for six months; they were finally driven off by African allies in the pay of the Consul, and the following year were punished by the *Investigator*. Owing to the difficulty experienced in affording efficient

[1] The chiefs of this tribe had signed a treaty in 1856 for the suppression of the traffic in slaves and the encouragement of legitimate trade.

[2] It was alleged that the West Africa Company had arranged for the natives of Brass to fire on all ships but theirs, on condition that the Company did not trade below Onitsha.

Richard Lander (died 1834).

1. Muhamad el Kanemi, Shehu of Bornu (died 1835).

Sir George Goldie (died 1925).

2.   Chief Jaja of Opobo (died 1891).

3.   Miss Mary Slessor (died 1915).

Photo: Church of Scotland

Left   Bishop Samuel Crowther (died 1891).

Photo: Church Missionary Society

Sir John Glover. (Kindly lent by...)

Sergeant-Major Belo Akure.

4.

5. Herbert Macaulay (died 1946).

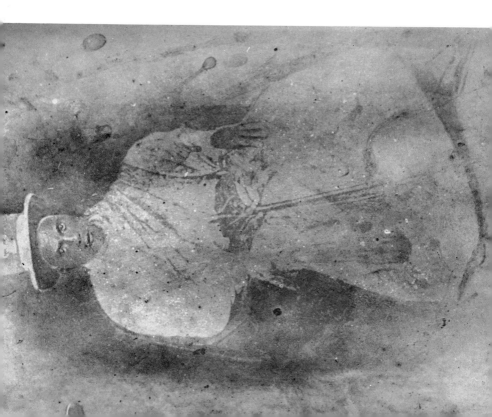

Left King Akitoye of Lagos (died 1853).

6. The first Governor-General of Nigeria. Sir Frederick (later Lord)
Lugard (died 1945).

7.   The present Governor-General of Nigeria. Dr. Nnamdi Azikiwe.

8. Sir Abubakar, Sultan of Sokoto

Photo : *Nigeria Magazine*

Alhaji Sir Abubakar Tafawa Balewa, Prime Minister of Nigeria

protection to the settlement, it was decided to close the Lokoja Consulate in 1869, but arrangements were made for King Masaba to give such protection as was possible to the traders who remained, and visits continued to be paid by ships-of-war and Government agents.[1]

It was, however, in the lower reaches of the river that the danger was greatest. In 1871, the naval escort for trading vessels having been given up, the steamer *Nelson* attempted to ascend the river independently, but was fired on and forced to retire; she struck a 'snag' during her hurried retreat and sank, the crew escaping in their boats under a heavy fire, two men being wounded. One steamer had no less than forty-three holes knocked in her hull while attempting to run past some well-placed batteries, and in 1875 and again in 1876, the steamer *Sultan of Sockotoo* was attacked so fiercely and so repeatedly that no other steamer dared to enter the river, and it became necessary for a naval force to punish the aggressors. Commodore Hewett accordingly proceeded to the spot with the gunboats *Cygnet* and *Ariel* and some hired steamers, and the towns of Agberi and Sabagrega were destroyed, a strong stockade having been rushed and captured with the loss of one man killed and fourteen wounded. It was said that the particularly violent attacks made on the *Sultan of Sockotoo* were in revenge for a breach of faith of which a former master of this steamer had been guilty. He had agreed to ransom, with a number of demi-johns of rum, a European who was a prisoner of one of the tribes, and the rum was duly landed and placed on the river bank, but when the prisoner had been handed over and was safely on board, the ship opened fire on the demi-johns and destroyed them, at the same time wounding many of the tribesmen. It is good to know that the master was dismissed by his employers directly this story came to their ears.

The powers of the Consul for the Bights of Benin and Biafra had at first been but vaguely defined, but in 1872 an Order in Council[2] was issued which conferred upon him certain judicial and administrative powers which had previously been exercised without any legal authority, and at the same time the Courts

[1] In 1871 Mr W. H. Simpson visited the Niger and made an interesting report.

[2] See extracts from this Order in Appendix E.

of Equity were legalized and regulated. Although the Consul's position was by this Order considerably strengthened in theory, he was still comparatively helpless in the matter of enforcing his own decisions. He could rely on naval aid from time to time for the punishment of any gross outrage, but the ships were not always available, and in any case their effectiveness was limited to the coast-line and the banks of the navigable rivers. These intermittent manifestations of force had little lasting effect and, as the Consul had no police, many minor crimes went unpunished. In 1862 a fine was imposed on one of the Benin river tribes in consequence of an outrage at the factory[1] of a Mr Henry, but as no warship was available the fine was not paid; the result of this was another attack on the same factory in 1864, the agent in charge being wounded and carried off and not released until a ransom had been paid.

The Consul himself was not always at his post. The climate made it necessary for him to be frequently in England on leave, and it was not always possible to find a substitute when the Consul died or was invalided.[2] In 1884 the merchants in the Benin river complained that no Consul had visited that river for five years, and in 1885 merchants on other rivers pointed out to the Home Government that no Consul had been on the coast 'for a long time'. Considering how much they had to do, and how little real power they possessed, it is remarkable what influence the Consuls of those days acquired among the Africans. Such men as Beecroft, Hopkins, and Hewett were respected, even if they were not always obeyed, and by their personality and sterling qualities they laid the foundation of a deep respect for the British administration. Writing in 1883 Consul Hewett said:

. . . No nation has taken the interest in the welfare of the natives that we have. . . . For many years past there has been a British Consul appointed to reside among them . . . he settles disputes, not only between traders and natives, but, at the request of the natives, he decides in cases where differences between tribes have arisen . . .

[1] Stores and shops in Nigeria are still spoken of as 'factories'.
[2] When Sir Richard Burton was appointed Consul at Fernando Po in 1861, he said: 'They want me to die, but I intend to live, just to spite the devils.' See *The Life of Sir Richard Burton* (1906), by T. Wright, p. 176. See Appendix M for list of Consuls.

natives having grievances claim it as a right to appeal to the Consul, and consider it his duty to listen to the story of their woes, and to check and punish where injustice has been done. . . . Unwittingly, but in effect, we have led them to rely too much, if not entirely, on us. As an instance of this, I would mention that . . . this year a French gunboat went to Bonny with the view to making a treaty. When spoken to by the Captain on the subject, the answer the Bonny-men gave was to the effect that they would do nothing till they had seen the Consul; he was their father and looked after them.[1]

For all this, there was very little effective control. In 1875 the Brassmen seized a French brig, and for this and other breaches of their treaty with the British they were punished by a naval expedition. A fine of twenty-five puncheons of oil was imposed by the Consul for the seizure of the brig, but as the naval force had left the river there were no means of enforcing the penalty, and the fine was never paid. In 1885 we find the Court of Equity on the Brass river being bullied by the chiefs and forced to reverse its own decisions. One of the members of the Court, a Mr Townsend, who was bold enough to protest against the intrusion of a large and disorderly crowd on his 'beach' at unreasonable hours, was fined by the chiefs two puncheons of palm oil 'for being proud'. He apparently learnt to be more humble, for it is recorded that the two puncheons were returned to him two months later. In every way the British Consuls sought to placate the chiefs and to avoid the necessity for recourse to a force which it was not always possible to command. At Bonny and Brass, for instance, the monitor lizard and the python respectively were regarded as sacred and were allowed to crawl throughout the towns, no one being allowed to kill or in any way interfere with them; so real was this animal worship till about 1878, that British subjects were actually fined by the Consul for molesting the sacred reptiles.[2]

---

[1] See *Further Correspondence* re *Oil Rivers* (1883), p. 5.

[2] 'In the year 1787 two of the seamen of a Liverpool ship trading at Bonny, being ashore watering, had the misfortune to kill a guana as they were rolling a cask to the beach. . . . The offenders, being carried before the king, or chief man of the place, were adjudged to die. However, the severity of justice being softened by a bribe from the Captain, the sentence was at length changed to the following, that they should pay a fine of 700 bars (about £175) and remain in the country as slaves to the king until the money should be raised. The Captain, not being willing to advance so large a sum

On the main stream of the Niger, above the delta, which was even less accessible to the Consul and naval ships, the merchants had to depend still more on their own resources, and it was obvious that the lack of unity among them weakened their position *vis-à-vis* the Africans, while keen competition reduced their profits considerably. Other nations were beginning to take an interest in the palm-oil trade, and a French company was established on the lower Niger when, in 1877, Mr G. Goldie Taubman, later and better known as Sir George Goldie,[1] visited the river. He had already some experience of Africa, and was now interested in one of the companies trading on the Niger; it was clear to him that the existing conditions were impossible, and that unity was necessary if the British companies were to hold their own against foreign competitors and hostile tribes. As a result of his persuasions all the firms trading on the river agreed to amalgamate,[2] and the United African Company came into existence in 1879, being reorganized and incorporated as the National African Company Limited, three years later.

Up to this time European interest in western Africa had been connected almost entirely with slavery, at first with the idea of profiting by the slave-trade, and later, in a chastened spirit, to put a stop to it. When the traffic was made illegal for British subjects, British merchants turned at once to legitimate trade and developed it in spite of every obstacle and with little support from the Government. The possession of colonies in such an unhealthy part of the world was not valued, and the House of Commons had adopted in 1865 the report of a Committee which advised:

That all further extension of territory or assumption of government, or new treaties offering any protection to native tribes, would be inexpedient, and that the object of our policy should be to en-

for the redemption of these poor wretches, sailed without them, and what became of them afterwards I have not heard.' See Bryan Edwards, *op. cit.*, vol. ii, p. 77.

[1] Sir George Dashwood Taubman Goldie was born in 1846, and died in 1925. He served in the Royal Engineers before he became interested in Nigeria. See *Sir George Goldie and the Making of Nigeria* (1960), by John E. Flint.

[2] The firms were the West African Company, the Central African Company, Miller Brothers, and James Pinnock.

courage in the natives the exercise of those qualities which may render it possible for us more and more to transfer to them the administration of all the governments, with a view to our ultimate withdrawal from all, except, probably, Sierra Leone.[1]

It was, however, not so easy to escape from responsibilities which had once been assumed, and within a few years the attitude of the European nations had changed, the desire for 'a place in the sun' resulting in a 'scramble for Africa'.

The French made vain attempts to secure treaties with the chiefs of the Oil Rivers, and on the western frontier of Lagos Colony there was constant friction owing to French intrigues and claims to territory which was considered part of the British sphere. Porto Novo, and at a later date Dahomey, came under the French flag, attempts were made to secure a treaty with the Egba chiefs, and even land to the east of Badagri was claimed for France. The frontier was at last roughly adjusted, but even then difficulties arose over the passage of French troops through the inland waters of Lagos Colony,[2] and much of the early correspondence reflects the general uneasiness that was felt in Lagos regarding the possibilities of French aggression. It was, however, on the Niger that the French made their most determined bid for a share of Nigeria, and it was only through the energy of Mr Goldie Taubman that this was defeated. With the encouragement, if not under the patronage, of Gambetta,[3] a large company was formed in Paris bearing the name 'Compagnie française de l'Afrique équatoriale', with a subscribed capital of £600,000, and this company at once began its operations on the river. To this the National African Company replied by raising its capital to a million sterling and, after a hard commercial struggle, the French company was finally bought out in October 1884.

In the Cameroons, where British influence had been paramount for many years, and where the chiefs had repeatedly offered to place their territories under British protection, the decision to establish a Protectorate came too late, British envoys being forestalled by a few days by the Germans, who

[1] Adopted by the House of Commons on June 26, 1865.
[2] The traffic through the creeks between Lagos and Dahomey was later regulated by treaty.
[3] The French statesman was at this time at the zenith of his power.

obtained a treaty from the chiefs in 1885.[1] In the same year
Herr G. L. Gaiser, a Hamburg merchant trading at Lagos, purchased from the chief of the Mahin country a tract of land
known as Mahin Beach; a few months later Dr N. G. Nachti-
gal, Imperial German Consul and Commissioner for the West
Coast of Africa, signed a treaty with the chief and took the
country under German protection. The British Government
protested that the Mahin country lay within the Lagos territories, and the German authorities did not ratify the treaty,
but Herr Gaiser's claim was recognized, and he received a sum
of money in compensation for the loss of the land he had purchased.

In the meantime the British Consul had succeeded in obtaining treaties from the chiefs of the Oil Rivers, placing their territories under British protection. Similar treaties were obtained
from the chiefs of the tribes on either bank of the Niger[2] and
from the Fulani Sultans of Sokoto[3] and Gando, and at the
Berlin Conference of 1885 the British representatives were able
successfully to claim that British interests were supreme on the
lower Niger and in the Oil Rivers. Subject to an agreement
embodied in the 'Berlin Act'[4] regarding the free navigation of
the Niger and its tributaries by the ships of other nations, the
British claim to Nigeria was recognized by the Conference,
and a notification was accordingly published in the *London
Gazette* of June 5, 1885, declaring the establishment of a

[1] Colonel Nicholls, the British representative at Fernando Po, concluded
a treaty with the Cameroons chiefs and hoisted the British flag in their
territory about the year 1835. In 1848 Mr Alfred Saker founded the town of
Victoria, in Ambas Bay, and started a Baptist mission, and a little later the
British Consul presided over a Court of Equity at Victoria. The Baptists
were bought out by the Germans in 1887, and the British claim to Ambas
Bay was withdrawn.

[2] See Appendix F for a specimen. Some of the treaties were obtained by
the National African Company.

[3] See Appendices G and H. In the opinion of Lord Lugard these treaties
were often misunderstood by the chiefs who signed them, owing to faulty
interpretation. 'The Sultan of Sokoto, for instance, regarded the subsidy
promised to him by the Chartered Company as tribute from a vassal.' See
The Dual Mandate, p. 15.

[4] On February 26, 1885, the General Act of the Berlin Conference
was signed, chapter v of which contained an 'Act of Navigation for the
Niger'. Hertslet's *Map of Africa by Treaty*, second edition (1896), p. 440.

protectorate over the 'Niger Districts'. These 'Districts' were defined as including 'the territories on the line of coast between the British Protectorate of Lagos and the right or western bank of the Rio del Rey', and the 'territories on both banks of the Niger, from its confluence with the River Benue at Lukoja to the sea, as well as the territories on both banks of the River Benue, from the confluence up to and including Ibi'.

For the next six years the Oil Rivers Protectorate existed only on paper, nothing being done to make it really effective, and the Consul continuing to exercise a more or less nominal authority. Even at this date some of the chiefs were of such importance that the Consul was glad enough to make use of them in the government of the country. Such a chief was Nana of the Benin river who, although merely the hereditary Governor of the Itsekiris, and nominally a vassal of the King of Benin, was in point of fact practically an independent sovereign. A dispute with another chief over the distribution of the 'comey' paid by the Benin river merchants was settled in 1885 by the recognition of Nana as the 'Governor' of Benin river. In that year the Consul visited the river, and on the quarter-deck of a British man-of-war Nana was solemnly presented with a staff of office and declared to be the 'executive power through which decrees of Her Majesty's Government and of the Consular Court are to be exercised and enforced'. It was only nine years later that Nana defied the British Government!

Another powerful chief was Jaja of Opobo. Bought in an Ibo slave-market at the age of twelve and taken to Bonny, his ability soon enabled him to acquire wealth and influence, and he became a serious rival to the chief of Bonny. At length, in 1872, Jaja and his followers found it advisable to escape from Bonny and, receiving the necessary permission from the owners of the land, established themselves at Opobo. Here they were attacked, and would have been destroyed by the Bonny chief save for the intervention of some European traders. A treaty was agreed to, and Jaja's position as chief of Opobo was acknowledged by his rivals and recognized by the Commodore on the station on behalf of the British Government. British merchants settled at Opobo, and 'comey' was paid to Jaja in accordance with the usual custom. Now that he was established as an independent ruler Jaja's energy and acumen had full scope. His wealth was considerably increased by trade, and this permitted him to acquire sufficient force to strengthen his position and to establish a monopoly in the districts claimed by him. In 1875 he was awarded a sword of honour by Queen Victoria in recognition of his services during the Ashanti War, to which he sent a contingent of fifty of his fighting men. He was occasionally made use of by the Consul as an arbitrator in disputes between rival tribes, and his hospitality to British traders and officials impressed the neighbouring chiefs with the belief that he was in high favour with the British Government. But in order to keep the trade in his own hands he refused to allow the European merchants to have access to the interior markets,[1] and he attacked and punished any tribe which attempted to deal directly with the Europeans. In 1881 he raided the country of the Kwa Ibos, an independent tribe whose territories he claimed as lying within his sphere of power. His war canoes were armed with cannon, and flew the blue ensign in order to make his opponents believe that he was acting with the Consul's sanction; over a hundred of his prisoners were butchered in cold blood on the return of the expedition to Opobo. His cruelties to other Africans were notorious, and although he dared not at first take any action against the Europeans his arrogance increased daily, and even the Consul was publicly insulted by his followers. As early as 1883 Consul Hewett urged on the Government the necessity for banishing Jaja from the country, but nothing was done beyond warning him. In 1884, among the treaties obtained from the various chiefs in the Oil Rivers, was one signed by Jaja placing his country under the protection of

[1] Even the Consul had to ask permission to pass through the creeks, as will be seen from the following letter:

'BONNY RIVER,
'March 26, 1875.
'KING JAJA,
'I have been requested by Commodore Sir W. N. Hewett to deliver to you a sword which Her Majesty the Queen of England has been pleased to award you in recognition of your services during the late Ashanti War.
'I therefore purpose visiting Opobo next week, travelling through the creeks in the steam launch. . . . It is, however, necessary that I am informed before doing so whether the Bonny people or yourself have any objection to my passing through these creeks on an occasion like the present. . . .
'G. HARTLEY,
'H.B.M.'s Consul.'

Great Britain; from this treaty, however, the usual article providing for the freedom of trade was deliberately omitted in consequence of Jaja's insistence on his monopoly in that part of the country.[1] The following year, by the terms of the Treaty of Berlin, freedom of navigation in the Niger and the connected rivers was provided for and, on the establishment of the British Protectorate, the Consul decided that the European merchants were within their rights in visiting the interior markets. This decision was strongly resented by Jaja, who appealed to the Secretary of State, and in the meantime took steps to prevent the Consul's ruling being made use of by forbidding the people of the upper river from trading.

This political trouble was aggravated by an economic dispute. In 1884, owing to the high prices being paid by the merchants for palm oil on account of the severe competition, it was agreed among them not to give more than a certain figure. This was, not unnaturally, objected to by the Africans, and Jaja was able to persuade Messrs A. Miller Brothers and Company to withdraw from the agreement, using his influence to secure that the whole trade of the river went to this firm, the other merchants being boycotted; at the same time he began to ship palm oil to England himself in large quantities. The boycotted firms were now compelled to go up the river in search of new markets, but they were followed everywhere by Jaja's spies, who threatened the people with the vengeance of their master if they dared to trade direct with the Europeans. In 1887 the Consul decided that 'comey' need no longer be paid to Jaja, as he was shipping produce himself and therefore competing unfairly with those who paid 'comey', and further because his territory was now included in a protectorate.[2] Jaja again appealed to the Secretary of State, and sent a deputation to England to press his claims.

[1] See Appendices I and J.
[2] In this connexion the following letter from the Consul to King Jaja is of interest:

'H.M.S. "FLIRT", OPOBO RIVER,
'*July 1, 1884.*

'DEAR SIR,

'I write as you request with reference to the word "protection" as used in the proposed Treaty that the Queen does not want to take your country or your markets, but at the same time is anxious that no other nation should

The European merchants were now being interfered with in every way, and canoes conveying their mails through the creeks were stopped, if not by Jaja's followers, at any rate by his orders. The acting Consul at this time was Mr H. H. Johnston,[1] and he at once took steps to put a stop to Jaja's aggression. A meeting was called at Opobo in July 1887, at which Jaja admitted that he had made the up-river tribes swear not to trade with the Europeans, and at a later meeting on August 5th, after being threatened with a naval expedition, Jaja signed an agreement to allow free trade in all the markets. He protested bitterly against being compelled to sign away what he regarded as his rights, and addressed another petition to the Secretary of State. On August 15th, Mr Johnston went up the river, but encountered opposition, a boom being placed across the stream and armed warriors assuming a threatening attitude; this the Consul attributed to Jaja's influence and forbade him to trade in any way until the matter was satisfactorily settled.

Mr Johnston now telegraphed to the Foreign Office for permission to deport Jaja, and a telegram being received by him which appeared to give the necessary approval, steps were taken to carry out the deportation. H.M.S. *Goshawk* entered the river, and Jaja was summoned to a meeting at the 'beach' of Messrs Harrison, one of the English firms on the Opobo river. He refused to attend until the Consul had pledged his word that he would not be detained against his will and that he would be free to go after the meeting.[2] On these conditions

take them. She undertakes to extend her gracious favour and protection, which will leave your country still under your government.

'She has no wish to disturb your rule, though she is anxious to see your country get up as well as the countries of the other tribes with whom her people have so long been trading.   'Faithfully yours,
                                    'EDWARD HYDE HEWETT,
                                                'Consul.'

[1] Afterwards Sir Harry Johnston. See Chapter VIII.
[2] The following was the Consul's letter to Jaja:
                                    'OPOBO RIVER,
                                        'September 18, 1887.
'SIR,
  'In reply to your note I beg to say that whatever Uranta may or may not have said to you is of no importance, and can affect in no way the issue of tomorrow's meetings.
  'I have summoned you to attend in a friendly spirit. I hereby *assure* you

he attended, was informed that it was necessary for the peace of the river that he should be removed, and he was invited to go on board the *Goshawk* and proceed to Accra for trial. He was given an hour to decide, and warned that if he refused he would be treated as an enemy and attacked by the naval forces. Jaja was unable within the hour allowed him to escape from the position in which he now found himself. Menaced by the guns of the *Goshawk* and cut off from his base by tribes friendly to the British and opposed to him, he had no choice but to surrender. He was removed to Accra and tried there by the Admiral, who found him guilty of various charges and, as soon as arrangements could be made, he was removed to the island of St Vincent in the West Indies. While there he was under no restraint, and a sum of £800 a year was allowed to him from 'comey' collected from the Opobo merchants. He appealed repeatedly to be allowed to return to Opobo, and in 1891 it was decided that it would be safe for him to go back, but he died at Teneriffe on the voyage home; his body was subsequently removed to Opobo and buried there.

There can be no doubt that the removal of Jaja was a great benefit to the trade of Opobo and its vicinity, and that his cruelties richly deserved punishment, but it is impossible not to feel sympathy for him in the struggle to maintain what he had won by the force of his own personality. The unfortunate thing is that the manner in which he was removed from Opobo caused a suspicion of the good faith of the Government which still survives. The people of Opobo, and most of the people of

that whether you accept or reject my proposals tomorrow no restraint whatever will be put upon you, you will be free to go as soon as you have heard the message of the Government.

'If you do not attend the meeting no further consideration will be shown you, and you will be simply treated as an enemy of the British Government. I shall proclaim your deposition, and hand your markets over to the Bonny men.

'If you attend tomorrow *I pledge you my word* that you will be free to come and go, but if you do not attend I shall conclude you to be guilty of the charges brought against you and shall immediately proceed to carry out your punishment.

'I am, yours obediently,

'H. H. JOHNSTON,

'*Acting Consul.*'

the Oil Rivers,[1] firmly believed that the Consul's promise of a safe conduct had not been honoured, and that Jaja had been entrapped, and to this day the feeling at Opobo is very bitter in this connexion. Had Jaja been ten times more guilty than he was, it would have been better that he should have gone free than that there should have been the least ground for suspicion that the plighted word of the Government's representative had been broken, either in the letter or in the spirit.

In 1889 there was some more trouble at Opobo, another attempt being made to hold up the trade with the interior markets, a boom being placed across a creek to stop the boats of the merchants. A naval force effected a bloodless blockade and compelled the surrender of 24 guns, 442 rifles, and 26 war-canoes. This completed the pacification of the river.

[1] In 1894 Chief Nana, of the Benin river, refused to attend a meeting with the Consul for fear that he would be seized and deported as Jaja had been. See Chapter XIV.

CHAPTER XIII

THE ROYAL NIGER COMPANY

Some men make gain a fountain, whence proceeds
A stream of liberal and heroic deeds.

W. COWPER: *Charity*

While the British Government was taking slow and reluctant steps towards an efficient administration in the Oil Rivers, a trading company was showing the way on the Niger. From soon after the formation of the National African Company, Mr Goldie Taubman had been endeavouring to secure a Charter which would consolidate the position the Company had won for itself and permit the establishment of a form of government suited to pioneer conditions. Government by means of chartered companies was nothing new in the Empire, and the system offered a means of asserting British sovereignty without the expense and immediate responsibility that such sovereignty usually connotes.

In actual fact, the Company had since 1870 assumed a practical though unofficial control of the Niger waterway and the banks of the river. In 1881 and 1882 material help was given to the Emir of Nupe in his struggle with rebels, and the treaties obtained from the riverain tribes in 1884, placing their territories under British protection, were in many cases signed by the representatives of the Company and merely witnessed by the Consul. When an attempt was made by the Germans, through Herr Flegel, to secure control of the Nigerian hinterland, it was a representative of the Company, Mr Joseph Thomson,[1] who visited Sokoto and Gando and secured from the two sultans treaties in favour of the British. On his way down the river, after securing these treaties, Mr Thomson met a German expedition ascending, bound on a similar errand and unaware that the race had already been won.

The first request for a Charter in 1881 was refused, the Government hesitating on account of the small capital of the Com-

[1] See Chapter VIII.

pany and the presence of the rival French firm on the river. These objections had, however, been removed, and the status of Great Britain in the Niger territories had been recognized by the Berlin Conference. A British Protectorate existed on paper, but the Government was not yet prepared to provide the costly administration that would be necessary if these immense areas were to be brought under control. It was better to hand over responsibility to those who were willing and anxious to accept it, and accordingly, on July 10, 1886, a Royal Charter was granted to the National African Company Limited, the name of which was soon afterwards changed to the Royal Niger Company, Chartered and Limited. The following were the principal clauses of the Charter:

The Company shall, to the best of its power, discourage and, as far as may be practicable, abolish by degrees any system of domestic servitude existing among the native inhabitants; and no foreigner, whether European or other, shall be allowed to own slaves of any kind in the Company's territories.

The Company as such, or its officers as such, shall not in any way interfere with the religion of any class or tribe of the people of its territories, or of any of the inhabitants thereof, except so far as may be necessary in the interests of humanity; and all forms of religious worship and religious ordinances may be exercised within the said territories, and no hindrance shall be offered thereto except as aforesaid.

In the administration of Justice by the Company to the peoples of its territories, or to any of the inhabitants thereof, careful regard shall always be had to the customs and laws of the class, or tribe, or nation to which the parties respectively belong, especially with respect to the holding, possession, transfer, and disposition of lands and goods, and testate or intestate succession thereto, and marriage, divorce, and legitimacy, and other rights of property and personal rights.

Nothing in this Our Charter shall be deemed to authorize the Company to set up or grant any monopoly of trade; and subject only to customs duties and charges as hereby authorized, and to restrictions on importation similar in character to those applicable in Our United Kingdom, trade with the Company's territories under Our protection shall be free and there shall be no differential treatment of the subjects of any Power as to settlement or access to markets, but foreigners alike with British subjects will be subject to administrative dispositions in the interests of commerce and order.

The customs duties and charges hereby authorized shall be levied and applied solely for the purpose of defraying the necessary expenses of government, including the administration of justice, the maintenance of order, and the performance of treaty obligations, as herein mentioned, and including provision to such extent and in such manner as Our Secretary of State may from time to time allow for repayment of expenses already incurred for the like purposes or otherwise, in relation to the acquisition, maintenance, and executing of Treaty rights.

The delta tribes who had objected to the European merchants trading to the interior were still more hostile when the different firms were amalgamated into one powerful Company, and they did not cease in their efforts to hamper its trade. On the whole the Company proved too strong for them, but from time to time stations were sacked by the up-country tribes at their instigation, and the Company suffered. Especially before the grant of the Charter determined attempts were made to drive the Company from the river. So hostile were the people at Onitsha in 1879 that it was decided to evacuate the station there, but the trade goods were only removed after some fighting and under the covering fire of the guns of H.M.S. *Pioneer*, which happened to be there at the time. In 1882 H.M.S. *Flirt* destroyed Asaba and some neighbouring towns which had been implicated in the destruction of the Company's store at that place, while in 1883 a small naval squadron had to punish the towns of Idah and Abo in reprisal for further outrages; on this occasion the Africans fought with a reckless disregard of the immense odds against them, and hundreds were killed by gun and rifle fire, three British sailors being killed and a few wounded. Again in 1886 a naval force attacked some villages in the delta in consequence of hostile action against the Company's vessels.

The grant of the Charter, of course, strengthened the position of the Company enormously, and steps were at once taken for the establishment of the usual Government services, with headquarters at Asaba. Courts of Justice were instituted, and an armed constabulary, with British officers, was raised for the protection of the territories. Customs duties and trade licences were imposed to provide the funds necessary for administration, and we shall see later how these pressed on the people of

Brass, whose worst fears were realized. The Royal Niger Company exercised an effective control over a very small proportion of the vast territory that was nominally under their government. Along the banks of the Niger and Benue and their navigable tributaries, within range of the guns on the river steamers, their authority was supreme, but no attempt was made at first to deal with the powerful Fulani states, where misgovernment and tyranny flourished unchecked, accompanied by the worst form of slave-raiding.

The initial difficulties of the Chartered Company were international. In 1887 a German merchant, named Hoenigsberg, with the avowed intention of falling foul of the Company and 'bursting up their Charter', entered the Niger in a vessel with a cargo of salt, which was seized on account of his deliberate infringement of the Customs regulations. Arriving at Nupe, he began to intrigue against the Company, but he was arrested, tried at Asaba, and found guilty by Sir James Marshall, the Chief Justice of the Niger Company's administration, and ordered to leave the country. The case was taken up by the German Government, and Von Puttkamer,[1] the German Consul at Lagos, visited Nupe late in 1889 to investigate. He did not enter the Niger by the recognized route via Akassa, and in other ways broke the regulations, no doubt intentionally. It is probable that German hostility to the Company was due to the fact that the importation of spirits into the greater part of their territories was prohibited, and the basis of German trade with West Africa had always been the gin exported from Hamburg. At any rate, Major Macdonald,[2] who also visited the country in 1889 as a Special Commissioner, did not consider that Hoenigsberg was entitled to any compensation. Agreements were made by the British and German Governments in 1885, 1886, 1890, and 1893, settling the boundary between Nigeria and the Cameroons and, following the 'Heligoland' agreement of 1890, there was little further friction with the Germans, in spite of the fact that the position of a Chartered Company performing the functions of a Government was a difficult one as regards its foreign relations.

[1] A nephew of Bismarck.
[2] Afterwards Sir Claude Macdonald, Commissioner and Consul-General, Niger Coast Protectorate.

With the French, however, there were grave difficulties. France was supreme on the upper Niger, and there were grandiose Gallic visions of an immense Central African empire under the Tricolour, which would compensate France for the loss of Alsace and Lorraine. The Company had foiled French efforts to obtain a footing on the lower Niger by means of trade, but it was obvious that effective occupation of the vast hinterland to which the Company laid claim had not been achieved, and it was hoped that French influence might be extended by treaty over those areas which lay on the confines of the British Protectorate. In 1889 Lieutenant Mizon and a small party of Frenchmen and Africans were brought to one of the mouths of the Niger in a French warship, and entered the delta in a steam launch armed with a hotchkiss gun and towing some small boats. They soon fell foul of the hostile Patani tribe and in the fighting which ensued Mizon and some of his followers were wounded; they were in a very precarious position, without fuel or the means of obtaining it, when they were rescued by an official of the Company and brought by him to Akassa, where the wounded received surgical aid. As soon as these were sufficiently recovered the party proceeded up the Niger and Benue, and an attempt was made to secure a treaty from the Emir of Yola, but so far from succeeding they were ordered to leave the Emir's territories. On his return to France in 1892 Lieutenant Mizon, to cover the complete failure of his expedition, asserted that the Company had instigated the attack by the Patanis and had placed every obstacle in his way. He speedily became a national hero, and was sent out again with a party, permission being asked by the French Government for his armed party to pass through the Niger territories. This permission was given by the Foreign Office in spite of the protests of the Company. Arriving at Muri, with which Emirate the British already had a treaty, Mizon secured a treaty for the French and, in order to please the Emir, agreed to attack the pagan town of Kwana. The town was shelled and stormed by the French force, and the inhabitants who survived the fighting were sold into slavery by the Emir of Muri, who was no doubt highly delighted with his accommodating French friend. It is only fair to add that Mizon's companions did not approve of his actions, and the French newspapers,

F

which a few months before had acclaimed him as a hero, now openly condemned him.

It was, however, on the western frontier of Nigeria that French aggression was most marked. In 1890 a Declaration was signed which contained the following clause:

The Government of Her Britannic Majesty recognizes the sphere of influence of France to the south of her Mediterranean Possessions up to a line from Say on the Niger to Barrawa on Lake Tchad, drawn in such manner as to comprise in the sphere of action of the Niger Company all that fairly belongs to the kingdom of Sokoto, the line to be determined by Commissioners to be appointed.

In 1893 a French Protectorate was declared over Dahomey, and an attempt was made to extend this Protectorate to the north-east so as to include Borgu (now part of Nigeria), which the French maintained was not within the territories of the Company. The claim of the Company to Borgu was based on a treaty which had been signed with the chief of Bussa, but it was now asserted that the Bussa chief was no more than the vassal of the chief of Nikki (a town later within the French sphere), who alone had the power to sign treaties on behalf of Borgu, and Captain Decœur left France with a large party on July 24, 1894, to obtain a treaty from the Nikki chief. The news of his departure stirred the Company to action, and on July 28th Captain Lugard, who was destined later to be High Commissioner of Northern Nigeria and Governor-General of Nigeria, left England on a similar mission. The race was a close one, but Captain Lugard, with his escort of forty men, reached Nikki first, and a treaty was signed on November 10th placing Borgu under British protection; five days later, after Captain Lugard had left with the signed treaty in his pocket, Captain Decœur arrived at Nikki with 500 Senegalese troops only to find that he was too late and that Borgu was lost to France. Relations between England and France now became very strained. The loss of Borgu was bitterly resented, and expeditions, ostensibly private, sought to obtain territory in other parts of the country within the boundaries of the Company's sphere.

For a while, however, international complications were forgotten owing to a serious internal crisis. We have seen that the tribes of the lower Niger and the Oil Rivers, and more particularly the Brassmen, had resented from the beginning the visits of European traders to the interior markets as threatening their commercial advantages as middlemen. They had been able to hamper considerably the activities of individual firms, but as soon as the Royal Niger Company had obtained its Charter sufficient force was provided to prevent any recurrence of piratical attacks on its river steamers, and a series of stringent Customs regulations virtually excluded the inhabitants of Brass from their former markets. In 1889 they made a formal complaint to Major Macdonald, the Special Commissioner who had been sent out by Her Majesty's Government to investigate certain allegations against the Company, but nothing was done for them as the Company was strictly within its legal rights in enforcing the regulations of which the Brassmen complained. There is no doubt, however, that these regulations did operate unfairly against them. In his report in 1895 on the Akassa outrage[1] Sir John Kirk,[2] the Special Commissioner sent out by the Foreign Office, wrote as follows:

With reference to the complaint that the Brass people have been excluded by the regulations of the Royal Niger Company from their old trade markets on the Niger, and that they have no others open to them, it is first necessary to bear in mind that the Rules they complain of were approved by Her Majesty's Government five years before what is now known as the 'Niger Coast Protectorate' was established, or the present boundary-line defined which cuts them off. The Agent-General of the Company stated, in the presence of the Chiefs of Brass, in answer to questions put by me, that, in order to be able to trade legally on the Niger, any native of Brass, being technically regarded under the Company's laws as a foreigner in the Company's territory, would be required to comply with the same rules as affect the largest trading Corporation. He would thus, I was told, be required to pay yearly a sum of £50 for licence to trade, with a further sum of £10, also yearly, for every station he traded at, and he would then only be allowed to trade at such stations as had been declared open for that purpose, and nowhere else. He would next be required to pay £100 annually if he intended to trade in spirits, without which, I may remark, trade in the Delta is at

---

[1] See below.
[2] Born 1832; died 1922. Sir John Kirk served under the Foreign Office for many years, principally in Zanzibar. He was an eminent naturalist and geographer.

present impossible.[1] Having thus acquired the right to commence trade in the Niger Territory, he would on first entering have to report his arrival and obtain a clearance either at Akassa or higher up at the mouth of the Ekole Creek, and pay the Company's duties. . . . It will thus be seen that the Rules in force are practically prohibitory to native trade, and the Brassmen are right in saying that this is so. They are for all intents and purposes excluded from the Niger if they are to respect these Regulations, for how could they possibly pay such a heavy licence tax and sell at a profit goods on which duty had previously been paid to the Protectorate, thus placing them at a disadvantage . . . to those who introduced the same article at Akassa or through Forcados at Ganagana, and paid duty to the Company's revenue only? Had the Brassmen been originally included in the Niger Territory . . . none of the above onerous Rules would have applied.

It was not the fault of the Company that Brass was not included in its territory, nor was it fair to the men of Brass that the establishment of an artificial boundary should exclude them from their former markets. Some satisfactory solution of the difficulty could no doubt have been found, but there was, unfortunately, a traditional hostility between the Brassmen and all Europeans who traded to the Niger above the delta which prevented any compromise. The Brassmen smuggled and evaded the Company's regulations, and frankly admitted that they did so. The Company enforced the regulations as far as it was able, and some of its servants were perhaps not over-tender to law-breakers who hailed from Brass. The mutual resentment increased, and there were frequent threats that Akassa, the Company's trade headquarters, would be attacked. Writing to his Admiral on July 9, 1887, from H.M.S. *Royalist*, in the Bonny river, Captain Hand reported: 'During my stay at Brass I was told by a good authority that the Brass chiefs were actually meditating an attack on Akassa.' However, as years passed by and nothing happened, little attention was paid to these threats, which were interpreted as representing rather the wishes than the intentions of the people. On January 27, 1895, Mr Harrison, the Vice-Consul at Brass, received an anonymous letter in the following terms:

[1] Because spirits were then, and continued to be for many years, the most popular currency.

Brass people leaving tomorrow to destroy Royal Niger Company's factories and lives at Akassa on Tuesday morning. Be sure you send at once to stop them.

AN OBSERVER.

Mr Harrison had only just arrived in the district and knew nothing of the conditions; he had no troops, no reliable interpreter, and no means of visiting the Brass chiefs at their town of Nimbe except in a canoe. Not believing the story told in the anonymous letter, he merely forwarded it to the Agent-General of the Company at Akassa for what it was worth.

The Agent-General himself did not think it probable that an attack would be made, but certain precautions were taken, a gun being placed to command the river and a steamer got ready and sent to patrol the creek. Before daylight on January 29th a fleet of canoes, containing over 1,500 men, left the various towns of Brass and, passing quietly by the Consulate and the merchants' factories at Brass, entered the waters within the sphere of the Company. The patrolling steamer was easily evaded in the darkness and the heavy mist on the river, and Akassa was suddenly attacked. The Agent-General escaped in a steamer and the other Europeans successfully defended themselves in a house, but the African servants of the Company, mostly Krumen, were not so fortunate, about twenty-four being killed and over sixty carried off as prisoners. Most of the Company's property at Akassa was destroyed or plundered, several of the delta tribes joining in the looting after the fighting was over, and only the timely appearance in the offing of a steamer, which was mistaken for a ship-of-war, put an end to the raid.

The heads of the Krumen killed in the fighting were carried off to Nimbe as trophies and forty-three of the captives were butchered in cold blood and eaten. Some of the Christian chiefs refused to join in the cannibal feast, nor would they surrender their prisoners to provide a meal for those who were less squeamish, and these prisoners were afterwards released. Father Bubendorf, a Roman Catholic priest who was at Nimbe before and after the raid on Akassa, was a witness of the feast, and he relates that a young man, the son of one of the chiefs, who had been educated for some years at a mission school in the Isle of Man and professed to be a Christian, joined in the feast and actually invited the priest to share his portion of human flesh.

Two years before the Akassa incident there had been a threat of an attack on the Government station at Brass and the merchants established there, but now the Consul was assured that the Brassmen were in no way hostile to the 'Queen's Government', and that 'we did not kill the Queen's men at all'. The Royal Niger Company they regarded as their oppressor and their enemy, and there could be no peace between them, but the Consul was their father and him they would obey.

In spite, however, of these loyal sentiments, a punitive expedition was necessary, but as the Royal Niger Company was not immediately concerned with this it will be better to discuss it in the next chapter. The necessary punishment having been meted out to the Brassmen, Sir John Kirk was sent out as a Commissioner to inquire into the causes of the raid. His report[1] made it clear that the Company had acted strictly within its legal rights, but that the natives of Brass had undoubtedly suffered as a result.

Soon afterwards the Company was involved in a struggle with the Fulani Emirs of Nupe and Ilorin, who raided for slaves even the villages along the banks of the Niger which were under the Company's protection. All efforts to secure a peaceful settlement having proved fruitless, the Company was forced to take action. On Janary 6, 1897, a force of 500 men of the Royal Niger Constabulary, with twenty-five British officers, two guns, and over 800 carriers,[2] marched westwards from Lokoja in pursuit of a portion of the Nupe army which was raiding for slaves in the district south of the Niger. The force was under the command of Major Arnold, and was accompanied by the Governor of the Company, Sir George Taubman Goldie. The war camp of the raiders was discovered and de-

---

[1] *Report of Sir John Kirk on the Disturbances at Brass, Africa*, No. 3 (1896), (Cd. 7977).

[2] All the provisions, ammunition, and stores of a military expedition in West Africa used to be carried on the heads of men, the paths being too narrow for wheeled transport. Thousands of carriers were used during the war of 1914–18 in West and East Africa.

stroyed, but they themselves scattered and fled before the troops, while a strong flotilla on the river prevented the fugitives from crossing to join the main Nupe army at Bida. On January 23rd the Company's forces crossed the Niger and advanced towards Bida, and in spite of determined resistance by the Emir's followers, estimated at about 30,000 men, the town was taken four days later, with the loss of one officer (Lieutenant Thomson) and seven men killed, and nine men wounded. Another Emir was installed in the place of the former one, who had fled before the town was occupied, and the expedition recrossed the Niger and moved on Ilorin. An attempt was made to avert hostilities, but the war party refused all overtures made by the Company's representatives, and the troops were suddenly attacked by about 8,000 men, of whom some 800 were mounted. The fire of the guns and maxims, as at Bida, proved decisive, and Ilorin was occupied on February 16th, the only casualties being one officer and three men wounded; a few days later the Emir surrendered and was reinstated on his signing a treaty.[1] The terms imposed on Nupe and Ilorin included the recognition of the Company's suzerainty, while the Company took over Kabba, the Nupe province on the south bank of the Niger. Opportunity was at the same time taken to warn the Emirs against slave-raiding, and the legal status of slavery was declared to be abolished within the territories of the Company.

In the meanwhile French aggression on the western boundaries of the Company's territory was becoming more and more serious, and in 1897 it was decided to raise a local military force, financed by the Imperial Government and officered from the British Army, to protect the frontiers of the British Protectorates.[2] Captain Lugard, who was given the rank of Brigadier-General, was sent out to raise the force, which was known as the West African Frontier Force,[3] and headquarters were established at Jebba. For some months the British and French forces faced one another, and it seemed as though a conflict was inevitable; national feelings ran high, and the

---

[1] See *Campaigning on the Upper Nile and Niger* (1898), by S. Vandeleur.
[2] Three companies of the West India Regiment were sent to Lagos for the same purpose.
[3] Later the Royal West African Frontier Force.

rivalry, both on the borders of Nigeria and in the Egyptian Sudan,[1] nearly provoked a war. Wiser counsels, however, prevailed, and an international agreement was arrived at in June 1898, by which the western frontier of Nigeria, as it at present exists, was amicably settled.

The time had, however, arrived when the existence of the Chartered Company could no longer be justified. As early as 1889 Major Macdonald had been sent out to inquire into certain allegations as to the way in which the Company used its administrative position to safeguard itself against commercial competition and, although the Company's actions were proved to have been entirely legal, their rivals still maintained that freedom of trade on the Niger and Benue was merely nominal, and that in fact a virtual monopoly existed. The attack on Akassa by the Brassmen had attracted public attention to the undoubted hardship involved to some of the inhabitants of the country by the existence of the Chartered Company, and the maintenance of the West African Frontier Force gave the British taxpayer a direct interest in the matter, for, as Lady Lugard says in her book, 'it was undesirable that territories, of which the defence was provided at public expense, should be administered at private discretion'.[2] It was in 1899 that the Government decided that the Charter should be revoked, and the reasons for this decision were set out in a letter from the Foreign Office to the Secretary of the Treasury, dated June 15, 1899:[3]

The Marquess of Salisbury has for some time past had under consideration the question of approaching the Niger Company with a view to relieving them of their rights and functions of administration on reasonable terms. His Lordship has arrived at the opinion that it is desirable on grounds of national policy that these rights and functions should be taken over by Her Majesty's Government now that the ratifications of the Anglo-French Convention of June 14, 1898, have been exchanged, and that the frontiers of the two countries have been clearly established in the neighbourhood of the territories administered by the Company. The state of affairs created by this Convention makes it incumbent on Her Majesty's Govern-

[1] The Fashoda incident occurred in 1898.

[2] Lady Lugard, *op. cit.*, p. 362.

[3] See *Papers relating to the Surrender of the Charter of the Royal Niger Company*, 1899 (C. 9372).

ment to maintain an immediate control over the frontier and fiscal policy of British Nigeria such as cannot be exercised so long as that policy is dictated and executed by a Company which combines commercial profit with administrative responsibilities. The possibility of the early claim by the French Government to profit by the advantages in the Lower Niger which are secured to them by the Convention makes it essential that an Imperial Authority should be on the spot to control the development of the policy which actuated Her Majesty's Government in granting these advantages, and to prevent the difficulties which would be sure to arise were the Company's officials alone to represent British interests.

There are, moreover, other cogent reasons for the step now contemplated. The West African Frontier Force, now under Imperial officers, calls for direct Imperial control; the situation created towards other firms by the commercial position of the Company, which, although strictly within the right devolving upon it by Charter, has succeeded in establishing a practical monopoly of trade; the manner in which this commercial monopoly presses on the native traders, as exemplified by the rising in Brass, which called for the mission of inquiry entrusted to Sir John Kirk in 1895, are some of the arguments which have influenced his Lordship. . . .

In revoking the Charter the Government felt that the Company was entitled to full recognition of the position which it had created for itself and to the rights which it had acquired in its territories, and accordingly payment was made to the Company of a sum of £450,000 as compensation and for expenses incurred by it in connexion with the administration of the country. The Government also took over all buildings and stores required for administrative or military purposes at a cost of £115,000 and assumed responsibility for a public debt of £250,000. Moreover, the Government undertook to impose royalties on minerals won between the Niger and a line drawn from Yola to Zinder, and to pay to the Company, for a period of ninety-nine years from the revocation of the Charter, one-half of the receipts from these royalties.[1] In return for these

---

[1] The existence of tin in northern Nigeria was known of as early as 1885, but the exact location of the tin fields was not discovered until after the revocation of the Niger Company's Charter. In 1949 the Government of Nigeria purchased for one million pounds from the United Africa Company (as successors of the Royal Niger Company) the rights to these royalties, which had still some fifty years to run.

payments and concessions the Company assigned to the Government the benefits of all its treaties, and all the land (other than trading stations) and mining rights it had acquired. On these terms, and in spite of some opposition in Parliament, the Charter was revoked, and Government assumed the direct control of the Company's territories on January 1, 1900.

How far the Royal Niger Company's administration was of benefit to the country is a matter of opinion. From a mixture of patriotic and commercial motives it ensured that the rich hinterland of Nigeria should be added to the British Empire, and the prosperity of the territory is due in no small measure to its pioneering enterprise. With its limited resources it did its utmost to restrict the slave-traffic and to carry out its international obligations as custodian of the Niger waterway. At the same time, while keeping strictly within the letter of the Charter and its legal rights, it established a practical monopoly which infringed the spirit of free trade which it professed to recognize. It must, however, remain for all time to the credit of the Company that it brought to the people of the interior the benefits of British justice, before any direct form of government could be provided, and that it resolutely refused to increase its profits by any traffic in spirits.

Sir George Goldie, from whose inspiration the Royal Niger Company was born, and who guided its policy throughout its administrative life; Lord Aberdare, the first Governor of the Company; Mr David McIntosh; Mr Joseph Flint; Mr William Wallace,[1] and other local representatives, must be ranked high among the builders of Nigeria. The Royal Niger Company, Chartered and Limited, filled a great and responsible position in Nigeria from 1887 to the end of 1899, and the legend on the Company's flag, 'Ars, Pax, Jus', stood for achievement as well as for hope. On the revocation of the Charter it became an ordinary trading company, and its name was changed to the Niger Company Limited. In 1920 control of the Niger Company was acquired by Lever Brothers Limited, and the Company was later absorbed into the United Africa Company.

[1] Afterwards Sir William Wallace. Born 1856; died 1916.

CHAPTER XIV

THE NIGER COAST PROTECTORATE

The years came, and the years went,
The wheel full-circle rolled;
The tyrant's neck must yet be bent,
The price of blood be told.

H. NEWBOLT: *Seringapatam*

It was not until some years after the inauguration of the Niger Company's administration that the government of the Oil Rivers was seriously taken in hand. We have seen that a British Consul was first appointed in 1849, and that in 1885 the establishment of a Protectorate had been proclaimed, but no steps were taken to make this effective. In 1887 Mr Johnston, the acting Consul, recognizing the need for some attempt at practical government, endeavoured to introduce 'Governing Councils,' a development of the Courts of Equity, composed of European traders and African chiefs; the Foreign Office, however, did not look with favour on the scheme. At last, in 1891, six years after the establishment of the Protectorate, a system of government was adopted, Consuls and Vice-Consuls being appointed to the various rivers under a Commissioner and Consul-General resident at Old Calabar.[1] A force of armed constabulary was raised and armed launches were provided by which the consular officials could visit the districts under their control. In 1893, by an Order in Council, the Protectorate was extended over the hinterland and renamed the Niger Coast Protectorate.

During the same year there was trouble on the Cross river. One of the chiefs of the Akunas, who did not approve of his people trading with the down-river tribes, deliberately murdered five inoffensive Ibo traders with the intention of provoking an inter-tribal war and thus putting a stop to trade. He was completely successful in his plan, and a force of constabulary

---

[1] The first Consul-General was Major (afterwards Sir Claude) Macdonald, who was appointed on January 1, 1891. He was succeeded by Mr (afterwards Sir Ralph) Moor in 1896.

had to be dispatched up the river to put a stop to the disorder and reopen the way to trade. In this they succeeded, but the Commandant, Captain Price, was killed at the beginning of the fighting. The chief, however, was captured, tried and hanged.

The following year the Government was forced to take action against the Itsekiri chief Nana, who had taken advantage of his position as the recognized 'Governor' of the Benin river[1] to acquire considerable power and wealth. A clever and enterprising man, he carried on an extensive trade in slaves, his war-canoes ascending the Ethiope river, where the unfortunate inhabitants were seized and carried off to his headquarters at Brohemie; trade was practically stopped as a result of the terror inspired. Mr (afterwards Sir Ralph) Moor, the acting Consul-General, proceded to the Benin river and wrote to Nana, requesting his attendance to answer the charges against him. To this Nana sent excuses, and he was then ordered to withdraw his war-canoes from the Ethiope. At the end of a fortnight the war-canoes were still carrying on their depredations, and Mr Moor therefore forbade Nana's followers from trading and began to seize the canoes. Troops of the Niger Coast Constabulary were brought to the Benin river and H.M.S. *Alecto* arrived. A meeting of the chiefs was summoned, but Nana again refused to attend, stating that he was afraid of being seized and deported (as Jaja of Opobo had been) in spite of the safe-conduct offered. In defiance of the order that all the waterways in the district were to be free, a strong barrier was erected across the creek leading to Brohemie; this barrier was blown up by a force from the *Alecto*, which was fired on by Nana's men, and as hostilities were now inevitable Brohemie was closely blockaded.

On August 25th a reconnoitring party in the *Alecto's* steam-cutter was fired on by a masked battery, one bluejacket being killed, Captain Lalor of the Protectorate forces fatally wounded, and two other officers and five men wounded. On the 28th, H.M.S. *Phoebe* having arrived, a force of about 200 men from the ships, with 150 men of the Constabulary, two seven-pounder guns, and a rocket-tube, landed and advanced against Brohemie. In spite of the thick bush and swamp and

[1] See Chapter XII.

the creeks which had to be crossed, the force got within a few hundred yards of the town, capturing on the way a strong stockade, in which were mounted twenty-three heavy cannon, but a further advance was not practicable on account of the swampy ground. The force accordingly retired to the ships, but by this time the tide had risen and it was impossible to bring the guns back across the creeks; they were accordingly spiked and thrown into deep water. During the day one African soldier was killed and one officer and one bluejacket wounded.

A bombardment of the town was now commenced, the firing being directed from a crow's-nest on a spar rigged above the fore-topmast of the *Phoebe*, from which a view of the houses could be obtained over the tops of the mangrove-trees. In response to a request for further naval assistance, Rear-Admiral Bedford arrived in H.M.S. *Philomel*, and he was soon followed by H.M.S. *Widgeon*. On September 25, 1894, a naval force, with the Protectorate troops and guns, made a second advance against Brohemie and captured it without casualties, the fire of the defenders, although heavy, being very badly directed. Nana and most of his people had fled before the town was taken, and it was found that a desperate attempt had been made to cut a canal from the Brohemie creek into a creek behind the town, in order that their property could be removed in canoes, hundreds of slaves being employed on this work under the lash. The pursuit, however, was too swift, and Nana was only able to escape in a small canoe by night, accompanied by a few followers; this canoe was captured by a patrolling launch and with it all of Nana's papers. He himself jumped overboard and escaped, travelling later to Lagos, where he gave himself up to the authorities. He was tried and deported to the Gold Coast, where he was detained until 1906, in which year he was allowed to return and settle at a village called America, some miles above Brohemie on the Benin river. He died in 1916.

The most remarkable achievement of Nana was the complete concealment of the strength of Brohemie. No stranger was permitted to approach the town, which was so little known that it did not appear on any chart, yet it was more strongly fortified and contained more munitions of war than any town in Nigeria. One hundred and six cannon (two of which had a bore of six inches), a machine-gun, 445 blunderbusses with swivels for mounting on war-canoes, 1,500 flintlock guns, 14 tons of gunpowder, and hundreds of rounds of case-shot, made up in cylinders of split bamboo and filled with iron balls and pieces of scrap-iron, were among the warlike stores found in Brohemie, and it is astonishing that the British forces suffered such a small number of casualties in the taking of a place so strongly fortified. The merchandise found in the town was valued at thousands of pounds, there being over 8,300 cases of gin alone.[1] The slaves, more than 5,000, were released and sent to their homes, and the rooting out of this nest of pirates had a marked effect throughout the district.

No sooner had Nana been disposed of than the Protectorate Government was called upon to avenge the raid by the Brass tribe on the Niger Company's headquarters at Akassa. The raid had taken place at the end of January 1895, and early the following month the Consul-General arrived in the Brass river and summoned the chiefs to surrender, demanding from them all their war-canoes and guns, the restoration of all property taken from Akassa, and a reasonable fine. To this they replied that they had no quarrel with the Queen, but that they would continue to wage war against the Niger Company until their markets were restored to them. A naval force now assembled in the river under the command of Admiral Sir Frederick Bedford in H.M.S. *St George*, and an ultimatum was sent to the chiefs informing them that the Admiral had received orders from the Queen to punish them severely if they did not at once comply with the terms offered. King Koko of Nimbe sent a reply asking for time to think the matter over, but as it was reported that the creeks were being blocked and stockades prepared, an immediate advance was decided on. The force consisted of H.M.S. *Widgeon* and H.M.S. *Thrush*, with armed boats from the larger ships of the squadron, and a detachment of Protectorate troops with guns. A skilfully constructed bar-

---

[1] Gin was then, and continued to be for many years, a most useful form of currency and a popular investment. Owing to the policy of the Government steadily to increase the rate of duty on spirits imported, the value of such an investment always appreciated, and many chiefs possessed large stocks of gin until 1914, when the importation of spirits was cut down.

rier in the Nimbe creek was blown up, and the main force
landed at Sacrifice Island in the creek, when an attack was
made by about twenty canoes, which advanced with colours
flying and tom-toms beating and opened a heavy rifle and
cannon fire. The canoes were driven off with some loss.

The following morning a final ultimatum was addressed to
the chiefs, who were informed that they had fired on the forces
of the Queen and that their town would be burnt unless they
at once submitted. The chiefs replied that they were sorry to
have fired on the Queen's men, but that they had mistaken the
white ensign for the flag of the Royal Niger Company (which
much resembled it), and would surrender their war-canoes and
loot if the force would withdraw and if they were given more
time. As any delay would merely give time for a further
strengthening of the defences, orders were given for an immediate advance on the town, which was captured and burnt
after some severe fighting on February 22, 1895. The towns
of Twon and Fishtown, the people of which had joined in the
raid on Akassa, were also destroyed, and the resistance collapsed. The Brass people were now disarmed, and in due
course their chiefs appeared before the Special Commissioner,
Sir John Kirk, who was sent out to inquire into the circumstances. In a few years, by the cancellation of the Royal Niger
Company's Charter, their grievances were removed.

While the rest of the country was being gradually brought
under control, Benin still held itself aloof from the Government, and terrible tales were told of the wholesale human sacrifices that took place there annually. Benin had been at one
time a place of considerable importance, but a severe blow had
been struck at its prosperity by the suppression of the slave-
trade, and the resentment of the king was expressed by an
order which closed his country to trade of all kinds. In 1892
Captain Galway,[1] Vice-Consul of the Benin river district,
visited Benin city and persuaded Overami, the king, to sign
a treaty placing his country under British protection and binding himself to abolish the slave-trade and human sacrifice. A
limited amount of trading was now permitted, but after the
overthrow of Nana it was again stopped, and it became evident

[1] Afterwards Sir Henry Galway, Governor of St Helena, of the Gambia,
and of South Australia. Born 1859; died 1949.

that Overami had no intention of abiding by the terms of the treaty. He was remonstrated with by the Consul and grudgingly consented to reopen the markets on payment of higher tribute from the Benin river chiefs. Nothing came of this, and at last, in 1896, the acting Consul-General, Mr Phillips, informed the king that he would like to pay him a visit to discuss the question of trade and the abolition of human sacrifice. Overami replied that he was then celebrating the 'custom', or anniversary festival, of his father's death, but would be glad to see the Consul-General in a few months' time.

Mr Phillips had in the meantime asked the Secretary of State to obtain for him sufficient naval or military escort to enable him safely to visit Benin, but it was not possible to arrange for this and, unless the mission was to be abandoned althogether, the alternative was to take up a small escort of the Protectorate Constabulary or to proceed to Benin without escort of any kind, trusting that the peaceful nature of the mission would be sufficient protection. In spite of warning to the contrary from experienced Europeans and loyal chiefs, Mr Phillips decided on the latter alternative, and informed the king that he proposed to visit him immediately, as he could not wait until the end of the 'custom'. He also informed the king that he would be accompanied by a few other Europeans and the necessary African servants and carriers, but that none of the party would be armed. To this Overami replied that messengers and guides would be sent to meet the party.

Mr Phillips's decision to visit Benin without an adequate escort has been much criticized, but it must be remembered that Benin had been visited by Captain Galway as recently as 1892,[1] and that British officials had frequently placed themselves in the power of African despots without ever finding their confidence misplaced. If there were those who advised him not to go, there were other experienced men, merchants and officials, who were willing and anxious to accompany him. On January 2, 1897, the acting Consul-General and his party left Sapele by launch for Gwato, from which place the expedition was to start for Benin. On the way they were met by Chief

[1] Mr MacTaggart, an official of the Royal Niger Company, entered the Benin country in 1894 with an armed party, an act which called forth a protest from the Government of the Niger Coast Protectorate.

Dore,[1] the Government's most trustworthy political agent in the district, who on his knees implored Mr Phillips not to proceed, maintaining that it would be certain death to do so. Mr Phillips, however, insisted on carrying out his plan, agreeing only not to take the Constabulary band, which it had been arranged should accompany him; the band therefore was sent back in Dore's canoe to Sapele, and the rest of the party went to their fate.

Gwato was reached next day, and there the Consul-General received a friendly welcome from messengers sent by the King of Benin. On January 4th a start was made for Benin, the party consisting of Mr Phillips, Major Copland-Crawford, Mr Locke, Mr Campbell, Captain Boisragon (Commandant of the Constabulary), Mr Maling, and Dr Elliott, all Government officials; Mr Powis and Mr Gordon, agents of two of the trading companies; two African clerks, and about 230 other Africans, mostly Itsekiri and Kru carriers. None of the party was armed, even the revolvers of the officers being left in their baggage, and in no way did it appear to be a military force. At about four o'clock in the afternoon the party was suddenly fired on from the bush on either side of the narrow path. Mr Phillips, who was in front, was killed almost immediately, and the other Europeans then endeavoured to get back to the carriers to obtain their revolvers. The carriers, however, were already scattered, a heavy fire having been opened on them, and Major Copland-Crawford received a severe wound; the others tried to help him along, but he was again fatally wounded, and one by one the other white men were hit. At length only Mr Locke and Captain Boisragon were left alive, although both were badly wounded, and they crept into the bush and hid themselves. After wandering about for five days, living on green plantain and the dew from leaves, they at last reached the Gwato creek, and were brought away in a canoe by a friendly African. A few of the carriers were rescued by canoes sent up the creek by Chief Dore, who at once dispatched a messenger to inform the District Commissioner at Sapele of the disaster.

[1] For his services in rescuing the few survivors of the massacre and other faithful work, Chief Dore Numa was rewarded by the Government. In 1914 he was made a member of the Nigerian Council, and in 1925 he received the King's Medal for Chiefs. He died in 1932.

The information was received at Sapele on the morning of January 7th, and was forwarded to Bonny. On January 10th a telegram was received in England from Lieutenant Child,[1] RN (Retired), of the Protectorate yacht *Ivy*, reporting the massacre. Immediate steps were taken to deal with the situation. The Consul-General, Mr Moor, who was on leave in England, proceeded at once to the Protectorate, and carriers were provided from the Gold Coast and Sierra Leone. The troops of the Royal Niger Company were employed on a campaign in Nupe and, for fear that the Brass people would seize the opportunity again to attack Akassa while the Protectorate forces were at Benin, a detachment of the West India Regiment was used to garrison some stations in the Niger delta. A naval force, under the command of Rear-Admiral Rawson, consisting of Her Majesty's ships *St George*, *Philomel*, *Phoebe*, *Barrosa*, *Magpie*, *Widgeon*, and *Alecto*, of the Cape Squadron, with *Theseus* and *Forte* from the Mediterranean, and the hospital ship *Malacca* with marines from England, was concentrated in a remarkably short time, and Lieutenant-Colonel Hamilton was sent out to command the Protectorate troops.

The line of the Jamieson river, to the east of Benin city, was held by a small naval detachment, while another attacked and captured Gwato on the west. On February 10th the main naval force was landed at Warrigi and advanced to Ceri, which had already been occupied by the Protectorate troops. Much fighting occurred in the thick bush, and the advance was also hampered by the shortage of water, which became so serious that Admiral Rawson decided to leave a portion of his force behind and push on with a flying column. On the 16th, therefore, a column of about 250 seamen and marines, with a slightly larger number of Protectorate troops, made the final start for Benin, which after severe fighting was captured on February 18, 1897, just over six weeks from the date of the massacre of Mr Phillips and his companions. The casualties amounted to three officers, ten seamen and marines and four Africans killed or died of sunstroke, and five officers,

[1] Lieutenant Child was afterwards Director of the Nigerian Marine, which he brought to a high standard of efficiency. He was drowned in 1914, during the Cameroons campaign, when endeavouring to find a safe crossing on a river bar for the troops to land.

twenty-two seamen and marines and twenty-three Africans wounded.

Admiral Rawson expressed his admiration for the Protectorate troops in a letter to Lieutenant-Colonel Hamilton, their temporary commander:

On leaving the Niger Coast Protectorate Force after the joint expedition to Benin City, I wish to bear record to the exceedingly zealous and able manner in which the officers and men of that force have carried out their most arduous and trying duties. Hardly seeing an enemy, yet always in the advance guard, and bearing the brunt of the fighting, they have proved themselves a very valuable force; and I request that you will convey to them my cordial thanks and appreciation for the willing manner in which they have throughout carried out my orders, taking as they did extra guards and extra duties to relieve the white force.

The naval force was re-embarked on February 27th, a garrison of Protectorate troops being left in a fortified position at Benin.

The condition of the city when it was entered by the British was shocking. Captain Boisragon gives a vivid description:

. . . Altars covered with streams of dried human blood, the stench of which was awful . . . huge pits, forty to fifty feet deep, were found filled with human bodies, dead and dying, and a few wretched captives were rescued alive . . . everywhere sacrificial trees on which were the corpses of the latest victims—everywhere, on each path, were newly sacrificed corpses. On the principal sacrificial tree, facing the main gate of the King's Compound, there were two crucified bodies, at the foot of the tree seventeen newly decapitated bodies and forty-three more in various stages of decomposition. On another tree a wretched woman was found crucified, whilst at its foot were four more decapitated bodies. To the westward of the King's house was a large open space, about three hundred yards in length, simply covered with the remains of some hundreds of human sacrifices in all stages of decomposition. The same sights were met with all over the city.[1]

Other witnesses, and the official reports[2] of the Consul-General, gave details as horrible, and there is no doubt that the occupa-

---

[1] *The Benin Massacre* (1898), by Captain A. Boisragon, p. 187.
[2] *Papers Relating to the Massacre of British Officials near Benin, and the Consequent Punitive Expedition, Africa*, No. 6 (1897), C. 8677. Also circulated as C. 8440 (1897).

tion of Benin by the British put an end to a bloodthirsty tyranny as terrible as there has ever been. In the words of the Consul-General, the

. . . result was the freeing of a very large population of natives from a most appalling yoke of pagan Ju-Juism, which deadened every feeling of right and crushed out all desire for improvement. Under this rule no man's life was safe, and the very possession of riches or property was an incentive to the rulers to remove the owner by sacrifice or murder so that his riches might be confiscated to the use of the King and his myrmidons. It is impossible in a report of this nature to detail the state of oppression in which these people lived and the absolute terror of the fetish and Ju-Ju of the King, but I suppose that no worse state has ever existed in any country or at any time.[1]

Before the capture of the city, the king, with his chiefs and fetish-priests, had escaped, and as soon as the position had been consolidated a small column set out in pursuit. A town which was being built by the refugees was discovered and destroyed, but once again the king escaped. Some of the people, however, began to come in and surrender, and at length the king and some of his chiefs followed their example. A judicial inquiry took place; those of the chiefs who were directly responsible for the massacre of Mr Phillips's party were executed, and Overami, the king, was deported to Calabar, where he died in 1914. There still remained in the bush an irreconcilable party, led by Ologbosheri, the chief most directly implicated in the massacre, but after some arduous operations, accompanied by hard fighting, all were eventually captured.

Ologbosheri was tried by the Consul-General, assisted by the chiefs of the Native Council, on June 27, 1899. Mr Moor invited the chiefs to say, after hearing the evidence, whether Ologbosheri and those with him were sent to fight men coming into the country by force of arms, or whether they were authorized to kill any white men, with or without arms. To this the chiefs replied: 'Ologbosheri was not sent to kill white men—and we therefore decide that according to native law his life is forfeited.' He was duly executed the following morning.

[1] *Annual Report on the Niger Coast Protectorate for the Year 1896–7*, Africa No. 3 (1898), C. 8775, p. 14.

The settlement of the Benin country was the last important act of the Niger Coast Protectorate Government, which had been conducted under the supervision of the Foreign Office. The few years of its existence had been spent in a continual struggle with the barbarous and warlike tribes which inhabited the banks of the rivers, and having no particular objection to the establishment of a British Protectorate, yet objected to the restrictions imposed by the Government on their time-honoured customs. Inter-tribal war, slave-raiding, cannibalism, and human sacrifice were ingrained in the people who had known nothing better for centuries, and found it difficult to understand the prejudice of British officials against these practices. If these evils were not entirely stamped out, they could at least no longer be practised openly, and a beginning had been made of ordered administration.

CHAPTER XV

THE PROTECTORATE OF NORTHERN NIGERIA

Just a thought for the workers of yesterday.
The men on whose bones we build.

E. C. Adams: *Juggernaut*

We have seen in Chapter XIII the circumstances in which the Charter of the Royal Niger Company was cancelled. On January 1, 1900, the Union Jack was hoisted at Lokoja in place of the Company's flag, and the Protectorate of Northern Nigeria came into being with Sir Frederick Lugard as the first High Commissioner. The Niger Company's territories south of Idah were included in the Niger Coast Protectorate (the name of which was changed to Southern Nigeria), and the remainder, including the vast hinterland which the Company had never attempted to administer, became the new Protectorate. Ilorin, Kabba, and Borgu were to some extent under control, but elsewhere British power did not extend very far from the banks of the Niger and Benue, and the Emirs of Kontagora and Nupe were raiding for slaves to within a few miles of the former river and not far from the garrison at Jebba. The new Administration was handicapped at first by the necessity that arose of sending a strong contingent of troops to take part in the Ashanti campaign,[1] and it was impossible to put a stop to the outrages which were being committed so close at hand. Encouraged by the inactivity of the small British forces, and confident that they were powerless except on the river itself,[2] the combined armies of Nupe and Kontagora actually threatened the small garrison at Wushishi, and Ilorin was invited to throw off the yoke of the infidel and join in the holy work of driving him from the country. Ilorin was, however, kept quiet by the influ-

[1] The contingent was commanded by Colonel (afterwards General Sir James) Willcocks, and distinguished itself greatly in the campaign.

[2] The Emir of Kontagora told his people that the British were a species of fish, and would die if they left the banks of the Niger.

ence of the Resident,[1] and the troops were at length permitted to attack the enemy, on whom they inflicted severe losses in several skirmishes. In December Major O'Neill with a small force defeated the Nupe cavalry and pursued them to the walls of Bida, and then with only thirty men he actually entered the town and endeavoured to arrest the Emir. The odds, however, were too great, and the party barely escaped annihilation, Major O'Neill himself being badly wounded in his gallant though reckless attempt.

The troops having returned from Ashanti, an expedition against Kontagora and Nupe was undertaken in 1901. Under the command of Colonel Kemball, the acting Commandant, the troops advanced on Kontagora, and after a severe defeat had been inflicted on the Fulani cavalry, the town was occupied without resistance; the Emir fled, and in spite of a close pursuit succeeded in escaping. He was one of the worst of the slave-raiding Emirs, and was nick-named '*Na-Gwamachi*' and 'King of the Sudan'. When, some time later, he was captured, the opportunity was taken to impress upon him the evils of slave-raiding which he was advised to abandon, but his only reply was: 'Can you stop a cat from mousing? When I die I shall be found with a slave in my mouth.'

Leaving a garrison at Kontagora, the force then marched on Bida, receiving from the villagers as they passed congratulations and thanks for the defeat of '*Na-Gwamachi*'. The Emir of Nupe, the same one who had been driven out by the Royal Niger Company in 1897 and had since returned, refused to meet the High Commissioner, in spite of promises of a safe-conduct, and fled from Bida, closely pursued by some of the British troops. The remainder of the force entered the town without resistance, and the High Commissioner publicly invested the Emir who had been appointed by the Company, and later driven out by his rival, and proclaimed him Emir of Nupe. A 'letter of appointment' was given him which laid down the conditions on which he held the Emirate: he was required to recognize the Protectorate Government and obey the High Commissioner, to rule his people justly, and to put down slave-

[1] Each province, as it was brought under control, was placed in the charge of a British 'Resident', who was responsible to the High Commissioner.

raiding. A letter was also sent to the Sultan of Sokoto in the following terms:[1]

> In the name of the Most Merciful God,
> Peace be to the Generous Prophet.
> Salutations, peace, and numberless honours.

To the Emir of Mussulmans in Sokoto, whose name is Abdullahi, the son of the late Emir of Mussulmans, whose name is Atiku.

I desire to inform you who are head of the Mohammedans and to whom the Fulani rulers in this country look for advice and guidance that the Emirs of Bida and Kontagora have during many years acted as oppressors of the people and shown themselves unfit to rule. More especially in these latter days they have raided the towns and villages in the districts close to their own cities, and have depopulated vast areas so that the fields are lying uncultivated and the people are destroyed or fled. Moreover, they have gratuitously attacked my men when proceeding with mails or canoes, and have seized the mails and stolen or destroyed goods in the canoes. I have therefore found it necessary to depose both these Emirs, and to place troops near their respective cities, to keep the peace and protect the people.

In the case of the Emir of Bida, I have made the Makum Emir instead of Abu-Bakri, which proves to you that I have no hostility to the Fulanis or to your religion, provided only that the Emir of a country rules justly and without oppression. In the case of Kontagora, many evil people tried to burn the town. It may have been the slaves who had been ill-treated by their masters, or it may have been the carriers with my troops. But through all the night the Commander of the Force made the soldiers and carriers extinguish the flames, so that the town has not suffered.

I desire that the people shall return and live in peace under a just ruler, and I write to you to appoint a man who will rule justly, and if he does so I will support him and uphold his power; send him to me with a letter and I will install him as Emir of Kontagora with pomp and honour. But warn him that if he acts treacherously and with deceit, he will share the fate of Kontagora the *Gwamachi*.

With peace from your friend Governor Lugard.

March 18, 1901.   F. D. LUGARD.

To this friendly letter, which, it was hoped, would placate the Sultan of Sokoto and establish peaceful relations, no defin-

[1] See Appendix I to *Report on Northern Nigeria, 1902* (Colonial Reports, Annual, No. 409).

ite reply was received, and the throne of Kontagora remained empty for some time. The defeat of the two Emirs, however, had a marked effect. Ilorin accepted the inevitable, and the agitators who had been busy there were quieted; slave-raiding ceased in the conquered territories and the harassed people looked with gratitude and hope to their deliverers. The only sufferers from the conquest were the deposed Emirs and their Fulani horsemen, the people who had taken part in and had prospered by the slave-raids of the past.

It next became necessary for the Government to deal with the Emir of Yola, a well-educated and able man, but so fanatical a Muslim that he was intolerant of any intercourse with European 'infidels'. The Niger Company was compelled to stop trading in his territory, the trade routes were closed, and an extensive traffic in slaves from the Cameroons territory to the east of Yola was carried on. In September 1901 Colonel Morland,[1] with a force of twenty-two Europeans, 365 African rank and file, four guns and four maxims, ascended the Benue and, after a fruitless attempt to open negotiations, attacked the town. The Emir had two cannon,[2] which were effectively used with grape, and he had the assistance of sixty deserters from Rabeh's army who were in possession of modern rifles. The town was finally captured with the loss of two men killed and two officers and thirty-seven men wounded. The Emir fled, and his heir was installed in his place on similar terms to those imposed on the Emir of Nupe.

The intervention of the French into Bornu politics, referred to in Chapter IV, showed that it was time for the British Protectorate to be made effective over that country. Major McClintock, by direction of the acting High Commissioner, had visited Bornu in 1901 and formed so high an opinion of Fad-el-Allah, Rabeh's son, by whom he had been well received, that he recommended his recognition as ruler of Bornu. Not long afterwards, however, Fad-el-Allah was defeated and killed by the French. A military force was now organized to restore order. In February 1902 this force, which consisted of twenty-one Europeans, 515 African rank and file, two guns and four maxims,

[1] Afterwards General Sir T. L. N. Morland. Born 1865; died 1925.
[2] Presented to him in 1892 by the French officer, Lieutenant Mizon, who is referred to in Chapter XIII.

left Ibi, on the Benue, for Bauchi. It was under the command of Colonel Morland, and was accompanied as far as Bauchi by Mr William Wallace[1] as chief Political Officer. Preparations had been made by the Emir of Bauchi, a notorious slave-raider, to resist the advance of the troops, but the size of the force overawed the people and the hostile intentions were abandoned. The Emir and some of his immediate followers fled from the town, but at the request of Mr Wallace the chief men named his heir, who was duly installed, on the usual terms, as Emir. Public notification was given that the late Emir had been deposed on account of his misdeeds, of which the chief was a treacherous attack on a friendly town two years before, when the inhabitants had been massacred or carried off as slaves. A small garrison was left at Bauchi with Mr Temple[2] as Resident, and efforts were made by him to get into touch with the neighbouring pagan tribes, in some cases successful, but in others involving punitive expeditions.

In the meantime the force under Colonel Morland advanced into Bornu. On the way it was suddenly attacked by a party of about 700 fanatics, led by Mallam Jibrella, who had recently declared himself to be the Mahdi[3] and had terrorized the country, and the advance guard had rapidly to form square to repel the assault. Luckily the enemy did little firing, and lost heavily in their attempts to rush the square, while the troops lost only two men wounded, and the attack was eventually repulsed. The Mallam's following now scattered, small parties being pursued for some days by the troops, and Lieutenant Dyer, who rode seventy miles in seventeen hours, personally captured their leader.

The force met with no further resistance, and Bornu was occupied effectively with little trouble. The Shehu of Bornu, Abubekr Garbai,[4] was at Dikwa awaiting the collection from

[1] Formerly in the employ of the Royal Niger Company.

[2] Born 1871. Afterwards Lieutenant-Governor of the Northern Provinces of Nigeria, 1914–17. Author of *Native Races and Their Rulers* (1918). Died 1929.

[3] A number of Mahdis appeared from time to time after the establishment of the British Protectorate over Northern Nigeria. They were invariably dealt with, in an effective manner, by the Fulani Emirs themselves.

[4] He received the C B E in recognition of his loyal services in 1914. He died in 1922.

the impoverished people of the balance of 6,500 dollars of the indemnity of 80,000 dollars demanded from him by the French as the price of their defeating Rabeh and his son. Colonel Morland sent him a message telling him that he would be recognized as the ruler of British Bornu if he would stop the collection of the French indemnity and return to his country. The offer was gratefully accepted, and the Shehu remained for the rest of his life a loyal and enlightened ruler under the British Government. The French appointed a rival Shehu for Dikwa and the small portion of the Bornu empire that lay beyond the British border,[1] but soon afterwards the Germans occupied the country, which lay within their agreed sphere of influence, and the French retired into their own territory east of the Shari.

While the troops were still in Bornu the Government took action against the late Emirs of Kontagora and Bida who, with a large following, were ravaging the country around Zaria, carrying off as slaves both pagans and Muhammadans. Orders from the Sultan of Sokoto and remonstrances from their other co-religionists were alike unavailing, and at length the Emir of Zaria appealed to the High Commissioner for aid. A small force was at once dispatched, and by a number of forced marches the raiders were caught up and defeated after a little fighting. The Emir of Kontagora was captured and kept in custody for a while, his followers scattering and returning to their homes.

The attention of the Government was next directed to the clearing up of the country along the north bank of the Benue. The troops marched from Bornu to Yola, and a column moved west from the latter place, meeting with some opposition from the pagan tribes, who were notorious robbers and head-hunters, but effecting its purpose after a number of skirmishes. The trade routes from Kano and Zaria to the Benue were practically closed by bands of robbers in the western part of Nassarawa, and a strong force was sent into the country to clear it up. Abuja, the principal nest of the brigands, was captured, and after several arrests had been made the column returned to Lokoja.

[1] This country was administered by the British after the war of 1914–18 (at first under a Mandate, and later under a Trusteeship agreement), and was added, for administrative purposes, to Bornu Province. It is now part of Nigeria.

While this strong force was in the neighbourhood, the Resident of Nassarawa made an attempt to put a stop to the intrigues of the Magaji of Keffi, who had obtained complete control over the weak old King of Keffi, and was himself a robber chief and slave-raider. Captain Moloney, the Resident, went to the king's house and summoned the Magaji to his presence. He declined to attend, and Mr Webster,[1] the Assistant Resident, was sent to fetch him. Owing, however, to a misunderstanding, or misled deliberately by the African Government Agent, Mr Webster entered the private apartments of the Magaji, whence he was forcibly ejected by armed men. The Resident now sent Mr Webster to call the troops, but before they could arrive the Magaji and his followers rushed out of the house and killed Captain Moloney. The Magaji fled with a few men, closely pursued by troops, but he was able to reach Kano, where he was received with honour by the Emir, who was always bitterly opposed to the British. 'If a little town like Keffi could do so much', the Emir is reported to have said in speaking of the murder of Captain Moloney, 'what could not Kano do?'

The time had now come when the relative strength of the Government and the Fulani empire had to be settled. It was believed (and subsequently proved) that the sympathies of the peasantry would be with the British in a struggle with the slave-raiders. The Fulani were aliens ruling over a subject people whom they had antagonized by decades of slave-raiding and injustice. The effects of the constant raids for slaves are described in the next chapter, and Lady Lugard gives a graphic picture of the abuses prevalent during the closing years of the Fulani tyranny:

The judicial system of the Hausas, already founded on Mohammedan institutions, and adopted in the first instance by the conquerors, was allowed to fall into disuse. Courts continued to exist, but the Alkalis who should have presided over them and dispensed justice according to Koranic law, irremovable from their positions as the judges of Great Britain, were either disregarded, as in some cases by the great chiefs who held their own courts and gave decisions at their own will, or overruled by the Emir, or worse still, subjected to the authority of the Emir's favourite slaves, who decreed to their enemies inhuman punishments of their own

[1] Afterwards a Resident in Nigeria.

invention. For the nails to be torn out with red-hot pincers, for the limbs to be pounded one by one in a mortar while the victims were still alive, for important people who had offended to be built up alive gradually in the town walls, till, after a period of agony, the head of the dying man was finally walled up, were among the punishments well attested to have been inflicted in the decadence of Fulani power. . . . Impalements and mutilation were among the penalties of lesser offences. . . . The public prisons became places of public torture, from which few who were confined in them could escape alive.[1]

The hostility of the Sultan of Sokoto and his vassal, the Emir of Kano, was beyond doubt. The High Commissioner's messenger announcing the inauguration of the Protectorate at the beginning of 1900 had been treated with indignity by the Sultan; no reply had been received to the letter asking him to nominate a successor to the dethroned Emir of Kontagora, and a letter informing him of the British action in Bauchi received a most unfriendly reply. The following letter[2] from the Sultan settled any possible doubt:

From us to you. I do not consent that any one from you should ever dwell with us. I will never agree with you. I will have nothing ever to do with you. Between us and you there are no dealings except as between Mussulmans and Unbelievers, War, as God Almighty has enjoined on us. There is no power or strength save in God on high.
This with salutations.

A demand that the murderer of Captain Moloney should be surrendered was refused by the Emir of Kano, who actually marched out to attack the British garrison at Zaria, and only desisted on the refusal of the Emir of Katsena to join him in the enterprise. A garrison had been installed at Zaria after the successful expedition against *Na-Gwamachi* and his followers, which had been undertaken at the request of the Emir of Zaria. On account of his cruelties and suspected intrigues this Emir was deposed and removed from the town, the British garrison being strongly reinforced in view of the hostile attitude of Kano.
Sir Frederick Lugard now collected a force of about 1,000

[1] Lady Lugard, *op. cit.*, p. 401.
[2] See Appendix I to *Report on Northern Nigeria, 1902* (Colonial Reports, Annual, No. 409).

African troops, with Colonel Morland in command, and concentrated it at Zaria. Brigadier-General Kemball,[1] Inspector-
General of the West African Frontier Force, who was then at
Lagos, was instructed by the British Government to take command, and 600 men from the Lagos and Southern Nigerian
Regiments were ordered north as reserves. Before any of these
could arrive, however, Sir Frederick Lugard instructed Colonel
Morland to advance,[2] and the Kano territory was accordingly
entered by a force of over 700 African rank and file, with thirty-
eight Europeans, four guns and four maxims. The first resistance offered was at the walled town of Bebeji, 8 miles within
the frontier, which was summoned to surrender, but the inhabitants replied that the Emir had threatened them with death
if they gave in. However, a shell blew in the gate, killing the
chief men of the town, and the storming party met with little
opposition, the town being quietly occupied without harm to
the people. The effect on other towns was profound. In spite
of the recently repaired walls and deep ditches which had been
got ready when the imminence of the British advance was
realized, the inhabitants would not fight, and their Fulani head-
men retired in haste to Kano before the advancing troops.
Town after town opened its gates to the invaders, and such was
the confidence of the people in the discipline of the soldiers and
the justice of their British leaders that there was no panic, food
and other supplies being brought in for the men and paid for
by them without any untoward incidents. On February 3,
1903, five days after leaving Zaria, Kano was reached and captured. 'The wall of the town, of which the circumference was
eleven miles, was forty feet thick at the base, and from thirty to
fifty feet high. It was loopholed, and strengthened in front
by a double ditch. Its thirteen gates had been lately rebuilt,
and some of them were designed in a re-entrant angle, so that
access to them was enfiladed by fire from the walls on either
side, while the ditch was full of live thorns and very deep. The
fortifications were such that, had there been any determined
resistance on the part of the defenders, the town might have

---

[1] Born 1859. Later Major-General Sir George Kemball, KCMG, CB, DSO.
[2] Lord Lugard himself said, in the West African Supplement to *The Times*
of October 30, 1928, that he 'was rightly censured for acting without prior
approval, but the situation was saved'.

stood an almost interminable siege.'[1] As it turned out, there was little opposition. A heavy fire was opened from the walls, but the guns soon effected a breach, and the defenders fled as soon as the storming-party appeared, losing heavily in their flight from the town at the hands of the troops sent to cut them off. The British casualties consisted of fourteen wounded.

As soon as the town was occupied, the head-men of each quarter were made responsible for good order, and the life of the people went on with little interruption, the great market being re-opened and trade fully resumed within three days. The slave-market had been automatically suspended on the arrival of the British and the notorious prison was cleared. Lord Lugard wrote of this place:

I visited the dungeon myself. A small doorway 2 feet 6 inches by 1 foot 6 inches gives access into it. The interior is divided (by a thick mud wall, with a similar hole through it) into two compart-ments, each 17 feet by 7 feet and 11 feet high. This wall was pierced with holes at its base through which the legs of those sentenced to death were thrust up to the thigh, and they were left to be trodden on by the mass of the other prisoners till they died of thirst and starvation. The place is entirely air-tight and unventi-lated except for the one small doorway, or rather hole in the wall, through which you creep. The total space inside is 2,618 cubic feet, and at the time we took Kano 135 human beings were con-fined here each night, being let out during the day to cook their food, etc., in a small adjoining area. Recently, as many as 200 have been interned at one time. As the superficial ground area was only 238 square feet, there was not, of course, even standing room. Victims were crushed to death every night, and their corpses were hauled out each morning. . . . One of the great pools in the city is marked as the place where men's heads were cut off, another near the great market is the site where limbs were amputated almost daily.[2]

It was found that the Emir of Kano had left his city some weeks earlier to pay a visit to the Sultan of Sokoto, but he now returned towards Kano with a large army, determined to fight. His chiefs, however, were not anxious for battle, and a consider-able portion of the army deserted him. Leaving the still loyal

[1] Lady Lugard, *op. cit.*, p. 443.
[2] *Report on Northern Nigeria, 1902*, para. 45 (Colonial Reports, Annual, No. 409).

portion under the command of the Waziri, he fled to Gobir, where he was subsequently captured, and the Waziri's troops were opposed by the British force, which moved out of Kano in search of them. A reconnoitring party of forty-five Mounted Infantry, under the command of Captain Wright[1] and Lieutenant Wells, repulsed with great gallantry the attack of over 1,000 Fulani horsemen and twice that number of foot-soldiers, led by the Waziri in person. 'Fortunately there was a little scrub around, of which during the action a zariba was made. Ten times the little square was charged, and yet the men held their ground with perfect steadiness, firing only at fifty yards' range to save their ammunition, and only by word of command. Each charge was repulsed, though many of the enemy were shot only fifteen feet from the rifles. The Waziri and seven other principal chiefs were killed, and the attack was beaten off with only one man wounded and three horses killed on our side. The enemy lost very heavily. Had the square once been broken or the leaders lost their heads or been wounded, the little force would have been obliterated. The enemy retired in good order to the village named Chamberawa, where Captain Porter, with another small detachment of Mounted Infantry, came upon them and charged incontinently, taking them completely by surprise and routing the whole force. . . . A notable incident proving the attitude of the people towards us was the fact that at one time Lieutenant Wells was cut off, and would undoubtedly have been killed with the handful of men with him, had it not been for the action of a small village named Shankra, whose inhabitants, seeing his danger, came to his assistance, received him within their walls, and shut their gates in the face of the Kano army. This was a gallant act, since they could hardly expect that the handful of British would win, and our defeat would mean their own annihilation.'[2]

The British force, now under the command of General Kemball, advanced towards Sokoto, being joined on the way by 200 men who had been acting as escort to the Anglo-French Boundary Commission. Friendly messages to the Sultan received

[1] Afterwards Brigadier-General Wallace Wright, VC, CB, CMG, DSO; died 1953.
[2] Report on Northern Nigeria, 1902, para. 48 (Colonial Reports, Annual, No. 409).

only evasive replies, and the troops were opposed before Sokoto by a force of about 1,500 horse and 3,000 foot. Fanatics charged the British square in twos and threes, but there was little real resistance, the Government casualties amounting to one carrier killed and two wounded. The enemy losses were about 70 killed and 200 wounded. The Sultan fled before the battle and did not return, but a few days later most of the Sokoto chiefs tendered their submission to the High Commissioner, who had followed the troops, with a small escort, first to Kano and then to Sokoto. The chiefs were now asked to nominate a successor to the fugitive Sultan, and their choice being approved by the High Commissioner, the new Sultan, Atahiru,[1] was installed with full ceremonial, after the terms on which he was appointed had been carefully explained to him. These included the abolition of slave-raiding and the recognition of British suzerainty, and were coupled with an assurance that the existing system of law and the Muhammadan religion would not be interfered with. The statement by the High Commissioner that their religion would be respected was received with audible expressions of pleasure and satisfaction by the large crowd which witnessed the installation. Sir Frederick Lugard then proceeded to Katsena, where the Emir peaceably accepted the Government's terms, and to Kano, where a new Emir was installed on the usual conditions.

The effect of the easy conquest of Kano and Sokoto was immediate. The desert tribes tendered their submission, a new Emir was installed at Zaria, and *Na-Gwamachi*, chastened by adversity, was reinstated at Kontagora.[2] The people were delighted with the overthrow of their old oppressors, and the Fulani themselves, who had held the country by right of conquest and were now conquered in their turn, accepted with resignation, if not with gratitude, the not too onerous terms of their conquerors. The ex-Sultan of Sokoto, the Magaji of Keffi, and a few of the irreconcilable chiefs of Bida, Kano, and Sokoto, alone held out and refused to recognize the new power. The ex-Sultan announced that he was starting on a pilgrimage to Mecca, and called on the people to follow him, but he was obeyed only by a mob of unarmed peasants and some women.

[1] Died 1915. See Appendix A for genealogy of Sultans of Sokoto.
[2] His later conduct was satisfactory, and he reigned for many years.

G

Hustled eastwards by the garrisons from Sokoto and Zaria, he was pursued by troops from Kano and Bauchi as far as the town of Burmi, on the borders of Bornu, where he was received by a son of Mallam Jibrella, who had taken refuge there with the remnant of his father's followers after their defeat the previous year. Captain Sword, commanding the pursuing troops, immediately attacked the town, but having no gun to breach the wall he was repulsed with the loss of four men killed and two Europeans and sixty rank and file wounded. A large force was now organized, and in spite of a message from the ex-Sultan that he had no wish for further fighting, the people of Burmi made a determined resistance. The town was taken on July 27, 1903, with the loss of Major Marsh (commanding) and ten men killed, and three officers and sixty-nine men wounded; but the loss to the enemy was much more severe, amounting to at least 700 men killed, including the ex-Sultan, the Magaji of Keffi, and most of the other irreconcilable chiefs.

Later in the year a small party of soldiers and police, under the command of Captain O'Riordan, the Resident of Bassa Province, and Mr Amyatt-Burney, Police Officer, was attacked and massacred by the Okpotos, who were punished by a military expedition in 1904. In the same year the Emir of Katsena was deposed on account of his extortion and oppression of the people, and the Emir of Hadeija, who had shown a hostile attitude, was temporarily cowed by a show of force and the warnings of the loyal Emir of Kano. A typical instance of the loyal manner in which most of the Fulani chiefs accepted the British rule is given in one of the official reports. The High Commissioner had arrived at Katagum on a visit and summoned the neighbouring chiefs to meet him in durbar. The Emir of Katagum and the Chief of Gummel had presented themselves and taken the oath of allegiance, but the Emir of Hadeija, whose attitude was doubtful, did not at first appear. In the words of Lord Lugard, 'he, however, elected to come and make submission, and arrived on the morning of my departure with a great throng of horsemen in shirts of mail,[1] with spears and

---

[1] Chain armour is still worn by the horsemen of the Fulani chiefs on ceremonial occasions. Although some of the suits are, no doubt, modern imitations, a number are genuine, and were probably brought across the desert about the time of the Crusades.

swords. Meanwhile the Chiefs of Katagum and Gummel, who had been told to dismiss their 1,000 odd horsemen, fearing, perhaps, some ill intention on the part of Hadeija (many of whose chiefs and warriors bore a truculent and even insolent demeanour), had on their own accord stayed on, and to my surprise I found them drawn up in a great crescent formation beyond my own escort and the ranks of the garrison, as a threat on Hadeija's flank.'[1]

Early in 1906 a quarrel between some Hausa traders and the Jukon inhabitants of Abinsi developed into a battle, and the Jukons, getting the worst of it, called the Tiv tribe to their assistance. The Tivs attacked and overwhelmed the Hausas, carrying off a number as slaves, and then sacked and burned the Niger Company's store. A strong expedition was sent against them, to which the Tivs offered little resistance; but the Home Government would not permit the operations to be extended so as to open up the whole Tiv country, and the recall of the troops for action at Satiru prevented the accomplishment of much more than the release of the Hausa prisoners taken at Abinsi.

[1] *Report on Northern Nigeria, 1904*, para. 93 (Colonial Reports, Annual, No. 476).

CHAPTER XVI

THE PROTECTORATE OF NORTHERN
NIGERIA (*continued*)

Remember, Lord, the years of faith,
The spirits humbly brave,
The strength that died defying death,
The love that loved the slave.

H. NEWBOLT: *Hymn*

The Satiru incident of 1906 afforded fresh evidence of the loyalty of most of the Fulani rulers, men who had been in arms against the British only a few years before. In 1904 the chief of the village of Satiru, fourteen miles south of Sokoto, had proclaimed himself the Mahdi, but was arrested by the Sultan and died in prison before trial. His son was then sworn on the Koran to attempt no further sedition, but in 1906 Dan Mai-kafo, an outlaw from French territory, arrived at his village and persuaded him to lead a rising. Major Burdon,[1] the Resident, had already left Sokoto on his way down country in order to proceed on leave, and Mr Hillary, who was acting for him, sent a message after him with news of the reported rising and a police escort to take him through the danger zone. Major Burdon, however, attached no importance to the report, and did not consider it necessary to return to Sokoto. Mr Hillary, in the meantime, proceeded towards Satiru with a company of Mounted Infantry and, hoping to avert bloodshed, rode forward to the village in front of the troops, accompanied only by Mr Scott, the Assistant Resident, and an interpreter, shouting that he had come in peace and wished to talk with the leaders of the people. Lieutenant Blackwood, commanding the troops, thinking that the civil officers had advanced too far, brought up his men at the gallop and formed square, but as the Satiru people had begun to charge and the civil officers were still in advance of the square and in considerable danger, he attempted to move the square forward towards them. Before the square

[1] Afterwards Sir John Alder Burdon, KBE, CMG, Governor of British Honduras. Died 1933.

could reform properly the enemy, who had charged over 800 yards of ground, had broken into it. Hillary, Scott, Blackwood, and twenty-five soldiers fell in the mêlée that followed, Dr Ellis was severely wounded, and the only other Englishman present, Sergeant Gosling, was unable to rally the men, most of whom fled in panic. One soldier made a gallant attempt to save Mr Scott, and the same man helped Dr Ellis on to a horse and got him away in safety with Sergeant Gosling and a few men. Another soldier at great risk went back and rescued a comrade who had been unhorsed, and the African sergeant-major collected a few stragglers and retired to Sokoto in good order. The maxim, which had been left behind owing to the rapid advance of the square, was captured and taken to Satiru.

Sergeant Slack, who had been left at Sokoto with a gun, prepared to start for the scene with his detachment, but as the survivors arrived with the full tale of the disaster it became obvious that nothing could be accomplished with the small force available. The Sultan and his chiefs assembled their followers for the defence of Sokoto, and the principal war-chief led some 3,000 men against the rebels, but was easily defeated, his followers refusing to face fanatics who had overcome well-armed troops and killed three white officers. The situation was fraught with great danger. The followers of the Satiru chief were elated with success and promised themselves further crushing victories over the 'infidel'. The Emirs of Gando and Hadeija, never very loyal, were now openly hostile. Several other 'Mahdis' had arisen simultaneously in other parts of the Protectorate, and the main body of the troops was engaged against the Tivs. Above all things prompt action was necessary, and it was taken. The garrison at Hadeija could not be moved, but the garrisons of Zungeru[1] and Lokoja were at once dispatched towards Sokoto, and troops from Jega and Kontagora moved north to join them; the troops in the Tiv country were recalled and 250 men were sent from Lagos as a reserve. Major Burdon had returned to Sokoto as soon as he heard of the disaster and the loyal chiefs were co-operating with him in the defence of the town. The Governor-General of

---

[1] Zungeru became the headquarters of Northern Nigeria in 1902. In 1917 the headquarters of the Northern Provinces of Nigeria were moved to Kaduna, and Zungeru was practically abandoned.

the French Sudan offered assistance, which was not, luckily, required.

On March 10th, less than a month after their victory, the Satiru rebels were engaged by a force of 570 men, with thirty Europeans, a gun and several maxims, under the command of Major Goodwin. The rebel force, which numbered about 2,000, charged at once against the Mounted Infantry, who had advanced in front of the British line to draw them on; the Mounted Infantry immediately wheeled to the side, thus affording the infantry behind an opportunity to pour in a tremendous fire, which shattered the attack. In several desperate charges, and in hand-to-hand fighting in the village, the rebels fought with great gallantry, but at length they were forced to fly, pursued by the British troops and the Sokoto horsemen, who had not been allowed to take part in the main battle. The British casualties included three officers wounded; the enemy lost very heavily.

Six of the ringleaders were convicted by the Sokoto Native Court and condemned to death, the village of Satiru was destroyed, and the Sultan, as Sarkin Musulmi, pronounced a curse on anyone who should rebuild it or till its fields. The rebels —and it must not be forgotten that they were rebels against their own Sultan as well as against the British—had received severe punishment, but they had murdered those who would not join their forces and had destroyed a neighbouring village against which they bore a grudge. The troops from the Tiv country and from Lagos had not proved to be necessary, but the former accomplished a great feat in marching 312 miles in 12½ days, at the hottest time of the year and across very difficult and rugged country.

Throughout this critical period the loyalty of most of the chiefs and people was remarkable. The Emir of Nupe offered armed horsemen to assist, the troops from Jega were joined by 150 horsemen from the town of Tambawel, the chiefs from the towns around Sokoto came in to offer help, and from Ilorin to Yola the Emirs publicly demonstrated their loyalty, while the 'Mahdis' who had arisen in the other parts of the country were seized and executed by the native authorities. The old Emir of Gando had to be removed and replaced by someone more loyal, and an ultimatum was delivered to the Emir of Hadeija who, however, elected to fight. The British forces had possession of one of the gates of his town, and the troops entered and occupied the large open space within the walls; here they were charged by the Emir's mounted men, who were repulsed, and following some hours' street fighting, in which the townsmen suffered very heavily, the Emir and three of his sons were killed after a gallant stand against heavy odds in the citadel. A new Emir was at once installed, and by the next morning the market had reopened and the life of the city continued as though there had been no change.

With the successful action against the Satiru rebels and the defeat of Hadeija, the conquest of Northern Nigeria may be considered to have closed, and from this time there was no armed resistance from any of the great Muslim chiefs. From time to time small pagan tribes defied the Government and were punished by armed patrols, but such revolts were characterized less by a zeal for independence than by a desire to continue the habits of murder, robbery, and cannibalism,[1] which had become the second nature of these primitive people. There was also a not unnatural suspicion among these pagans of the good faith of the British. Accustomed for centuries to be raided for slaves, during the last hundred years they had been harried even more persistently and systematically by the Fulani, and had learned to retaliate on traders and others who were not protected by the Fulani troops. Whether the British would raid for slaves or not they could not tell, but they had found out by bitter experience that it was unwise to trust anyone stronger than themselves. Moreover, the British had taken up the wholly unreasonable attitude that the Fulani and Hausa traders, their old enemies and legitimate prey, were not to be murdered or robbed, and were actually establishing friendly relations with the Muslim Emirs. The savage distrusts anything that he cannot understand, and these strange white men were certainly beyond comprehension. In the first year of the Protectorate, 1900, six British officers were wounded in attacks made by pagans on surveying parties, whose curious

[1] Speaking of these tribes, Lord Lugard says: 'In one such case I received a reply that they had eaten every kind of man except a white man, and they invited me to come that they might see what I tasted like.' *The Dual Mandate,* p. 581.

instruments and mysterious actions were regarded with alarm. Year by year small military patrols had to be sent out to punish some outbreak of lawlessness. In 1904 the Montoils, Gurkawa, and Yergums were attacked. These tribes, after committing many other murders, killed and ate a Government messenger.[1] The following year the Lakai tribe killed and ate seven Yergums and enslaved others. The Yergums, who had been promised protection if they behaved themselves, appealed for aid, and the Lakais were punished. In 1906 the escort of a Resident, Major Sharpe, was attacked and the Resident himself severely wounded. The same year the Chibbuk clan of the Marghi tribe, who had for some time been robbing and murdering traders on the Bornu–Yola road, were attacked in their mountain fastnesses. For months, in spite of the fact that they were armed only with bows and poisoned arrows, they defied the troops in an extraordinary network of tunnels which penetrated the hills, and in the first attack, which lasted for eleven days, the British casualties amounted to ten men killed and two officers and forty men wounded. 'In most cases the arrows were shot at a range of from five to twenty yards through rocky apertures, from unseen foes, in passages to which daylight did not penetrate.'[2] The Chibbuks were finally subdued only through a systematic picketing of the hills and the accidental discovery of their water supply.

In 1908 the Dakkakerri tribe, who had robbed and murdered traders and fired on Political Officers, finally attacked a joint military and police patrol, killing Captain Briggs of the police and an African soldier with their poisoned arrows: they were defeated only after some hard fighting. In 1909 the Gwari town of Gussoro was punished for an attack on a small force of police, in which a Political Officer, Mr Vanrenen, and several constables were killed.

Every military expedition or patrol was accompanied by a responsible Political Officer, whose duty it was to get into touch with the people and endeavour to find a peaceful solution to whatever difficulty existed, or if this were impossible to bring hostilities to a close at the earliest opportunity and to see that

[1] As late as the year 1916 the Montoils killed and ate a British official.

[2] *Report on Northern Nigeria, 1906–7*, Part V (Colonial Reports, Annual, No. 551).

bloodshed was avoided if it could be done. In all cases the operations were carried out with great humanity and with comparatively little loss of life, the discipline of the troops ensuring that there was no indiscriminate slaughter.

Although military events loom large in the history of the first few years of the Northern Nigeria Protectorate, there was a considerable amount of work done on the civil side, in spite of the shortage of funds and the corresponding lack of an adequate staff. A grant from the Imperial Treasury to balance the annual deficit involved a control over the finances which seriously handicapped the young Administration, and many necessary and urgent works had inevitably to be postponed. In spite of this a great deal was accomplished.

One of the first laws of the Protectorate was the Slavery Proclamation, which abolished the legal status of slavery, prohibited slave-dealing, and declared all children born after April 1, 1901, to be free. The Proclamation did not make the holding of slaves illegal, the abolition of the legal status merely preventing a master from recovering a runaway slave through the medium of the Courts, and enabling a slave to leave his master and claim his freedom whenever he chose. It was not considered expedient to abolish domestic slavery at once, for had this been done a very serious problem would have arisen. The social scheme of the people would have been rudely shattered, slaves thrown on their own resources and deprived of the protection of their former masters would have starved or taken to brigandry, and the prosperity of the country would have been ruined by an arbitrary act, utterly incomprehensible at that time in Northern Nigeria and uncalled for by public opinion there. Although to many it may seem a disgrace that slavery in any form should have been tolerated for a moment in a British Protectorate, it cannot be too often repeated that on this point the European and the African at that period thought entirely differently.[1]

There were three principal reasons for the existence of slavery in Nigeria, namely, the total absence of free labour, the practical

---

[1] See *The Dual Mandate*, by Lord Lugard, p. 365. Zebehr Pasha admitted the evils of slavery, but pointed to the condition of the workers in British steam factories in the nineteenth century, and asked whether steam should be abolished on account of the evils existing in the factories.

absence of coin currency, and the need for a convenient form of transport. The demand for slaves for human sacrifices or as eunuchs need not be considered; the priests and chiefs would not have hesitated to take free men for these purposes had slavery not existed. Where the requirements of everyday life are very primitive and the means of satisfying them easily obtained, there is no need for one man to work for another; enough need only be done to provide the necessaries of life for the immediate family of the worker, and where no luxuries can be obtained there is no incentive to work for a wage. Such was the point of view of the savage who inhabited the fastnesses of mountain and forest, who worked how and when he pleased, for himself and his family, and for no one else except under compulsion. In the more open and fertile country there was enough land for all, and each peasant cultivated his own small patch and provided for his own simple wants without any necessity to earn a wage. The chiefs and rich Africans, on the other hand, needed labour to cultivate their farms and to perform the daily work of their households and, no free labour existing, they could see no alternative to slavery.[1] Slaves, again, provided the currency that was not otherwise available and, being mobile, soon became the principal medium of exchange, the rich man amassing slaves as his European counterpart amasses money. Lastly, the prevalence of the tsetse fly, which makes animal transport impossible in large sections of Nigeria, and the absence of any form of wheeled traffic until comparatively recently, made it necessary to employ carriers for the conveyance of merchandise.

It must be borne in mind that, although the European nations were entirely responsible for the oversea slave-traffic and encouraged the evils of slave-raiding, they did not introduce slavery to the innocent African, nor did the cessation of the export of slaves put a stop to the traffic. Domestic slavery

[1] It is, however, an economic fact that paid labour is more productive than slave labour. This was clearly proved in Zanzibar, where it was found that plantations worked by free labour did better than those which employed slaves so much so that 'the Arab clove-owners started a new policy. They paid their slaves, whether formally freed or not, in cash for every day's work done by them during the clove-picking season, thus stimulating their efficiency as workmen and compensating themselves for the outlay involved in the payment of their wages.' See *A Diplomatist in the East* (1928), by Sir Arthur Hardinge, p. 207.

is an old and well-organized institution in Africa, and the enslavement of prisoners-of-war and the selling of malefactors had probably existed for ages before the first Europeans visited Nigeria.[1] In a country where the patriarchal system is well established and the powers of the head of the family are practically unlimited, the position of a slave was not so very different from that of a free man, and the slaves were on the whole well treated.[2] Public opinion, and in those parts where Islam held sway, even religion, secured fair treatment for a slave,[3] who might, moreover, rise to a position of great influence, acquire wealth, and himself become the owner of slaves.

As a matter of fact, were it not for the attendant evil of slave-raiding, there would not be much to say against slavery as it existed in Northern Nigeria[4] at the beginning of the British occupation, except that it was repugnant to our ideals. But slave-raiding was a very different affair. In 1901 the High Commissioner wrote as follows:

There is, probably, no part of the 'Dark Continent' in which the worst forms of slave-raiding still exist to so terrible an extent, and are prosecuted on so large and systematic a scale, as in the

[1] One writer, endeavouring to justify the oversea slave-trade, tried to prove that the prisoner and malefactor would not have escaped death but for it. ' . . . tho' to traffick in human creatures may at first sight appear barbarous; inhuman, and unnatural; yet the Traders herein have as much to plead in their Excuse, as can be said for some other Branches of Trade, namely, the *Advantage* of it: And that not only in regard of the Merchants, but also of the Slaves themselves, as will plainly appear from these following Reasons.' The reasons given are that captives taken in war would be slain if they could not be disposed of to European dealers, and that criminals sold to Europeans are 'transported never to return again; a Benefit which we very much want here'. See *A New Account of Some Parts of Guinea and the Slave Trade*, by Captain William Snelgrave, London (1734), pp. 160–1. See also Captain Crow: 'It has always been my decided opinion that the traffic in negroes is permitted by that Providence that rules over all, as a necessary evil.' *Memoirs*, p. 132.

[2] 'Everywhere in the Moslem East the slave holds himself superior to the menial freeman, a fact that I would impress upon the several Anti-Slavery Societies, honest men whose zeal mostly exceeds their knowledge, and whose energy their discretion.' Sir Richard Burton in a note in the *Arabian Nights*.

[3] By Muhammadan law an owner is bound to provide for his slave, and a slave may be freed by judicial authority on the grounds of ill-treatment by his owner.

[4] In Southern Nigeria, where human sacrifice and cannibalism were practised, the situation was entirely different.

British Protectorate of Northern Nigeria. Each year, as the grass dries up, armies take the field to collect slaves. Nor are they even provident of their hunting-grounds, for those who are useless as slaves are killed in large numbers, the villages burnt, and the fugitives left to starve in the bush . . . the country is depopulated and hundreds of ruins attest the former existence of a population and a prosperity which have gone.[1]

Further testimony to the effects of slave-raiding is supplied by Sir Charles Orr:

Perpetual slave-raids and internecine wars, with their concomitant miseries, were the established order of things; the strong preyed upon the weak; whole towns were blotted out in intertribal warfare, the inhabitants being either killed or carried off into slavery, and it is one of the commonest sights in African travel to come across the crumbling walls of some deserted town which only a few years before had been the home of a thriving community.[2]

And again:

It is impossible for any one who has not travelled through and lived in districts in Central Africa which have suffered from slave-raids and internecine war to realize the conditions to which they can be reduced by these means. One may travel for miles over fertile plains and see nothing but weeds and scrub growing up, with every now and then the ruins of some farmstead or village, forming a pathetic indication of the population which once called these crumbling walls their home.[3]

These evils had to be, and were, removed at once, but the abolition of domestic slavery was only gradual.

For this policy there were serious practical reasons. To have given monetary compensation to the owners, had all the slaves been freed, would have been beyond the financial power of the Protectorate, and would have been a serious matter even for the Imperial Treasury. Had the slaves been liberated without compensation there would have been brought into active opposition to the Government even the best and most enlightened Africans, who had acquired the only form of wealth known to them, in good faith and with never a thought that they were doing anything wrong. Indeed, if a Muhammadan, the slave-owner had the sanction of his religion, which recognized and

[1] *Report on Northern Nigeria for the Period 1st January, 1900, to 31st March, 1901* (Colonial Reports, Annual, No. 346).

[2] Orr, *op. cit.*, p. 48.   [3] *Ibid.*, p. 113.

permitted the ownership of slaves and, especially in the Fulani Emirates, a considerable army would have been required to enforce a law providing for the immediate abolition of slavery.

In any case, a great deal was accomplished. Of those who were slaves before April 1, 1901, many were voluntarily freed by their masters and many more, who could prove oppression by their owners or could purchase their freedom, were set free by the Courts.[1] Homes for freed slaves were established and maintained by the Government for some years, being finally handed over to a missionary society.

In 1904 a serious famine occurred throughout the greater part of the Protectorate, especially in Yola and Bauchi, and considerable assistance was given to the starving people by the Government. So serious was the shortage of food that the pagan inhabitants sold their children in large numbers to secure food for themselves and, perhaps, to ensure that the children should not die of starvation; it was reported that the price of a child varied from 1s. 6d. to 2s.[2]

It was, however, to the developing and improving of the administration that the energies of the Government were at first mainly directed. When the Protectorate was inaugurated in 1900 the territory under control consisted only of Borgu, which had been occupied by the West African Frontier Force at the time of the French boundary crisis and had since been administered by the military, Ilorin, and Kabba, which had been subdued by the Royal Niger Company, and the actual banks of the navigable rivers. None of the Niger Company's posts had been established more than fifty miles from the Niger or Benue, and their authority in the Fulani empire and Bornu was merely nominal. As the country was opened up by military force British officials were stationed at the capitals of the different states as Residents, and the Protectorate was divided

[1] 37,998 slaves were recorded as having been freed by the Courts between 1900 and 1914, and this 'is, of course, very far from including all who have been liberated, since large numbers were, no doubt, omitted from the records of the native Courts, especially in the earlier years, when these were very imperfect; and very many (probably many thousands) were at that time set free or left their masters without the knowledge of Government, as the result of the conquest of each Emirate'. *Report on Nigeria for 1914* (Colonial Reports, Annual, No. 878).

[2] Lady Lugard, *op. cit.*, p. 259. There was another serious famine in 1914.

into a number of provinces, the Resident of each being responsible to the High Commissioner at headquarters. As the administration became more developed some of these provinces were
amalgamated into larger units, some of the old names dis-
appearing in the amalgamation or being changed. The provinces of the Middle Niger, Upper Benue, and Lower Benue
ceased to exist at an early date; Borgu was included first in
Kontagora and later in Ilorin, Bassa in Munshi, and Katagum
in Kano. But throughout the history of the Protectorate, in
spite of the changes in the names and areas of the administrative divisions, the policy of the Government remained the same.
This was to support the African rulers, their councils and their
Courts, their customs and their traditions, so long as these were
not repugnant to British ideals of humanity and justice. Advantage was taken of the intelligence and governing ability of
the Fulani chiefs, and they were retained as a class in the
positions which they had won before the arrival of the British.
Checked by the close supervision of European officials from
relapsing into the tyranny and cruelties of their predecessors,
they have proved themselves capable of ruling the people in a
just and enlightened manner. The British Resident and his
assistants acted as advisers to the native administration,[1]
the two forming a single Government, of which the British
and African officials were complementary to one another,
working and co-operating for the common good.

The abuses which had crept in and ruined the Fulani empire
in its later years were removed, fief-holders were compelled to
live in their districts and look after them or surrender their sine-
cures, the Courts of Justice were reorganized and a check was
put to the bribery of the judges, and the multitude of arbitrary
and illegal taxes were swept away and replaced by a single
tax based on a personal assessment by the Resident and his
staff. As the organization progressed each native administration was provided with its own treasury, locally known as *Beit-
el-Mal*, budgets were properly prepared, and all officials from
the Emir downwards were placed on fixed salaries.[2] A propor-

---

[1] This is the system of government generally known as 'Indirect Rule'.

[2] The Sultan of Sokoto, the Emir of Kano, and the Shehu of Bornu
received each a salary of £6,000 a year, in addition to an establishment
allowance of £3,000 a year to the Sultan and £1,500 a year to the others.

tion of the tax was assigned to the native administration, the balance being paid to the Protectorate Government, but the collection was invariably left to the native administration.[1]

'The most serious obstacle experienced in Nigeria when the tax was inaugurated was the difficulty of suppressing personation. A credulous and illiterate people, long accustomed to oppression, were easily victimized by any scoundrel who, producing an old envelope picked up in a deserted camp, or even a piece of newspaper, as his credentials, would declare himself to be the authorized emissary of the Government and demand what he chose. If the villagers demurred he would threaten their extermination by Government, or bring lying accusations of disaffection'.[2] These people would demand food and lodging for months, obtaining from the terrified villagers all sorts of property, and even their wives and daughters.[3] Two trusted African Political Agents were convicted in 1902 of acquiring slaves illegally in the name of the Government; in addition to those disposed of before they were arrested, one was found to have sixty-five slaves and the other thirty, and these, mostly girls, had been obtained either on the statement that the Resident wanted them or by threats of false reports which, so it was represented, would involve terrible punishments.[4] It was only by the constant touring of the Administrative Officers that the crime of impersonation could be kept in check, a crime productive of considerable suffering to the people and danger to the Government, which incurred much undeserved odium on account of the rapacity of the scoundrels who alleged that they were acting in its name.

In those parts of the country where there was no strong central authority, chiefly on the Bauchi plateau and along the valley of the Benue, where the small pagan tribes were situated, it was, of course, impossible to govern on the lines adopted in the more advanced Muhammadan states. The rule of the Administrative Officer here became more direct, but efforts were made to build up among these primitive people

[1] The Native Treasuries later received the whole tax.
[2] Lord Lugard. *The Dual Mandate*, p. 252.
[3] *Report on Northern Nigeria, 1900–1* (Colonial Reports, Annual, No. 346).
[4] *Report on Northern Nigeria, 1902*, para. 71 (Colonial Reports, Annual, No. 409).

some idea of the meaning of responsibility and to support the power of any influential head-man who showed a capacity to rule.

One of the main obstacles to the effective pacification and administration of the Protectorate was the difficulty of transportation away from the navigable rivers. For this reason the capital was originally established at Lokoja, and a site was selected at Quendon, some thirty miles below the confluence of the Niger and Benue, but in January 1900 it was transferred to Jebba. In September 1902 it was possible to move headquarters to a more central position at Zungeru, a light railway being constructed to connect that town with Barijuko, the highest navigable point on the Kaduna river. Rough roads were driven in all directions, rocks and 'snags' on the Niger were blown up or buoyed, and an unsuccessful attempt was made (in 1909) to dredge some of the shallow crossings on the river.

In 1906 Sir Frederick Lugard resigned his appointment as High Commissioner of Northern Nigeria,[1] and was succeeded by Sir Percy Girouard,[2] a former officer of the Royal Engineers, with considerable railway experience. Under his supervision the construction was begun in January 1908 of a railway from Baro, on the Niger, which reached Kano, 350 miles away, in March 1911. The Lagos railway was extended northwards to join this line at Minna, and a light railway was constructed from Zaria, on the main line, to the Bauchi plateau.

In 1908 the title of High Commissioner was abolished, and Sir Percy Girouard became the first Governor of Northern Nigeria. In 1909 he was succeeded by Sir Hesketh Bell,[3] and he was in his turn succeeded by Sir Frederick Lugard, who in 1912 was appointed simultaneously Governor of both Northern and Southern Nigeria. On January 1, 1914, the Protectorate of Northern Nigeria was amalgamated with the Colony and Protectorate of Southern Nigeria as a single Government under

---

[1] Sir Frederick Lugard was appointed Governor of Hong Kong in 1907.

[2] Born 1867; died 1932. Sir Percy Girouard had been Director of Soudan Railways and President of the Egyptian Railway Board from 1896 to 1899, and Director of Railways in South Africa from 1899 to 1904. He was Governor of British East Africa from 1909 to 1912.

[3] Born 1864. Governor of Uganda 1905–9; of the Leeward Islands 1912–15; of Mauritius 1915–24. Died 1952.

the control of Sir Frederick Lugard as Governor-General.[1] In 1900 an unsubdued and undeveloped country had been taken over from the Royal Niger Company, and in the fourteen years of its existence it had changed from a land of cruel despotisms and savage warfare into a peaceful British Protectorate of great promise, inhabited for the most part by a contented and industrious people. The man who was mainly responsible for this improvement was Sir Frederick Lugard.

[1] This title was personal to Sir Frederick Lugard; his successors until 1954 bore the title of Governor.

CHAPTER XVII

THE LAGOS AND SOUTHERN NIGERIA PROTECTORATES

Nation shall not lift up sword against nation, neither shall they learn war any more.

ISAIAH ii. 4

In Yorubaland, meanwhile, British influence was being steadily extended. We have seen that arbitrators appointed by the Governor of Lagos had succeeded in 1886 in bringing to a close the internecine strife that had raged intermittently among the Yoruba tribes for half a century. In 1889 an attempt was made to arrange a peace between the Fulani of Ilorin and the Ibadans, but a European officer who was sent up to negotiate was not even allowed to reach the Ilorin camp. The same year, however, Major Macdonald[1] visited Ilorin from the Niger, and the Emir undertook to withdraw his army if the Ibadans would withdraw theirs, but mutual distrust prevented anything being done.

The time had now arrived when the British Government was to take control of the Yoruba country. In 1888 the report that French emissaries were endeavouring to conclude a treaty with the Egbas occasioned some anxiety at Lagos, and in order to prevent the hinterland of the Colony falling into alien hands a treaty was signed with the Alafin of Oyo by which the whole of Yorubaland was placed under British protection.

The Egbados, who occupied the south-west corner of Yorubaland, had been conquered by the Egbas when the latter were driven south about the year 1830, and had ever since been forced to pay tribute to their conquerors. Oppressed by the Egbas and raided by the Dahomey armies, they appealed to the Lagos Government for protection, which was not, however, afforded them until the fear of the establishment of a French Protectorate induced the British to extend their frontiers. The British flag was hoisted at Ilaro and Oke Odan in 1891, with

[1] Afterwards Sir Claude Macdonald, Commissioner and Consul-General, Niger Coast Protectorate.

the full consent of the Egbados, but to the intense indignation of the Egba chiefs, who threatened to attack Ilaro. To meet this danger a garrison was thrown into Ilaro, and the Egbas replied by blocking the trade routes to Lagos, refusing all offers for negotiation. Not long afterwards the Ijebus closed the trade routes through their country, denying to the Oyos and Ibadans any access to the sea. Peaceful overtures from the Lagos Government were disregarded, and the acting Governor was treated with scant courtesy when he endeavoured personally to negotiate. Towards the end of 1891 Mr G. T. Carter,[1] the newly appointed Governor, arrived in Lagos, and negotiations were reopened. The Ijebu authorities were required to apologize for the insult to the acting Governor, and they agreed to open the trade routes and abolish human sacrifices, a treaty to this effect being signed, the Lagos Government binding itself to an annual payment in lieu of the tolls hitherto received by the Ijebus.

There was never any intention of abiding by the treaty, and very soon the Ijebus made this manifest, all trade being brought to a standstill. An ultimatum was ignored, and on May 13, 1892 an expedition left Lagos and landed at Epe. The force, which was under the command of Colonel F. C. Scott, CB, of the Gold Coast Constabulary, consisted of a company of the West India Regiment, about 150 Hausas of the Gold Coast Force, a similar number of the Lagos Constabulary, and about 100 Ibadan auxiliaries. The only serious resistance met with was at a river, where the Ijebus were strongly posted; but they were shelled out of their position and on May 20th Ijebu Ode was entered. The British casualties consisted of an African officer[2] and three men killed, and three European officers and twenty-five men wounded. The Awujale (king) was found in Ijebu Ode with a few of his followers, most of the people having fled. There was little doubt that he was opposed to the war party which insisted on fighting the British, and he was therefore allowed to retain his position, a garrison and a

[1] Afterwards Sir Gilbert Carter, Governor of the Bahamas and Barbados. Born 1848; died 1927.

[2] This officer belonged to the well-known Willoughby family, of which several generations have served the Government in Lagos with loyalty and ability.

British Resident being left to preserve order. The Egbas, who had sympathized with the Ijebus, and had even offered them military aid, now tendered their submission to the Lagos Government and removed all restrictions on trade.

Early in 1893 Governor Carter, with an escort of Hausas, proceeded to Abeokuta, and there a treaty was signed providing for freedom of trade through the Egba territories and guaranteeing the independence of Egbaland.[1] The Governor next visited Oyo, where he was well received and a treaty was signed, and thence proceeded to Ilorin and obtained from the Emir assurances of friendship. The Governor's party then took up a position between the Ilorin and Ibadan camps, and after some negotiations with the leaders on either side the rival armies were persuaded to withdraw. The Governor now travelled to Ibadan, but he was unable to get the chiefs of that town to sign a treaty or to agree to receive a British Resident, and this was the only disappointment he suffered in his progress through the country. However, a few months later the Ibadan chiefs reconsidered the matter and asked that the question should again be opened; the acting Governor proceeded to Ibadan, and a treaty was duly signed. Soon afterwards Captain R. L. Bower was appointed Resident and Travelling Commissioner, and with a company of the Lagos Constabulary he established his headquarters at Ibadan.

The Alafin of Oyo, who regarded the rising power of Ibadan and his own consequent loss of prestige with jealous eyes, had long secretly sympathized with the Emir of Ilorin, with whom it is alleged he had been conspiring against Ibadan. British interference now seemed to be robbing him of the last remains of his dwindling power, and his attitude to the authorities was not a friendly one. In 1895 he was involved in some intrigues which resulted in trouble at the town of Okeho, and a man accused of having intercourse with one of the wives of a provincial 'king' was sent to Oyo, and there made into a eunuch by order of the Alafin. Captain Bower proceeded to Oyo with about sixty soldiers to demand an explanation, and an unsatisfactory meeting was held. Next morning Captain Bower and

[1] See Appendix K. In 1904 a Judical Agreement was signed, giving the British Courts jurisdiction in cases affecting non-natives in Egbaland. Similar agreements were made with Oyo, Ibadan, Ife, and Ijebu.

his men were waiting for a further interview, when they were suddenly attacked by a large crowd armed with guns and cut-lasses; a few shots were fired which cooled the ardour of the mob, which finally dispersed through the persuasions of a Roman Catholic missionary. Captain Bower demanded an apology from the Alafin, and asked that certain persons should be delivered to him for trial within two days. Guns were sent for from Ibadan, and, as the terms were not complied with, Oyo was bombarded. The troops then entered the town, and under a heavy fire destroyed the Alafin's palace and the houses of his chiefs. The same day the chiefs sent to Captain Bower some 'ducks with their wing-feathers cut in token of submission'. A few months later the Governor visited Oyo and received the submission of the Alafin, coupled with a full apology for the attack on Captain Bower, and a garrison was retained temporarily at Oyo.

In the meantime the Emir of Ilorin, with whom friendly rela-tions had been established, had been killed, and his successor was bitterly hostile to the British authorities, who had asso-ciated themselves with Ibadan, and whose military detach-ments on the northern frontier of Yorubaland interfered with his slave-raiding habits. All attempts at negotiations having been repulsed, the roads from Ilorin southwards were block-aded, in the hope that the loss of trade would bring the Emir to reason. This, however, was not the case. In March and April 1896 surprise attacks were made by Ilorin warriors on the town of Odo Otin, which was garrisoned by the Lagos Constabulary. The attacks were driven off, and in January 1897 a similar attack was repulsed by a small outpost party under an African sergeant-major. The blockade had in the meantime been raised at the request of the Lagos merchants, and in February 1897 Ilorin was attacked and captured by the forces of the Royal Niger Company, as described in Chapter XIII.

The whole of Yorubaland was now under control and attached as a Protectorate to the Colony of Lagos. The cessa-tion of civil war resulted in an immediate increase in the pros-perity of the people, and this was reflected in a marked degree in Lagos which, as the capital and port of the Colony, rapidly gained in importance. The streets of Lagos were first lit by electricity in 1898, and two years later the bridges between

Lagos and Iddo islands (Carter Bridge, 2,600 feet) and Iddo and the mainland (Denton Bridge, 917 feet)[1] were completed. The railway from Lagos to Ibadan was opened in 1900, construction having begun in 1896. A considerable amount of swamp on Lagos island was reclaimed, in some cases by offering swamp land to private individuals on condition that the swamp should be filled up to a certain level, but for the most part by the Government. A canal was also cut through the island to drain the swamp area between the town and Ikoyi; this is known as the MacGregor Canal,[2] and is much used by canoes.

Meanwhile considerable political changes were taking place in the country to the east of the Lagos Protectorate. On April 1, 1899 the Foreign Office handed over to the Colonial Office the control of the Niger Coast Protectorate, and on January 1, 1900 this territory was renamed the Southern Nigeria Protectorate, the delta of the Niger and the land on either bank of the river as far north as Idah being included. This addition coincided with the cancellation of the Royal Niger Company's Charter and the establishment of the Protectorate of Northern Nigeria. The titles of 'Consul-General' and 'Consul' were abolished, a High Commissioner being appointed to Southern Nigeria with Commissioners under him.

The new administration was soon faced with the problem of slavery. The Slave-Dealing Proclamation of 1901 made the offence penal, but the same year saw the legalizing of a curious local institution known as 'House Rule'. It was thought that 'the advantages and . . . the guarantees afforded by it for the thrifty management of property and the resulting absence of pauperism among the lower social grades of the natives' justified the Government in strengthening the 'quasi-parental authority of the Representatives of "Houses"'.[3] 'House' was defined in the law as a group of persons subject by native law

---

[1] Carter Bridge was rebuilt in 1931, and Denton Bridge was replaced by a causeway.

[2] After the Governor, Sir William MacGregor (1899–1904).

[3] *Report on Southern Nigeria for 1901* (Colonial Reports, Annual, No. 381, Cd. 1388). Dr Dike, writing of it as it existed before 1885, says that 'if house rule may be judged from its practical results, on the whole it met the needs of the day'. Dike, *op. cit.*, p. 36.

and custom to the control, authority and rule of a chief, known as the 'Head of the House', and the preamble ran as follows:

Whereas it is expedient for the preservation of peace and good order in the Protectorate to make provision for the maintenance of the authorities vested in the Heads of Houses by native law and custom.

The law laid down that every member of the 'House' should be subject to the native law and custom relating to 'Houses' (so long as this was not repugnant to natural justice), that runaway members of 'Houses' might be arrested and restored, and that no one might employ a member without the consent of the 'Head of the House'. The duty of the 'Head' to look after and provide for the interests of the members of the 'House' was also expressly stated. This institution differed little, except in name, from that of slavery, and in fact was a legalized form of slavery which gave to the 'Heads of Houses' far more power than was left to the slave-owners of Northern Nigeria. This anomaly was not done away with until 1914, when the House Rule Proclamation was repealed, in spite of the protests of some of the chiefs who complained that their influence was being undermined.

With slave-dealing, however, the Government would allow no compromise, and it was necessary in 1902 to attack the powerful Aro tribe, which was still unsubdued. This tribe exerted a tremendous influence over a vast extent of country between the Niger and the Cross rivers owing to their control of an important oracle (the Long Juju) at Aro Chuku. The Aros were not a military race, but owed their power to their relatively great intelligence as compared with the neighbouring tribes; they seldom fought themselves, but dealt with their enemies by sending against them the warlike tribes under their influence, recompensing their mercenaries with the loot obtained from their vanquished foes.

No dispute could be settled save by reference to the oracle. . . . Each of the contending parties attempted to propitiate this oracle by large offerings, and the party against whom judgment was pronounced was believed by his tribe to have been destroyed by the hidden power, while, in reality, he was almost invariably sold secretly into slavery.[1]

[1] *Report on Southern Nigeria for 1902* (Colonial Reports, Annual, No. 405).

As the Aros refused to abandon these practices, a strong expedition, to which contingents from Lagos and Northern Nigeria were attached, marched to Aro Chuku in converging columns and overcame all resistance. The Aros gave fresh indication of their intelligence by immediately accepting the new conditions and taking advantage of the increased trade caused by the opening up of their country.

There now remained no single tribe of any importance which was not under control, but much remained to be done before the country could be pacified. The small tribes on either bank of the Cross river, and the various clans of the Ibo tribe which inhabited the wild forest country to the east of the Niger, continued to give sporadic trouble, and numerous small expeditions were necessary to put a stop to inter-tribal fighting or to avenge the murder of and assaults on officials. In 1905 a Medical Officer, Dr Stewart, while travelling in the country to the east of Onitsha, lost his way and wandered into a hostile village, where he was killed and eaten; a strong expedition inflicted the necessary punishment after some severe fighting. In 1906 Mr Crewe-Read, an Assistant District Commissioner, was murdered at Owa; the town was captured after a stubborn resistance. The same year saw the punishment of the Kwale tribe, which a few months before had defeated a small force of troops sent against it.

On May 1, 1906 the Colony of Lagos and its protected territory were amalgamated with the Protectorate of Southern Nigeria under one administration, and designated the Colony and Protectorate of Southern Nigeria, with Lagos as the seat of Government. The first Governor was Sir Walter Egerton, who had been appointed to the double post of Governor of Lagos and High Commissioner of Southern Nigeria in 1904, in order that he might arrange for the amalgamation. The country was divided into three provinces, Western, Central, and Eastern, under Provincial Commissioners, Warri being the headquarters of the Central Province and Calabar of the Eastern.

The next few years were spent in building up a system of communications. In 1907 the great work was begun of making the harbour of Lagos accessible to ocean-going vessels by the construction of moles on either side of the entrance and the dredging of the sandbar which caused an obstruction at the mouth, preventing steamers drawing more than nine feet from entering the port. Today large vessels can enter and lie along-side the wharves, but until 1914 all cargo for Lagos was taken to Forcados, and brought from there to Lagos in small 'branch boats'. The railway from Lagos to Ibadan was pushed on to join the Northern Nigerian Railway at Minna, trains being ferried across the Niger at Jebba until the completion of the railway bridge in 1916. Broad main roads, which remain today as monuments to Sir Walter Egerton's progressive policy, were driven in all directions, and telegraph lines were constructed between important centres. The influence of these public works on the African population was very great. Apart from the civilizing effect of easier communication, there was a marked increase in trade and in the circulation of coin. Thou-sands worked for the Government, and were paid in money with which they were able to purchase for themselves both necessaries and luxuries, returning to their villages to boast of their adventures and to show off their recently acquired finery to their less sophisticated brothers. There is no doubt that this free labour, which became increasingly popular, did a great deal towards the suppression of slavery and the improvement of trade.

It had long been foreseen that the eventual amalgamation of Northern and Southern Nigeria was inevitable, and with a view to this Sir Frederick Lugard was appointed in 1912 Gover-nor of both Administrations. It is important to remember that, save in Lagos, which became a Colony in 1862, there was no real Government in Nigeria till 1885; in fifteen years between 1885 and 1900 the Government was divided between three different groups of officials, responsible respectively to the Colonial Office, the Foreign Office, and the Directors of the Royal Niger Company. Each Administration settled its prob-lems independently and on its own lines, and mutual support was not easily arranged for. To the inhabitants the three Ad-ministrations, each professing to represent the almost mythical Queen of England, must have been puzzling and, in the case of the Brassmen, extremely irritating. However, in spite of different methods, each Government exercised towards the ever-present problems of slave-dealing and internecine war the same deliberate and unrelenting hostility, and the result affords the best justification for their existence. In 1900, when the Royal Niger Company as a governing body disappeared, there still remained three Administrations, reduced in 1906 to two, and now at last to be made into a single entity. A beginning was made in 1913 by the union of some of the important departments, such as the Railway and the Customs, and on January 1, 1914 the Colony and Protectorate of Nigeria was formally inaugurated under the authority of Royal Letters Patent and Orders in Council.

CHAPTER XVIII

THE COLONY AND PROTECTORATE
OF NIGERIA

Sons of the Island Race, wherever ye dwell,
Who speak of your fathers' battles with lips that burn,
The deeds of an alien legion hear me tell.

H. NEWBOLT: *The Guides at Cabul*

The Letters Patent and Order in Council which set up the
Colony and Protectorate of Nigeria with effect from January 1, 1914, divided the country, for purposes of administration, into three main portions, the Colony of Nigeria[1] and two
groups of Provinces, known as the Northern and Southern Provinces, which together formed the Protectorate.[2] (On April
1, 1939, the Southern Provinces were divided into two groups,
known respectively as the Western and Eastern Provinces.)

The Colony was practically identical with the former
Colony of Lagos, and the Northern and Southern Provinces
with the Protectorates of Northern and Southern Nigeria

---

[1] Boundaries defined by the Colony of Nigeria Boundaries Order in
Council, 1913, dated November 22, 1913.

[2] There is no statutory or authoritative definition of the term 'Protectorate'. Protectorates are not British territory in the strict sense but it is
understood that no other Power will interfere in their affairs. They are
administered under the provisions of the Orders in Council issued by
virtue of the powers conferred upon the Crown by the Foreign Jurisdiction
Act, 1890, 'or otherwise vested in Her Majesty', which latter phrase may be
taken to be intended to bring in aid any exercise of the Royal prerogative
that may be necessary to supplement the Crown's statutory powers. The
preamble to the Order in Council 'providing for the exercise of His Majesty's
jurisdiction in the Protectorate of Nigeria' ran as follows:

'Whereas by the Foreign Jurisdiction Act, 1890, it is, among other things,
enacted that it shall be lawful for His Majesty the King to hold, exercise,
and enjoy any jurisdiction which His Majesty now has or may at any time
hereafter have with a foreign country in the same and as ample a manner as
if His Majesty had acquired that jurisdiction by the cession or conquest of
territory:

'And whereas by treaty, grant, usage, sufferance and other lawful means
His Majesty has power and jurisdiction within the territories known as the
Protectorate of Nigeria. . . . '

respectively. Although outwardly and in practice there was little to distinguish the Colony from the Protectorate, there was in law a considerable difference. Natives of the Colony, for instance, were British subjects while natives of the Protectorate were 'British-protected persons'. The Colony of Nigeria was a part of the dominions of the Sovereign: the Protectorate was, as it were, an appendage to those dominions.

An Administrator was placed in immediate control of the Colony,[1] and the Northern Provinces and Southern Provinces were each placed under the control of a Lieutenant-Governor; these officers were all responsible to the Governor.[2] After a few years the title of Lieutenant-Governor was for a while changed to that of Chief Commissioner, but the former title was later restored. An Executive Council, consisting of the Chief Secretary to the Government[3] and other senior officials served as an advisory body to the Governor, and, should the Governor decide to act contrary to the advice of a majority of the Council in any matter, he was bound to report the circumstances to the Secretary of State for the Colonies. A larger advisory and deliberative body, known as the Nigerian Council, was established at the amalgamation; it was composed of the Governor, the members of the Executive Council, the Senior Residents,[4] and a number of unofficial members, both African and European, nominated by the Governor. This Council was devised to afford an opportunity for the expression of public opinion, but it possessed no power over the legislation or the finances of the country, and merely afforded an opportunity for the Governor, in his address at the annual meeting, 'to give a summary of matters of interest during the past year, to review and forecast the position of

[1] Mr, afterwards Sir Frederick Seton, James, was appointed Administrator. After his transfer in 1916 to the Straits Settlements, no separate appointment to the post was made until 1927, the Lieutenant-Governor of the Southern Provinces holding in addition the office of Administrator of the Colony. The post of Administrator was later abolished.

[2] Sir Frederick Lugard had the personal title of Governor-General.

[3] This office was created on the January 1, 1921, the former post of Central Secretary being abolished.

[4] Each of the Provinces, and for a few years the Colony, was placed under the immediate control of a Resident, styled at first, in the Southern Provinces, Provincial Commissioner.

trade and finance, and to emphasize and explain any questions of policy and legislation of importance'.[1] The Nigerian Council was abolished in 1922. There was, in addition, a small Legislative Council for the Colony, composed of the Governor and certain officials, with four unofficial members nominated by the Governor, two of these being, as a rule, Africans. The attention of this Legislative Council was confined rigidly to the Colony, the Protectorate being entirely beyond its purview. Laws affecting the Colony were passed 'with the advice and consent of the Legislative Council,' which was also allowed to scrutinize the estimates of expenditure for purely Colony services; there was at all times an official majority on the Council. This Council, like the Nigerian Council, was abolished in 1922, its place being taken by a larger and more representative body, which will be referred to later.

The months that followed the amalgamation of Northern and Southern Nigeria were occupied in adjusting the differences that existed between the two Administrations, between which there were wide divergencies of policy, law, and systems of government, and negotiations were carried on with the State of Egba in order to put an end to its anomalous position as an independent enclave within the British Protectorate. The treaty of 1893 had expressly recognized the independence of Egbaland, and the Government of that State had established a fiscal frontier and collected customs duties on certain articles. The government was conducted in the name of the Alake of Abeokuta by a bureaucracy which strove to imitate the methods of British colonial administration, but was unable to eradicate bribery in the Courts and extortion from the peasantry. In 1912 and 1913 there had been risings at Abeokuta against the Egba Government and in response to appeals for help troops were sent from Lagos to restore order.[2] A riot ensued, in which there was some loss of life. The employment of Government forces for the suppression of revolts, the real reasons for which were unknown to the British authorities, was very unsatisfactory, as it might have resulted in the support of a rule which was causing great suffering and

---

[1] *Report by Sir F. D.* (later Lord) *Lugard on the Amalgamation of Northern and Southern Nigeria and Administration, 1912–19* (Cmd. 468, 1920), p. 19.

[2] Similar help had been given in 1898 and 1901.

reasonable discontent among the people. In these circumstances the Nigerian Government suggested to the Alake and his chiefs that the treaty should be annulled, and this was agreed to, Egbaland being placed on September 16, 1914 'unreservedly under the Government of the Protectorate of Nigeria'.[1]

The outbreak of the war with Germany in August 1914 so soon after the inauguration of the new Administration, was particularly unfortunate for Nigeria. Construction work on a new railway from Port Harcourt to the interior had been begun, but it was impossible to carry on with the entire scheme, which was reduced to a line of 151 miles to the coal-fields of Udi. The trade with Germany, which in 1913 amounted to 14 per cent of the total commercial imports and 44 per cent of the exports of the country, came to an abrupt end, and the shortage of shipping almost paralysed the commercial life of Nigeria. A more immediate problem was presented by the existence, on the eastern frontier, of the large German Colony of the Cameroons and the reported presence of German gunboats in the Gulf of Guinea. The Nigeria Regiment[2] was immediately mobilized, European officials and merchants were enrolled as volunteers in a force known as the Nigeria Land Contingent,[3] a Marine Contingent, consisting of the European officers and African ratings of the Marine Department, was organized, and a large number of African gentlemen were sworn in as Special Constables in Lagos and other places. From all quarters came manifestations of the loyalty of the African population. The chiefs offered financial assistance to the Government and large contributions were made to the Prince of Wales's Fund and other war charities. The Planters' Union at Agege sent corn for the troops, and the war chiefs of Abeokuta offered their services in the defence of Lagos. The entry of Turkey into the

[1] Agreement for the abrogation of the Egba Treaty of 1893, dated September 16, 1914.

[2] At the amalgamation the separate regiments of Northern and Southern Nigeria were formed into the Nigeria Regiment of the West African Frontier Force. The regiment consisted of two batteries of artillery, one mounted infantry battalion, and four battalions of infantry. Since 1956 the regiment has been called the Queen's Own Nigeria Regiment.

[3] In this Contingent several officers were trained who afterwards served with the Nigeria Regiment. It was reconstructed in 1918 as the Nigerian Volunteers.

war called forth from the Muhammadan section of the population fresh protestations of loyalty to the British cause. The
Tripoli Arabs resident in Kano assured the Governor-General
in a letter that 'we have nothing to do with the enemies of
England, nor do we agree to the thing which the Turkish Government has done'. The Sultan of Sokoto, the leader of Islam
in Nigeria, expressed his grateful thanks for the many benefits
conferred on himself, his people, and his country, and gave
assurances of his steadfast loyalty to the British at this crisis
and at all times. The Muhammadans of Lagos and of other
towns publicly demonstrated their loyalty, and the Shehu of
Bornu kept an army of mallams praying in his courtyard for
the success of the British arms. The Shehu of Bornu and the
Emir of Yola,[1] although their territories marched with the
Cameroons and Nigerian operations on the frontier were not at
first successful, gave the greatest assistance in obtaining information of the enemy's movements and furnishing transport and
supplies for the troops. Typical of the letters received from the
Muhammadan chiefs is the following from

Shehu Bakr Garbai, the humble slave of Allah, Emir of Bornu by
the power of the King of England.
I salute Governor Lugard, the representative of the King of
England. May God prolong his days.
After that we know that the King of England is waging war
against the Germans. The war is close to us at Mora. Who knoweth
the ways of Allah? We are warring against proud and stiff-necked
people as the Germans are. In such a case Allah is on our side.
Our Lord Muhammad saith: 'Those who break friendship, kill
them like pagans. If you kill them perhaps they will repent.'
I have assisted the Resident with all that has been required, horses,
donkeys, bullocks, carriers and corn, and everything that he
asked for. The Resident told me that the King of England wanted
them. I am the King of England's servant. Why should I not
help him?

And again:

The Resident has told us that the Germans have compelled the
Sultan of Stamboul to take up arms against the King of England,

[1] Both of these chiefs were awarded the CBE in recognition of the loyal
assistance given by them.

our master. We grieve to hear this news; but we ask you to assure the King that our hearts are set in all obedience to him: we wish but for peace under the King and not under the Germans. We, the people of Bornu, are of the school of Ibn Malik[1] may God have mercy on him, and we know that our country is Dar el-Islam and not Dar el-Harb[2]: we are Muslims and not pagans, for we are free to worship in our own way, and our religion is not interfered with. And so we pray God to prosper the King and to give him long life. We ask you, Governor Lugard, to lay this our message of loyalty before the King.

It was not long before Nigerian forces were in action against the enemy. A detachment of the Nigeria Regiment was sent to Togoland to assist the Gold Coast troops, who, with the French, were attacking that German Colony. The Germans, however, surrendered on August 29, 1914 and the troops from Nigeria took no part in the fighting. The campaign in the Cameroons was longer and more arduous. A Mounted Infantry detachment of the Nigeria Regiment crossed the frontier and occupied the German post of Tepe, attacked the station of Garua, on the River Benue, on August 29th and succeeded in capturing one of the forts; on the following day, however, the Germans counterattacked in force and inflicted a severe defeat on the British, driving the Mounted Infantry back to Nigerian soil, the officer commanding, Lieutenant-Colonel Maclear, being killed. At this early stage, and in the hour of defeat, the African soldiers of the Nigeria Regiment gave convincing proof of their gallantry and of their loyal devotion to their officers. When Major Lord Henry Seymour had been severely wounded, Sergeant Chiroma and Private Audu Sakadade remained with him, covering him with their bodies from the hail of bullets. In the same action Lance-Corporal Sanni Zozo and Private Sadieko stood over Lieutenant Sherlock, who was wounded and lying within twenty yards of the enemy, and remained there firing until the end of the engagement.

In the south the British troops were at first no more successful. A force ascended the Cross river, entered the Cameroons,

[1] The author of the *Muwatta*, a work founded upon the traditions which centred round Muhammad, containing all the fundamental principles of the Maliki school.
[2] The country of infidels.

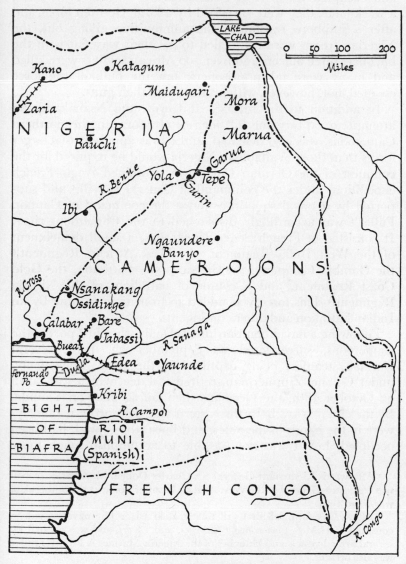

The Cameroons in 1914.

and occupied the post of Nsanakang on August 30th. Here, a week later, they were surprised by a large German force, and after a stubborn resistance, the ammunition giving out, the Nigerian troops were compelled to cut their way out with the bayonet; three officers and over 100 African soldiers were killed and many were taken prisoners, but the bulk of the force escaped, not, however, without the loss of their guns.

In addition to the reverses at Garua and Nsanakang, an attempt to capture the hill fortress of Mora, in the northern Cameroons, was also defeated, and it was apparent that larger forces than those available in Nigeria would be required for the conquest of the German Colony. A combined Anglo-French expedition, under the command of General Dobell,[1] and supported by a naval squadron under the command of Captain Fuller,[2] was accordingly dispatched to the Cameroons river. It consisted of French Senegalese troops, a small detachment of the West India Regiment, the West African Regiment,[3] the Gambia Company, the Sierra Leone Battalion, the Gold Coast Regiment, and a couple of battalions of the Nigeria Regiment.[4] This force was added to from time to time by an Indian battalion and other contingents.

Following a naval bombardment, Duala, the chief port of the Cameroons, surrendered on September 27, 1914, several German steamers being captured in the river. The enemy, under Colonel Zimmerman, retired to Edea, which was taken on October 26th, the Germans then falling back on Yaunde. By the end of 1914 both the eastern and the northern railways were in the hands of the allies, and Buea, the capital, had been occupied, but it was not possible to accomplish much more

[1] Afterwards Lieutenant-General Sir Charles Dobell. Sir Charles Dobell was Inspector-General of the West African Frontier Force at the outbreak of war. Died 1954.

[2] Afterwards Admiral Sir Cyril Fuller; died 1942. The naval squadron consisted of H.M.S. *Cumberland*, *Challenger*, and *Dwarf*, and was assisted by several armed vessels and launches of the Nigeria Marine. A French cruiser was also present.

[3] An Imperial regiment with British officers and African rank and file recruited in Sierra Leone. This regiment was generally stationed at Freetown, and was disbanded in 1928.

[4] The troops of the four Colonies mentioned together formed the West African Frontier Force.

until after the conclusion of the rainy season. In the north, however, Colonel Cunliffe,[1] Commandant of the Nigeria Regiment, with the assistance of a French column, moved against Garua, which surrendered on June 11, 1915. Sweeping south, Cunliffe captured Ngaundere, an important station in the central Cameroons, on June 29th, and put an end to the danger of enemy raids into Nigeria. The most serious of these raids was the attack on the small post of Gurin in April 1915; the little garrison held out for seven hours, and finally beat off the enemy, after suffering many casualties. The officer commanding the troops was killed, but Captain J. F. J. Fitzpatrick, a Political Officer, took charge and remained in command until the post was relieved.

Two further attempts to storm Mora, on August 23rd and September 15, 1915, were unsuccessful, but Colonel Cunliffe succeeded on November 6th in capturing the hill fortress of Banyo, after an action which was described as one of the most arduous ever fought by African troops. Meanwhile, in the south, General Dobell's forces were advancing eastwards on Yaunde, while French columns from the south and east were converging on the same place, and Cunliffe's force from the north was fighting its way down. On January 1, 1916, General Dobell's troops, who had met with serious resistance in November and December, entered Yaunde unopposed, and within a few days the four converging columns had joined hands. The German troops retired to the south-westward towards Spanish territory, and in spite of pursuit succeeded in reaching Rio Muni, where they were disarmed. They were subsequently interned at Fernando Po where, owing to the small numbers of the Spanish garrison, they remained a constant menace to the security of Nigeria for the remainder of the war. On February 18, 1916, Captain von Raben, the gallant defender of Mora, surrendered on terms, and the conquest of the Cameroons was complete.

Throughout this campaign the conduct of the African soldiers of the Nigeria Regiment, and indeed of all the West African Frontier Force, was beyond praise. General Dobell said of them that 'no day appears to be too long, no task too difficult', while Colonel Cunliffe wrote as follows:

[1] Later Brigadier-General. Born 1861, died 1955.

. . . . They have been called upon to take part in a great struggle, the rights and wrongs of which they can scarcely have been expected dimly to perceive. They have been through the, to them, extremely novel experience of facing an enemy armed with modern weapons and led by highly trained officers. Their rations have been scanty, their barefoot marches long and trying, and their fighting at times extremely arduous, yet they have not been found wanting either in discipline, devotion to their officers, or personal courage.

Such devotion, such discipline, and such courage, speak well for the type of officer who trained these men in peace and led them in war.

Although the Germans in the Cameroons were outnumbered by the allies, the nature of the country and the torrential rains that fell afforded every advantage to the defenders. The colony was a large one, food was plentiful, and the thick forest and undergrowth afforded cover for snipers and facilitated rear-guard actions, while disease attacked the British and French troops, who were unaccustomed to the conditions. The troops from the open, sandy country of the north suffered severely in the humid forests, and one battalion was for a short period made practically immobile by the attacks of jiggers[1] and the clumsy efforts of the men to remove these annoying insects from their feet. The troops of Colonel Cunliffe's column marched and fought for over 600 miles in three and a half months, and entered Yaunde only a few days after the town had been occupied by General Dobell.

Dozens of instances could be given of the gallantry of the troops. Two will suffice. Private Osuman Gombe, of the 1st Battalion of the Nigeria Regiment, was wounded in the face at Jabassi, on October 15, 1914, while trying to remedy a jam in a maxim gun; he remained at his post until he got the gun working; his wound was then dressed, and he returned to his post. Company Sergeant-Major Belo Akure, of the 2nd Battalion, who was already in possession of the Distinguished

---

[1] The jigger (or chigoe) is a burrowing flea which penetrates the skin of the foot and lays a large number of eggs. Unless carefully removed, great discomfort is caused, and there is danger of blood-poison. An experienced African can remove the jigger and its eggs with a needle almost painlessly.

Conduct Medal for bravery in the field, was awarded a clasp to the medal for the services which were thus described in the *Nigeria Gazette*:[1]

At Mbongo on November 4, 1914, his behaviour was particularly cool and courageous. He received orders to conduct the retirement of an advanced post which was being heavily attacked by the enemy. The post was separated from the main position by an unfordable river 35 yards in width. Sergeant-Major Belo Akure got his men into the only available canoe, and, finding it would founder if he entered it himself, with great self-devotion he lay on the bank and covered its retirement, being all the time submitted to a heavy fire, one bullet penetrating his sleeve. When the canoe landed he ordered the men into their trenches and swam the river to join them.

Not to the troops alone was gallantry confined. The lack of roads in the Cameroons made necessary the employment of thousands of carriers, who bore their heavy loads of stores and ammunition for hundreds of miles along narrow bush paths, through rivers and streams, under the blazing sun or torrential rains. Although they were non-combatants, they were frequently under fire, and many were killed in action or succumbed to the hardships of the campaign. They received little honour and their services were too often overlooked, but without them the troops would have been helpless. The officers and men of the Nigerian Marine also distinguished themselves in many a skirmish along the rivers and creeks of the Cameroons and, as long as the campaign was confined to the banks of the navigable rivers, provided a reliable and efficient transport service.

As soon as the Cameroons campaign was concluded steps were taken to organize a Nigerian Brigade for service in German East Africa. Under the command of Brigadier-General Cunliffe, four battalions and a large carrier corps proceeded overseas in 1916 and served in East Africa till 1918, earning fresh laurels for the regiment and the high admiration of all officers who saw them in action. The casualties in this campaign were very heavy, the carriers especially dying in large numbers. Constant drafts kept the Brigade up to strength.

[1] Of November 25, 1915.

When the troops returned from East Africa they were reorganized for further service in Palestine, but the end of the war came before they were ready to embark.

The services of the Nigeria Regiment were recognized by the award of Colours to each of the infantry battalions,[1] and the West African Frontier Force, of which the Nigeria Regiment was the largest part, was honoured by His Majesty the King becoming its Colonel-in-Chief and the word 'Royal' being added to its name.

The Nigeria Regiment may be said to have dated from the year 1864, when Sir John Glover raised the Lagos Constabulary; this force consisted of 100 armed Hausas, who performed police as well as military duties, and were under the immediate command of the Governor of Lagos, who was assisted by African officers.[2] In 1895 the Lagos Constabulary was divided into a purely military body, known as the Hausa Force, and a separate civil police detachment. The Oil Rivers Irregulars,[3] raised by Sir Ralph Moor in 1892, became later the Niger Coast Constabulary. The Royal Niger Company's Constabulary was raised soon after the grant of the Company's Charter in 1886. As we have seen, Sir Frederick Lugard raised an Imperial force in 1898, which was styled the West African Frontier Force, all the Colonial troops in West Africa being later included in this force. In 1900, when the Charter of the Royal Niger Company was revoked, a portion of their constabulary was combined with the Imperial force to form the Northern Nigeria Regiment, while the rest was combined with the Niger Coast Constabulary to form the Southern Nigeria Regiment. The latter regiment was later amalgamated with the Lagos Battalion. In 1914 all the Nigerian forces were formed into a single

---

[1] The regimental Colours are of Muhammadan green, and bear the motto, in Arabic, 'Victory is from God alone'. The battle honours are: Ashantee, 1873–4'; 'Ashanti, 1900'; 'Duala', 'Garua', 'Banyo', 'Cameroons, 1914–16'; 'Behobeho', 'Nyangao', 'East Africa, 1916–18'. In respect of the Second World War the following Battle Honours have been awarded: 'Marda Pass', 'Babile Gap', 'Colito', 'Abyssinia, 1940–41', 'Kaladan', 'Myohaung', 'Dalet', 'Chindits, 1944', 'Burma, 1943–45'.

[2] One of these, named Yakuba, was a man of great influence, and helped Sir John Glover to raise the force.

[3] The force consisted at first of forty men. Their conduct left a great deal to be desired, and they were known locally as 'The forty thieves'.

regiment, the Nigeria Regiment of the West African Frontier Force, comprising two batteries of artillery, one mounted infantry battalion and four battalions of infantry.

After the war of 1914–18 the regiment was reorganized, the mounted infantry battalion being disbanded and the number of infantry battalions increased from four to six. The achievements of the Nigeria Regiment in the war of 1939–45 are referred to in Chapter XX.

CHAPTER XIX

THE COLONY AND PROTECTORATE OF NIGERIA (*continued*)

It is the mission of Great Britain to work continuously for the training and education of the Africans towards a higher intellectual, moral, and economic level than that which they had reached when the Crown assumed the responsibility for the administration of this territory.   Cmd. 1922 (*Indians in Kenya*)

Although Nigeria suffered no violation of its territory other than a couple of raids across the frontier from the Cameroons, the effect of the war of 1914–18 was profoundly felt. At the very beginning a Committee of Control had to be set up to regulate the prices and distribution of foodstuffs and necessaries, and this control was continued, in various forms, throughout the war. The large number of German firms in Nigeria, the basis of whose trade was the cheap gin imported from Germany and Holland, employed for the most part German agents and assistants; these were for a time allowed to remain at liberty and to continue their business, but all were finally interned in camps at Ibadan and other centres until they could be deported to England. The revenue suffered considerably from the abrupt check to the importation of 'trade spirits.'[1] In 1913 the sum yielded by duties on spirits amounted to £1,140,000, or over 30 per cent of the total revenue for the year, but in 1917 the receipts from this source had shrunk to £89,000. There was, moreover, a serious dislocation of the export trade and a shortage of shipping, but as the war continued and the demand for vegetable oils became greater in the United Kingdom, the necessary shipping was provided, and an export tax on produce furnished an increasing revenue. By the middle of 1916 the colliery at Udi had been reached by the railway from Port Harcourt, and what might have proved a serious difficulty was avoided by the use of Nigerian coal on the railway and local craft.

[1] It was found very difficult to give a satisfactory definition of 'trade spirits'. In an Ordinance passed in 1919 they were defined as 'spirits imported, or of a kind previously imported, for sale to natives, and not generally consumed by Europeans'.

The greatest problem was caused by the shortage of staff in the civil departments. A number of officials were attached to the Nigeria Regiment or seconded for war duties under the Imperial Government and many of these rendered valuable and important services to the empire.[1] Over 100 officials perished at sea through the sinking of mail steamers,[2] and it was, of course, impossible to replace any of these or to make good the ordinary wastage. The remainder of the civil staff, in order to carry on the administration of the country, willingly undertook prolonged tours of service and much additional work, but in spite of this the departments were throughout the war hopelessly undermanned. In these circumstances it is remarkable that there was so little serious internal trouble, and in view of the absence on active service of a large proportion of the Nigeria Regiment it was extremely fortunate.

Largely at the instigation of the German traders, who were still at large in Nigeria, the people of Kwale rose in revolt in October 1914 and murdered a number of inoffensive Africans who were in the neighbourhood. A strong force was at once dispatched to the scene and the outbreak was crushed in spite of determined opposition. During the same month, and again at the instigation of German agents, who spread the report that the British had been defeated, there was a rising of some of the Bassa tribes, which was, however, easily dealt with.[3] There were a few other slight and sporadic outbreaks, but they gave little trouble, owing to the loyalty of the principal chiefs.

[1] These included Brigadier-General R. H. W. Hughes, C B, C S I, C M G, D S O, R D (afterwards Director of Marine and a Captain R N R) who was Director of Inland Water Transport in Mesopotamia; Major-General A. S. Collard, C B, C V O, and Brigadier-General A. S. Cooper C B, C M G, both of whom served as Director of Inland Waterways and Docks; and Sir John Eaglesome, K C M G, who served with the Ministry of Munitions.

[2] The *Falaba* (1915), *Abosso, Tarquah, Karina, Umgeni, Apapa* (1917), and *Burutu* (1918). The *Appam* was captured in January 1916 by the German raider *Moewe*.

[3] Mr Meek relates, as an example of the chivalrous courtesy of the fighting tribes of Nigeria, the following incident: ' . . . In 1914, when the Basa believed all the British to be dead, they sent word to the chief of Koton Karifi that they would attack his town in four days' time. They kept their word, and were greatly surprised to find that they had to deal not merely with the chief of Koton Karifi, but with a British District Officer and Government police armed with rifles!' Meek, *op. cit.*, p. 301.

In the meantime an event of great significance had taken place at Benin. Overami, the King of Benin, who had been removed in 1897,[1] died in 1914 at Calabar and, by the wish of his people, his son was installed as Oba (king) with full ceremony. His appointment was conditional on his recognition of the suzerain power of the Nigerian Government, and the opportunity was taken to inaugurate a native administration on the lines of those which had proved successful in the Northern Provinces. This departure, which involved the principle of direct taxation, was readily accepted in Benin, but in Yorubaland similar innovations were not accepted so readily. The Alafin of Oyo was quick to grasp the advantages of a native administration, but this was opposed by several of the subordinate chiefs and by certain sections of the Yoruba people. There was a serious rising at Iseyin in 1916, in which many persons were murdered, but the revolt was soon crushed, and the position of the Alafin was strengthened.

In 1916 there was a riot in Lagos in connexion with the collection of the water-rate, which was easily dealt with by the police. As far back as 1897 there had been some agitation against a proposed water-rate, but it is doubtful whether the people had really any strong feelings in the matter. There has always been in Lagos a small band of disaffected persons, ever ready to stir up trouble in the capital or in the hinterland; but luckily the common sense of the people prevents any real harm being done.

In 1916 an outbreak occurred among the Montoils, a pagan cannibal tribe of the Northern Provinces, who suddenly attacked and murdered Mr Maltby, an Assistant District Officer, and his unarmed party, among whom were several chiefs of other friendly tribes. The Montoils were punished by a military expedition.

In 1917 the French troops in the territories north of Nigeria suffered a severe reverse at the hands of the nomad tribes said to have been inspired by the Senussi movement. All the available forces were moved north in support of the French columns, and as the bulk of the Nigeria Regiment was in East Africa, four companies of the West African Regiment were sent from Sierra Leone as reserves. With the help thus provided the

[1] See Chapter XIV.

French were able to defeat the tribes and to relieve the beleaguered garrisons at Agadez and other posts.

By far the most serious trouble, however, occurred in the Egba territory in 1918. For reasons which are not even now very clear, but which were not unconnected with the imposition of taxes and the intrigues of agitators from Lagos, there was a sudden rising in June. Sections of the railway and telegraph lines were destroyed and railway stations burnt and looted. The Alake of Abeokuta narrowly escaped with his life, and one European trader was brutally murdered. A police detachment of twelve men was employed as an escort on a train carrying specie; the train was derailed, and for a day and a night the escort defended the van containing the money, seven men being wounded. The money was safely conveyed to Olumu station, where there was a stronger force of police, but the station, which had been hurriedly fortified, was besieged by the Egbas for some days, and was finally relieved by columns operating from Lagos and the north. A large force was now concentrated, and there was some severe fighting until the end of July, when the resistance suddenly collapsed. Had this rising taken place a few months earlier, before the troops had returned from the East African campaign, the situation would have been very grave. As it was, after the first surprise the Egba fighters had no chance against the well-armed veterans of the Cameroons and East Africa.

The only other event of interest during the war was the curious religious revival in the Opobo district in 1915. An African named Gabriel Braid declared himself to be the second Elijah, forbade the drinking of spirits, and started propaganda against the British Administration and the African chiefs. No action was taken by the Government until his followers began to wreck the ju-ju houses and idols of the pagans, but Braid was finally arrested and convicted on charges of extortion and sedition. The movement, however, continued under other leadership, and developed into a schism which was called 'Christ's Army', and later the 'Delta Church'.

The end of the war synchronized with the departure from Nigeria of Sir Frederick Lugard, whose term of Governorship expired in the middle of 1919. As we have seen, he first visited Nigeria in 1894 on behalf of the Royal Niger Company, when he negotiated treaties between the Company and the chiefs of Borgu; in 1897 he was sent out by the Imperial Government to raise the West African Frontier Force; from 1900 to 1906 he served as High Commissioner of Northern Nigeria; and from 1912 to 1918 he ruled over the Colony and Protectorate of Nigeria, after being responsible for the amalgamation of the two Administrations which had previously existed.[1] He was succeeded as Governor of Nigeria in August 1919 by Sir Hugh Clifford.

The eighteen months that followed the termination of the war was a period of unparalleled prosperity in Nigeria. The great boom in trade throughout the world was reflected in the high prices paid for West African produce, and the value of the exports from Nigeria in 1919 and 1920 reached the record figures of £14,600,000 and £16,800,000 respectively. Only too soon this period of prosperity came to an end. Towards the end of 1920 not only did the prices of produce fall considerably, but the demand itself almost disappeared; firms were left with large, unsaleable stocks on their hands, and heavy losses were experienced by all. The Government was faced with a serious shrinkage of revenue, due in the first place to the decision of the Imperial Government to prohibit the importation into West Africa of 'trade spirits', the duty on which, before the war, had formed a large proportion of the total revenues of Nigeria. The traffic in these spirits had existed in Nigeria for a long time,[2]

[1] Before he came to Nigeria Sir Frederick Lugard had already earned a great reputation in East and Central Africa. Born in 1858, he joined the army and served in the Afghan War of 1879, the Sudan campaign of 1885, and the Burma campaign of 1886. In 1888 he was severely wounded in an expedition against Arab slave-traders on Lake Nyasa, and for the next three years he was employed by the British East African Company in opening up and governing Uganda. He received the gold medal of the Royal Geographical Society for his expedition across the Kalahari desert in 1896. He received the DSO in 1887, the CB in 1895, the GCMG in 1911, and was made a Privy Councillor in 1920. From 1907 to 1912 he was Governor of Hong Kong. His publications include *Our East African Empire* (1893), and *The Dual Mandate in British Tropical Africa* (1922). From 1922 to 1936 he was a member of the Permanent Mandates Commission of the League of Nations. He was created a peer on January 1, 1928, and died in 1945. His biography is contained in two volumes, *Lugard* (1956, 1960) by M. Perham.

[2] Early in the nineteenth century an African chief stated his mercantile views in these words: 'We want three things, powder, ball, and brandy; and we have three things to sell, men, women, and children.' Buxton, *op. cit.*, p. 280.

and for a period almost as long had proved a very vexed question. The bulk of the 'trade spirits' came from Hamburg and Holland,[1] and consisted of cheap gin and rum. It had for many years been a medium of exchange in a country where trade was almost entirely confined to barter, and many chiefs possessed large stores of gin, which represented, in some cases, their entire wealth.[2] The Royal Niger Company, even before the grant of a Charter, discouraged the trade in spirits on the Niger, and as soon as they had the power to do so absolutely prohibited it. In 1890 the international Brussels Act[3] forbade the importation of 'trade spirits' into those territories where their sale was not already established and, owing to the action of the Royal Niger Company, the hinterland of Nigeria remained innocent of the traffic. Missionary and philanthropic bodies pressed for the abolition of the trade in Southern Nigeria, where it was well established and increasing from year to year, and in 1909 the Government sent to Nigeria a strong Committee, under the chairmanship of Sir Mackenzie Chalmers,[4] to inquire into the matter.

After hearing the evidence of 171 witnesses, African and European, officials and missionaries, medical men and chiefs, and obtaining written statements from sixty-four others, the Committee reported that

There is absolutely no evidence of race deterioration due to drink. In Southern Nigeria mortality is high and disease is rife, but drink is only an insignificant factor in producing these results. There is hardly any alcoholic disease amongst the native population, and, with the exception of one or two isolated cases, we found no connexion between drink and crime. On the occasions of feasts and festivals the natives often drink more than is good for them, both of trade spirits and native liquors. Individuals injure themselves both morally and physically by indulgence in drink, but the

[1] The trade with Holland had long been in existence. In 1790 Captain Crow went in a British slave-ship to load spirits at Rotterdam before sailing for West Africa. *Memoirs*, p. 32.

[2] *Report of the Committee of Inquiry into the Liquor Trade of Southern Nigeria*, 1909 (Cd. 4906), p. 7.

[3] Ratified 1892. Also forbade the importation of arms and ammunition, and laid down regulations for the restriction of the slave-trade. Other international conventions, in 1899 and 1906, amended the original Act.

[4] Born 1847; died 1927. Served in India and in the Home Civil Service.

people generally are a sober people, who are able to drink in moderation without falling into excess. There appears, however, to be a tendency among some of the natives who have received a certain amount of European education to acquire drinking habits, but the prohibition of the import of trade spirits would not do much to diminish this evil. As education progresses, this tendency will doubtless be carefully watched. The expert evidence taken in England shows that there is nothing to complain of as regards the quality of the spirits imported into Nigeria.[1]

Several specific statements, by well-meaning but somewhat prejudiced missionaries, as to the prevalence and immediate effects of drink in Southern Nigeria, were carefully examined and proved on investigation to be without foundation,[2] and the fable as to the bad quality of the 'trade spirits' was completely exploded by the reports of the officials of the Government Laboratory in England.[3]

In consequence of the Committee's report, the liquor traffic was allowed to continue, but the policy was followed of steadily increasing the import duties on spirits. In 1894 the duty in the Niger Coast Protectorate was 1s. a proof gallon on spirits; by 1906 it had reached 3s. 6d. a proof gallon, and the rate of increase was accelerated until in 1918 the duty was fixed at 10s. a proof gallon. When the importation of spirits was curtailed by the outbreak of war in 1914, the loss to the revenue was considerable, and in 1916 export duties on local produce were imposed to make good this loss. Owing to the demand for tropical products during the war and the high prices ruling, the export duties did not appear at first to be a very heavy burden to the trade of the country, and it seemed that a satisfactory source of revenue had been found in the place of the import duty on spirits. Sir Frederick Lugard, who had always been opposed to the importation of 'trade spirits', thought that

[1] *Report of the Committee of Inquiry into the Liquor Trade in Southern Nigeria,* 1909 (Cd. 4906), p. 18.

[2] *Ibid.,* pp. 14–17.

[3] *Ibid.,* p. 15. 125 samples of gin were analysed, and it was reported that 'the spirits from which these gins have been prepared are, as a whole, clean and well rectified and of fair quality. The majority of the gins are similar to what is sold in ordinary public-houses in this country.' It was also found that the 'trade' rum did not compare unfavourably with the cheaper rum sold in England.

it was 'a disgrace to an Administration that the bulk of its Customs, and nearly half its revenue, should be derived from such a source',[1] and expressed the opinion 'that the Government of Nigeria can dispense with revenue derived from spirits'.[2]

Accordingly, in 1919, the Imperial Government concluded the Convention of St Germain, by which the French and British bound themselves to exclude 'trade spirits' from their West African dependencies, and an Ordinance was passed prohibiting the importation of these spirits into Nigeria. In the same year the duty on 'European' spirits was doubled.[3] The French Government did not, at first, fulfil its obligation, a decree being passed prohibiting the importation of all foreign spirits, but permitting spirits manufactured in France or French colonies to enter French West Africa regardless of quality. A protest by the British Government at this breach of the terms of the Convention resulted in the abrogation of the decree, but no further steps were taken until 1922 as the French Government was unable to find a suitable definition for 'trade spirits'. The British definition, though theoretically unsound, proved adequate in practice.[4] In the meantime these spirits were imported in large quantities into French West

[1] *Report by Sir F. D. Lugard on the Amalgamation of Northern and Southern Nigeria and Administration, 1912–19* (Cmd. 468), para. 145.

[2] *Ibid.*, para. 150. It is interesting to compare this with the opinion expressed by Sir Claude Macdonald, Commissioner of the Niger Coast Protectorate, in 1894: 'It must be remembered that this liquor traffic has formed a very considerable part of the import trade . . . for upwards of a century, and that to suddenly put a complete stop to it would very seriously affect the entire conditions of trade if it did not paralyse them altogether, and would certainly not assist the cause of temperance to an appreciable degree, for the natives manufacture a liquor from the palm-tree which is as potent under certain conditions of fermentation as anything that has ever been imported into the Protectorate. In the present conditions of trade it would be impossible to substitute any other import duty without altogether ruining the trade of the Protectorate. It must be remembered that it is the liquor traffic that supplies a revenue which enables the Administration to deal with the many crying evils on which I have touched.' *Report on the Administration of the Niger Coast Protectorate*, 1891–4 (C. 7596), pp. 7–8.

[3] It has since been further increased.

[4] 'Spirits imported, or of a kind previously imported, for sale to natives, and not generally consumed by Europeans.' A later definition made all spirits 'trade spirits' except such as come up to a definite fixed standard.

Africa, and not a little was smuggled from Dahomey into Nigeria.[1]

Whether the importation of 'trade spirits' was doing much harm to the inhabitants of Nigeria is a matter of opinion, but there is no doubt that without it the African is not entirely destitute of the means of getting intoxicated. In the Northern Region liquor is obtained from guinea-corn and other grain, and after the harvest there is among many of the pagan communities a long-drawn-out orgy of intoxication.[2] 'Trade spirits' have never penetrated to these people, and the prohibition of importation has not resulted, and cannot result, in the reduction of drunkenness amongst them. In the south, the population, deprived of the gin and rum to which it had been accustomed for generations, is tapping (and damaging)[3] the palm trees in order to obtain palm wine, which when fermented is a very powerful intoxicant, and a beer made from grain is also drunk.[4] The assertion has been made that the law prohibiting the importation of 'trade spirits' is a piece of class legislation which permits the European and rich African to drink expensive spirits and excludes the cheaper kind of liquor which would be within the reach of all.[5]

With the slump that followed the 'boom' years of 1919 and 1920[6] there arose a demand for the reduction of the export

[1] *Report of a Committee on Trade and Taxation for British West Africa*, 1922 (Cmd. 1600), para. 71.

[2] 'The extent of their orgies must be seen to be appreciated. I have entered a village at 8 a.m. and found every one of the two or three hundred inhabitants, men, women, boys and girls, and children in arms, all in a state of drunkenness, mostly quite insensible.' *Native Races and their Rulers* (1918), by C. L. Temple, p. 173.

[3] See *Report of the Committee of Inquiry into the Liquor Trade in Southern Nigeria*, 1909 (Cd. 4906), p. 10, and evidence referred to there.

[4] This beer is called 'peto', and the wine made from the palm is known as 'tombo' or 'mimbo'.

[5] A similar charge was made against the Prohibition Law of the United States; in that case, however, the law made no distinction in theory, but owing to inefficient administration it was easy for the wealthy citizen to evade it.

[6] In 1919 and 1920 the average price in Liverpool per ton of palm kernels was over £36; of palm oil nearly £70; and of ground-nuts about £40. In 1918 the average prices were £26, £48, and £32 respectively. In 1938 the prices were £9, £14, and £10. 'Producer prices' in 1960 were about £30, £40, and £37 respectively.

duties that had been imposed during the war, as they formed a severe handicap to the struggling trade. Towards the end of 1921 a Committee was appointed by the Secretary of State for the Colonies to report on the systems of trade and taxation in British West Africa; the Committee, which was under the chairmanship of Sir Hugh Clifford, consisted of official representatives from the colonies concerned and delegates from the principal bodies in England which were interested in the West African trade. In their report,[1] which was signed on December 15, 1921, the Committee stated that it was 'unable to recommend any immediate reduction of the existing export duties, or any alternative means of raising revenue which, while meeting the financial necessities of these colonies, and proving at once adequate and stable, will be less injurious to trade and industry than are the export duties on produce'.[2] At the same time the Committee was of opinion that as soon as possible it should be the endeavour of Government to decrease and even to abolish the export duties. Export duties on produce are still charged.

There was another form of export duty, imposed for political rather than for financial reasons, which was in force from 1919 to 1922, and provoked even more adverse criticism. This was the differential duty of £2 a ton on all palm kernels exported from the British West African colonies which were not shipped under a guarantee that they would be crushed in some place within the Empire. This duty was imposed on the recommendation of a Committee which sat in 1915 and 1916,[3] and was originally intended to be in force for five years from the termination of the war. It was designed to divert the trade in palm kernels 'from German to British ports, and to establish the kernel-crushing industry firmly in Great Britain,'[4] affording a measure of protection to British companies which had

[1] *Report of a Committee on Trade and Taxation for British West Africa,* 1922 (Cmd. 1600).

[2] *Ibid.,* para. 189.

[3] *Report of Committee on Edible and Oil-producing Nuts and Seeds,* 1916 (Cd. 8247).

[4] In 1913, out of 174,000 tons of palm kernels exported from Nigeria, 131,000 tons went to Germany and only 30,000 tons to the United Kingdom, and from this last figure must be deducted the large proportion that was re-exported to Germany.

erected crushing mills during the war at a heavy cost. The differential duty imposed, however, a serious handicap on British West Africa *vis-à-vis* other West African kernel-producing countries and, moreover, did not have the effect for which it was designed.

The chief focus for political trouble after the war was Lagos. Here Eshugbayi Eleko, the titular King of Lagos, had permitted his position to be exploited by political adventurers. He was the descendant of the King Dosumu who ceded Lagos to the British Crown in 1861, and as an act of grace he had received an annual grant from the Government and a certain amount of courtesy recognition. Repeated warnings were of no avail and finally, towards the end of 1920, his stipend was stopped and all official recognition was withdrawn. Until this time the Eleko had received scanty acknowledgement and respect from his 'subjects', but he now became a political martyr, and numerous attempts were made to persuade the Government to reinstate him. At last, in 1925, as intrigues continued to centre round him, he was deported, and Ibikunle Akitoye was installed as Eleko in his place. On Empire Day 1926, when Akitoye was returning from the official celebration, an organized attack was made upon him, but he escaped injury. By his patience and tact he was gradually strengthening his position and satisfying his opponents, but he died in 1928 and was succeeded by Sanusi Olusi. In 1931, the deportation order having been cancelled, Sanusi Olusi retired from his position and Eshugbayi returned to Lagos, where he died the following year. His successor was recognized as 'Oba' of Lagos, and peace was gradually restored between the factions which for so many years caused trouble in Lagos.

For some years also there was a bitter feud between two sections of the Muhammadan community in Lagos, and on more than one occasion it was necessary for the police to interfere to put a stop to fighting. In one instance the mosque had to be cleared by the police, and considerable difficulty was experienced in preventing a clash between the rival parties at the times of the great feasts. At last, in 1925, after much litigation, the disputing factions separated and agreed to worship at different mosques.

From time to time political capital was made of the long-drawn-out litigation over certain lands, claimed by one of the 'white cap' chiefs, Oluwa, which had been expropriated by the Government in 1913 for public purposes. This case was referred to the Judicial Committee of the Privy Council, which decided in favour of Oluwa. In this case Oluwa was greatly helped by Mr Herbert Macaulay,[1] a prominent journalist and political leader.

It was particularly in connexion with the reorganization of the administrative machine, and the reconstitution of the Legislature, that Sir Hugh Clifford was engaged in the first years of his administration. The Nigerian Council devised by Sir Frederick Lugard was considered a failure, as its members would not take seriously their position on what they regarded as little more than a debating society. The small Legislative Council of the Colony, with its extremely limited powers, was also unpopular, and it was decided to find some other means of obtaining the advice of responsible members of the community and of satisfying the demand of the people for some form of representative Government. On the advice, therefore, of Sir Hugh Clifford, the Nigerian Council and the small (Colony) Legislative Council were abolished by Order in Council in 1922 and a larger Legislative Council for the whole country substituted for them, including, for the first time in the history of British West Africa, a limited number of elected members. The first elections took place in September 1923, and the Council was inaugurated by the Governor the following month. The Council consisted of thirty official members, including the Governor, three unofficial members elected to represent the municipal area of Lagos, one elected to represent the municipal area of Calabar, and not more than fifteen unofficials nominated by the Governor. These fifteen were selected to include nominees of the four Chambers of Commerce and the Chamber of Mines, together with banking and shipping interests, and African members selected to represent the interests of those parts of the Colony and Southern Provinces not represented by elected members. The franchise was limited to males who were British subjects or natives of the Protectorate. An elector had to have a twelve months' residential qualification and an income of not less than £100 a year. The Council

[1] Born 1864; died 1946.

legislated only for the Colony and the Southern Provinces, and had no power to impose taxation in the Northern Provinces; but no money could be expended in the Northern Provinces from the public treasury without the sanction of the Council. For the later constitutions see Chapter XX.

In July 1922 Great Britain received a Mandate[1] from the League of Nations to administer that small portion of the Cameroons which had been assigned provisionally to the British after the conquest of the country.[2] By authority of an Order in Council which came into operation in February 1924 the mandated territory was administered as though it were an integral part of Nigeria, the southern portion being treated as one of the Southern Provinces, while the northern portion was divided between the Northern Provinces of Adamawa and Bornu. Most of the laws of Nigeria applied to the British sphere of the Cameroons. When the Cameroons was conquered a large number of German-owned plantations, in the neighbourhood of Victoria and Kumba, were taken over by representatives of the Nigerian Government and vested in the public custodian of enemy property. They were later sold by public auction, and in 1925 were handed over to their purchasers, most of whom were Germans. At the outbreak of war in 1939 they were again taken over, and in 1947 were leased to a corporation as described in Chapter XX.

After the war of 1914–18 there was a series of epidemics in Nigeria, which affected the African inhabitants in even greater degree than the Europeans. In 1918 the world-wide epidemic of influenza reached Nigeria and took a heavy toll of life. All sorts of curious reasons for its prevalence were believed by the more ignorant sections of the population, and in one locality it was attributed to the fumes of petrol from motor-cars. In 1920 there was a serious epidemic of cerebro-spinal meningitis in Sokoto and neighbouring provinces. Relapsing fever and small-pox also took a heavy toll. In 1924 there was an outbreak of bubonic plague in Lagos, and sporadic cases occurred for

[1] A Trusteeship Agreement with the United Nations replaced in 1947 the Mandate from the League of Nations; it terminated in 1961.

[2] It had an area of 34,081 square miles, and included the port of Victoria and the lofty Cameroons mountain, an active volcano, on the lower slopes of which is situated Buea, the former German capital of the Cameroons.

some time in that neighbourhood, especially in the province of Ijebu-Ode. Following on the report of Sir Edward Thornton,[1] who visited Nigeria in 1926, a special sanitary staff was appointed for anti-plague work. Yellow fever, which appears in Nigeria from time to time, assumed epidemic form in 1925. Vigorous measures were taken to stamp out these and other diseases,[2] but the disregard of the people for the first principles of sanitation was a great handicap. Leprosy presents a serious problem; it is estimated that there are nearly half a million lepers in Nigeria, of whom only a small proportion are segregated or receiving treatment.

Of other outstanding events, the most notable were the killing in January 1924, of Major Rewcastle, a police officer, in an ambush at Ochima, in Onitsha Province, and the consequent punitive expedition; the participation of Nigeria in the British Empire Exhibition in 1924 and 1925; the visit of the Prince of Wales in 1925; and of Mr Ormsby-Gore, Parliamentary Under-Secretary of State for the Colonies, in 1926.[3] The visit of the Prince of Wales was the occasion for remarkable demonstrations of loyalty by the chiefs and people of Nigeria. At Lagos, where the Prince was unable to land on his first arrival on account of the presence of plague, the inhabitants lined the shore for miles, many standing waist-deep in the water to greet the King's son. At Kano a Durbar was held which was attended by practically all the chiefs of the Northern Provinces with their followers, many of the tribes which met on this occasion being traditional enemies now united in a common allegiance. At Ibadan the Prince was met by all the leading Yoruba chiefs, and all along his route chiefs and people met to do him honour.

In 1929, owing to dissatisfaction with the existing Native Administrations and the unfounded fear that women were going to be taxed, there were serious disturbances, generally known as the 'women's rising' or the 'Aba riots', in the Owerri and Calabar Provinces. Troops had to be employed in support of the police and many women were killed and injured before

---

[1] Sir Edward Thornton, KBE, was the Director of Medical Services Union Defence Forces, South Africa.
[2] Work has been carried on for many years on the investigation of the tsetse fly and trypanosomiasis.
[3] See *Report of Visit*, 1926 (Cmd. 2744).

order was restored. These disturbances resulted in a reorganization of the Native Administrations in the areas affected to base them more closely on the indigenous customs of the people.

In 1925 Sir Hugh Clifford[1] left Nigeria on his appointment as Governor of Ceylon. He was succeeded by Sir Graeme Thomson,[2] formerly Governor of British Guiana who served in Nigeria until 1931. Sir Donald Cameron,[3] formerly Chief Secretary to the Government of Nigeria and afterwards Governor of Tanganyika, was Governor of Nigeria from 1931 to 1935. He was succeeded by Sir Bernard Bourdillon,[4] formerly Governor of Uganda, who retired in 1943.

[1] Appointed Governor of the Straits Settlements and High Commissioner for the Malay States in 1927, where he served until 1929. Sir Hugh Clifford, GCMG, GBE, was born in 1866, and served with distinction in the Malay States, Trinidad, and Ceylon, being appointed Governor of the Gold Coast in 1912. He wrote many excellent books, and managed to impart interest even to official documents by his vigorous style. He died in 1941.

[2] Sir Graeme Thomson, GCMG, KCB, was born in 1875. He served in the Admiralty, as Colonial Secretary of Ceylon, Governor of British Guiana, Nigeria, and Ceylon. He died in 1933.

[3] Sir Donald Cameron, GCMG, KBE, was born in 1872. He served in British Guiana, Newfoundland, Mauritius and Nigeria, where he became Chief Secretary to the Government in 1921. He was Governor of Tanganyika from 1924 to 1931. No abler official has ever served Nigeria. He died in 1948.

[4] Sir Bernard Bourdillon, GCMG, KBE, was born in 1883. He served in India, Iraq, and Ceylon, and was Governor of Uganda from 1932 to 1935. He was appointed Governor-General of the Sudan in 1939, but owing to the war did not take up the appointment. He died in 1948.

CHAPTER XX

POST-WAR NIGERIA

For, so the Ark be borne to Zion, who
  Heeds how they perished or were paid who bore it?
For, so the Shrine abide, what shame—what pride
  If we, the priests, were bound or crowned before it?

R. KIPLING: *The Pro-Consuls.*

The outbreak of the Second World War in 1939 found Nigeria in what seemed at first to be a much better position than in 1914, as there was on this occasion no hostile German colony on her eastern frontier. But the fall of France in 1940 changed the situation. The French Cameroons remained faithful to the allied cause, but to the north and west of Nigeria there lay French territories which had thrown in their lot with Vichy; until the successful landings in North Africa destroyed Vichy influence in French West Africa, these territories remained a potential danger which could not be ignored, although in fact no hostilities occurred.

The Nigeria Regiment was mobilized, and its strength considerably increased by voluntary recruitment. Altogether fifteen battalions were raised. A strong detachment was sent (with units from the other West African colonies) to take part in the fighting against the Italians in Somaliland and Ethiopia, and bore a worthy part in the defeat of the Italian forces. At a later date two Divisions (the 81st and the 82nd) of West African troops, of which the Nigerian Brigades comprised about two-thirds, won a high reputation for themselves in Burma in severe fighting against the Japanese. Smaller units served in the Middle East.

When the Mediterranean route was closed through the entry of Italy into the war, the West African colonies became important links in the line of communications with Egypt and the Far East. A few aerodromes had been constructed in Nigeria before the war, and these were rapidly extended and added to. A regular air-transport service was established between Nigeria and Khartoum and Cairo, and many distinguished allied commanders and political leaders made use of this service during the war. A constant stream of fighting and bombing aircraft passed through Nigeria (from the Gold Coast and elsewhere) to Egypt and India to reinforce the Royal Air Force and the American Air Force, and service personnel and warlike stores also went by this route.

Some naval units were stationed at Lagos to meet the submarine menace, but in spite of this several steamers were torpedoed close to the Nigerian shores, and floating mines rendered navigation still more unsafe; a large dredger was sunk by a mine at the entrance to Lagos harbour.

One of the most important contributions of Nigeria to the allied cause was the supply of raw materials, principally palm oil and kernels, ground-nuts, rubber and tin. Before the war there had been set up a Governors' Conference,[1] comprising the Governors of the four British West African colonies, with the Governor of Nigeria as chairman, and this organization was able at the beginning of the war to co-ordinate the actions of the various governments, especially in their relations with the fighting services. In 1942 Viscount Swinton was appointed Resident Minister for West Africa and established his headquarters at Accra, in the Gold Coast. He set up a War Council, into which the Governors' Conference was absorbed, and also included the heads of the three services. Under Lord Swinton's direction the production of raw materials was greatly stimulated and the war effort of the colonies increased; he was succeeded as Resident Minister in 1944 by Captain Harold Balfour (now Lord Balfour of Inchrye), and the post of Resident Minister was abolished in 1945.

When the Resident Minister's office was abolished there was set up a West African Council, under the chairmanship of the Secretary of State for the Colonies,[2] with the Governors of the British West African colonies as members; a permanent secretariat[3] was established at Accra, under a Chief Secretary.[4]

As we have seen, the estates owned by Germans in the

[1] Generally known as 'Wagon'.
[2] The first meeting, at Accra, in 1946, was presided over by Mr George (now Viscount) Hall, then Secretary of State.
[3] Generally known as 'Ofwac'.
[4] The first Chief Secretary was Sir Gerald Creasy, afterwards Governor of the Gold Coast.

Cameroons were taken over by the Government in 1939, and were finally, in 1946, purchased by the Government of Nigeria and leased in the following year to the Cameroons Developmen Corporation.[1] This Corporation, the members of which were appointed by the Governor, was responsible for the working and development of the lands leased, and the profits on the working were used for the benefit of the inhabitants of the British sphere of the Cameroons.

In 1947 a Trusteeship Agreement with the United Nations replaced the Mandate for the Cameroons received from the League of Nations in 1922. Under this Agreement the Trust Territory of the Cameroons[2] continued to be administered as though it were an integral part of Nigeria. While the northern portions of the Trust Territory remained attached for administrative purposes to the Northern Provinces of Adamawa and Bornu, the Southern Cameroons were separated from the Eastern Region under the 1954[3] Constitution, and administered by a Commissioner who was directly responsible to the Governor-General.[4]

Towards the end of the war and in the period following the termination of hostilities, there was considerable labour and political unrest, in many cases encouraged and directed by a section of the Nigerian press, which also succeeded in whipping up anti-white feeling and exacerbating racial prejudice. There was a serious wave of inter-tribal animosity in Lagos which led to the banning of processions and assemblies in public places, while at Abeokuta political agitation terminated in the abdication of the Alake, who was later restored.

During 1946 a number of persons were convicted of so-called 'leopard murders', of which more than 150 were reported to the police in Calabar Province. The victims received injuries resembling those which might be inflicted by the claws of a leopard.

On August 4 and 5, 1949 men of the Kalabari tribe attacked

[1] Established by Ordinance No. 39 of 1946.
[2] The French sphere of the Cameroons was also placed under Trusteeship.
[3] See below.
[4] The northern part of the Trust Territory is now included in Nigeria; the Southern Cameroons has joined the Republic of Cameroun. See Chapter XXI.

some Okrika fishermen in consequence of a dispute regarding fishing grounds. It was reported that in the massacre which followed over 100 Okrikas were killed. As the Kalabaris refused to co-operate with the police in identifying those guilty, and deliberately suppressed evidence, the tribe was fined £20,000, of which £12,000 was awarded as compensation to the Okrikas.

On November 18, 1949, following a labour dispute which ended in a strike at the Enugu Colliery, the police opened fire on a mob of miners, and twenty-one persons lost their lives. This was followed by disturbances at Aba, Calabar, Onitsha and Port Harcourt. A Commission of Inquiry reported that these disturbances were inspired by political agitators who used the economic tension which existed for their own ends. The non-official members of the Eastern House of Assembly unanimously adopted a vote of confidence in the Chief Commissioner in respect of the action taken by him during these disturbances.

In 1950 there were some inter-tribal clashes in the hilly areas of the Gwoza district of Dikwa Division.

In 1951 the elections in Benin Province had to be postponed in consequence of serious disorders.

In 1953 there was a serious inter-tribal riot at Kano in which fifteen northerners and twenty-one southerners lost their lives and a number of other persons were injured; some of those killed were brutally mutilated. The causes of this riot appear to have been the insults offered by Lagos hooligans to northern representatives after a meeting of the legislature early in April 1953, and attacks on northern rulers and ministers in the Lagos press. These incidents exacerbated the smouldering feeling that existed between north and south and, on May 16th, the arrival of a Southern political leader at Kano precipitated an attack by local hooligans and other northerners on the Ibo and Yoruba residents in the suburbs of Kano. These southerners defended themselves and (particularly the Ibos) counter-attacked. In spite of the efforts of the police, who did not use firearms, order was not restored for some days.

Sir Arthur Richards[1] succeeded Sir Bernard Bourdillon as Governor of Nigeria in 1943, and was himself succeeded by Sir

[1] Later Lord Milverton, G C M G. Born in 1885; served in Malaya and as Governor of North Borneo, Gambia, Fiji and Jamaica.

John Macpherson in 1948[1]. In 1954, when the constitution was changed, as described below, Sir John Macpherson became Governor-General and was succeeded as such by Sir James Robertson[2] in 1955.

The post-war period has been chiefly remarkable for the constitutional changes that have been made, no less than four new constitutions having been introduced in ten years. The first momentous change was made by the so-called 'Richards Constitution' of 1947, which replaced that of 1922. In addition to a central Legislative Council for Nigeria and the Cameroons, there were set up, by Letters Patent and Orders in Council, Houses of Assembly for the Northern Provinces (or Region), the Western Provinces (or Region) and the Eastern Provinces (or Region), respectively, as well as a Council of Chiefs for the Northern Region. In all these Houses there was an unofficial majority, and for the first time in Nigerian history there was a majority of unofficials in the central Legislative Council. The Governor possessed certain 'reserve powers'. The first session of the Legislative Council under the new constitution was opened on March 20, 1947.

Although it had been intended that the 1947 Constitution should run for six years, it was replaced in 1951 by a new constitution, which established as a central legislature a House of Representatives consisting of a President, six *ex-officio* Members, 136 Representative Members, and not more than six Special Members appointed by the Governor to represent interests or communities not otherwise adequately represented. Of the Representative Members sixty-eight were chosen by the Joint Council of the North, thirty-one by the Western House of Assembly, three by the Western House of Chiefs, and thirty-four by the Eastern House of Assembly. The members of the Regional legislatures were elected by Electoral Colleges formed by a number of intermediate stages through primary elections at which all male adult taxpayers could vote.

A Council of Ministers was established as the principal instrument of policy in Nigeria. The Council of Ministers consisted of the Governor, six Official Members, and twelve Ministers

[1] Born 1898; served in Malaya, the Colonial office, Nigeria (1937–39), Palestine and the West Indies, and after retirement from Nigeria as Permanent Under-Secretary of State for the Colonies.

[2] Born 1899; served in Sudan 1922–53.

appointed by the Governor; of the Ministers four were appointed from each of the Regions from those chosen by the Regional legislatures to be members of the House of Representatives.

A Public Service Commission was also established to advise the Governor on matters affecting the public service.

It was not long before the 1951 Constitution was found to be unworkable, and it was decided to amend it so as to provide for greater Regional autonomy and for the removal of powers of intervention by the central government in matters which could, without detriment to other Regions, be placed entirely within Regional competence. After protracted discussions in London and Lagos in 1953 and 1954, between the Secretary of State for the Colonies, the Governor, and Nigerian leaders from all the Regions, a new constitution was agreed upon, and this came into operation on October 1, 1954.[1] One of the most difficult problems to be solved in these discussions was the future of Lagos, the capital of the country, which was claimed by the representatives of the Western Region as a Yoruba town which should properly form a part of the Western Region; it was finally decided to make the town of Lagos federal territory. It was also decided to separate the Southern Cameroons from the Eastern Region.

Under the new constitution the Federation of Nigeria was established, to consist of the Northern Region of Nigeria, the Western Region of Nigeria, the Eastern Region of Nigeria, the Southern Cameroons, and the Federal Territory of Lagos. The office of Governor-General of the Federation was constituted, with Governors in charge of the three Regions and a Commissioner in charge of the Cameroons.

The legislature of the Federation was styled the House of Representatives. It consisted of a Speaker appointed by the Governor-General, three *ex-officio* Members (the Chief Secretary, Attorney-General and Financial Secretary of the Federation), 184 Representative Members, and not more than six Special Members appointed by the Governor-General to represent interests or communities not otherwise adequately represented. Of the Representative Members ninety-two were elected in the

[1] Under the authority of the Nigeria (Constitution) Order in Council, 1954, and the Nigeria (Offices of Governor-General and Governors) Order in Council, 1954, both dated August 30, 1954.

Northern Region, forty-two in the Western Region, forty-two in the Eastern Region, six in the Southern Cameroons, and two in Lagos.

The members of the Northern House of Chiefs were the Governor, as President of the House, all first-class chiefs and thirty-seven other chiefs, those members of the Executive Council of the Northern Region who were members of the Northern House of Assembly, and an adviser on Muslim law appointed by the Governor. The members of the Northern House of Assembly were four Official Members appointed by the Governor, 131 Elected Members, and not more than five Special Members. The President of the House of Assembly was appointed by the Governor.

The members of the Western House of Chiefs were not more than fifty head chiefs and other chiefs, those members of the Executive Council of the Western Region who were members of the House of Assembly, and not more than four chiefs as Special Members. The President of the House of Chiefs was elected by the House. The members of the Western House of Assembly were eighty Elected Members and not more than three Special Members appointed by the Governor. The Speaker was elected by the House.

The Eastern House of Assembly consisted of eighty-four Elected Members. The Speaker was appointed by the Governor.

The House of Assembly of the Southern Cameroons consisted of the Commissioner of the Cameroons, who was President of the House, three *ex-officio* Members, thirteen Elected Members, six Members representing the Native Authorities of the Southern Cameroons, and not more than two Special Members appointed by the Governor-General.

The legislative powers of the House of Representatives and the other legislatures were laid down in the Constitution, which provided for an exclusive legislative list of subjects for which the Federal House of Representatives alone could legislate, and a Concurrent Legislative List of subjects which could be dealt with either by the House of Representatives or one of the other legislatures. The official languages in the two Houses of the Northern Region were English and Hausa; in all the other legislatures the official language was English only.

There was a Council of Ministers for the Federation which was the principal instrument of policy for Nigeria. It consisted of the Governor-General, who was President of the Council, three *ex-officio* Members (the Chief Secretary, the Attorney-General, and the Financial Secretary of the Federation), and ten Ministers, of whom three were chosen by the Governor-General from among the Representative Members of the legislatures of each of the three Regions, and one from among the Representative Members of the legislature of the Southern Cameroons. The Governor-General could charge any Minister with responsibility for any matter or department of government, except legal matters which were the responsibility of the Attorney-General. The Governor-General retained control of the police.

In each of the three Regions there was an Executive Council consisting of the Governor, who was President of the Council, a Premier of the Region appointed by the Governor, and a number of other Regional Ministers appointed by the Governor from among the members of the legislature on the recommendation of the Premier. In the Northern Region there were three *ex-officio* Members and thirteen Ministers (including the Premier); in the Western Region and the Eastern Region not less than nine members in each case (including the Premier). The Executive Council of the Southern Cameroons consisted of the Commissioner of the Cameroons, three *ex-officio* and four Unofficial Members appointed by the Governor-General from among the members of the Southern Cameroons House of Assembly.

The Constitution further provided for a Federal Supreme Court and High Courts for the Regions, the Southern Cameroons and Lagos; for the distribution and control of the revenues of Nigeria; for Public Service Commissions for the Federation and the Regions; and for the control of the Public Service and the pensions of officials.

In 1950 the Lagos Town Council was reconstituted on a purely elective basis, the twenty-four members being elected on a universal adult franchise. Serious complaints having been made against the Council, a Commission was appointed in 1952 to inquire into its administration. The Commissioner found that the Council had failed to discharge its functions in a manner conducive to the welfare of the town of Lagos, and that corruption existed amongst members of the Council. The Council was subsequently dissolved and the town's affairs taken over by a Committee of Management.

CHAPTER XXI

INDEPENDENT NIGERIA

Independence is not an end in itself. It is the means whereby we are determined
to ensure that Nigeria plays her full part in world affairs and whereby Nigerians
are enabled to enjoy a higher standard of living both materially and spiritually.
In working for independence we are creating a national self-respect.

The Prime Minister of Nigeria (1959)

During January and February 1956 Nigeria was visited by Her
Majesty the Queen and His Royal Highness Prince Philip,
Duke of Edinburgh. At Lagos the Queen received a Loyal
Address from the Federal Parliament and visits were paid to the
three Regional capitals, Kaduna, Ibadan and Enugu, as well
as to other important centres. Everywhere the Queen and the
Prince received a tremendous welcome. In a speech at Guildhall
on February 22, 1956, when the Queen was entertained by the
Lord Mayor and the Corporation of the City of London, Her
Majesty said:

'We have seen a great deal [of Nigeria] and we have seen enough
to take away a conviction that its future is full of promise and that
its people—the memory of whose warm-hearted welcome will
always be with us—are steadily working their way forward along
the hard but rewarding path of progress . . .

'But perhaps even more striking was the sense of purpose and
determination, particularly in the intellectual field, which is so
evident among the people of Nigeria. They know what they want;
they are pushing forward with education, and schools are multi-
plying.'

Her Royal Highness the Princess Royal visited Nigeria in
1957, and conveyed messages from the Queen to the legislatures of Eastern and Western Nigeria on the attainment by
these Regions of self-government. Their Royal Highnesses the
Duke and Duchess of Gloucester attended the celebration in
1959 of self-government by the Northern Region.

In May and June of 1957 a Constitutional Conference

was held at Lancaster House in London which was attended by representatives of all the political parties in Nigeria and by representatives of the United Kingdom Government. This Conference resulted in further constitutional advance for Nigeria. The offices of Chief Secretary and Financial Secretary of the Federation were abolished and the Attorney-General ceased to be a member of the Council of Ministers, which then consisted entirely of Nigerians except for the Governor-General who continued as President. A Federal Prime Minister was appointed for the first time, as was a Minister of Finance, who replaced the former Financial Secretary. The Prime Minister was Alhaji Abubakar Tafawa Balewa[1] and the Minister of Finance was Chief Festus Okotie-Eboh. The Prime Minister formed an all-party government, consisting of members of the Northern Peoples Congress, the National Council of Nigeria and the Cameroons, and the Action Group. Special commissions were set up to advise on problems of minorities, electoral boundaries, and fiscal matters.

The Eastern and Western Regions became self-governing on August 8, 1957, and the constitution of the Southern Cameroons was changed to one similar to the Regional constitutions of 1954.

The move towards independence now became more rapid. The Constitutional Conference was resumed in 1958 to discuss the reports of the special commissions referred to above, and it was arranged that the Northern Region should become self-governing in 1959. It was further agreed that if independence were asked for by the Nigerian legislature it would be granted in 1960.

In 1958 the control of the military forces of Nigeria passed to the Federal Government and the Nigeria Navy was created. A Central Bank of Nigeria was formally opened in 1959 and a new Nigerian currency issued.[2] On March 15, 1959, the Northern Region became self-governing and in December there were federal elections to an enlarged House of Representatives and members of a new Senate were appointed.

Early in 1960 the Federal House of Representatives passed a motion requesting Her Majesty's Government to grant

[1] Born 1912. He was knighted in 1960.
[2] The Nigerian pound is at par with the pound sterling.

independence to Nigeria as from October 1, 1960, and an Independence Act was passed by both Houses of the United Kingdom Parliament in July 1960, receiving the Royal Assent on July 29th.

On September 12th the Queen approved The Nigeria (Constitution) Order in Council, 1960, which was laid before the United Kingdom Parliament four days later, and was to come into operation on October 1, 1960. By this Order the independent Federation of Nigeria was set up, to consist of Northern Nigeria, Western Nigeria, Eastern Nigeria, and the

I

Federal Territory of Lagos. In separate schedules to the Order
were set out the constitutions of the Federation and its com-
ponent territories. The Order also provided for a Niger
Delta Development Board, responsible for advising the Government of the Federation and the Governments of Eastern and
Western Nigeria with respect to the physical development of
the delta area.

Provision was also made for facilitating the inclusion in the
Federation of Nigeria of the Trusteeship Territory of the Camer-
oons under British Administration if the inhabitants of that
territory elected, by referendum, to throw in their lot with
Nigeria. In the event, the people of the northern part of the
Cameroons voted to join Nigeria and their territory became a
province of the Northern Region on June 1, 1961. The Southern
Cameroons, on the other hand, voted to join the Republic of
Cameroun, and its official connection with Nigeria ceased on
October 1, 1961.

Under the constitution set up by the Order in Council,
which came into existence at independence, the Parliament
of the Federation consists of Her Majesty the Queen, a Senate,
and a House of Representatives. There is a Governor-General
appointed by the Queen who exercises, on behalf of Her
Majesty, the executive authority of the Federation, acting on
the advice of the Council of Ministers (the Federal Cabinet)
over which the Prime Minister presides.

The Federal Senate consists of (a) twelve senators represent-
ing each Region, selected at a joint sitting of the legislative
Houses of the Region from among persons nominated by the
Governor of that Region; (b) four senators representing the
Federal Territory, including ex officio the Oba of Lagos and a
chief selected by the White-Cap Chiefs and War Chiefs of
Lagos; and (c) four senators selected by the Governor-General
on the advice of the Prime Minister.

The Federal House of Representatives consists of 312
members, of whom 174 come from Northern Nigeria, seventy-
three from Eastern Nigeria, sixty-two from Western Nigeria,
and three from the Federal Territory of Lagos. All members
are elected by adult suffrage except in the Northern Region
where the suffrage is confined to adult males.

A Minister of the Federal Government may take part

in the proceedings of either House of Parliament notwithstanding that he may not be a member of that House, but may not vote unless he is a member.

Each Region is self-governing and in each there is a Governor, as the Queen's representative, a Premier, an Executive Council, a House of Chiefs and a House of Assembly. In Northern Nigeria the House of Chiefs consists of all first-class chiefs, 95 other chiefs, and an adviser on Muslim law; the House of Assembly of 170 elected members and not more than five special members appointed by the Governor. In Western Nigeria there is a House of Chiefs consisting of certain senior chiefs, 115 other chiefs having stipulated qualifications, and not more than four chiefs selected by the Governor; and a House of Assembly consisting of 124 elected members. In Eastern Nigeria the House of Chiefs consists of all traditional rulers, a certain number of first-class chiefs, and not more than five other persons selected by the Governor; the House of Assembly consists of 146 elected members.

The division of authority between Federal and Regional Governments is clearly defined. Exclusive authority lies with the Federal Government in defence, external affairs, communications, customs, banking, and other subjects affecting the country as a whole. The Schedule to the Nigeria (Constitution) Order in Council, 1960, contains an *Exclusive List* of subjects on which the Federal Parliament alone can make laws and a *Concurrent Legislative List* of subjects on which legislation may be enacted either by the Federal or a Regional legislature. If a law enacted by a Regional legislature is inconsistent with any law validly made by the Federal Parliament, the Federal law prevails and the Regional law is void. Subjects which are not included in either of the *Legislative Lists* are within the competency of the Regional legislatures.

The principal political parties at the time of independence were (*a*) the Northern Peoples' Congress (NPC), mainly Hausa and Fulani, which had an overwhelming majority in the House of Assembly of the Northern Region; (*b*) the National Council of Nigeria and the Cameroons[1] (NCNC) mainly Ibo,

[1] This party was formed before the separation of the Southern Cameroons from the Eastern Region. It is now called the National Council of Nigerian Citizens.

which had a large majority in the Eastern House of Assembly, and (c) the Action Group, which also had a large majority in the House of Assembly of the Western Region.

At the elections held in December 1959 for the Federal House of Representatives the results were:

Northern Peoples' Congress	142
National Council of Nigeria and the Cameroons	89
Action Group (and allies)	72
Independents	9
	312

Following this election a coalition government was formed, of the Northern Peoples' Congress and the National Council of Nigeria and the Cameroons, with the Action Group as the opposition. It was this Government which was in power when Nigeria attained independence.

Nigeria duly became independent, with the constitution described above, on October 1, 1960. At 10.30 p.m. on September 30th there began a Searchlight Tattoo on the Racecourse at Lagos in the presence of Her Royal Highness the Princess Alexandra of Kent, who had been appointed by the Queen to represent Her Majesty at the independence celebrations. In addition to detachments of the Royal Nigeria Military and Naval Forces and Police, there were present representative detachments of the Forces of the Commonwealth. Just before midnight the Anglican Bishop of Lagos, the Roman Catholic Archbishop of Lagos, and the Chief Imam offered prayers of dedication, and at midnight the Union Flag was lowered and the Flag of the Federation of Nigeria was hoisted. (Three equal vertical bands, of green, white and green.) A few hours later, at a ceremony on the Racecourse, after Sir James Robertson had been sworn in as Governor-General, Princess Alexandra addressed a large gathering and presented the Constitutional Instruments to the Prime Minister, Alhaji Sir Abubakar Tafawa Balewa.

On October 3rd Her Royal Highness, by command of Her Majesty the Queen, opened the first Parliament of the independent Federation of Nigeria.

Throughout the independence celebrations, which were the occasion of great popular rejoicing, there was a marked spirit of dignity and restraint. It was, as the Prime Minister pointed out,[1] an occasion for pride for Nigerians, 'but', he said, 'do not mistake our pride for arrogance. It is tempered by feelings of sincere gratitude to all who have shared in the task of developing Nigeria politically, socially and economically. We are grateful to the British officers whom we have known, first as masters and then as leaders and finally as partners, but always as friends. And there have been countless missionaries who have laboured unceasingly in the cause of education and to whom we owe many of our medical services. We are grateful also to those who have brought modern methods of banking and commerce, and new industries. I wish to pay tribute to all of these people and to declare our everlasting admiration for their devotion to duty.' In the opinion of the Prime Minister, 'history will show that the building of our nation proceeded at the wisest pace: it has been thorough and Nigeria now stands well-built upon firm foundations'. *The Times* expressed the view that is very widely felt, that 'rarely, if ever, can the end of an empire have been announced with so much dignity and good will'.

Shortly after independence Sir James Robertson left Nigeria and was succeeded as Governor-General, on October 16, 1961, by Dr Nnamdi Azikiwe,[2] formerly President of the Senate.

Nigeria was recognized at independence as a member State of the Commonwealth and on October 7, 1960, became a member of the United Nations. High Commissioners represent Nigeria in the United Kingdom and other Commonwealth countries and Nigerian Ambassadors are stationed in various foreign capitals; several Commonwealth High Commissioners and foreign Ambassadors have their offices in Lagos.

[1] A complete copy of the Prime Minister's speech is at Appendix L.
[2] Born 1904.

CHAPTER XXII

RELIGION AND EDUCATION

Make knowledge circle with the winds;
But let her herald, Reverence, fly
Before her to whatever sky
Bear seed of men and growth of minds.

LORD TENNYSON: *Love thou thy Land*

The greater number of the pure Negro inhabitants of Nigeria are pagans,[1] while among the Negroid and Berber tribes of the north the majority are Muhammadans. Christianity has made slow progress in the country save in the comparatively few localities where missionaries have worked for long periods.

In considering the pagan beliefs of the people it is important to realize that the existence of a Supreme Being is appreciated practically throughout the country, even by the most backward tribes. This Supreme Being, however, is invisible and remote, and little likely to interfere much in the petty concerns of the individual and, therefore, though He is not forgotten, more attention is paid to minor deities, good and evil, who are considered to have a greater interest in human affairs. But even these are held to be spirits, and the images which the people venerate are but the representations of the spirits and not the gods themselves. In most cases there is a tribal god, a lesser god for each village of the tribe, a household god for every family in the village, and a personal god for every member of the family. Add to these a god or devil for every striking object of nature, for every river or stream, for every hill or grove, and for every large or remarkable tree, and it will be understood how complicated is the Africans' mythology.

As by far the greater number of these spirits are malevolent, the unfortunate who believes in them is constrained to constant sacrifices to avert their evil influence. Along the banks of the rivers and creeks are to be seen the sticks and rags which represent the fishermen's offerings to the water-gods. Similar offerings are everywhere, and throughout his life the pagan never

[1] See note on p. 35.

ceases in his efforts to avert the wrath of the gods. His religion, such as it is, is very real to him, and in his superstition he allows himself in many instances to be exploited by the 'juju' priests. These men, who profess to be on terms more or less intimate with the gods, have a powerful position in the community. They are in a position to terrorize the people by threats of supernatural vengeance unless the wishes of the gods, which coincide in a remarkable manner with their own, are complied with, and the very kings and chiefs have often been wax in their hands. In 1897 the most powerful potentate in Southern Nigeria, the King of Benin, was a mere puppet in the hands of the priests, and a few years later it was necessary to break up the influence of the Aros, who by the possession of a 'Long Juju' of extraordinary power kept the surrounding country in a state of terror and reduced the neighbouring tribes to a condition of abject submission. Should a crime be committed, the culprit is 'discovered' by the 'juju' priest, who is regarded as infallible in such cases, and the importance of keeping on friendly terms with such a person is obvious. The faith of the people in the power of others to work magic against them is unbounded, and sudden or unaccountable death is invariably attributed to the black art of an enemy, who must be 'smelt out' by the 'juju' priest.

We have seen that in many of the tribes there are initiation ceremonies for boys and girls attaining the age of puberty; there are societies, claiming religious sanction, whose object is the intimidation of the women and the aggrandisement of the male sex; and there are rules which originally were made for the benefit of the people's health, and have now become a part of their religious life. Such is the 'yam custom' or 'yam festival', which originated in a wise provision against the eating of the immature yams. At Bonny and Brass, as stated above, the monitor lizard and the python were worshipped as gods and moved with impunity about the houses. It was not till about 1884 that the missionaries prevailed upon their converts at Bonny to celebrate Easter Sunday by a massacre of all the monitor lizards in the town. Many tribes have their totems, and there is a widespread belief in the power of certain men and women to change themselves at will into animals.[1] In some

[1] See note, p. 61.

districts it is believed that the killing of a wild animal will result in the death of the person whose soul is occupying either temporarily or permanently the body of the beast.

Cannibalism was widely practised in the past and existed in remote districts until comparatively recently.[1] As late as 1918 it was reported that head-hunting was practised in the Okigi district and the Ogoja country,[2] while on the Bauchi plateau there were indications that the eating of human flesh had not then ceased. In some cases cannibalism is of religious significance; in others it is due to a desire to acquire certain merits which belonged to the person whose body is eaten. For instance, a warrior would eat the heart of a vanquished enemy to improve his own courage, while the Yoruba chiefs in ancient times would eat the heart or tongue of their predecessor that they might more surely inherit the magical and other virtues of the royal line.[3]

Although the change is slow, it is unquestionable that paganism is gradually yielding in Nigeria to the influence of Islam and Christianity, partly perhaps on account of the social and political advantages of these religions. It is estimated that in Negro Africa, where Christian and Muslim missionaries are in competition, ten heathens embrace the doctrines of Islam for every one who becomes a Christian.[4] For this there are many reasons. To begin with, although there is little love lost between the different Muslim sects, to the heathen Islam presents a united front, while sectarian differences tend to weaken the Christian force and puzzle the pagan mind.[5] Again, the doctrines of Muhammad are spread by Africans who can penetrate freely into any part of the country and get in touch with the people, while Christianity is generally preached by European missionaries who have not this advantage. Moreover, every Muslim proselytizes as a matter of course; the Christian leaves this duty to his priests.

[1] See *Annual Report* for 1924 (No. 1245), p. 11.
[2] *Police Report for Southern Provinces of Nigeria, 1918.*
[3] This is the origin of the saying, 'He has eaten the king', to signify that a man has succeeded to the throne. See *The Golden Bough* (abridged edition, 1922) by Sir J. G. Frazer, p. 295.   [4] De Lacy O'Leary, *op. cit.*, p. 59.
[5] 'Unless the Christian Church can exhibit a brotherhood as real as that of Islam, we cannot be surprised if the latter is more successful in winning the allegiance of pagan peoples.' See Oldham, *op. cit.*, p. 263.

The chief reason for the greater success of Islam is, however, that it is better adapted than Christianity to the African life. The native of Nigeria, as he advances in knowledge and becomes more civilized, ceases to believe in the numberless gods of his pagan ancestors and looks around for something better.[1] There is offered to him the choice of the Cross or the Crescent. Both involve strange doctrines which he scarcely understands, but while one forbids him to possess more than one wife,[2] the other imposes no such restriction. Polygamy is an old-established custom throughout Nigeria, and to the African it appears not only a reasonable but almost an essential institution. The number of a man's wives provides an indication of his wealth, in which form it is often entirely invested, and the labour of his wives adds to his income and permits of further investments.[3] Children are not a financial burden in West Africa, but add to the wealth of the father, so there is no economic disadvantage in large families. Daughters are easily marketable as wives at an early age, and sons provide an unpaid labour supply. But apart from the financial advantages of a plurality of wives, there is the fact that mothers in most parts of Nigeria nurse their children till they are from two to three years of age, and deny themselves to their husbands during this period. With monogamy the rule, such a custom might in time disappear, but it appears at present to be an insuperable difficulty.

Muhammadanism has existed in the north of Nigeria for many centuries, and was certainly introduced before the year 1400. It was adopted by the town-living Fulani some time after their arrival in Hausaland, and under the inspired leadership of Othman dan Fodio, with the co-operation of their fanatical

---

[1] Mr C. K. Meek says, however, that the Muhammadans in Nigeria retain many of the older pagan beliefs and superstitions, and that 'on the spiritual side Islam in Nigeria is but a poor imitation of the lofty religion of the Prophet'. See Meek, op. cit., vol. ii, p. 4.

[2] The Native African Church, modelled on the Church of England, permits polygamy among its members, and has therefore attracted to itself many African Christians.

[3] Wives, besides their value as potential mothers, perform most of the manual labour in the home and on the family farms. It is doubtful whether any but the then favourite wife would object to the addition of others to their lord's seraglio, as extra hands would lighten the work.

neighbours, they were able early in the nineteenth century to overthrow the pagan state of Gobir and to subdue those Muhammadan cities which conformed too laxly to the rules of the Prophet. Using their religious zeal as a cloak to their ambition, the Fulani leaders waged endless war against the pagan tribes. 'God has given me all the land of the infidels', said Sultan Bello to Clapperton in 1824, and with this comforting knowledge he acquired as much of the infidels' territories as he could. But not only against the infidel did Bello fight. Bornu had been a Muhammadan state for centuries when it was invaded by the Fulani, and even when the 'Servant of God', Muhammad el Kanemi, a man of unquestioned sanctity and austerity, had driven the invaders from Bornu and abolished the abuses of the past, wars between the Fulani and Bornu were always breaking out.

With the establishment of the British administration the spread of Islam by force of arms was put a stop to, but it has not ceased to spread by more peaceful means. Today more than half of the inhabitants of Lagos are Muslims, and elsewhere the religion is gaining ground rapidly. The statement has been made in the past that the Nigerian Government prevented Christian missions from operating in the Muhammadan Emirates, and that Christian missionaries had been excluded even from pagan areas to which the preachers of Islam had been admitted. This was met by the argument that the Government had given a solemn promise to the people when British rule was extended to the north that the Muhammadan religion would not be interfered with and that all men would be free to worship God as they chose.[1]

As regards the pagan areas, the Government always fostered and assisted missionary enterprise, provided it was confined to those districts which were sufficiently under control to be devoid of danger to the missionaries themselves. Today, missions are established throughout Nigeria.

It is unfortunately true that friction existed in the past between the Government and the missionaries. We have seen in Chapter XI that the missionaries prejudiced the Egbas

[1] Speech made by the High Commissioner of Northern Nigeria, Sir Frederick (later Lord) Lugard, on March 22, 1903, at the installation of the new Sultan after the capture of Sokoto.

against the newly established Colony of Lagos, and much injury was caused to the British administration by articles inserted in the newspaper *Iwe Irohin*,[1] which was printed by the missionaries at Abeokuta. Although it was alleged from time to time that the missionaries were still prone to interfere in political and judicial matters which did not concern them,[2] and to encourage the recently converted Africans to ignore their tribal rulers, there was later a much better spirit of co-operation.

Among the missionaries themselves, however, there has been in the past not a little jealousy. There are Church of England, Roman Catholic, Wesleyan, Presbyterian, Baptist, and other missions, each with little love for the other. The wonder is that so much has been done with such divided counsels. What has been done has been done very largely by the schools. From early years mission schools have given to those who attended them a Christian education, and the only form of education available, as the Muhammadan schools give little but religious instruction.[3] The people have been, and are more than ever now, keen on acquiring knowledge, and with the knowledge those who used the mission schools have acquired Christianity, in many cases a mere veneer over the old paganism, but none the less a start. We have seen that in 1895 the son of a chief of Brass took part in a cannibal feast on the captives taken during

[1] See particularly the issue of October 4, 1862.

[2] *Report on the Amalgamation of Northern and Southern Nigeria and Administration, 1912–19*, paras. 183–4. See also *Report on the Eastern Provinces of Nigeria*, by the Secretary for Native Affairs, 1922, pp. 15–18. This was not peculiar to Nigeria; not very long ago the Attorney-General of Uganda stated that he had never read a more grossly improper letter than one written by the Archdeacon of that diocese to the authorities of a native court on behalf of certain employees of the Church Missionary Society. The Chief Justice said he was willing to believe that the grave irregularity and impropriety of writing such a letter had not been realized, but issued a warning against further interference with judicial proceedings.

[3] In Muhammadan schools the pupils learn the Koran by heart, and are instructed in their religion, but there is little or no education in the Western sense. 'The average Muslim regards Western scientific education simply as a species of craftsmanship, a knowledge extremely useful for certain purposes, and especially so for the pursuit of wealth and ambition, but in no sense connected with learning or scholarship, which are to be found in the mosque, and not in the English or American school.' See De Lacy O'Leary, *op. cit.*, p. 64.

the raid on Akassa; this young man had been educated for some years at a missionary training-college in the Isle of Man, but in his case the veneer was not able to restrain the savage within. Nevertheless, it must not be forgotten that the Christian chiefs of Brass, on the same occasion, at great personal risk, refused to join in the feast or to give up their prisoners to be massacred. There are many African clergymen and African bishops who have earned the respect both of the Europeans and of their own countrymen. Bishop Crowther was a man of exceptionally high character and attainments, while the eloquence of Bishop Oluwole will never be forgotten by those who were privileged to hear his sermon in Lagos on January 6, 1918.

There are also numerous European missionaries throughout Nigeria who are preaching the Gospel, educating the people, and alleviating their physical sufferings by medical work. There are men—and women—of high character, undoubted piety, and thorough devotion to their mission. Typical of these was Miss Mary Slessor, a Presbyterian missionary, who lived among the Africans from 1876 to 1915 and devoted herself to saving twins and their mothers from the death to which a cruel superstition would have doomed them. The official tribute paid to her memory in the *Nigeria Gazette* is worthy of reproduction:

It is with the deepest regret that His Excellency the Governor-General has to announce the death at Itu, on January 13th (1915), of Miss Mary Mitchell Slessor, Honorary Associate of the Order of the Hospital of Saint John of Jerusalem in England.

For thirty-nine years, with brief and infrequent visits to England, Miss Slessor has laboured among the people of the Eastern Provinces in the South of Nigeria.

By her enthusiasm, self-sacrifice, and greatness of character she has earned the devotion of thousands of the natives among whom she worked and the love and esteem of all Europeans, irrespective of class or creed, with whom she came in contact.

She has died, as she herself wished, on the scene of her labours, but her memory will live long in the hearts of her friends, native and European, in Nigeria.[1]

---

[1] The *Nigeria Gazette* of January 21, 1915. A biography of Miss Slessor, by W. P. Livingstone, has been published.

The first European missionaries to work in Nigeria, if we except the Portuguese Roman Catholic priests who were at Benin and Warri in the fifteenth and sixteenth centuries, were Wesleyan missionaries who visited Badagri and Abeokuta in 1841, and the members of the Church Missionary Society who landed at Badagri in 1842 and reached Abeokuta in 1846.[1] In 1846 the Presbyterians began work at Calabar, and two years later a Baptist mission was started at Victoria, which is now included in the Republic of Cameroun.

Although with the missions religious training was naturally the first object, the country still owes to them a great debt of gratitude for the work they have accomplished in laying the foundations of education in Nigeria. They have frequently been charged with giving to the Africans the wrong type of education and turning out from their schools a large number of semi-literate youths with untrained characters. It is true that in the past many of these youths were too ill-educated for any but the lowest form of clerical work, that they looked with contempt on any form of manual labour, that they lacked discipline, and were often idle, useless, and immoral. The reason for this is not far to seek. Until comparatively recently education was left almost entirely in the hands of the missionaries and, indeed, the first Government school was not founded until 1899. The demand for any form of education was tremendous,[2] and the missions were unable adequately to staff their schools or to afford the supervision which was so necessary.

The first problem that presented itself to the newly formed Administrations of Nigeria was the lack of a native-born clerical staff. Europeans in West Africa, owing to the necessity for frequent leave of absence in a temperate climate, were too expensive for any but the senior posts, and clerks from the Gold Coast and Sierra Leone,[3] though less expensive than Europeans, still required many compensations for leaving their

[1] Mr (afterwards Bishop) Crowther accompanied the Niger Expedition of 1841; see Chapter VIII.

[2] Dr Dike says that 'the children were sent to mission schools for one purpose only: that they might learn the business methods of the West. Instances of this abound in contemporary records'. Dike, *op. cit.*, p. 161.

[3] Nigeria owes much to the African clerks from these two colonies, men who were invaluable to the Government in the early days, and set a high example of loyalty and integrity to those who followed them.

more civilized homes for the unsettled territories of Nigeria.[1] In these circumstances the various Governments, and to a lesser degree the trading firms, were only too anxious to employ anyone who could read and write, and as the country developed the demand increased far more rapidly than the supply. Lord Lugard has said in this connexion that

the result of this demand and inadequate supply has been not merely to raise the pay disproportionately to the qualifications of the candidates, but to tempt boys who can neither read nor write properly to leave school for lucrative employ, and withdraw them from parental discipline. . . . The standard of the native official service was thus permanently lowered, and the majority of the candidates were unfitted for posts of responsibility.[2]

The solution was not an easy one to find. A clerical staff was absolutely necessary, and for those who filled it, and for others who sought a higher education with a view to professional life, a literary training was required which would ensure at least a sound knowledge of English and some arithmetical skill. Excellent secondary schools and training colleges conducted by various missions for a number of years, together with Government colleges and schools, did a great deal of good. The Yaba Higher College was opened in 1934. The pupils from most of the other schools were lacking in book-learning, and still worse off as regards character and discipline, while the tendency of all semi-educated youths to break away completely from the ordinary life of the community and from any tribal control has been commented on.[3]

In 1914 Mr Sapara Williams, CMG, senior African member of the Legislative Council, declared at a public meeting in Lagos that the indiscipline and vanity of the young men produced by the schools had become so intolerable that parents were discussing the withdrawal of their sons. Dr Henry Carr, CBE, ISO, a distinguished African who held a senior

[1] For a long time it was difficult to persuade a Lagos-born clerk to accept a transfer to a post in the hinterland, even if such transfer involved promotion.
[2] Report on the Amalgamation of Northern and Southern Nigeria and Administration. 1912–19, p. 61.
[3] Report on the Eastern Provinces (of Nigeria) by the Secretary for Native Affairs, 1922, p. 15.

post in the Education Department for many years, described these youths as ill-educated, unreliable, and lacking in self-control.[1]

In these circumstances it is not to be wondered at that there was for a time a decided reaction against a literary education for the people, and that many thoughtful persons urged greater concentration on technical and manual training and the teaching of crafts. Dealing with a similar problem in East Africa, a Commission sounded a note of warning:

We do not suggest for one moment that what is termed literary education can be entirely dispensed with; a knowledge of the three R's is essential. But the danger is lest we import into Africa nineteenth century English Board School education with its obsolete emphasis on the earning of marks and the passing of written examinations, and still more with the excessive importance attached to the knowledge and parrot-like repetition of textbooks on foreign history and geography. The African should be taught geography and history, but they should be the geography and history of his own country.[2]

It will, unfortunately, take some time to combat the idea that has grown up that manual labour and agricultural pursuits are undignified, and that the scantiest amount of book-learning confers upon its possessor a social status and a claim upon the Government that would otherwise be lacking.

The question of language is of great importance to education in Nigeria. The East Africa Commission considered that during the elementary and primary stages it was 'essential that the medium of education should be a native language, and that English should be introduced only at a later stage. . . . When English is taught at all, it must be taught thoroughly and completely, and only to such pupils as are undergoing a period of school-life long enough to enable English to be learnt properly.'[3] Anyone who has heard 'pidgin English' spoken will agree with this.[4] Dr Jesse Jones, of the Phelps-

[1] *Report by Sir F. D.* [later Lord] *Lugard on the Amalgamation of Northern and Southern Nigeria and Administration, 1912–19*, p. 60.
[2] *Report of the East Africa Commission*, p. 52 (Cmd. 2387).
[3] *Ibid.*, p. 51.
[4] The following 'Story of the Creation told by a Kruboy' was quoted in a memorandum published by the Advisory Committee on Native Education

Stokes Education Commission, has said that the vernacular 'is one of the chief means of preserving what is more important than all else, namely native self-respect'.[1] Lord Lugard has, however, pointed out the great difficulty caused in Nigeria by the numerous languages and dialects,[2] and the absence of any vernacular with a literature of its own.[3]

As a result of a visit to West Africa in 1944 by a Commission appointed by the Secretary of State for the Colonies to report on the question of higher education, and after further investigation and discussions, it was decided to establish a University College at Ibadan. The Yaba Higher College was closed and on January 18, 1948, 104 students began their first term as undergraduates at Ibadan, the formal opening of the University College taking place on March 25th of that year. The University College, which is in association with the University of London, includes courses of study in the faculties of Agriculture, Arts, Medicine and Science. About 1,200 students were enrolled during the academic year 1960–61. There is also a Department of Extra-Mural Studies and an Institute of Social and Economic Research.

in Tropical Africa (see *Nigeria Gazette* of March 4, 1926) as an example of 'pidgin English':

'Then He begin, He make oll thing, He make eny kind beef, He make bush, He make farm, too. After wats He say: "how, I no get people?" Then He take some ground for hand, He mass him, He make him turn op like man He col him, say "be Kruboy!" Befor he put him for some big big garden; plenty chop live there inside, plenty planten, plenty makabo, plenty fruits, plenty palmoil, eny kind beef too he live, das oll; work no live! so them place be fine too much.

'Then he tok for them Kruboy; "I give you this fine place for sit down, oll thing I dash you!" So them Kruboy, he sit down for them garden, he waka there, he waka so oll for him self, he waka so-o-o-te-e-e, he tired.

'One day he com for God, he say: "Massa, I com for You, I get some p'lava for tell You; no be You, You make me? No be You, You don't put me for them garden? You no luk out for me, becos You be massa for me? Them garden, You don't put me, he fine too much, I like him bad; plenty chop live, but oll them chop he live for spoil, becos I no get woman for cook him; I think better You dash me some!" '

[1] *Education in East Africa*, chap. ii, p. 19.

[2] Over sixty distinct languages have been identified in a single province.

[3] *Report on the Amalgamation of Northern and Southern Nigeria and Administration, 1912–19*, p. 61.

The University of Nigeria was opened at Nsukka in October 1960, with about 200 students, and the Ahmadu Bello University of Northern Nigeria at Zaria a year later.

There is also a Nigerian College of Arts, Science and Technology, with headquarters at Zaria and branches at Enugu and Ibadan; this provides specialized instruction in various forms of engineering, pharmacy, accountancy, secretaryship, administration, etc. There are in addition technical institutes, commercial schools, and other vocational institutes, as well as a number of teacher training schools.

There are over 500 secondary schools in Nigeria, as well as more than 16,000 primary schools. Adult literacy and mass education schemes have made considerable progress, and scholarships are offered to suitable candidates which are tenable at local and overseas institutions of higher education.

CHAPTER XXIII

LAND TENURE

Make ye sure to each his own
That he reap where he hath sown.

R. KIPLING: *A Song of the English*

Practically the only thing that is common to all the peoples who inhabit Nigeria is the communal ownership of land, and the absence of any conception of individual possession. The whole question of land tenure in Northern Nigeria was fully investigated by a Committee appointed by the Secretary of State for the Colonies in 1910, and 'it was clearly established by the evidence before the Committee that the use of land by the inhabitants throughout the Protectorate could be, and was by custom, transferred and inherited, but that it was the use of the land, and not the land itself, which was thus dealt with. . . . The actual difference lay in the power to revoke the original grant, and the evidence was overwhelming that this power always remained in the hands of the paramount chief.'[1] In Southern Nigeria the position was the same, and throughout the country the chiefs are considered as the trustees of the people, who are as a body the owners of the land. Among the Yorubas land belongs, superficially, to the family and not to the tribe, the individual being entitled to the use of a portion of his family's estate; the principle, however, is identical, the family being merely the tribe on a smaller scale, and the family itself having the use of the land by permission of the state, to whom the land would revert in the event of the extinction or outlawry of the family. 'The native conception appears to be that each head of a family is entitled to the enjoyment of sufficient land within the limits of the village or other community to which he belongs for the support of his household. If the land he has occupied is exhausted, he is entitled to permission to occupy fresh land. If he has no land, for instance, when he

[1] Orr, *op. cit.*, p. 248.

grows up and has a family of his own, he is entitled to permission to cultivate a new piece of land.[1]

The use of this land was granted by the chiefs or elders of the tribe during the good behaviour of the grantee, and could at any time be taken away from him if he failed in his duty to the state;[2] but so long as his obligations were met there was little danger of his being dispossessed, public opinion being too strong to be overridden by any but the most reckless tyrants. Indeed, the use of a farm often descends from father to son through many generations without in any way impairing the title of the tribe to the land or placing the later users in any stronger position as regards ownership of the farm than that of their ancestor who first was granted the use of it. The user is not permitted, in any circumstances, to sell the land, or even transfer it to the use of another, without the sanction of the tribal trustees, the chiefs. 'According to native customary law, land is inalienable, and . . . the sale of land is a crime against the state.'[3] Indeed, 'all those acts of native chiefs, which, by means of treaties made with strangers, alienated the tribal lands, are . . . according to native law and custom, *ultra vires*'.[4]

It was the aim of the British administration in Nigeria to support the African idea of land tenure and to preserve for future generations the unlimited ownership of the land by the tribe as against any form of freehold. The opening up of the country and the influx of European money and ideas would, without Government control, undoubtedly have resulted in the rapid acquisition by capitalists and speculators of the people's land. For very little would the improvident African barter away the morrow's happiness, and comparatively trifling sums would have sufficed in the past to purchase from some of the chiefs the land they held in trust for their people and their

[1] *Report of Northern Nigeria Lands Committee, 1910* (Cd. 5102). A Committee was also appointed to inquire into the conditions of land tenure in Southern Nigeria, but this Committee never reported.

[2] As the principal duty was that of fighting for the defence or aggrandisement of the tribe, there is little difference between this and the feudal system which formerly existed in England. Cf. *Native Races and their Rulers* (1918), by C. L. Temple, p. 141.

[3] *Nigerian Studies* (1910), by R. E. Dennett, p. 208.

[4] *Native Races and their Rulers*, by C. L. Temple, p. 140.

people's children. Public opinion could not restrain them, as the tribe would probably be ignorant of the meaning of the sale, or possibly unaware of the sale itself, till long after the transaction was complete, while the proceeds of the sale would become the property of the chiefs and not of the people—the real owners of the land. Owing to the climatic conditions in Nigeria, the country did not attract to it European settlers, and as a result of this Nigeria has escaped the serious problems of land tenure which have arisen in East Africa. There have, however, been demands from commercial companies for freehold sites for business purposes and, in at least one case, for ranching; these demands were invariably rejected.

Freehold property existed therefore only in the Colony (except in the case of the freeholds vested in the Niger Company when their Charter was revoked). Grants of land had been made by the King of Lagos before its cession in 1861, and these had been authenticated by the stamp of the British Consul; after the cession these grants were replaced by Crown grants which gave titles to the land. Lands in the Colony which were not included in Crown grants were held in communal tenure.[1]

In the Northern Region the law vested the ownership of all land in the Governor, as trustee for the people, and the Governor had the right of leasing such land to non-natives for a definite term of years. Land has thus been alienated to non-natives, to a very limited extent, for the purpose of tin-mining and for the building of business premises. So far as the people of the country are concerned, the settlement of land disputes was left to the Native Authorities and the Native Courts, which gave full consideration to customary rights and preserved the native conception of land tenure.

In the Western and Eastern Regions 'absolute ownership by non-natives has in some cases in the past been recognized by Government, but, broadly speaking, it may be said that the only title that Government recognizes in a non-native is a leasehold

---

[1] Two important cases relating to land in the Colony were decided by the Judicial Committee of the Privy Council in 1915 and 1921. (Attorney-General of Southern Nigeria and John Holt and Co., Liverpool, Ltd., A.C. 599; and Amodu Tijani v. The Secretary, Southern Nigeria, 2 A.C. 399.)

title'.[1] Some long leases have been obtained by non-native corporations for rubber and oil-palm plantations, but these are exceptional and practically all the land remains in the hands of native owners.

[1] *Titles to Land in Nigeria, a Collection of the Principal Enactments relating to* (1916), p. xiii.

CHAPTER XXIV

THE JUDICIAL SYSTEM

But is this law?
Ay, marry, is't.
W. SHAKESPEARE: *Hamlet*

The Common Law, doctrines of Equity, and the Statutes of general application which were in force in England on January 1, 1900 were brought into force throughout Nigeria on that date, and certain Imperial Acts have been applied to Nigeria since then by Order in Council.

Most of the statute law of Nigeria, however, is contained in Ordinances passed by the local legislatures. The competence of the Federal and Regional legislatures under the existing constitution, relating to the enactment of laws, is referred to in Chapter XXI.

There were, of course, separate laws in force in the two administrations of Northern and Southern Nigeria prior to the amalgamation of 1914, but these were replaced by a single body of Nigerian laws which were published in a revised form in 1923. The laws have been further revised since then.

Until 1946, the Legislative Council of Nigeria had no power of legislation for the Northern Provinces, the laws for which were enacted by the Governor, but most of the laws passed by the Legislative Council were, in fact, enacted by the Governor for the Northern Provinces, and many were applied to the British sphere of the Cameroons by special Ordinance. There were very few Ordinances which applied to the Northern Provinces only.

The 1954 Constitution provided that laws made by the Federal House of Representatives should apply to the whole of Nigeria, while laws made by the Regional legislatures applied only to the Regions.

In addition to the statute law of Nigeria there is in force such of the native law and custom as is not repugnant to the ideals of humanity and justice. The most important part of this is the Muhammadan law, which has effect in those parts of the country where the bulk of the people follow the religion of Islam. This law, of course, is based on the teachings of the Prophet as contained in the Koran and handed down by tradition, and in Nigeria the interpretations of the Maliki school[1] are accepted. Where Muhammadan law is not in force there is no written native law of any kind, but immemorial custom has given the force of law to the rules which govern the lives of the people in their dealings with one another. Especially is this the case with regard to their complicated matrimonial affairs, debt, and the occupation of land; the rules governing these and other important matters are not the less binding because they are unwritten, nor are they lacking in reason and justice. The cruel system of trial by ordeal, and the persecution of reputed 'witches', are no longer permitted.

To administer the various forms of law there are distinct classes of courts in Nigeria, namely, the Federal Supreme Court and the Regional High Courts (with their subordinate courts), and the Native Courts. The last named vary considerably in their personnel and powers, and are graded accordingly. Among the pagan tribes the Native Courts consist of a number of chiefs sitting together as joint judges; their powers are strictly limited and although their judicial ability is not very great they possess a thorough acquaintance with the locality and the people and a knowledge of the traditional customs of the tribes which would make them difficult to replace. The Native Courts of Southern Nigeria before 1914 were presided over by the District Commissioners,[2] and, although the decisions were in theory those of the entire court, they were, in fact, largely influenced by the District Commissioners. In the absence of these officers, the Native Courts were controlled in many cases by their clerks. The chiefs were, as a rule, illiterate, and the clerks, who had some sort of education and could write a kind of English, soon attained a dominance which did no good and, where the clerk was dishonest, as he frequently was, was an actual danger. The duties of the District Officers with regard

[1] See *Maliki Law* (1916), by F. H. Ruxton, C M G, formerly Lieutenant Governor Southern Provinces, Nigeria.

[2] Miss Mary Slessor, the celebrated lady missionary, was for some time the President of a Native Court.

to these courts were later confined to supervision and, by a simplification of procedure, the clerk was made the servant and not the master of the court.

The higher grades of Native Courts, to which much more power and responsibility are entrusted, are either presided over by a trained African judge or by a paramount chief with his principal officials as members; in the latter case such a court is styled a judicial council. Most of these higher grade courts administer Muhammadan law, and the Alkali of such a court is, as a rule, a man of considerable knowledge of law, and with access to useful reference libraries containing the works of Muhammadan jurists. Such judges receive adequate salaries, and are prohibited from accepting the presents and bribes which, in the days of the Fulani empire, formed their principal emolument. Christian and pagan communities are not compelled against their will to be subject to the jurisdiction of Muhammadan courts, but in districts where the population is partly Muhammadan and partly pagan, non-Muslim assessors sit with the Alkali in cases where pagans are concerned; this is important on account of the close connexion between religion and law in the eyes of Muhammadans, and affords a valuable protection to 'unbelievers'. Certain of the higher grade courts have the power of imposing the death sentence.

The advantages of these Native Courts in Nigeria are very great. At the present time they fill a gap in the judicial system which could not otherwise be filled save at a prohibitive cost and, moreover, they do the work allotted to them more efficiently than it could be performed by most magistrates. The courts are presided over by men of the same tribe as the litigants, speaking the same language and thinking along similar lines. In the past, a mistake made by a British official in a case affecting land, marriage, or any other of the subjects governed by native law, would have been regarded by the unsuccessful litigant and his friends as the result of ignorance, or the malicious interference of the official with the customs and rights of the people; the political effect of a number of such mistakes might have been far-reaching and disastrous. On the other hand, a similar mistake by a native court would be regarded by the losing party and by the public as an unfortunate happening due to the machinations of an evil spirit or to bribery, and the loser would accept the decision with the resolve that on the next occasion he would out-bribe his opponent or offer to the local deity such a sacrifice as would ensure a favourable verdict. In the greater part of the Northern Region the Muhammadan courts have been established for centuries and, save for the abolition of abuses, there has been no break in their traditions.

Until 1934 there were 'Provincial Courts' in the Provinces, presided over by the Residents and their officers. Few of these officers had any legal training, but against this disability must be set their knowledge of the people and the language, advantages which few Supreme Court judges would attain. It was therefore considered necessary to prohibit legal practitioners from appearing in the Provincial Courts,[1] and this was undoubtedly the cause of most of the criticism directed at these courts in the Southern Provinces.[2] In this connexion Lord Lugard says:

There can be no doubt that the appearance of Counsel in the District Courts—and even in the Native Courts—under the old system, had led to the fomenting of litigation by lawyers' agents, especially in land cases, with disastrous results to the ignorant people who had spent their substance in bootless litigation.[3]

The lawyers and their friends maintained that, by the exclusion of counsel from the courts, the public was deprived of the best advice and ignorant litigants were unable to secure justice; this was denied by experienced judges and by many senior administrative officers, and it is significant that when the judicial agreements with the Egbas and other Yoruba tribes were being negotiated, the representatives of these tribes of their own accord insisted that lawyers should not be allowed in the courts within their territories.[4]

[1] Nor in the Native Courts, where the procedure is in no way modelled on that of British courts.

[2] *Report by Sir F. D.* (later Lord) *Lugard on the Amalgamation of Northern and Southern Nigeria and Administration, 1912–19*, para. 54. The Provincial Court system, which had existed in Northern Nigeria before 1914, was only extended to the Southern Provinces after the amalgamation.

[3] *Ibid.*, para. 50. (See also *The Native Problem in Africa* (1928) by R. L. Buell, vol. 1, p. 651.)

[4] *Ibid.*, para. 50. The Hausa says 'ya yi mani lawya' (lit., he did to me lawyer) in describing how he has been tricked.

In 1934 the Provincial Courts were abolished and replaced by a High Court for the Protectorate, with qualified judges, and legal practitioners were allowed to appear before this court except in certain classes of cases; the High Court was abolished in 1943.

There is now a Federal Supreme Court for Nigeria consisting of the Chief Justice of the Federation, a number of Federal Justices, and the Chief Justices of each of the High Courts. There is a High Court for each of the Regions and for the Federal Territory of Lagos, each with a chief justice and other judges.

These High Courts, in addition to original jurisdiction, hear appeals from subordinate courts in their territories, but in the Northern Region there is also a Sharia Court of Appeal with power to hear appeals from subordinate courts on any question relating to Muslim matters.

In addition to extensive original jurisdiction, which includes jurisdiction in disputes between the Federation and a Region, or between Regions, the Federal Supreme Court has jurisdiction to decide appeals from the High Courts and from the Sharia Court of Appeal.

Appeals from the decisions of the Federal Supreme Court may be carried to Her Majesty in Council (the Judicial Committee of the Privy Council).

The Supreme Court and the High Courts differ little in their procedures from English Courts of Law. Judges wear the usual wig and gown and listen to the arguments of barristers, African and European, members of the same Inns of Court, and robed alike in conventional fashion. Witnesses who profess the Christian religion are sworn on the Bible, Muhammadans on the Koran, and pagans generally on a sword or knife.

The number of criminal cases brought before the courts continues to increase, but this is probably due to the more efficient administration of the country and not to any increase of crime. In the more backward provinces a great many murders are committed, many of them for apparently trifling causes, and until recently a certain amount of trading in young children still went on. On the whole, however, slave-trading may be said to have been stamped out.

There is a regular armed police force in Nigeria, and in addition an unarmed police force maintained by some of the Native

Administrations.[1] In the same way there are, in the Northern Provinces, in addition to the regular Government prisons, a number of prisons maintained by the Native Administrations, in which prisoners convicted by the Native Courts are confined.

Prisoners are not treated with severity, and the native of Nigeria sees no particular reason for avoiding the risk of a temporary sojourn in a Government prison. Comparing the former African punishments with those inflicted by the Lagos courts, Sir Gilbert Carter says:

> Crucifixion is not a pleasant sequel to the unlawful acquisition of a pot of palm oil, but a few months' residence in Lagos prison, which is far more comfortable and well regulated than any king's palace, is a welcome change as a fresh experience with regular meals. But for the isolation at night and a wearisome exercise known as 'shotdrill', there would be a scramble for cells which Lagos would find it hard to satisfy.[2]

Lord Lugard points out that

> prison life, so far from being deterrent, is even popular. That it is not looked on as degrading may be judged by the respectful salute paid by a warder to a prisoner of petty rank, and by the terms of fellowship and equality which often exist between the prisoners and their guardians.[3]

Save for his enforced separation from his wives, the prisoner has little to complain of, and there have not been wanting instances where he has implored, at the expiration of the term of his sentence, to be allowed to remain in prison. There is no doubt that some of the prisoners regard themselves as the servants of the Government, whose uniform they wear with little less pride than do the soldiers and police. There is a story that a passer-by was once assaulted by a member of a prison gang, who, on being interrogated as to the cause for the apparently unprovoked assault, explained that the man had failed to 'salute His Majesty's prisoners'. Lord Lugard records that

---

[1] In the Hausa speaking districts the native police are known as *dogarai*. These men do all the police work over very large areas.

[2] *African West*, No. 509 (1896).

[3] Lord Lugard, *The Dual Mandate*, p. 559.

on one occasion a prisoner, working in a gang away from the prison, seized an opportunity to run away.

The single constable in charge ran after him, and failing to capture him and fearing the consequences, he laid down his rifle and equipment and bolted himself; whereupon a prisoner marched his fellow-convicts back to prison, bringing the constable's arms with them.[1]

It is not uncommon, when a gang is under the nominal control of an inefficient warder, for some prisoner to assume the command and direct the work in hand. Some years ago a notorious burglar was convicted and committed to a provincial prison to serve a long sentence. He persuaded the warders to release him at night to carry on his profession, on the understanding that he would return before daylight and that they would receive a share of his takings. The bargain was loyally kept, the warders receiving £30 as their share of the first night's work; but a quarrel among the warders themselves over the spoils led to the discovery of the plot, and the enterprising burglar was removed to another prison.

[1] Lord Lugard, *The Dual Mandate*, p. 559.

CHAPTER XXV

THE CIVIL SERVICE

And some there be which have no memorial; who are perished as though
they had never been; . . . but these were merciful men, whose righteousness
hath not been forgotten.   ECCLESIASTICUS xliv, 9-10.

In the Nigerian Civil Service, as in those of the other West
African Colonies and Protectorates, the African and European
staffs were formerly distinct, although there were always a few
Africans filling what were then called 'European posts'. As we
have seen, the African staff was in former years recruited very
largely from the Gold Coast and Sierra Leone, whence a number of men of sufficient education could be obtained for the
Services of the newly organized Governments of Nigeria.
These valuable civil servants gave loyal and efficient help to the
British administration in its early years. As the administration
expanded, and the demand for clerical assistance became more
and more insistent, a large number of Nigerians, trained in the
Government and mission schools, entered the Government
offices as clerks. Few of these were well educated and many
were unfitted for any but the lowest positions; their inefficiency
was injurious not only to themselves but to the whole of the
African staff of which they were too often taken as examples.
So little reliance could be placed on the majority of the Nigerian
staff in the early days that practically no responsible work
was ever allotted to them, with the consequence that those who
had ability were given little opportunity for proving their
worth.

Many of the Africans in the Service in those days had
left school at an early age and made no effort afterwards to
improve their minds. The local papers did not fail to deplore
the fact that so many young Africans started in life with an
insufficient education, but did not seem to realize that this was
the reason why practically all the higher posts in the Civil Service were filled by Europeans. There was a continuous agitation for the appointment of more Africans to the better paid
and more responsible offices, and it was maintained that there

were many Africans, in the Service and out of it, who were capable of filling senior posts. Some of the junior civil servants, who had but a smattering of book-learning, were fully satisfied that they were completely educated and fitted for the highest positions, and many of those who knew better took no trouble to undeceive them. Nor was it fully appreciated that even educational and professional qualifications are insufficient in themselves to fit a man for a responsible post. Strength of character and personal integrity were disregarded as qualifications.

Many responsible officials, by no means antagonistic to African aspirations, felt that the efficiency and the reputation for integrity of the Service would suffer if insufficiently qualified men, of uncertain character, were placed in positions of responsibility and trust.

It was not only in Government departments that these fears existed and the inefficiency of African employees as a class was realized. Mercantile establishments were in no better position and were compelled, as business grew, to employ Europeans in ever increasing numbers. Whatever might be thought of the Government's employment policy, it is unlikely that commercial firms, with an eye to profits, would have employed expensive European staffs if a sufficient number of capable Africans had been available locally. For some years after the First World War an African merchant, a shrewd and successful man, felt obliged to employ Europeans in his business; an able man himself, and full of confidence in the future of his race, he realized with regret that there were not at that time a sufficient number of Africans available for all the positions of trust and responsibility that had to be filled.

Notwithstanding the difficulties, appointments were made to senior posts whenever suitable Africans could be found. Several Africans filled responsible posts in Nigeria in former years, the best known being the late Dr Henry Carr, who held a very senior position in the Nigerian administrative service after many years as Deputy Director of Education.

Since the last war the position has changed considerably. In 1948 a Commission which included a majority of African members submitted a unanimous report recommending that certain principles of policy should be accepted, the chief being that no non-Nigerian should be recruited for any Government post unless no suitable and qualified Nigerian was available to fill it. The Commission also recommended that Public Service Boards with non-official majorities should select candidates for senior posts in the Government Service and that a large number of scholarship grants should be made with a view to training Nigerians for responsible positions. These and other recommendations were adopted by the Government, which provided large sums for scholarships at the University College, Ibadan, and at universities in the United Kingdom and the United States of America. Today the Civil Service is staffed almost entirely by Nigerians.

In the past, Europeans appointed to the Nigerian Service were recruited as a rule in the United Kingdom. Candidates were selected by the Secretary of State for the Colonies, or in some cases by the Crown Agents for the Colonies, and were formally appointed by the Governor. Some were employed on temporary agreements for fixed periods or for some specific work, but the majority of the officials were appointed to the permanent staff subject to a probationary period of three years. Appointments were made either to the Administrative Service or to one of the Departments. Officers were sometimes transferred on promotion to other colonial territories but most of the Europeans appointed to Nigeria remained there throughout their official lives.

Before taking up their appointments in Nigeria, the officers of some branches of the Government were required to take a special course of training in England, which included the study of tropical hygiene, criminal law, Muhammadan law, accounting, ethnology and surveying. Officers were also required to begin the study of one of the Nigerian languages, and within a certain period to pass examinations in this language. In some parts of the country, and especially in the Hausa-speaking districts, the officers stationed there acquired a thorough mastery of the language, but unfortunately there are so many dialects and distinct tongues in Nigeria that it was impossible to allot to every district an officer who could speak the local language.

The most important branch of the European staff was the Administrative Service, which included the Secretariat and the

Political Officers. The latter were the backbone of the administration. Each of the provinces[1] of Nigeria was under the control of a Resident, responsible to the Lieutenant-Governor of the group of provinces concerned.[2] The province contained two or more 'divisions', each being in the charge of a senior District Officer assisted by other Political Officers stationed at various towns in the division. The duties of these Political Officers—Residents, District Officers, Assistant District Officers and Cadets—were innumerable. They sat as judicial officers to hear criminal and civil cases, and they exercised a general supervision over the Native Courts. They directed and controlled, in the absence of a police officer, the constabulary stationed in the various divisions, and they supervised the local prisons. They overlooked the construction of local roads by the Native Administrations and encouraged the chiefs to provide labour for the building of Government roads and railways. In those areas where direct taxation was in force they personally surveyed the properties of the taxpayers. They acted as local treasurers at their stations, receiving revenue and paying wages to Government employees; much of their time was occupied (or wasted) in keeping accounts and prepar-

---

[1] The names and the boundaries of the provinces have been changed from time to time. The present provinces are: *Northern Region:* Adamawa, Bauchi, Benue, Bornu, Ilorin, Kabba, Kano, Katsina, Niger, Plateau, Sardauna, Sokoto, Zaria. *Western Region:* Abeokuta, Benin, Colony, Delta, Ibadan, Ijebu, Ondo, Oyo. *Eastern Region:* Abakaliki, Annang, Calabar, Degema, Enugu, Ogoja, Onitsha, Owerri, Port Harcourt, Umuahia, Uyo, Yenagoa.

[2] From 1914 to 1933 the officer in charge of the Northern Provinces (now the Northern Region) was styled Lieutenant-Governor. From 1933 to 1951 he was styled Chief Commissioner and from 1951 to 1954 the title of Lieutenant-Governor was revived. From 1954 there was a Governor in charge of the Northern Region.

From 1914 to 1935 there was a Lieutenant-Governor in charge of the Southern Provinces, and a Chief Commissioner from 1935 to 1939. In 1939 the Southern Provinces were divided into two groups, the Western Provinces (now the Western Region) and the Eastern Provinces (now the Eastern Region), each under a Chief Commissioner until 1951 when the officers in charge were styled Lieutenant-Governors. From 1954 there was a Governor in charge of the Western Region and another in charge of the Eastern Region.

Until 1954 the Southern Cameroons was included in the Southern Provinces or the Eastern Provinces.

ing returns. They made plans and sketches of the country and descriptions of routes. They settled boundary disputes and the endless squabbles of neighbouring tribes and villages.

A Political Officer accompanied every military force dispatched on a punitive expedition, and endeavoured to persuade the people to submit without fighting. It was in a vain attempt to effect a peaceful settlement and to avert the bloodshed that was inevitable if the Protectorate troops came into contact with the rebels that Mr Hillary and Mr Scott, two Political Officers, were killed at Satiru in 1906. Many others have perished at the hands of ignorant and savage tribes, by whom they were held responsible for grievances real or imaginary. Phillips and his comrades on the road to Benin in 1897, Moloney at Keffi in 1902, Crewe-Read at Owa in 1906, Maltby in the Montoil country in 1916, are examples of Political Officers who have lost their lives in the execution of their duty. Many others have escaped narrowly from death, saved by their courage or resource, or more often by sheer good fortune; and Lord Lugard has said:

Not once, but very many times I have known an officer, with an armed escort at his heels, expose his life recklessly to a shower of poisoned arrows, a scratch from one of which would probably mean death, rather than fire a shot, in the conviction that he would presently be able to settle matters without bloodshed. And I have sometimes wondered whether those who without knowledge accuse him of carelessness of human life would have stood the test themselves.[1]

The Political Officers lived in lonely stations, with little or no protection, they travelled alone or with but a scanty escort, and that so few were in real danger was due to the great respect felt for them by the people generally and the personal affection they frequently inspired in the people under their charge. The value of their work was very great, but it was less than the value of their reputation and prestige, for to a large section of the population they—and they alone—represented the Government. To quote Lord Lugard once again:

The way in which turbulent and sometimes treacherous tribes have been converted into staunch friends—fairly law-abiding and

[1] *Lord Lugard, The Dual Mandate*, p. 578.

K

progressive—by the sympathy and personal courage of the British District Officer is nothing short of amazing.[1]

More recently, Miss Margery Perham paid the following tribute to officers of the District Administration, in the fifth of her Reith Lectures, on December 10, 1961:

The office of District Commissioner should stand out in history as one of the supreme types developed by Britain to meet a special demand . . . The District Commissioner was for years the un-crowned king of his district, the would-be father of his people, the jack of all trades; a unit in a service of reliable and interchangeable parts who were not yet robots. He could be relied upon to be humane, uncorrupt, and diligent, even when left alone quite unsupervised in the outer parts of a very testing continent. . . .

I have not forgotten the letter I had from one of the first Africans to become an Assistant District Commissioner and who was posted to some remote sub-station. 'I marvel', he wrote, 'that an English graduate can endure to live alone in such a place for £400 a year.'

[1] Lord Lugard, *The Dual Mandate*, p. 585.

CHAPTER XXVI

COMMUNICATIONS

Clear the land of evil, drive the road and bridge the ford.
R. KIPLING: *A Song of the English*

Until the shores of the Gulf of Guinea had been explored by Portuguese navigators in the fifteenth century, the only communication between Nigeria and the outside world was across the Sahara desert. The routes followed by the explorers Denham and Clapperton,[1] and later by Barth and his companions,[2] had been well known for centuries, and for centuries caravans had taken the products of Hausaland and Bornu northwards to Tripoli and Tunis across the sea of sand which lay between. The principal export of those times consisted of slaves, and the routes were marked by the bones of men and women who had died of thirst and fatigue on the terrible journey.[3]

From the middle of the fifteenth century the coast of Nigeria was in touch with Europe. The sea-borne traffic, small at first, grew rapidly as the slave-trade developed. Vessels sailed from European ports for the estuaries of the rivers between Lagos and the Cameroons, loaded there with slaves for America or the West Indies, and returned thence to their home ports loaded with sugar or other products of the western hemisphere. It was easy to get from England to Nigeria by sea, but until the nineteenth century was well advanced the return journey almost invariably had to be made by way of America or the West Indies.[4] However, when the slave-trade had been made illegal for British subjects, and a trade in the products of the oil-palm had sprung up in its stead, communication between

[1] See Chapter VII.
[2] See Chapter VIII.
[3] See quotation from Denham and Clapperton's *Narrative* in Chapter VII.
[4] Mungo Park in 1797 and Richard Lander in 1831, after their adventurous travels in Africa, had to return to England by way of the West Indies and Rio Janeiro respectively.

Nigeria and England became less difficult. In 1852, largely through the exertions of Mr Macgregor Laird,[1] the African Steamship Company[2] received a Charter, and a regular service began. There are now frequent and reliable services by comfortable, well-equipped steamers between England and Nigeria, the voyage taking thirteen days. There are also direct services between Nigeria and South African, European and American ports.

All the ports of Nigeria are situated on rivers, at the mouths of which are shifting sandbars. The principal port is Lagos, which, as the result of extensive harbour works, is now accessible to large ocean-going vessels. In 1907, when dredging operations began, the draught on the bar at Lagos did not exceed nine or ten feet, and it was not until 1914 that large vessels were able to enter the harbour. Until that date all cargo for Lagos was transferred at Forcados from the ocean steamer to a 'branch boat' small enough to cross the Lagos bar in safety. Passengers were transferred from the mail steamers to a tender in the open roadstead off Lagos under conditions of considerable discomfort and some danger. They were lowered over the side of the mail steamer, three or four at a time, in a 'mammy-chair',[3] into a surf-boat, which rose and fell on a sea which was never still: crouched on the thwarts of the surf-boat as the 'mammy-chair' was lowered again with another load, paddled across by half-naked Krumen to the tender and hoisted aboard in another 'mammy-chair', when they were finally landed on the wharf at Lagos they were hot, tired, and not infrequently soaked to the skin.

The Lagos harbour works consist of two long moles, one on either side of the entrance to the harbour, and training banks

[1] For an account of Mr Laird's activities in Nigeria, see Chapters VII and XII.

[2] The African Steamship Company has maintained since 1852 an uninterrupted association with West Africa. This Company's steamers, together with those of the British and African Steam Navigation Company Limited, run regularly to Nigeria, the joint service being managed by Messrs Elder Dempster Lines Limited.

[3] The 'mammy-chair' is a wooden box, with two seats facing one another, each seat being able, with difficulty, to accommodate two persons. From each corner of the box is a rope or iron bar, joined overhead. Suspended by these ropes or bars the 'mammy-chair' is lowered from a derrick.

within to control the scouring currents.[1] Several powerful
dredgers are employed on the bar and in maintaining the
channels within the harbour. At Apapa, on the mainland
opposite Lagos, there are quays and warehouses capable of
dealing with the cargoes of the largest vessels, with accommodation for the reception and departure of passengers. More than
six million tons of shipping are handled in the port of Lagos/
Apapa each year.

Further east is Port Harcourt, situated on the Bonny River,
about thirty-five miles from the sea. Although the place was
practically unknown before the First World War, it is now the
second port of Nigeria. It is the terminus of the eastern division
of the railway and, being only 150 miles from the Udi coal-
field, is also a coaling port. The port of Bonny, at the mouth
of the river, is the terminal of the crude oil pipeline.

Between Lagos and Port Harcourt lies the Niger Delta,
in which are the ports of Burutu, Warri, Sapele and Koko.
Forcados, situated on what was once the principal outlet of
the Niger, is now of little importance. Burutu is the point
of departure for the river steamers which visit the various
stations on the Niger and Benue. A deep channel is being
dredged across the bar at the mouth of the River Escravos
in order to provide better access to these delta ports.

Calabar, formerly known as Old Calabar, is on the Calabar
River, a tributary of the Cross River, some forty miles from
the open sea. Other ports are Degema, Akassa, Brass and
Opobo, all of considerable importance in the early years of
the Niger Coast Protectorate but now overshadowed by Lagos
and Port Harcourt.

All Nigerian ports are under the control of the Nigeria
Ports Authority, while the Inland Waterways Department is
responsible for maintaining rivers and other inland waterways
in a navigable condition.

These inland waterways are of great importance, and until
the completion of the railway from Lagos to Kano in 1911
the Niger and Benue rivers formed the principal means of
communication with the interior. It was not until after the

---

[1] The stone for the construction of the moles and training banks had to be
obtained from a quarry at Aro, some 60 miles from Lagos. The longer of
the two moles is over 7,000 feet.

successful expedition of the *Pleiad* up these rivers in 1854[1] that a successful trade was established by British merchants in the hinterland, but once begun it developed rapidly. For centuries before, however, the natives of the country had used these great rivers for the transport of their goods in canoes and indeed, in the absence of any roads, water transport was a necessity. Nigeria is particularly fortunate in this respect. Innumerable rivers, navigable by canoes even in the dry season, and connected, in their lower reaches, one with another, by a network of creeks and lagoons, afforded the inhabitants an ideal and comparatively safe way of carrying their produce to the main markets.

In the extreme north camels and donkeys were used as beasts of burden, but further south, owing to the prevalence of the tsetse fly, animal transport was out of the question, and where canoes could not be used, everything had to be carried on the heads of men. As there was no wheeled traffic, 'bush paths', narrow tracks which did not permit of two men walking abreast, were a sufficient substitute for roads, and every village and farm was connected by these paths, which traversed the thickest forests and the densest bush.

A railway to develop the hinterland of Lagos had long been considered, but it was not until 1896 that construction was begun, from Ebute Metta, on the mainland opposite Lagos, towards the interior. In 1900 the line was open for traffic as far as Ibadan (120 miles), and was extended to Jebba, on the Niger, by the end of 1909. In the meantime a railway was begun, in 1907, from Baro, 130 miles below Jebba on the Niger, towards Kano. The railway was pushed on from Jebba and connected with the latter line at Minna, 462 miles from Lagos. A railway bridge had in the meantime been constructed between Ebute Metta and Iddo Island, which was itself connected with Lagos by another bridge, and Iddo became the southern terminus of the railway.[2]

A branch line (now abandoned) was constructed from Zaria, on the main line, to Jos, which is situated on the Bauchi plateau among the tin-fields, and this line proved of great benefit to the

---

[1] See Chapter VIII.

[2] The trains connecting with the mail steamers now use the Apapa terminus.

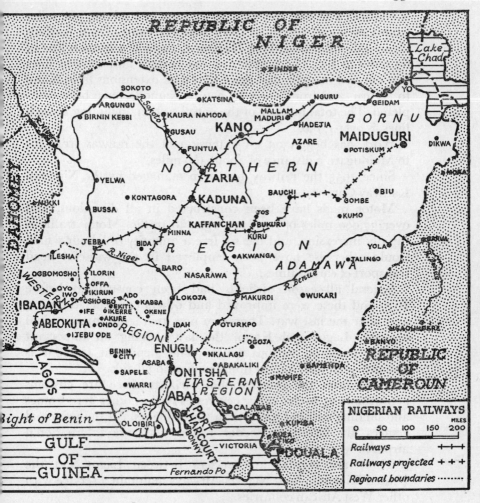

mining industry. The gauge of this branch line was 2 feet
6 inches; all the other lines in Nigeria are of 3 feet 6 inches
gauge. The trains were at first ferried across the Niger at
Jebba, but in 1916 a railway bridge over the river was completed in spite of serious engineering difficulties.

The eastern division of the railway begins at Port Harcourt
and, passing the coal-field at Enugu (151 miles), reaches the
Benue at Makurdi. Here the river is crossed by a railway bridge
opened in 1932. From the north bank of the Benue the railway

is continued to join the western division at Kaduna, 566 miles from Lagos and 569 miles from Port Harcourt. From Kaffan-chan, 458 miles from Port Harcourt, there is a branch line of 63 miles to Jos. The junction of the eastern and western lines was effected in 1926, and since that date extensions from Kano to Nguru, and from Zaria to Kaura-Namoda have been completed. The total mileage of the entire system, including branch lines, is over 1,750.

Work has begun on an extension of the railway from Jos to Maidugari, a distance of about 400 miles.

Since 1955 the railway has been managed by the Nigerian Railway Corporation.

Motor roads have been constructed in all directions, and over 37,000 miles of road are open to traffic. Motor traffic is rapidly increasing, and has set free a quantity of labour which would otherwise have been employed in the wasteful head transport of earlier times.

Several all-season airfields had been constructed before 1939 and these were improved and others constructed during and after the last war. There are now two large international airports, Lagos and Kano, the latter being an important staging point on various routes. The airport at Calabar is also provided with international navigational aids.

Apart from the international airports there are customs aerodromes at twelve other centres as well as other aerodromes and landing strips at more than thirty places. All the principal centres are linked by feeder routes with the international airports.

There are regular air services between Lagos and the United Kingdom, and Nigeria Airways maintain a service with other West African countries.

Every important town in Nigeria is now in telegraphic communication with Lagos and there are several miles of wire open for traffic in addition to wireless communications. There are also telephone exchanges in more than one hundred centres. Radio telephone services are available from Lagos to the United Kingdom, the United States, and other countries.

CHAPTER XXVII

TRADE AND INDUSTRY

If we listen to the voice of reason and duty . . . some of us may live to see the reverse of that picture from which we now turn our eyes with shame and regret. We may live to behold the natives of Africa engaged in the calm occupations of industry, in the pursuit of a just and legitimate commerce.

Speech by WILLIAM PITT, *in 1792, on the slave-trade.*

We have seen that the beginnings of trade between Europe and Nigeria in historical times were in the fifteenth and sixteenth centuries, when Portuguese and English mariners visited Benin and exchanged the products of their countries for pepper, 'elephants' teeth', and palm oil. Very soon the immense profits of the slave-trade practically destroyed all other business, and Negro slaves were bartered for spirits, fire-arms, ammunition, and other products of civilized Europe. When the slave-trade was declared illegal for British subjects at the beginning of the nineteenth century, British merchants took up the palm-oil trade, which increased rapidly in volume and in value. In 1806, 150 tons of palm oil were exported from the Oil Rivers to Liverpool; in 1839 the export had risen to 13,600 tons, and in 1960 no less than 183,000 tons of palm oil, valued at £13,181,000 were exported from Nigeria, in addition to the large quantity consumed locally. There is also a large export of palm kernels, 418,000 tons, valued at £25,097,000, being shipped in 1960.

Palm oil is extracted from the fruit of the oil-palm tree,[1] 'hard oil' being obtained from fermented fruit, and 'soft oil' without fermentation, the latter being the more valuable. The oil is obtained from the pericarp or fleshy exterior of the fruit, the nuts being then dried and cracked and the kernels extracted, both oil and kernels being then sold, generally through a middleman,[2] for export. Palm kernels exported to Europe

---

[1] *Elaeis guineensis.*

[2] The middleman has so often been abused as an unnecessary parasite on trade and industry that the views of Lord Lugard are interesting: 'The native middleman, who purchases in small quantities in distant markets and

are crushed by machinery, the oil extracted being more valuable than palm oil, while the cake or meal produced from the kernels after the extraction of the oil is useful as a food for cattle. The oil-palm tree is seldom planted but grows wild throughout a large area.

Next in importance to the products of the oil-palm are cocoa, groundnuts[1] and rubber. The quantity of hides and skins exported indicates the large number of livestock raised, principally in the north; it is estimated that there are in the country more than ten million cattle, fourteen million goats, and four and a half million sheep.

The oil-palm, cocoa and rubber grow chiefly in the south of Nigeria, whence come also crude oil and timber. From the north come groundnuts, cotton, benniseed, shea products and tin.

The quantity and value of the principal exports from Nigeria in 1938 (the last pre-war year) and 1960 are given in the table on the opposite page.

The total value of exports from Nigeria in the year 1900 was £1,858,000 as against £16,538,000 in 1926, £9,461,000 in 1938, and £160,897,000 in 1960. In the last-mentioned year the value of exports to the principal countries of destination was as follows:

	£
United Kingdom . .	77,551,000
Holland	20,718,000
United States of America .	15,596,000
Germany (West) . .	12,465,000

The import trade had grown in value from £1,735,000 in 1900 to £13,597,000 in 1926, £8,632,000 in 1938, and

sells in bulk, arranging for transport to the merchant's store, is often an agent no less indispensable than the merchant himself—especially in the Southern Provinces . . . the interference of middlemen where they are not required constitutes a burden on trade.' *Report on the Amalgamation of Northern and Southern Nigeria and Administration, 1912–19*, p. 42.

[1] The seed of the pod of *Arachis hypogoea*, known also as the monkey-nut or peanut.

	1938		1960	
	Quantity	Value	Quantity	Value
	tons	£	tons	£
Palm Kernels	312,048	2,168,366	418,040	25,097,000
Palm Oil	110,243	981,330	183,366	13,181,000
Cocoa	97,100	1,566,684	153,925	35,056,000
Groundnuts and Groundnut Cake	180,136	1,305,828	385,183	23,512,000
Rubber	3,135	135,797	57,227	14,256,000
Cotton Lint	5,729	246,856	26,865	5,905,000
Cotton Seed	6,859	24,857	39,937	1,039,000
Benniseed	17,743	152,200	27,280	1,832,000
Shea[1] products	3,088	21,876	2,544	76,000
Hides and Skins	5,845	515,788	9,479	4,520,000
Tin Ore	10,486	1,435,157	10,658	6,044,000
Crude Oil	—	—	827,702	4,408,000
Columbite	—	—	3,334	2,120,000
	Cub. ft.		Cub. ft.	
Mahogany Logs and Sawn Timber	602,628	50,415	—	—
	—	—	24,139,971	7,035,000

[1] *Butyrospermum Parkii.*

£212,908,000 in 1960. The value of importations from the principal countries in 1960 were as follows:

	£
United Kingdom	91,405,000
Japan	27,812,000
Germany (West)	15,210,000
Holland	11,608,000
United States of America	11,579,000
Norway	7,210,000
Italy	7,207,000
France	4,883,000
India	4,178,000

An important economic development since the war has been the establishment of Marketing Boards, which ensure the orderly marketing of crops and stable prices for the producers, besides contributing funds for research from their large accumulated reserves. The Cocoa Marketing Board was established in 1947 and three other Boards followed in 1949, the Oil-Palm Produce Marketing Board, the Cotton Marketing Board, and the Groundnut Marketing Board (which also deals with benniseed[1] and soya).

In the past, most of the trade of Nigeria was in the hands of large firms and combines, mainly British, the head offices of which were in England. Local agents, assisted by staffs of European and African clerks, represented the firms in Nigeria, but the control of business and the policy of the firms was retained by the principals in England. Commenting on this, Lord Lugard has said:

The day has passed when the West African merchant can remain in England and expect to conduct the trade of a country in which he has never resided, possibly never even visited for many years, if at all, and regarding which he is dependent for first-hand information on the agents whose responsibility to Government he denies. Such methods of carrying on business—peculiar, I think, to West Africa—are no longer appropriate now that the conditions of health and the amenities of life have so greatly improved.[2]

These arrangements were quite unnecessary as most of the local representatives of British firms were extremely able men, well qualified to take their proper place in helping to guide the economic destinies of Nigeria. The 'palm-oil ruffian' of early days had long passed away, and trade in Nigeria was conducted in recent years by men of a fine type, who were a credit to their race.

The existence of the 'palm-oil ruffian' was not a myth. Many of the men who had engaged in the slave-trade while yet it was legal remained to carry on one more legitimate, but they brought to their new business the cruelty, lack of scruple, and carelessness of human life which they had acquired in their

[1] Sim-sim.
[2] *Report on the Amalgamation of Northern and Southern Nigeria and Administration, 1912–19*, p. 35. See also the comments of Mr Ormsby-Gore in his *Report on Visit to West Africa, 1926* (Cmd. 2744), p. 169.

previous degrading occupation. An American captain, writing in 1805, said of the African slave-trade that it 'ruins the health or takes the lives of nine-tenths who are concerned in it, and poisons the morals of most of the survivors'.[1] The tradition was carried on by the palm-oil traders, who sometimes used force to help their business and whose transactions with the Africans were not always strictly honest. There were, of course, some notable exceptions, but generally speaking the British trader in Nigeria in the early days appears to have been an unpleasant person. As recently as 1904 a Governor pointed out the disadvantages of a system under which agents came out to Nigeria on agreement for fixed periods, with commissions on profits, with the results that they never looked beyond the immediate present and, indeed, opposed any measures designed to effect improvement in the future which might impose a temporary handicap on trade.

Trading by barter lingered on for years in some parts of the country, in spite of the Government's efforts to stop it. Lord Lugard says that 'There is abundant evidence to show that the attraction of the apparently "double profit" to be gained by ignoring currency as a medium of trade, and selling and buying in a single transaction, has done much to destroy trade'.[2] Currency is, however, becoming more popular. In former days slaves were used as currency; their place was subsequently taken by cases of gin, in which the wealth of many a powerful chief was invested. Cowries,[3] manillas,[4] brass rods,[5] and copper wires[6] were used until comparatively recently.

British gold and silver were for a long period legal tender in Nigeria. Most of the currency, however, consisted of special West African silver and alloy coins, and Nigerian nickel-

---

[1] *The Romance of an Old-time Shipmaster* (Captain John Willard Russell), edited by Ralph D. Paine, New York (1907), p. 164.

[2] *Report on the Amalgamation of Northern and Southern Nigeria and Administration, 1912–19*, p. 43.

[3] Small shells (*Cypraea moneta*), about half an inch in length, fastened together, as a rule, in strings of 40 to 100 each. Generally imported from the East Indies.

[4] A heavy horseshoe-shaped piece of metal, of brass and alloy.

[5] About the size of a small stair-carpet rod, but bent over so that the two ends nearly meet.

[6] Or 'cheethams'.

bronze coins. The latter had a round hole in the centre which
prevented them being passed off as coins of a higher value.
When the small coin of the nominal value of one-tenth of a
penny (a convenient sum in a cheap country) was first issued a
large number were used as washers under the nails by which
corrugated iron roofs were secured.

So often, in the early days of the British Protectorate, was
the ignorant peasant 'done' by his more sophisticated African
brother, that he was extremely suspicious of certain coins.
The similarity between the half-crown and the florin made it
easy for the unscrupulous to pass off large numbers of florins
as the higher-valued coin, with the result that no one would
willingly accept a half-crown at a value higher than two shillings. There was also a general suspicion of coins bearing the
head of Queen Victoria, the only reason given being that she
was dead. When during the war of 1914–18 the problem of
currency became acute, and the Government issued some
emergency notes bearing a facsimile of the signature of the
Treasurer, the Lagos market-women expressed some anxiety
for that officer's health, and viewed his departure for England
with profound misgiving.

The West African Currency Board was constituted in 1912
to provide for and to control the supply of currency to the
British West African Colonies and Protectorates. In addition
to the West African coins referred to above, the Board issued
a large number of currency notes which circulated freely in
Nigeria.

The currency of Nigeria today is the Nigerian pound which
is linked to sterling at par. Notes are issued by the Central
Bank of Nigeria in denominations of £5, £1, 10s. and 5s.,
and coins are in denominations of 2s., 1s., 6d., 3d., 1d., and ½d.
The currency issued by the West African Currency Board,
referred to above, is still legal tender but is being gradually
withdrawn from circulation.

In addition to the Central Bank, there are a number of
banks doing business in Nigeria. The first bank opened in the
country belonged to the African Banking Corporation, which
started business in Lagos in 1891, but did not last more than a
year. The Bank of Nigeria entered the field some years later
but was absorbed by the Bank of British West Africa[1] in 1912.

[1] Now the Bank of West Africa.

The Colonial Bank (now Barclays Bank, Dominion, Colonial and Overseas) began business in 1917. The following were operating in Nigeria in 1960: African Continental Bank, Agbonmagbe Bank, Bank of West Africa, Bank of Lagos, Bank of the North, Banque de L'Afrique Occidentale, Barclays Bank, D.C. & O., Berini Bank, British and French Bank, Merchants Bank, Muslim Bank (West Africa), and National Bank of Nigeria.

The people long regarded the banks with suspicion, and considerable quantities of coin were hoarded and hidden away. As education progresses this difficulty is being overcome.

There are still comparatively few large industrial undertakings in Nigeria, but the number is steadily increasing, and plans are being made for still more industrialization in the country. At Sapele there is one of the largest plywood and veneer factories in the world; at Kaduna a huge textile mill; at Apapa (near Lagos) a modern brewery; at Ibadan an up-to-date cigarette factory. At other centres there are cement, soap, shoe and various different factories.

In certain parts of the country leather is worked, and locally-made utensils of calabash, brass and earthenware are made everywhere for use and sale as curios. Most of these utensils are crude, and are decorated as a rule with geometrical designs. Before the advent of European trade goods several tribes worked the local iron into weapons and agricultural implements, but these cannot now compete with the cheaper and better-made articles. Cloth is woven on narrow hand-looms from the locally-grown cotton, and is generally durable, though coarse; it is often spoken of in a general way as 'Kano cloth'.

The inhabitants appear to have mined and used the tin deposits on the Bauchi plateau and the galena deposits near Abakaliki, but the minerals of the country were hardly touched until European companies with modern machinery were able to work at them. The tin-mines on the Bauchi plateau and in a few other places have proved of immense value to Nigeria, the ore, which is a high-grade concentrate of tin oxide with a metal equivalent of over seventy per cent, fetching, as a rule, a good price. Salt was formerly worked by some of the tribes, but has been unable to compete with the imported article. Gold in alluvial form has been found in various localities in small quantities, and lodes have been discovered but not developed.

There is a large coal-field in the vicinity of Enugu, east of the Niger, and Nigerian coal is used by the railway and Government vessels. Modern facilities have been provided at Port Harcourt (151 miles by rail from Enugu) for the loading and bunkering of vessels, and the tin-mines are now using Nigerian coal to work their machinery. Most of the work in the mines is performed by African labourers, who are rapidly improving in ability. The tribe from which this labour is drawn was in a very backward state when the mines were first opened, but has benefited greatly by contact with the outside world and the large sums earned in wages.

For many years exploration for oil was carried on without success, but in January 1956 oil was struck at Oloibiri, in the Niger delta, by the Shell-BP Petroleum Development Company. Further strikes in this neighbourhood were made later and pipelines were laid from the wells to Port Harcourt, where there are storage tanks. The port of Bonny is now the terminal of the oil pipeline. The first shipment of crude oil from Nigeria was made in February 1958.

Stock-raising is carried on entirely by the Africans, the Fulani especially possessing large herds of cattle which roam about the country seeking pasturage and water. Except for the dwarf 'pagan' cattle, which appear to be immune from trypanosomiasis, the herds suffer considerably from the attentions of the tsetse fly. There are several good breeds of horses, sheep (hair-producing), and goats, and swine are kept in the non-Muslim areas. Camels, oxen, and the small native donkeys are used as pack-animals. The Nigerian poultry is generally small and tough; in many parts of the country the Africans do not eat eggs but, knowing that white men have a curious partiality for them, will bring them in, for sale or as presents, long after they have ceased to be edible.

The principal occupation of the people of Nigeria is agriculture. The country is practically self-supporting in food, and there is a considerable internal trade in locally grown foodstuffs. Nearly all the cultivation, preparation and transport of export crops to port or rail is done by Nigerians.

It is a popular misconception that the African is lazy,

based no doubt on the fact that he frequently sleeps where everyone can see him, in broad daylight, and has a rooted objection to work in the hottest part of the day, the time generally selected by the inexperienced European for his most frantic exertions. The misconception probably first arose during the days of slavery, when the Negro was treated by his white master as a mere machine, to be driven at full pressure till it broke down. With no incentive to work save the fear of punishment, there is little wonder that the slave in the American or West Indian plantation was lazy and only worked when he had to. The enormous production in Nigeria is as much a tribute to the industry of its inhabitants as to the fertility of the soil.

Owing to the large amount of available land, the Nigerian farmers have resorted largely to 'shifting cultivation'. A space is cleared in the forest, generally by the means of fire, and crops are planted among the stumps of the great trees which are too difficult to remove; manure is not used, and when, after a short time, the soil is exhausted, the farm is abandoned and another clearing made. The damage to the forests caused by this method of farming is considerable, but it is difficult to see how it can be remedied at present. The plough is not often used, but the people have some notion of the advantages to be gained by the rotation of crops.

The possibilities of Nigeria are enormous. The land is fertile, the population large and industrious, and it is nearer to European markets than most of the countries whence tropical produce is exported. Writing in 1919, Lord Lugard said that 'Nigeria affords an immense field for British trade, and though it has developed at an extraordinary rate, it is capable of indefinite expansion'.[1]

[1] *Report on the Amalgamation of Northern and Southern Nigeria and Administration, 1912–19*, by Sir F. D. (later Lord) Lugard, p. 29.

CHAPTER XXVIII

CONCLUSION

O God of all creation,
  Grant this our one request,
Help us to build a nation
  Where no man is oppressed,
And so with peace and plenty
  Nigeria may be blessed.

A verse of the Nigerian *National Anthem*

Although Lagos became a Colony in 1862, it was only within the last sixty years before independence that British rule had become effective throughout Nigeria. What was accomplished within that period, and what justification was there for British rule? Imperialism is regarded in some quarters with such suspicion that it may be difficult to convince the prejudiced mind of the true motives that prompted the conquest of this vast territory. National acquisitiveness and commercial interests no doubt played a part, but in the case of Nigeria it may safely be said that the British entered on their great trust with reluctance and considerable hesitation, and that philanthropy was not the least of the influences that led us to take up the burden.

There is probably little to be gained by discussing, at this date, whether the British were right or wrong in taking Nigeria. No European nation had the right to assume sovereignty over the inhabitants of any part of Africa, and the claims put forward by the various Governments at the Berlin Conference in 1885 took little account of the rights of the people who lived in the territories claimed. As against the other European Powers, however, Great Britain had an undoubted claim to Nigeria, and this was readily admitted. As against the African inhabitants there could be no claim, but there was at least a good excuse. British rule, admittedly by force, gave the people good government in place of tyranny, abolished human sacrifice and slavery, and secured for the country a material prosperity which could never have been realized under the chaotic conditions that previously existed.

Enormous sums were spent by the British Government, with no possible selfish motive, in suppressing the oversea slave-trade. The cost of the preventive naval squadron which was maintained on the West Coast of Africa for over sixty years was very considerable, and the establishments at Sierra Leone and Fernando Po added to the expense. The attack on Lagos in 1851 was undertaken solely with a view to destroying the chief stronghold of the slave-traders in Nigeria, and when, ten years later, Lagos was annexed to the British Crown, its possible value as a Colony was not considered, and the suppression of slavery was once again the motive. Four years later, in 1865, a Committee of the House of Commons recommended the abandonment of all the British possessions in West Africa except Sierra Leone, and at this time Lagos was regarded frankly as an encumbrance. In the early 'eighties Europe suddenly awoke to a realization of the potential value of African colonies and the famous 'scramble for Africa' began, which resulted in the arrangement of spheres of influence at the Berlin Conference of 1885.

Slow to move, Great Britain lost the Cameroons, which was hers for the asking, and only the energies of private individuals and the long unofficial connection of the British with the coastal tribes of Nigeria prevented this country from falling to the French and Germans. Even then it was difficult to persuade the British people that the country was worth having, and successive Governments refused to commit themselves to the effective control of the immense territories involved. A 'dog in the manger' policy could not, however, be continued indefinitely, as Germany and France were still casting longing eyes on the rich lands which the British had failed to take, and at the close of the nineteenth century Great Britain became definitely committed to a more forward policy. Within a few years the whole of Nigeria was being administered by British officials, aided, whenever possible, by the African chiefs and their officials. The bloody tyranny of the King of Benin, the malign influence of the Aros, the oppression of the slave-raiding Fulani Emirs, were replaced by an ordered administration which stood between the long-suffering peasantry and their hereditary tyrants.

For the first time in the history of the country there was

peace and security for all. The farmer was able to reap where he had sown and the trader to move unmolested from one market to another. Fear, the fear of the sudden raid at midnight or the murderous ambush on the road, was swept away,[1] and under the *Pax Britannica* the country prospered and grew rich. When the testing time came, in 1914, and again in 1939, the people never wavered in their allegiance to the flag which had given them these benefits.

The demand for self-government and independence, however, was as insistent in Nigeria as in other parts of Africa, and was put to the United Kingdom Government by the political leaders of Nigeria with dignity and restraint. This demand has been met and the Nigerians are now responsible for the government of their own country. Nigeria has become independent without violence, and in a spirit of friendliness and moderation that has been most impressive. Owing to the good sense of the people and the ability of their leaders, the British officials have been able to hand over to their African successors a peaceful, prosperous, and well-developed territory, with a future that is full of hope. How have the people of the country been affected by the imposition of British rule which has now been removed?

The chiefs have had little to complain of. It is true that they were no longer permitted to amuse and enrich themselves with war and slave-raiding, but their position was more assured and their incomes more certain. They had no longer the fear of defeat by a stronger enemy, and there was far less chance of their being ousted from their positions by intrigue or violence. The Government recognized their position and supported them in it so long as they kept within the limits set by their advisers. Their religion, an important matter to the Muhammadan chiefs, was respected, their system of law was recognized, and their methods of administration, shorn of the abuses which even they in theory detested, have been preserved. Three years after the conquest of the Fulani empire the loyalty of the chiefs was tested by the Satiru disaster; again, during the wars of 1914–18 and 1939–45 there were favourable opportunities for an attempt at shaking off the British yoke; that none wavered is

[1] The more terrible fear of the supernatural still remains, and will remain until Christianity and education drive out superstition.

a sufficient answer to those who think that British government was not appreciated in Nigeria. For the rest, it may be sufficient to quote Sir Hugh Clifford, who says:

In the case of primitive peoples . . . unadulterated native rule is not popular or desired by the bulk of the natives. It means the oppression of the weak by the strong, the tyranny of might, the abnegation of law, the performance of various bloody rites, and perennial intertribal strife—in a word, all the things which are most abhorrent to the principles of democracy.[1]

No attempt was made to force upon Nigeria all of the doubtful advantages of modern civilization, but each tribe was permitted and encouraged to preserve such of its customs and ideas as were not repugnant to natural justice and humanity. It is true that the task of the Government was enormously simplified by the absence of European settlers who, in other colonial territories, caused much difficulty to those responsible for protecting the interests of the native inhabitants. It would, however, have been easy, at the beginnings of British administration, to have committed blunders which would have been fatal to success. Particularly in the matter of land tenure was there opportunity for blunder, but, in spite of some pressure, Government held firmly to the principle that the land is the property of the people and may not be alienated to settlers or speculators.

It was not, however, this policy that excluded settlers from Nigeria. For centuries West Africa was regarded as the 'White Man's Grave', and the mortality among Europeans in Nigeria up to the end of the nineteenth century did nothing to improve the reputation of the country, which was believed to possess the worst climate in the world. The causes of the various diseases which took so heavy a toll of human life in the past are now well known, and in most cases means have been devised to prevent them. The insects and microbes which carry these diseases can be destroyed or at any rate reduced in numbers, but even when malaria and other evils are abolished it is doubtful whether Europeans could ever live permanently in Nigeria and rear their children. The effect of the sun, and

[1] *German Colonies: A Plea for the Native Races* (1918), by Sir Hugh Clifford, p. 13.

the humidity that exists in certain parts of the country, combine to make it a land in which Europeans cannot permanently dwell.

There is, however, no longer any reason to regard a journey to Nigeria as a short cut to the grave. The days have long passed when, as in the Niger Expedition of 1841, 48 out of 145 men would die on the river in nine weeks. In Lagos, in 1896, 28 out of 150 Europeans died within a few months.[1] In 1951, out of an estimated European population for the whole of Nigeria of 15,000, there were only 47 deaths. Such an improvement is perhaps due to increased knowledge of how to live in the tropics and to better housing conditions as much as to medical discoveries.

Conditions for those of all races have improved enormously. The incidence of disease has been reduced and better housing and improved water supplies have increased both health and comfort. Broadcasting and television have added to the amenities, and sport of all kinds has been encouraged. There are good hotels for the accommodation of visitors.

As most of the inhabitants of Nigeria were infected with malaria, one of the methods adopted in the past for preserving the health of Europeans was segregation. Separate residential areas were laid out, where this was possible, for Europeans and Africans, generally with an intervening space of about a quarter of a mile which was kept clear of bush. By this arrangement the chances of infected mosquitoes biting Europeans was considerably reduced and a higher standard of sanitation could be maintained in the reservation than would have been possible in a 'mixed' neighbourhood. Although segregation had certain advantages for the African also, it was resented as a form of discrimination and has long been abandoned.

Relations between Africans and Europeans in Nigeria have in the past been reasonably harmonious. There have been exceptions, due in most cases to bad manners rather than to malice, but many personal friendships have existed between individuals of the two races and there is a general mutual respect. Let us hope that this mutual respect will remain and that Nigerians will believe, as the British are justified in

[1] Annual Report on Lagos for 1896, No. 219 (C. 8650–17).

believing, that Britain has little to be ashamed of in her past dealings with this great country. In the words of the Prime Minister of Nigeria, the British were known 'first as masters and then as leaders, and finally as partners, but always as friends'. Long may that friendship continue!

APPENDIX A—GENEALOGY OF THE SULTANS OF SOKOTO SINCE THE *JIHAD*

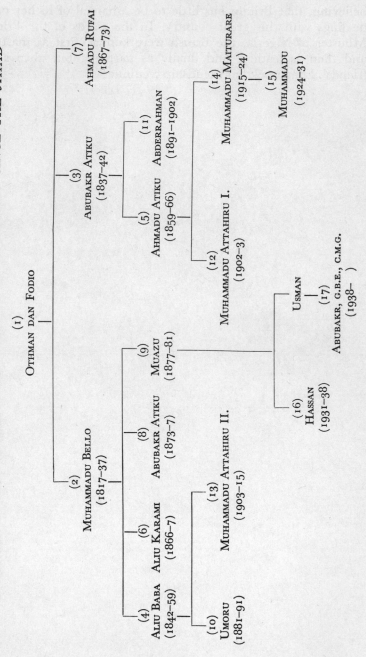

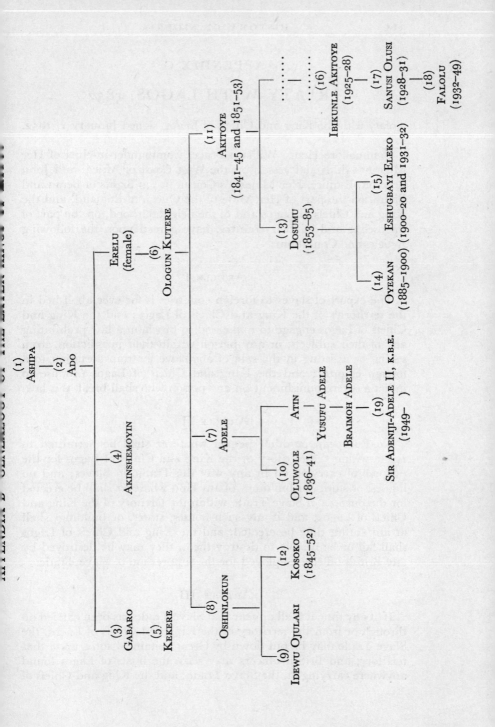

APPENDIX C

TREATY WITH LAGOS, 1852

Treaty with the King and Chiefs of Lagos, signed January 1, 1852.

Commodore Henry William Bruce, Commander-in-chief of Her Majesty's ships and vessels on the West Coast of Africa, and John Beecroft, Esquire, Her Majesty's Consul in the Bights of Benin and Biafra, on the part of Her Majesty the Queen of England, and the King and Chiefs of Lagos and of the neighbourhood, on the part of themselves and of their country, have agreed upon the following Articles and Conditions:—

ARTICLE I

The export of slaves to foreign countries is for ever abolished in the territories of the King and Chiefs of Lagos; and the King and Chiefs of Lagos engage to make and to proclaim a law prohibiting any of their subjects, or any person within their jurisdiction, from selling or assisting in the sale of any slave for transportation to a foreign country; and the King and Chiefs of Lagos promise to inflict a severe punishment on any person who shall break this law.

ARTICLE II

No European or other person whatever shall be permitted to reside within the territory of the King and Chiefs of Lagos for the purpose of carrying on in any way the Traffic in Slaves; and no houses, or stores, or buildings of any kind whatever shall be erected for the purpose of Slave Trade within the territory of the King and Chiefs of Lagos; and if any such houses, stores, or buildings shall at any future time be erected, and the King and Chiefs of Lagos shall fail or be unable to destroy them, they may be destroyed by any British officers employed for the suppression of Slave Trade.

ARTICLE III

If at any time it shall appear that Slave Trade has been carried on through or from the territory of the King and Chiefs of Lagos, the Slave Trade may be put down by Great Britain by force upon that territory, and British officers may seize the boats of Lagos found anywhere carrying on the Slave Trade; and the King and Chiefs of

Lagos will be subject to a severe act of displeasure on the part of the Queen of England.

ARTICLE IV

The slaves now held for exportation shall be delivered to any British officer duly authorized to receive them, for the purpose of being carried to a British Colony, and there liberated; and all the implements of Slave Trade, and the barracoons or buildings exclusively used in the Slave Trade, shall be forthwith destroyed.

ARTICLE V

Europeans or other persons now engaged in the Slave Trade are to be expelled the country; the houses, stores, or buildings hitherto employed as slave-factories, if not converted to lawful purposes within three months of the conclusion of this Engagement, are to be destroyed.

ARTICLE VI

The subjects of the Queen of England may always trade freely with the people of Lagos in every article they wish to buy and sell in all the places, and ports, and rivers within the territories of the King and Chiefs of Lagos, and throughout the whole of their dominions; and the King and Chiefs of Lagos pledge themselves to show no favour and give no privilege to the ships and traders of other countries which they do not show to those of England.

ARTICLE VII

The King and Chiefs of Lagos declare that no human being shall at any time be sacrificed within their territories on account of religious or other ceremonies; and that they will prevent the barbarous practice of murdering prisoners captured in war.

ARTICLE VIII

Complete protection shall be afforded to Missionaries or Ministers of the Gospel, of whatever nation or country, following their vocation of spreading the knowledge and doctrines of Christianity, and extending the benefits of civilization within the territory of the King and Chiefs of Lagos.

Encouragement shall be given to such Missionaries or Ministers in the pursuits of industry, in building houses for their residence, and schools and chapels. They shall not be hindered or molested in their endeavours to teach the doctrines of Christianity to all persons willing and desirous to be taught; nor shall any subject of the King and Chiefs of Lagos who may embrace the Christian faith be, on that account, or on account of the teaching or exercise thereof, molested or troubled in any manner whatsoever.

The King and Chiefs of Lagos further agree to set apart a piece of land, within a convenient distance of the principal towns, to be used as a burial-ground for Christian persons. And the funerals and sepulchres of the dead shall not be disturbed in any way or upon any account.

ARTICLE IX

Power is hereby expressly reserved to the Government of France to become a party to this Treaty, if it shall think fit, agreeably with the provisions contained in Article V of the Convention between Her Majesty and the King of the French for the suppression of the Traffic in Slaves, signed at London, May 22, 1845.

In faith of which we have hereunto set our hands and seals, at Lagos, on board Her Britannic Majesty's ship *Penelope*, January 1, 1852.

(L.S.)	H. W. BRUCE.
(L.S.)	JOHN BEECROFT.
(L.S.)	KING AKITOYE.
(L.S.)	ATCHOBOO.
(L.S.)	KOSAE.

APPENDIX D

TREATY WITH LAGOS, 1861

Treaty between Norman B. Bedingfield, Commander of Her
Majesty's ship *Prometheus*, and Senior Officer of the Bights
Division, and William McCoskry, Esquire, Her Britannic
Majesty's Acting Consul, on the part of Her Majesty the Queen
of Great Britain, and Docemo, King of Lagos, on the part of
himself and Chiefs.

ARTICLE I

In order that the Queen of England may be the better enabled to
assist, defend, and protect the inhabitants of Lagos, and to put an
end to the Slave Trade in this and the neighbouring countries, and
to prevent the destructive wars so frequently undertaken by
Dahomey and others for the capture of slaves, I, Docemo, do, with
the consent and advice of my Council, give, transfer, and by these
presents grant and confirm unto the Queen of Great Britain, her
heirs and successors for ever, the port and Island of Lagos, with
all the rights, profits, territories, and appurtenances whatsoever
thereunto belonging, and as well the profits and revenue as the
direct, full, and absolute dominion and sovereignty of the said port,
island, and premises, with all the royalties thereof, freely, fully,
entirely, and absolutely. I do also covenant and grant that the
quiet and peaceable possession thereof shall, with all possible
speed, be freely and effectually delivered to the Queen of Great
Britain, or such person as Her Majesty shall thereunto appoint for
her use in the performance of this grant; the inhabitants of the said
island and territories, as the Queen's subjects, and under her
sovereignty, Crown, jurisdiction, and government, being still
suffered to live there.

ARTICLE II

Docemo will be allowed the use of the title of King in its usual
African signification, and will be permitted to decide disputes
between natives of Lagos with their consent, subject to appeal to
British laws.

ARTICLE III

In the transfer of lands, the stamp of Docemo affixed to the docu-
ment will be proof that there are no other native claims upon it,
and for this purpose he will be permitted to use it as hitherto.

In consideration of the cession as before-mentioned of the port and island and territories of Lagos, the Representatives of the Queen of Great Britain do promise, subject to the approval of Her Majesty, that Docemo shall receive an annual pension from the Queen of Great Britain equal to the net revenue hitherto annually received by him; such pension to be paid at such periods and in such mode as may hereafter be determined.

LAGOS, *August* 6, 1861.

(*Signed*)   DOCEMO   his
                             ×
                             mark.

              TELAKE   his
                             ×
                             mark.

              ROCAMENA   his
                             ×
                             mark.

              OBALEKOW   his
                             ×
                             mark.

              ACHEBONG   his
                             ×
                             mark.

NORMAN B. BEDINGFIELD,
    Her Majesty's ship *Pro-metheus*, Senior Officer, Bights Division.

W. McCOSKRY,
    Acting Consul.

APPENDIX E

EXTRACTS FROM
ORDER IN COUNCIL OF
FEBRUARY 21, 1872

At the Court at *Osborne House, Isle of Wight*, the 21st day of February, 1872.

Present: The Queen's Most Excellent Majesty; His Royal Highness Prince Arthur; Lord President; Lord Steward; Mr. Forster.

Whereas by an Act of Parliament made and passed in the Session of Parliament holden in the 6th and 7th years of Her Majesty's reign, intituled 'An act to remove Doubts as to the Exercise of Power and Jurisdiction by Her Majesty within divers Countries and Places out of Her Majesty's Dominions, and to render the same more effectual', it is, amongst other things, enacted that it is and shall be lawful for Her Majesty to hold, exercise, and enjoy any power or jurisdiction which Her Majesty now hath, or may at any time hereafter have, within any country or place out of Her Majesty's dominions, in the same and as ample a manner as if Her Majesty had acquired such power or jurisdiction by the cession or conquest of territory:

And whereas Her Majesty hath by sufferance power and jurisdiction over her own subjects in the States and Territories hereinafter named:—

And whereas it is expedient to make provision for the due and effectual exercise of such power and jurisdiction:

1. Now, therefore, in pursuance and by virtue of the said recited Act of Parliament, Her Majesty is pleased, by and with the advice of Her Privy Council, to order, and it is hereby ordered, that Her Majesty's Consul or Consuls appointed to the places hereinafter named, shall have full power and authority to carry into effect, and to enforce by the means and in the manner hereinafter mentioned and provided, the observance of the stipulations of any Treaty, Convention, or Agreement, or of any Regulations appended to any Treaty, Convention, or Agreement now existing, or which may hereafter be made between Her Majesty, her heirs and successors, and the Chief or Chiefs of any of the territories situate upon the Old Calabar, Bonny, Cameroons, New Calabar, Brass, Opobo, Nun and Benin Rivers, or any part of the said territories; and to make and to

enforce, by fine, banishment, or imprisonment, Rules and Regulations for the observance of the stipulations of any such Treaty, Convention, or Agreement, and for the peace, order, and good government of Her Majesty's subjects being within the said territories.

*   *   *

3. And it is further ordered that it shall be lawful for Her
Majesty's Consul as aforesaid, upon information, or upon the complaint of any person that a British subject has violated any of the
stipulations of any Treaty, Convention, or Agreement, or of any
Regulations appended to any Treaty, Convention, or Agreement
between Her Majesty and the Chief or Chiefs of any of the States
aforesaid, or has disregarded or infringed any of the Rules or Regulations for the observance of the stipulations of any such Treaty,
Convention, or Agreement, affixed and exhibited according to the
provisions of the next preceding Article of this Order, to summon
before him the accused person, and to receive evidence and to
examine witnesses on oath, as to the guilt or innocence of such
person in regard to the offence laid to his charge, and to award
such penalty of fine or banishment against any person convicted
of an offence against any such Treaty, Convention, or Agreement,
or appended Regulations, or against the said Rules and Regulations
as may be specified therein respectively; and any charge against
a British subject for a breach of any such Treaty, Convention, or
Agreement, or appended Regulations, or for a breach of such
Rules and Regulations, for the observance of any such Treaty,
shall be heard and determined by the Consul without Assessors;
Provided always that in no case shall the penalty to be incurred
by a breach of such Rules and Regulations exceed £100, or banishment for three months.

4. And it is further ordered that any charge against a British
subject for a breach of Rules and Regulations other than those
relating to the observance of Treaties shall, in like manner, be
heard and determined by Her Majesty's Consul; and in all cases
in which the penalty shall not exceed £40, or banishment for one
calendar month, or imprisonment for a period not exceeding fourteen days, the Consul shall hear and determine the charge sum-
marily without the aid of Assessors; but where a penalty attached
to a breach of the Rules and Regulations other than those relating
to the observance of Treaties shall amount to more than £40, or to
banishment for more than one month, or imprisonment for more
than fourteen days, the Consul, before he shall proceed to hear the
charge, shall summon two disinterested British subjects of good
repute, being members of a Court of Equity, as hereinafter pro-

vided (see Section 5), to sit with him as Assessors, which Assessors, however, shall have no authority to decide on the innocence or guilt of the person charged, or on the amount of fine or punishment to be awarded to him on conviction, but it shall rest with the Consul to decide on the guilt or innocence of the person charged, and on the amount of fine or punishment to be awarded to him: Provided always, that in no case shall the penalty to be attached to a breach of Rules and Regulations other than those for the observance of Treaties exceed £100, or banishment for more than three calendar months, or imprisonment for more than twenty-one days and provided further, that in the event of the said Assessors, or either of them, dissenting from the conviction of the party charged, or from the penalty of fine or other punishment awarded to him by the Consul, the Consul shall take a note of such dissent, with the grounds thereof, and shall require good and sufficient security for the appearance of the person convicted at a future time, in order to undergo his sentence or receive his discharge; and in default of such security being given, it shall be lawful for the Consul to cause the person to be detained in custody until such security is given; and the Consul shall, with as little delay as possible, report his decision with all the particulars of the case, together with the dissent of the Assessors, or either of them, and the grounds for their dissent, to Her Majesty's Principal Secretary of State for Foreign Affairs, who shall have authority to confirm or vary or reverse the decision of the Consul as to him may seem fit.

5. And it is further ordered that it shall be lawful for Her Majesty's Consul to reorganize within the territories aforesaid, the local Courts, known as the Courts of Equity, appointed for the settlement, by permission of the Consul, of trading disputes between British subjects or between British traders and natives, such Courts of Equity to be composed of British agents and traders at the place where the Court is established, and out of their members to supply the Assessors required to assist the Consul in the trial of more important cases; and the Consul is hereby empowered carefully to lay down Regulations for the guidance of such Courts, whose decisions shall, after being submitted to and sanctioned by the Consul, be deemed and taken to be the decision of Her Majesty's Consul in such trading dispute or cause of litigation, and shall have the like effect and operation, and shall be entered and recorded as such, and shall be final and conclusive, and shall not be open to appeal: Provided always, and it is hereby ordered, that every British agent or trader, residing within any of the territories aforesaid, who shall, upon requisition from the Consul, refuse to be enrolled as a member of the Court of Equity

L

established at the place where he resides, shall, so long as he continue to refuse, forfeit his right to protection, as a British subject, in respect to any suit, dispute, or difficulty in which he may have been or may be engaged or involved within the territories aforesaid so long as he refuses to enrol himself as a member of such Court.

6. And it is further ordered, that all suits, disputes, differences, and causes of litigation of a civil nature arising between British subjects within the territories aforesaid, shall be heard and determined by Her Majesty's Consul, or in his absence and with the consent of the parties to the suit, by the local Court of Equity, whose decision must, however, in all cases be submitted to the Consul for his final sanction before it can be carried into effect.

7. And it is further ordered, and it shall be lawful for Her Majesty's Consul, or for the Court of Equity, but subject to the sanction of the Consul, in like manner to hear and determine any suit of a civil nature arising within the territories aforesaid between a British subject and a subject of the native Chief or Chiefs, or a subject or citizen of any other Foreign State or Government in amity with Her Majesty: Provided always that the native or other foreigner who may be party to such suit, either as Complainant or Defendant, shall have consented to submit to the jurisdiction of Her Majesty's Consul or of the Court of Equity, and will give sufficient security that he will abide by his decision, and will pay such expenses as the Consul or Court shall adjudge.

8. And it is further ordered, that it shall be lawful for Her Majesty's Consul to summon not less than two, and not more than four, disinterested British subjects of good repute, being members of a Court of Equity as hereinbefore provided, to sit with him as Assessors at the hearing of any suit, dispute, difference, or cause of litigation whatever of a civil nature brought before him for decision; and in case the sum sought to be recovered shall exceed £100, such suit shall not be heard by the Consul without Assessors, if within a reasonable time such Assessors can be procured; but the Assessors aforesaid shall have no authority to decide on the merits of such suit, but in the event of such Assessors, or any of them dissenting from the decision of the Consul, the Consul shall enter the fact of such dissent and the grounds thereof in the Minutes of the Proceedings.

*   *   *

15. And in order more effectually to repress crimes and offences on the part of British subjects within the territories aforesaid, it is further ordered, that it shall and may be lawful for Her Majesty's Consul to order by writing under his hand and seal any British sub-

ject who shall have been convicted twice before him of any crime and offence, and punished for the same, and who, after execution of the sentence of the Consul, on any second conviction, shall not be able to find good and sufficient security to the satisfaction of the Consul for his future good behaviour, or who, having been sent out of any of the aforesaid territories, under any sentence, shall, during such sentence, return, to be sent out of his Consular District; and to this end the Consul shall have power and authority, as soon as may be practicable after execution of the sentence on such second conviction, to give notice to any such twice-convicted party, or any person so returning as aforesaid, that he must leave his Consular District under penalty of a fine not exceeding £100, such fine to be increased, or a punishment not exceeding twenty-one days' imprisonment awarded, at the discretion of the Consul, in the event of the party refusing to obey such notice.

* * *

24. And it is further ordered, that it shall be lawful for Her Majesty's Consul, from time to time, to establish rules of procedure and practice to be observed in proceedings before him, or before the Courts of Equity, composed as aforesaid, and to make Regulations for defraying the expenses of witnesses in such proceedings, and the cost of criminal prosecutions, and also to establish rates and scales of fees to be taken in regard to civil suits heard and determined before the said Consul; and it shall be lawful for the said Consul to enforce by seizure and sale of goods, or, if there be no sufficient goods, by such other punishment as he may deem expedient, the payment of such established fees, and of such costs or expenses as may be adjudged against the parties, or any of them: Provided always that a table specifying the rates of fees to be so taken shall be affixed and kept exhibited in the public office of the said Consul.

25. And it is further ordered, that all fees, penalties, fines, and forfeitures levied under this Order, shall be paid to the public account, and shall be applied in diminution of the public expenditure on account of Her Majesty's Consulate in the territories aforesaid.

26. And it is further ordered, that it shall be lawful for Her Majesty's Consul, if called upon to do so, to grant probate of the will or letters of administration to the intestate estate of any British subject, or any native of a State or place under British protection, who shall die and leave property within any of the aforesaid territories; and if such probate or letters of administration shall not be applied for within thirty days after the death of the deceased person, it shall be lawful for the Consul to administer to the estate

of such person, and for so doing to reserve to himself out of the proceeds of such estate a commission not exceeding two and a half per cent on the amount thereof; and in case any agent for any firm in the United Kingdom shall die within the territories aforesaid, and there should be no person competent to take charge of his property or that of the firm, the Consul shall cause a full and true inventory to be made of all the property in charge of the deceased, and shall transmit such inventory, or a copy thereof, to the firm, and it shall also be lawful for the Consul in such case (if he shall think fit) to appoint any proper person to be the agent of the firm until the pleasure of such firm be ascertained.

27.   And it is further ordered, that a register shall be kept by Her Majesty's Consul of all British subjects residing within the territories aforesaid; and that every British subject now residing within those territories shall, within a reasonable time after the promulgation of this Order (such time to be specified in a notice affixed and publicly exhibited in the Consular Office), apply to the Consul to be enrolled in such register; and every British subject who may arrive within the said territories (except British subjects borne on the muster-roll of any British ship) shall, within a reasonable time after his arrival (such time to be specified as aforesaid), also apply to the Consul to be enrolled in such register; and any British subject who shall refuse or neglect to comply to be so enrolled as hereinbefore mentioned, and who shall not excuse such refusal or neglect to the satisfaction of the Consul, shall, so long as he refuses, not be entitled to be recognized or protected as a British subject in respect to any suit, dispute, or difficulty in which he may have been or may be engaged or involved within the territories aforesaid, at any time when he shall not have been or shall not be so enrolled.

28.   And it is further ordered, that Her Majesty's Consul shall and may exercise within his Consular District all or any of the powers which, by any Act or Acts of the Imperial Parliament for the regulation of merchant seamen, or for the regulation of the mercantile marine, or for the enforcement of regulations regarding quarantine, may now or at any time hereafter be exercised by any justice or justices of the peace within Her Majesty's dominions.

29.   And it is further ordered, that nothing in this Order contained shall be deemed or construed to prevent Her Majesty's Consul in the territories aforesaid from doing or performing any act whatsoever which British Consuls within any other State in amity with Her Majesty are by law, usage, or sufferance entitled or enabled to do or perform.

*   *   *

31. And it is further ordered, that the word 'Consul' in this Order shall include every person duly authorized to act in the aforesaid capacity within the territories specified in Article 1, and the term 'Court of Equity' shall be construed to include the principal resident British merchants and traders, duly authorized by the Consul to hear and entertain civil suits within their respective districts, as provided in Article 5; and that, in the construction of this Order, words importing the singular number shall, if necessary, be understood to include several persons, matters, or things; and words importing the masculine gender only shall, if necessary, be understood to import the feminine gender, unless there be something in the subject or context repugnant to such construction.

*   *   *

33. It is further ordered, that this Order shall take effect on and after the twenty-first day of February, one thousand eight hundred and seventy-two.

*   *   *

APPENDIX F

TREATY WITH ASABA, 1884

Treaty with Kings, Queen, and Chiefs of Asaba, signed at Asaba.

Her Majesty the Queen of the United Kingdom of Great Britain and Ireland, Empress of India, etc., and the Kings, Queen, and Chiefs of Asaba, being desirous of maintaining and strengthening the relations of peace and friendship which have for so long existed between them:

Her Britannic Majesty has named and appointed E. H. Hewett, Esq., her Consul for the Bights of Benin and Biafra, to conclude a Treaty for this purpose.

The said E. H. Hewett, Esq., and the said Kings, Queen, and Chiefs of Asaba have agreed upon and concluded the following Articles:—

ARTICLE I

Her Majesty the Queen of Great Britain and Ireland, etc., in compliance with the request of the Kings, Queen, Chiefs, and people of Asaba, hereby undertakes to extend to them, and to the territory under their authority and jurisdiction, her gracious favour and protection.

ARTICLE II

The Kings, Queen, and Chiefs of Asaba agree and promise to refrain from entering into any correspondence, Agreement, or Treaty with any foreign nation or Power, except with the knowledge and sanction of Her Britannic Majesty's Government.

ARTICLE III

It is agreed that full and exclusive jurisdiction, civil and criminal, over British subjects and their property in the territory of Asaba is reserved to Her Britannic Majesty, to be exercised by such Consular or other officers as Her Majesty shall appoint for that purpose.

The same jurisdiction is likewise reserved to Her Majesty in the said territory of Asaba over foreign subjects enjoying British protection, who shall be deemed to be included in the expression 'British subject' throughout this Treaty.

ARTICLE IV

All disputes between the Kings, Queen, and Chiefs of Asaba, or between them and British or foreign traders or between the aforesaid Kings, Queen, and Chiefs and neighbouring tribes, which cannot be settled amicably between the two parties, shall be submitted to the British Consular or other officers appointed by Her Britannic Majesty to exercise jurisdiction in Asaba territories for arbitration and decision, or for arrangement.

ARTICLE V

The Kings, Queen, and Chiefs of Asaba hereby engage to assist the British Consular or other officers in the execution of such duties as may be assigned to them; and, further, to act upon their advice in matters relating to the administration of justice, the development of the resources of the country, the interests of commerce, or in any other matter in relation to peace, order and good government, and the general progress of civilization.

ARTICLE VI

The subjects and citizens of all countries may freely carry on trade in every part of the territories of the Kings, Queen, and Chiefs parties hereto, and may have houses and factories therein, subject to the Agreement made on the 28th August, 1884, between the Kings, Queen, and Chiefs and the National African Company (Limited), of London.

ARTICLE VII

All ministers of the Christian religion shall be permitted to reside and exercise their calling within the territories of the aforesaid Kings, Queen, and Chiefs, who hereby guarantee to them full protection.

All forms of religious worship and religious ordinances may be exercised within the territories of the aforesaid Kings, Queen, and Chiefs, and no hindrance shall be offered thereto.

ARTICLE VIII

If any vessels should be wrecked within the Asaba territories, the Kings, Queen, and Chiefs will give them all the assistance in their power, will secure them from plunder, and also recover and deliver to the owners or agents all the property which can be saved.

If there are no such owners or agents on the spot, then the said property shall be delivered to the British Consular or other officer.

The Kings, Queen, and Chiefs further engage to do all in their power to protect the persons and property of the officers, crew, and others on board such wrecked vessels.

All claims for salvage dues in such cases shall, if disputed, be referred to the British Consular or other officer for arbitration and decision.

ARTICLE IX

This Treaty shall come into operation, so far as may be practicable, from the date of its signature.

Done in duplicate at Asaba, this 1st day of November, 1884.

(Signed)   EDWARD HYDE HEWETT.

KING OBI AKATA, his × mark.
KING OBI NEZA OMUKRORU, his × mark.
KING OBI WABUNI, his × mark.
KING OBI OSUDEBE, his × mark.
KING OBI RAPU OKOSA, his × mark.
KING OBI NTEE, his × mark.
KING OBI MEMEKA, his × mark.
KING OBI OGASIE, his × mark.
KING OBI CHEGEA, his × mark.
KING OBI NEYA, his × mark.
KING OBI AUBA, his × mark.
QUEEN OMU WANUKA, her × mark.
KING OBI ONACHIA, his × mark.
KING OBI EHBUAKA, his × mark.
CHIEF OSADEBE, his × mark.
CHIEF ITOR OMORDIE, his × mark.
CHIEF AFEHNAZA OMORDIE, his × mark.
CHIEF BALLIE OMORDIE, his × mark.
CHIEF MBA ODIE, his × mark.
CHIEF AWUNOR ODIE, his × mark.

Witness to the mark-signatures of the above thirteen Kings, of the Queen, and of the six Chiefs:

(Signed)   REGINALD GOUGH PAYNTER.

(Signature in Arabic of 'Mohamedu Shitta', a merchant of Lagos where he is also known as William Shitta.)

APPENDIX G

TREATY WITH SOKOTO, 1885

Copy of English duplicate of Treaty between Umoru, King of the Mussulmans of the Soudan and Sultan of Sokoto, for himself and Chiefs, on the one part, and those Europeans trading on the Kworra and Benué, under the name of the 'National African Company (Limited)', on the other part.

ARTICLE I

For the mutual advantage of ourselves and people, and those Europeans trading under the name of the 'National African Company (Limited),' I, Umoru, King of the Mussulmans of the Soudan, with the consent and advice of my Council, grant and transfer to the above people, or other with whom they may arrange, my entire rights to the country on both sides of the River Benué and rivers flowing into it throughout my dominions for such distance from its and their banks as they may desire.

ARTICLE II

We further grant to the above-mentioned Company the sole right, among foreigners, to trade in our territories, and the sole right, also among foreigners, to possess or work places from which are extracted articles such as lead and antimony.

ARTICLE III

We further declare that no communication will be held with foreigners coming from the rivers except through the above-mentioned Company.

ARTICLE IV

These grants we make for ourselves, our heirs, and successors for ever, and declare them to be irrevocable.

ARTICLE V

The Europeans above named, the National African Company (Limited), agree to make Umoru, Sultan of Sokoto, a yearly present of goods to the value of 3,000 bags of cowries, in return for the above grants.

Signed and sealed at Wurnu, the 1st June, 1885.

(Signature of the Sultan in Arabic.)
(Great seal of the Empire of Sokoto.)

For the National African Company (Limited).
JOSEPH THOMPSON, F R G S.

Witnesses:
W. J. SEAGO.
D. Z. VIERA.
T. JOSEPH.

(An Arabic duplicate was at the same time executed by both parties.)

APPENDIX H

TREATY WITH SOKOTO, 1890

Literal translation of second Treaty, in Arabic, between Umoru, King of the Mussulmans of the Soudan and Sokoto, on the one part, and the Royal Niger Company (Chartered and Limited) on the other part.

Be it known that I, Umoru, King of the Mussulmans, am desirous of introducing European trade in all parts of my dominions, so as to increase the prosperity of my people, and knowing that this cannot be effected except by securing to foreigners the protection of European government, with power of exercising jurisdiction over foreigners, as is the custom with them; also with the power of levying taxes upon foreigners as may be necessary for the exercise and support of this jurisdiction: I, Umoru, King of the Mussulmans of the Soudan, with the consent and advice of my Council agree and grant to the Royal Niger Company (Chartered and Limited)—formerly known as the 'National African Company (Limited)'—full and complete power and jurisdiction over all foreigners visiting or residing in any part of my dominions. I also grant you jurisdiction and full rights of protection over all foreigners; also power of raising taxes of any kind whatsoever from such foreigners.

No person shall exercise any jurisdiction over such foreigners, nor levy any tax whatsoever on such foreigners than the Royal Niger Company (Chartered and Limited).

These grants I make for myself, my heirs, and successors, and declare them to be unchangeable and irrevocable for ever.

I further confirm the Treaty made by me with the National African Company (Limited)—now known as the 'Royal Niger Company (Chartered and Limited)'—in the month of June, according to European reckoning, 1885.

Dated at Wurnu, this 15th day of April, 1890.

APPENDIX I

TREATY WITH OPOBO, 1884

Preliminary Treaty with the King and Chiefs of Opobo.

Her Majesty the Queen of the United Kingdom of Great Britain and Ireland, Empress of India, etc., and the King and Chiefs of Opobo, being desirous of maintaining and strengthening the relations of peace and friendship which have so long existed between them:

Her Britannic Majesty has named and appointed E. H. Hewett, Esq., Her Consul for the Bights of Benin and Biafra, to conclude a Treaty for this purpose.

The said E. H. Hewett, Esq., and the said King and Chiefs of Opobo have agreed upon and concluded the following Articles:—

ARTICLE I

Her Majesty the Queen of Great Britain and Ireland, etc., in compliance with the request of the King, Chiefs, and People of Opobo, hereby undertakes to extend to them and to the territory under their authority and jurisdiction Her Gracious favour and protection.

ARTICLE II

The King and Chiefs of Opobo agree and promise to refrain from entering into any correspondence, agreement, or Treaty with any foreign nation or Power except with the knowledge and sanction of Her Britannic Majesty's Government.

ARTICLE III

This Preliminary Treaty shall come into operation from the date of its signature.

Done in Duplicate the first day of July, 1884, on board her Britannic Majesty's Ship *Flirt*, anchored in Opobo River.

(*Signed*)   EDWARD HYDE HEWETT.
KING JA JA.
COOKEY.

Seal of the British
Consul for the
Bights of Benin and Biafra.

APPENDIX J

SECOND TREATY WITH OPOBO, 1884

Treaty with the King and Chiefs of Opobo, signed at Opobo.

Her Majesty the Queen of the United Kingdom of Great Britain and Ireland, Empress of India, etc., and the King and Chiefs of Opobo, being desirous of maintaining and strengthening the relations of peace and friendship which have so long existed between them:

Her Britannic Majesty has named and appointed E. H. HEWETT, Esq., her Consul for the Bights of Benin and Biafra, to conclude a Treaty for this purpose.

The said E. H. HEWETT, Esq., and the said Chiefs of Opobo have agreed upon and concluded the following articles:—

ARTICLE I

Her Majesty the Queen of Great Britain and Ireland, etc., in compliance with the request of the King, Chiefs, and People of Opobo, hereby undertakes to extend to them and to the Territory under their authority and jurisdiction Her Gracious favour and protection.

ARTICLE II

The King and Chiefs of Opobo agree and promise to refrain from entering into correspondence, agreement, or treaty with any foreign nation or Power except with the knowledge and sanction of Her Britannic Majesty's Government.

ARTICLE III

It is agreed that free and exclusive jurisdiction Civil and Criminal over British Subjects and their property in the territory of Opobo is reserved to Her Britannic Majesty to be exercised by such Consular or other Officer as Her Majesty shall appoint for that purpose.

The same Jurisdiction is likewise reserved to Her Majesty in the said territory of Opobo over Foreign Subjects enjoying British protection who shall be deemed to be included in the expression 'British Subjects' throughout this Treaty.

ARTICLE IV

All disputes between the King and Chiefs of Opobo, or between them or British or Foreign Traders, or between the aforesaid King and Chiefs and neighbouring tribes, which cannot be settled amicably between the two parties, shall be submitted to the British Consular or other Officers, appointed by Her Britannic Majesty to exercise Jurisdiction in Opobo territories, for arbitration and decision or for arrangement.

ARTICLE V

The King and Chiefs of Opobo hereby engage to assist the British Consular or other officers in the execution of such duties as may be assigned to them, and further to act upon their advice in matters relating to the administration of Justice, the development of the resources of the country, the interests of commerce, or in any matter in relation to peace, order, and Government and the general progress of civilization.

ARTICLE VI

(As printed in the treaty being expunged.)

ARTICLE VII

All white Ministers of the Christian Religion shall be permitted to exercise their calling within the territories of the aforesaid King and Chiefs, who hereby guarantee to them full protection.

ARTICLE VIII

If any vessels should be wrecked within the Opobo territories, the King and Chiefs will give them all the assistance in their power, will secure them from plunder, and also recover and deliver to the Owners or Agents all the Property which can be saved. If there are no such owners or agents on the spot, then the said property shall be delivered to the British Consular or other officer.

The King and Chiefs further engage to do all in their power to protect the persons and property of the officers, crew and others on board such wrecked vessels. All claims for salvage due in such cases shall, if disputed, be referred to the British Consular or other Officer for arbitration and decision.

ARTICLE IX

This Treaty shall come into operation so far as practicable from the date of its signature.

Done in duplicate at Opobo, this nineteenth day of December in the year one thousand eight hundred and eighty-four.

(*Signed*) EDWARD HYDE HEWETT.
JA JA.
COOKEY GAM.
PRINCE SATURDAY JA JA.
FINEBOURNE, his × mark.

JOHN AFRICA. ×	
HOW STRONGFACE. ×	
OGOLO. ×	Witnesses to the above marks.
WILLIAM OBANNEY. ×	
BLACK FOUBRAH. ×	
SHOO PETERSIDE. ×	
SAM ANNIE PEPPLE. ×	(*Signed*)—
THOMAS JA JA. ×	HAROLD E. WHITE,
SAM OKO EPELLA. ×	H.M. Vice-Consul.
DUKE OF NORFOLK. ×	
WILLIAM TOBY ×	R. D. BOLER,
JUNGI. ×	Chairman of the
CAPT. URANTA. ×	Court of Equity.
WARISOE. ×	
SAMUEL GEORGE TOBY. ×	

APPENDIX K

TREATY WITH ABEOKUTA, 1893

Treaty of Friendship and Commerce made at Abeokuta in the Egba country, this 18th (eighteenth) day of January, in the year 1893.

Between His Excellency Gilbert Thomas Carter, Esquire, Companion of the Most Distinguished Order of Saint Michael and Saint George, Governor and Commander-in-Chief of the Colony of Lagos, for and on behalf of Her Majesty the Queen of Great Britain and Ireland, Empress of India, etc., Her Heirs and Successors, on the one part, and the undersigned King (Alake) and Authorities of Abeokuta representing the Egba Kingdom, for and on behalf of their Heirs and Successors, on the other part.

We, the undersigned King and Authorities do, in the presence of the Elders, Headmen, and people assembled at this place hereby promise:—

1st. That there shall be peace and friendship between the subjects of the Queen and Egba subjects, and should any difference or dispute accidentally arise between us and the said subjects of the Queen, it shall be referred to the Governor of Lagos for settlement as may be deemed expedient.

2nd. That there shall be complete freedom of Trade between the Egba country and Lagos, and in view of the injury to commerce arising from the arbitrary closing of roads, we the said King and Authorities hereby declare that no roads shall in future be closed without the consent and approval of the Governor of Lagos.

3rd. That we the said King and Authorities pledge ourselves to use every means in our power to foster and promote trade with the countries adjoining Egba and with Lagos.

4th. That we the said King and Authorities will as heretofore afford complete protection, and every assistance and encouragement to all Ministers of the Christian Religion.

5th. It is further agreed and stipulated by the said Gilbert Thomas Carter on behalf of Her Majesty the Queen of England, that so long as the provisions of this Treaty are strictly kept, no annexation of any portion of the Egba country shall be made by Her Majesty's Government without the consent of the lawful Authorities of the Country, no aggressive action shall be taken against the said Country, and its independence shall be fully recognized.

6th. The said King and Authorities having promised that the practice of offering human sacrifices shall be abolished in the one township where it at present exists, and having explained that British subjects have already freedom to occupy land, build houses, and carry on trade and manufacture in any part of the Egba country, and likewise that there is no possibility of a cession of any portion of the Egba Country to a Foreign Power without the consent of Her Majesty's Government, it is desired that no special provision be made in regard to these subjects in this Treaty.

Done at Abeokuta this eighteenth day of January, 1893.

OSOKALU   his X mark.   KING ALAKE.

OSUNDARE ONLADO   his X mark.

SORUNKE JAGUNA   his X mark.   Representatives of King Alake and Egba United Kingdom.

OGUNDEYI MAGAJI   his X mark.

G. T. CARTER, Governor and Commander-in-Chief, Colony of Lagos.

Witnessed at Abeokuta this eighteenth day of January, 1893.

G. B. HADDON-SMITH, Political Officer.

R. L. BOWER, Captain, Asst. Inspector, Lagos Constabulary.

J. B. WOOD, Missionary of the Church Missionary Society.

A. L. HETHERSETT, Clerk and Interpreter, Governor's Office.

E. R. BICKERSTETH, Trader.

W. F. TINNEY SOMOYE, Clerk to the Egba Authorities.

I the undersigned do swear that I have truly and honestly interpreted the terms of the foregoing treaty to the contracting parties in the Yoruba language.

A. L. HETHERSETT.

Witness to the signature,

E. R. BICKERSTETH, Trader.

APPENDIX L

Speech by Sir Abubakar Tafawa Balewa, Prime Minister of Nigeria:

Today is Independence Day. October 1, 1960 is a date to which for two years every Nigerian has been eagerly looking forward. At last our great day has arrived and Nigeria is now indeed an independent sovereign nation.

Words cannot adequately express my joy and pride at being the Nigerian citizen privileged to accept from Her Royal Highness these Constitutional Instruments which are the symbols of Nigeria's independence. It is a unique privilege which I shall remember for ever, and it gives me strength and courage as I dedicate my life to the service of our country. This is a wonderful day, and is all the more wonderful because we have awaited it with increasing impatience, compelled to watch one country after another overtaking us on the road when we had so nearly reached our goal. But now we have acquired our rightful status and I feel sure that history will show that the building of our nation proceeded at the wisest pace: it has been thorough and Nigeria now stands well-built upon firm foundations.

Today's ceremony marks the culmination of a process which began fifteen years ago and has now reached a happy and a successful conclusion. It is with justifiable pride that we claim the achievement of our Independence to be unparalleled in the annals of history.

Each step of our constitutional advance has been purposefully and peacefully planned with full and open consultation, not only between representatives of all the various interests in Nigeria but in harmonious co-operation with the administering power which has today relinquished its authority.

At the time when our constitutional development entered upon its final phase the emphasis was largely upon self-government. We, the elected representatives of the people of Nigeria, concentrated on proving that we are fully capable of managing our own affairs both internally and as a nation.

However, we were not to be allowed the selfish luxury of focussing our interest on our own homes. In these days of rapid communications we cannot live in isolation apart from the rest of the world even if we wished to do so. All too soon it has become evident that for us Independence implies a great deal more than self-government. This great country, which has now emerged without bitterness or bloodshed, finds that she must at once be ready to deal with grave international issues.

This fact has of recent months been unhappily emphasized by the startling events which have occurred in this continent. I shall not labour the points but it would be unrealistic not to draw attention first to the awe-inspiring task confronting us at the very start of our nationhood. When this day in October 1960 was chosen for our Independence it seemed that we were destined to move with quiet dignity to our place on the world stage. Recent events have changed the scene beyond recognition so that we find ourselves today being tested to the utmost. We are called upon immediately to show that our claims to responsible government are well founded, and having been accepted as an independent state we must at once play an active part in maintaining the peace of the world and in preserving civilization. I promise you we shall not fail for want of determination.

And we come to this task better equipped than many. For this I pay tribute to the manner in which successive British Governments have gradually transferred the burden of responsibility to our shoulders. The assistance and unfailing encouragement which we have received from each Secretary of State for the Colonies and their intense personal interest in our development has immeasurably lightened that burden.

All our friends in the Colonial Office must today be proud of their handiwork and in the knowledge that they have helped to lay the foundations of a lasting friendship between our two nations. I have indeed every confidence that, based on the happy experience of a successful partnership, our future relations with the United Kingdom will be more cordial than ever, bound together as we shall be in the Commonwealth by a common allegiance to Her Majesty Queen Elizabeth whom today we proudly acclaim as Queen of Nigeria and Head of the Commonwealth.

Time will not permit the individual mention of all those friends, many of them Nigerians, whose selfless labours have contributed to our Independence. Some have not lived to see the fulfilment of their hopes—on them be peace—but nevertheless they are remembered here, and the names of buildings and streets and roads and bridges throughout the country recall to our minds their achievements, some of them on a national scale. Others confined perhaps to a small area in one Division, more humble but of equal value in the total.

Today we have with us representatives of those who have made Nigeria: representatives of the Regional Governments, of the Missionary Societies, and of the Banking and Commercial enterprises and members, both past and present, of the public service. We welcome you and we rejoice that you have been able to come and share in our celebrations.

We wish that it could have been possible for all of those whom you represent to be here today. Many, I know, will be disappointed to be absent but if they are listening to me now I say to them: 'Thank you on behalf of my countrymen. Thank you for your devoted service which helped to build up Nigeria into a nation. Today we are indeed proud to have achieved our independence, and proud that our efforts should have contributed to this happy event. But do not mistake our pride for arrogance. It is tempered by a feeling of sincere gratitude to all who have shared in the task of developing Nigeria politically, socially and economically. We are grateful to the British officers whom we have known, first as masters and then as leaders and finally as partners but always as friends. And there have been countless missionaries who have laboured unceasingly in the cause of education and to whom we owe many of our medical services. We are grateful also to those who have brought modern methods of banking and of commerce, and new industries. I wish to pay tribute to all of these people and to declare our everlasting admiration for their devotion to duty.'

And finally I must express our gratitude to Her Royal Highness the Princess Alexandra of Kent for personally bringing to us these symbols of our freedom, and especially for delivering the gracious message from Her Majesty the Queen.

And so, with the words 'God save our Queen' I open a new chapter in the history of Nigeria, and of the Commonwealth, and indeed of the world.

APPENDIX M

BRITISH CONSULS IN NIGERIA, 1849–1900

Consul for the Bights of Benin and Biafra (Territories lying between Cape St Paul and Cape St. John).
1849   J. BEECROFT.

Consuls for the Bight of Benin (Lagos):		*Consuls for the Bight of Biafra (Fernando Po):*	
1853	B. CAMPBELL.	1853	J. BEECROFT.
1859	G. BRAND.	1855	T. J. HUTCHINSON.
1860	H. G. FOOTE.	1861	CAPT. R. F. BURTON.
1861	H. S. FREEMAN.	1864	C. LIVINGSTONE.

(After Lagos became a Colony, the Governor was also for a few years Consul for the Bight of Benin.)

Consuls for the Bights of Benin and Biafra (Fernando Po):
1867   C. LIVINGSTONE.
1873   G. HARTLEY.
1878   D. HOPKINS.
1880   E. H. HEWETT.

(Headquarters transferred to Old Calabar in 1873, back to Fernando Po in 1875, and finally to Old Calabar in 1882.)

Commissioners and Consuls-General for the Oil Rivers and Niger Coast Protectorate (and Consuls for Fernando Po):
1891   MAJOR C. M. MACDONALD.
1896   R. D. R. MOOR.

Consul at Lokoja:
1866   J. L. McLEOD.
(Consulate closed in 1869.)

APPENDIX N

GOVERNORS AND HIGH COMMISSIONERS IN NIGERIA

Settlement of Lagos:

1862   Governor   H. S. FREEMAN.
1863   Lieutenant-Governor CAPTAIN W. R. MULLINE. R
1864   „   H. J. GLOVER.

(In 1866 Lagos was placed under the Governor of the West African Settlements, resident at Sierra Leone.)

1866   Administrator   ADMIRAL C. G. E. PATEY.
1866   „   J. H. GLOVER.
1872   „   G. BERKLEY.
1873   „   CAPTAIN G. C. STRAHAN.

(In 1874 Lagos was placed under the Governor of the Gold Coast Colony.)

1874   Lieutenant-Governor C. C. LEES.
1880   „   W. BRANDFORD GRIFFITH.

(In 1886 Lagos was separated from the Gold Coast.)

1886   Governor   SIR C. A. MOLONEY.
1891   „   SIR G. T. CARTER.
1897   „   SIR H. E. M'CALLUM.
1899   „   SIR W. MacGREGOR.
1904   „   SIR W. EGERTON.

From 1891 to 1900 the Oil Rivers and Niger Coast Protectorates were governed by Commissioners and Consuls-General (see Appendix M). In 1900 the Niger Coast Protectorate became

The Protectorate of Southern Nigeria:

1900   High Commissioner SIR R. D. R. MOOR.
1904   „   SIR W. EGERTON.

In 1906 Lagos and Southern Nigeria were amalgamated, and became

The Colony and Protectorate of Southern Nigeria:

1906   Governor   SIR W. EGERTON.
1912   „   SIR F. J. D. LUGARD.

In 1900, after the Royal Niger Company had surrendered their Charter, there was set up

The Protectorate of Northern Nigeria:

1900	High Commissioner	SIR F. J. D. LUGARD.
1907	Governor	SIR E. P. C. GIROUARD.
1909	,,	SIR H. HESKETH BELL.
1912	,,	SIR F. J. D. LUGARD.

In 1914 the two administrations of Northern and Southern Nigeria were amalgamated, and became

The Colony and Protectorate of Nigeria:

1914	Governor-General	SIR F. J. D. LUGARD.
1919	Governor	SIR H. C. CLIFFORD.
1925	,,	SIR G. THOMSON.
1931	,,	SIR D. C. CAMERON.
1935	,,	SIR B. H. BOURDILLON.
1943	,,	SIR A. F. RICHARDS (later LORD MILVERTON).
1948	,,	SIR J. S. MACPHERSON.

The constitution of 1954 provided for a Governor-General.

| 1954 | Governor-General | SIR J. S. MACPHERSON. |
| 1955 | ,, | SIR J. W. ROBERTSON. |

The Governors-General of the independent Federation of Nigeria:—

| 1960 | SIR J. W. ROBERTSON. |
| 1960 | DR NNAMDI AZIKIWE. |

From 1954 there has been a Governor in each of the Regions.

Northern Region:

1954	SIR B. E. SHARWOOD-SMITH.
1957	SIR G. W. BELL.
1962	SIR K. IBRAHIM.

Western Region:

| 1954 | SIR J. D. RANKINE. |
| 1960 | SIR A. ADEREMI. |

Eastern Region:

1954	SIR C. J. PLEASS.
1956	SIR R. DE S. STAPLEDON.
1960	SIR F. A. IBIAM.

INDEX

M

GEORGE ALLEN & UNWIN LTD
London: 40 Museum Street, W.C.1

Auckland: 24 Wyndham Street
Bombay: 15 Graham Road, Ballard Estate, Bombay 1
Buenos Aires: Escritorio 454–459, Florida 165
Calcutta: 17 Chittaranjan Avenue, Calcutta 13
Cape Town: 109 Long Street
Hong Kong: F1/12 Mirador Mansions, Kowloon
Ibadan: P.O. Box 62
Karachi: Karachi Chambers, McLeod Road
Madras: Mohan Mansions, 38c Mount Road, Madras 6
Mexico: Villalongin 32–10, Piso, Mexico 5, D.F.
Nairobi: P.O. Box 12446
New Delhi: 13–14 Asaf Ali Road, New Delhi 1
São Paulo: Avenida 9 de Julho 1138-Ap. 51
Singapore: 36c Prinsep Street, Singapore 7
Sydney: N.S.W.: Bradbury House, 55 York Street
Toronto: 91 Wellington Street West

A HISTORY OF GHANA
W. E. F. Ward

Originally published in 1948 as *A History of the Gold Coast*, this book has been completely revised and considerably expanded to take into account the momentous events of the last decade which culminated in Ghana's establishment as an independent state. Therefore it becomes in effect a new book.

The history of the land now known as Ghana is traced from a period before the arrival of the first Portuguese explorers to the present day. The author, who spent sixteen years in the country, makes use not only of the work of recent anthropologists, but also of his own researches into the unwritten historical traditions of the Ghana tribes.

He describes the early history of the peoples of the area, the rivalries of Portuguese, Dutch, British and others for the trade in gold and slaves, the rise of Ashanti and other native states, and the gradual consolidation of British authority. He concludes with a description of recent political and economic developments, which have ended with making Ghana the first African colony to achieve its independence, an occasion of the greatest significance for the whole continent and for the world.

'Sensible, reliable and clear . . . remains the standard work on its subject.'—*Times Literary Supplement*.

'No student of West African affairs can afford to neglect it.'— DONALD WOOD in *International Affairs*.

Demy 8vo   *Third Impression*   *25s. net*

RACE AND NATIONALISM
Thomas M. Franck

The emergence of a determined and vocal opposition to the anomalous situation of Federation in the Rhodesias and Nyasaland brings into sharp focus the commanding realities of the subjection of seven million Africans to the political, economic and social will of a quarter of a million Whites. The pressures built up by awakening African nationalism are threatening to explode the half-way house of Federation, established in 1953 to bring about the gradual growth of partnership between the races. With the Federation's Constitution coming up for revision, all those working on salvaging central Africa's uneasy experiment will have to face the facts as they are described in this book.

Demy 8vo   *30s. net*

SOUTH AFRICA IN MY TIME
G. Heaton Nicholls

A Londoner by birth, a wanderer and a South African settler by choice, and a politician perhaps by destiny, Heaton Nicholls' life might well be regarded as a success story with 'From Bugler Boy to Elder Statesman' as subtitle. His early years were restless ones. He nearly ran away to sea; he did run away and join the army, and having seen fighting in Burma and on the Northwest frontier of India, left the army in order to find congenial tasks in what is now Rhodesia, in the Australian farm country, and in New Guinea. When marriage ended the wandering, he settled down in Zululand to grow sugar in circumstances sufficiently hard to justify his proud claim to be a pioneer.

A constant process of self-education marked him out from the beginning of his settler days and it was less surprising than he thought in his modesty, that the other settlers should have chosen him to be their representative in the South African parliament. And in politics he remained until the end of his life.

His autobiography is not only a fascinating story of the ups and downs of a political career; it is also a book of first-class importance to the student of South Africa and its problems today.

Whether on the smaller stage of South Africa or the larger stage of the Commonwealth and of the United Nations, Heaton Nicholls made his mark—and made his notes—and though the notes, on the United Nations at a most interesting time, on London in the war years—when he was High Commissioner, on Ceylon's acquisition of independence, may lack the importance of those on South Africa, they make most entertaining and occasionally nostalgic reading.

Demy 8vo   *45s. net*

SOUTH AFRICA 1906-1961
Nicholas Mansergh

In 1906, four years after the ending of the Boer War, the Liberal Government restored self-government to the Transvaal and in so doing opened the way to Union in South Africa. Their magnanimous gesture had far-reaching consequences not only in South Africa but also, by force of example, in the shaping of the future British Commonwealth of Nations. The purpose of this study is to re-examine, in the light of documentary evidence recently made available, the aims of Liberal policy, the considerations which determined it, and the more important consequences that flowed from it in the broader perspective of history.

Crown 8vo   *Cloth 15s. net, Paper 9s. 6d. net*

RESTLESS NATIONS

A Study of World Tensions and Developments

The tensions which exist among and within the restless nations of the world and the need to establish workable partnerships between countries in various stages of development is one of the most pressing problems of our time. A group of distinguished leaders and influential thinkers, Paul Hoffman, Thorkil Kristensen, W. Arthur Lewis, Tom Mboya, B. K. Nehru, Barbara Ward and others, explore the issues raised by these tensions, particularly in relation to politics, economics and education. Their views, representing Africa, Asia, Europe, Latin and North America, were expressed at the Conference on Tensions in Development held at Oxford in 1961, and led, in the words of Lester Pearson, 'to a heightened understanding of many problems in terms of how they appeared to others. As a result, many of us are in a better position and more anxious to do our job more effectively in the complex partnerships on which development and the hopes of the world depend'.

Demy 8vo   *18s. net*

HIGH STREET AFRICA

Anthony Smith

Imagine being in Capetown and looking north—down at the docks and looking up the road which leads to Paarl, Worcester and beyond. See this road in its true perspective: the Great North Road that leads right to the Mediterranean. Then imagine a wallet filled with an accumulated salary, a timeless period stretching ahead with no commitments, no job to hurry to, no need to arrive on a definite day, or even during a definite month.

This was the framework of Anthony Smith's adventure. With money enough and time to spare, he decided to travel up through Africa by motor-cycle. Although he inevitably encountered hazards upon much of 'Africa's scleriotic arterial network', the journey itself is not allowed to dominate the book. Instead, he devotes most of his book to the people he met on the way. The 7,000 mile trip has been fashioned, for the most part, into a series of excellent short stories, each complete in their own way and each adding to the greater picture of the African continent.

Demy 8vo   *21s. net*

THE COLONIAL OFFICE
Sir Charles Jeffries

Recent decades have witnessed far-reaching changes in the work the Colonial Office has to perform and the ways in which its tasks are carried out. No longer is it mainly concerned with supervising the working of the dependent governments. It is today the headquarters of an all-out effort to develop the resources of the oversea territories and to free them from poverty, ignorance and other obstacles to their progress and welfare. Sir Charles Jeffries shows how this development has come about and how the Colonial Office is equipped to meet the changing needs of the territories; he also describes the organization and work of the Office.

The book opens with a brief introduction describing in broad outline the work and tradition of the Office. It then proceeds to consider the nature of the responsibilities of the Secretary of State and of the Office and follows this description with a survey of the various territories for whose good government they are concerned. After showing how the Office has expanded and adapted its organization to meet the changing demands made on it, the book describes the main aspects of its work today. A concluding chapter takes stock of developments over the last thirty years and suggests some possible lines of future evolution.

The New Whitehall Series

Demy 8vo   *18s. net*

THE GAMBIA
Lady Southorn

The Gambia is the most northerly of the four West African colonies. It is known as 'The Groundnut Colony' from its dependence economically on the groundnut crop and is the oldest British settlement in West Africa. Queen Elizabeth sent out roving merchants to the Gambia in search of gold and ivory, but the first permanent settlement was made at Fort James on a small island about twenty miles up-river. On this lonely spot 'The Royal Adventurers of England trading into Africa' established themselves in 1661 under the auspices of Charles II, James, Duke of York and Prince Rupert. Here for a century and a half the British struggled with the French for the mastery and the trade of the River Gambia.

Demy 8vo   *Illustrated*   *21s. net*

GEORGE ALLEN & UNWIN LIMITED